Jurisprudence

Jurisprudence: Themes and Concepts offers an original introduction to, and critical analysis of, the central themes studied in jurisprudence courses. The book is presented in three parts: the first two contain general themes with corresponding tutorial questions, and the third contains advanced topics. Every chapter in the book gives guidance on further reading.

Accessible, interdisciplinary and socially informed, this book has been revised to take into account the latest developments in jurisprudential scholarship.

Scott Veitch is Paul KC Chung Professor in Jurisprudence at the University of Hong Kong.

Emilios Christodoulidis is Chair of Jurisprudence at the University of Glasgow.

Marco Goldoni is Senior Lecturer in Legal Theory at the University of Glasgow.

Jurisprudence

Themes and Concepts

THIRD EDITION

Scott Veitch, Emilios Christodoulidis
and Marco Goldoni

Routledge
Taylor & Francis Group

LONDON AND NEW YORK

Third edition published 2018
by Routledge
2 Park Square, Milton Park, Abingdon, Oxon OX14 4RN

and by Routledge
711 Third Avenue, New York, NY 10017

Routledge is an imprint of the Taylor & Francis Group, an informa business

First edition published by Routledge-Cavendish 2007
Second edition published by Routledge 2012

British Library Cataloguing-in-Publication Data
A catalogue record for this book is available from the British Library

Library of Congress Cataloging-in-Publication Data
Names: Veitch, Scott, author. | Christodoulidis, Emilios A., author. |
   Goldoni, Marco, author.
Title: Jurisprudence : themes and concepts / Scott Veitch, Emilios
   Christodoulidis, Marco Goldoni.
Description: Third edition. | Milton Park, Abingdon, Oxon ; New York, NY :
   Routledge, [2018] | Includes bibliographical references and index.
Identifiers: LCCN 2017060233 | ISBN 9780415749640 (hbk) |
   ISBN 9780415749657 (pbk) | ISBN 9781317749219 (web pdf) |
   ISBN 9781317749202 (epub) | ISBN 9781317749196 (mobipocket) |
   ISBN 9781315795997 (master)
Subjects: LCSH: Jurisprudence. | Law—Philosophy.
Classification: LCC K237 .V45 2018 | DDC 340—dc23
LC record available at https://lccn.loc.gov/2017060233

ISBN: 978-0-415-74964-0 (hbk)
ISBN: 978-0-415-74965-7 (pbk)
ISBN: 978-1-315-79599-7 (ebk)

Typeset in Joanna MT
by Apex CoVantage, LLC
Printed and bound by CPI Group (UK) Ltd, Croydon, CR0 4YY

For Neil MacCormick (1941–2009), teacher and friend

Contents

Acknowledgements and attributions   xi
Abbreviations   xii

Introduction   1
The themes   3
How to use this book   4

PART I: LAW AND MODERNITY   7

I. THE ADVENT OF MODERNITY   9

1   Overview   11
The idea of progress   12
Specialisation of knowledge and the individual   13
Thinking about modern law   15

2   Social contract theory   17
The emergence of the sovereign state – Westphalia as
    marker of transition   17
Hobbes, theorist of the modern state   19
John Locke: social contract and the law of private property   24
Rousseau: law between equality and self-government   28

3   Law and the rise of the market system   35
The institutional dimension   37
The market system   39

4   Law and the political   45
Elements of the modern state   45
Sovereignty   47
Holding sovereign power to account   51

II. THEORISTS AND CRITICS OF MODERNITY   61

5   Law, class and conflict: Karl Marx   63
The function of law   66
Ideology   67

6   Law, legitimation and rationality: Max Weber   71
     Max Weber: modernity and formal legal rationality   71
     Forms of political authority   73
     Forms of legal rationality   74
     The development of legal modernity   77
     Modern law and the economic system   79
     Weber as theorist and as critic of modernity   81

7   Law, community and social solidarity: Emile Durkheim   83

III. TRANSFORMATIONS OF MODERN LAW   89

8   The rise and decline of the rule of law   91
     The materialisation of modern law   91
     Law in the welfare state   93
     Beyond the welfare state   97

9   Law and globalisation   100
     Sovereignty after globalisation   103
     Constitutionalism beyond the state   105
     'Unthinking' modern law   107

GENERAL PART I TUTORIALS   111
     Tutorial 1 Sovereignty   112
     Tutorial 2 Social contract   113
     Tutorial 3 Law and general will: Rousseau's social contract 114
     Tutorial 4 Property rights: justification and limits   115
     Tutorial 5 Property rights   117
     Tutorial 6 Understanding legal modernity   118
     Tutorial 7 Globalisation and regulation   121
     Tutorial 8 The structure of rights   123

PART II: LEGAL SYSTEM AND LEGAL REASONING   129

I. LEGALITY AND VALIDITY   131

10   The differentiation of law and morality   133

11   Identifying valid law: the positivist thesis   137
     Hart's concept of law   137
     Kelsen's 'pure' theory of law   140

12   The challenge of natural law   144
     The question of form   144
     The question of content   151

II. THEORIES OF LEGAL REASONING   161
     Introduction   163

13   Formalism and rule-scepticism   167
     The promise of formalism   167
     The challenge of American legal realism   173

14   The turn to interpretation   182
     Hart and the 'open texture' of legal language   182
     MacCormick and the limits of discretion   184
     Dworkin, justification and integrity   188

15   The politics of legal reasoning   193
     Critical legal theory   193
     The U.S. critical legal studies movement   194
     Feminist critiques of adjudication   198

GENERAL PART II TUTORIALS   205
     Tutorial 1 Legality and the rule of law   206
     Tutorial 2 Law, power and the rule of law   207
     Tutorial 3 Identifying valid law: legal positivism   208
     Tutorial 4 Identifying valid law: natural law   209
     Tutorial 5 Law and morality   210
     Tutorial 6 Interpreting or making the law? [1]   211
     Tutorial 7 Interpreting or making the law? [2]   215
     Tutorial 8 Discrimination and legal reasoning   219
     Tutorial 9 Legal reasoning and the scope of interpretation: Hart and Dworkin   220
     Tutorial 10 Essay questions on legal reasoning   221

PART III: ADVANCED TOPICS   227

1   Theories of justice   229
     Utilitarianism versus libertarianism   230
     Liberalism: Rawls's justice as fairness   234
     Socialism   237

2   Global justice   244
     The central issue and some terminology   244
     Content and scope of justice   244
     The conservative view   246
     The progressive view   247
     The way forward   248

3   Transitional jurisprudence and historic injustices   251
     The rule of law in political transitions   251
     Addressing colonialism: judging in an unjust society   257

4   Trials, facts and narratives   265
     The legacy of fact-scepticism   265
     Trials and perceptions of fact: language and narrative in the courtroom 268
     Trials, regulation and justice   270

5   Displacing the juridical: Foucault on power and discipline   274
    Power and the law   275
    Discipline   275
    Biopower   277
    Governmentality   278
    A theory of legal modernity?   279

6   Legal pluralism   282
    Classical and contemporary legal pluralism   283
    Strong and weak legal pluralism, and the position of the state 284
    Empirical, conceptual and political approaches to legal pluralism 286
    Future directions in legal pluralism   287

7   Legal institutionalism   290

8   Law and deconstruction   299

9   Juridification   312
    The meaning and scope of juridification   312
    Habermas on juridification   313
    Juridification and the 'regulatory trilemma'   315
    Juridification as depoliticisation   317
    A fifth epoch?   318

10 Autopoietic law   321
    The concept of autopoiesis   321
    An inventory of concepts   322
    The coding of social systems   324
    Society, sub-systems and the law   325
    How does 'the law think'?   327

Index   333

Acknowledgements and attributions

In writing the third edition of this book we have re-arranged the structure, updated the text and references and added several new sections. Our guiding ideas have, however, remained the same as in the previous editions. They are more fully explained in the Introduction. That we have been asked to do a further edition is, we hope, an indication that some students and teachers have enjoyed using the book and agree with its approach to the subject.

We have benefited greatly from the generosity of friends, colleagues and students and we are pleased to record our gratitude to them all. The substantial contributions of certain colleagues are recognised in the attributions below.

We are fortunate to have been joined by Marco Goldoni as co-author of this third edition. Marco, who joined the Glasgow School of Law staff a few years ago, has brought insights and great momentum to the third edition and a distinctive, 'Continental' approach which has significantly enriched the book, not least in its range.

There is one overriding debt to acknowledge, to our colleague and friend Lindsay Farmer, who is no longer amongst the co-authors of the third edition. His role in the conception, design and writing of the book was invaluable and we thank him for his past contributions and for ongoing engagement in our discussions.

In one instance the need to make updates ourselves was forced upon us by circumstances. Neil MacCormick, who contributed enormously to the first edition by providing sections on sovereignty and the rule of law, died in April 2009. We have continued to update and integrate these sections as seemed necessary. More generally, though, Neil demonstrated through his life and work how jurisprudence could be seen as part of the project of government broadly conceived, and he was always alert to the need to engage widely with political and social issues. It is in recognition of this enduring spirit that we, again, dedicate this third edition to him.

SV/EC/MG
November 2017
Glasgow and Hong Kong

In Part III: Advanced Topics, topic 5 ('Displacing the Juridical') was written for us by Lindsay Farmer, of the University of Glasgow; the sections on 'Legal Pluralism' and 'Law and Globalisation' have been updated from an original version written by Gavin Anderson, of the University of Glasgow; the section on 'Law and Deconstruction' was written by Johan van der Walt, of the University of Luxembourg; and the section on 'Global Justice' was written by George Pavlakos, of the University of Glasgow.

Abbreviations

ADR	alternative dispute resolution
CJ	Chief Justice
CLS	critical legal studies
EC	European Community
ECHR	European Convention on Human Rights
ECJ	European Court of Justice
EEC	European Economic Community
EU	European Union
GDP	gross domestic product
ICC	International Criminal Court
ILO	International Labour Organisation
IMF	International Monetary Fund
MEP	Member of European Parliament
MP	Member of Parliament
NGO	non-governmental organisation
PFIs	private finance initiatives
PPP	public private partnerships
PVS	persistent vegetative state
TRC	Truth and Reconciliation Commission (S Africa)
UDHR	Universal Declaration of Human Rights
UK	United Kingdom
UN	United Nations
UNIDROIT	International Institute for the Unification of Private Law (Fr)
US	United States
WTO	World Trade Organization

Introduction

In a series of lectures delivered at the University of Glasgow beginning in 1762, Adam Smith, the Professor of Moral Philosophy, delineated the province of jurisprudence. He defined it in general terms as 'the theory of the rules by which civil governments ought to be directed', otherwise, 'the theory of the general principles of law and government' (Smith 1978/1762, pp 5 and 398). This he saw as comprising four main objects: the maintenance of justice, the provision of police, the raising of revenue and the establishment of arms. What immediately strikes the modern reader of this definition is its breadth. He includes subjects such as taxation or police and security that obviously concern relations between state and citizen, but which are all too often viewed as purely technical areas of government. Just as importantly a theory of law and government for Smith requires that we attend not merely to matters of the definition or application of law, but also of how these relate to politics and the practice of governing. His approach to these questions is striking, for he approaches the topic with a method that is (in contemporary terms) both historical and sociological: that is to say that he is concerned with both the question of understanding the historical development of forms of law and government, and that of how it relates to stages of social and economic development of the society to be governed.

The contemporary study of jurisprudence rarely aspires to a comparable breadth in either subject matter or method. Anglo-American jurisprudence, indeed, has for a long time been more interested in law than government, has focused more on abstract rules than institutions, and has paid only patchy attention to the historical or sociological context within which law and legal and political institutions develop. While we do not have the space here to address the question of why it has come about that the scope of province of jurisprudence has narrowed so dramatically, we would argue that the contemporary approach is too narrow and too technical. It not only risks losing the interest of students, but more importantly risks undermining the relevance of the subject itself. The aim of this book, then, is to restore some of the breadth of subject matter and method that animated the studies of our illustrious predecessor at the University of Glasgow.

Our starting point in this enterprise is that jurisprudence is the study of law and legal institutions in their historical, philosophical and political contexts. The study of law in this sense cannot be abstracted from the questions of the nature and theory of government; indeed, the two must necessarily be considered in their relation to each other. This book offers a range of competing interpretations of how the role of law is best understood, considering among other things the relation between law and politics, law and the economy, law and moral values, the role of judges in a democracy, and the virtues of the rule of law and threats to its realisation in practice. The book provides students with an introduction to, and overview of, the historical and philosophical development of understandings of a range of profoundly important social concerns, with the aim of enabling them to analyse and reflect on the role of law and legal practice more broadly.

These are complex issues that invite complex answers. We have attempted to navigate through the complexity by organising the material around two broad thematic axes: law and modernity, and legal system and legal reasoning. The first seeks to locate the development of modern law within the ideas, institutions and social contexts of modernity; the second examines the systemic quality of law and its application in particular cases, with specific reference to their relation with other disciplines or rationalities. We shall have more to say about these themes shortly, but before doing so, we want to say a little more about our 'thematic' approach to this subject.

All too often, in our experience, jurisprudence is taught in one of two ways. Either it is presented as a series of imaginary debates between positions or approaches that seem to have little in common (natural law vs positivism, conceptualism vs realism, and so on), or it is taught as a stately progression from one great thinker to another (Bentham to Austin to Hart to Dworkin, and so on). The problem with the first approach is that it presents the debates in a rather abstract way, wrenching them out of any sort of context in which the debate might be considered meaningful. It is difficult, especially for a student encountering jurisprudence for the first time, to care much about the relative merits of natural law and positivism in the abstract, and so the exercise becomes one of the rote-learning of the 'strengths' and 'weaknesses' of the different positions. However, we consider that these kinds of debates can become much more meaningful when considered in the context of what they can say about different theories of sovereignty, of the relation between legal power and political power, or the day-to-day realities of the judicial interpretation and application of legal rules. Likewise, presenting ideas through the theories of thinkers who advanced them can make the study of jurisprudence seem a hermetically sealed world, developing with reference only to its own history and where jurists engage only with other jurists. Against this we would argue that it is important to understand something of the historical context in which particular theories were developed, or of the problems of state and law that the theorists were addressing. Jurisprudence, in other words, should be neither understood nor taught as a purely abstract or philosophical subject. The most important jurists and the major jurisprudential theories have much to say about the pressing legal and political issues of their, and our own, time.

The way in which we have sought to address these shortcomings in this book is to address theoretical debates and issues through the themes we have identified. The themes lay out certain broad contexts within which questions of law and legal institutions should be considered, with the aim of showing how particular concepts and debates, far from being abstract or distant from the 'real world', are often addressing matters of central political or legal concern. Our aim in doing this is to try and make the subject of jurisprudence easier to understand by relating it to the kind of subjects that are already being studied in the curriculum of the LLB, and doing so in such a way that the student can also see that these subjects are not just matters of technical, positive law, but are also related to contemporary social and political issues.

This has three other consequences that we should note. We have, so far as possible, eschewed an approach that looks at the 'complete' theory of a particular philosopher, or indeed (within limits) an approach that looks at discrete thinkers in the abstract. Instead, our thematic approach means that we focus primarily on issues, and thus what particular thinkers had to say about these issues, rather than addressing a corpus of thought. This means that the work of particular theorists appears at different places in the book, where we address different aspects of their overall work in order to illuminate the topic under discussion. What is lost in the failure to cover the 'complete' theory is hopefully made up for by the fact that we are able to present a range of positions in relation to the issues. This also has consequences for the way that certain concepts are addressed, as the thematic approach means that certain issues will appear more than once, in different sections of the book, and will be addressed differently in the light of the context established by the overall theme. This should underline the point that there is not necessarily a single correct approach to an issue, but that the approach or understanding might depend on the context or perspective from which it is addressed. The third consequence relates to the range of issues covered. The book misses out certain issues that might normally be covered in a jurisprudence course – such as theories of punishment – while also including others that are not, perhaps, part of the conventional course. This is not because we do not think that these things are important – far from it. However, in seeking to present a relatively short introduction to the subject we have preferred to focus on the issues that we take to be related to our central themes – and which are also related to our own research and writing in the area. We are not so much setting out to define the scope of the subject as to set out a method and themes that will whet the appetite of the student and hopefully lead them on to a fuller study of the subject.

In doing so we are thus moving away from what has become in recent decades an unfortunate tendency to channel jurisprudence through the distorting lens of analytical jurisprudence. This tendency has resulted both in an increasingly narrow specialisation which separates the study of jurisprudence from other disciplines, and its marginalisation from other parts of the law curriculum. By seeking to challenge these unhappy exclusions we hope to engage students' curiosity about the role and worth of law, its promises and its drawbacks, its history and the challenges it faces now and in the future.

The themes

As we have suggested above, each of the themes is intended to set out a broad framework or context within which we can address more specific issues about the role and function of law. Each theme thus sets out a general problematic – the contested development of law and legal institutions in modernity, and the nature of legal systems and legal reasoning or argumentation – and discusses a range of theoretical issues and perspectives with respect to each. There is a certain logic to this approach for it is our starting point (with Smith) that it is central to the method of jurisprudence that it should be historically and sociologically informed.

In Part I we set the thematic context of the book within an overarching account of modernity. What is meant by 'modernity' is set out in detail at the start of Part I, but suffice it to note for now that it is driven by the idea of progress; that it involves increasing specialisation and differentiation of social systems; and that it demands new accounts of power, sovereignty and citizenship. None of these is uncontested, however. And so we set out to explore these contestations around questions of the state, the economy and the political by engaging with some of the most enduringly influential modern accounts of these, exemplified in the writings of social contract theorists and theorists of conflict and consensus, and of rights and the rule of law. How, for example, has the relationship between law and politics, or the modern state, developed? How is this conception of the state related to the social and economic structures of society? How might it change in the context of developments such as globalisation? And what visions of society and accountability does modern law embody or eschew? These are, amongst others, the kinds of question that Part I raises and provides a range of answers to.

One aim here is to assess how and whether the projects and ends of modern law continue to be adequate in contemporary social conditions. Hence the articulation of law, economy, community and politics is central to legal and political theory's most perplexing questions. On the one hand, for example, law is an expression of political sovereignty, the product of political processes of will-formation and entrusted to the political apparatus of the state for its administration and enforcement. And yet at the same time it claims autonomy from politics, an objective meaning of its own, an expression of principle, even justice, somehow above and beyond the 'messy' world of politics. Moreover, in recent decades, legal organisation and society generally have seen massive shifts in the political and economic landscape through the emergence of global, sectoral and regional institutions (such as the European Union), as well as the contradictory pressures that are associated with processes of globalisation and national populism. How law is involved in, and responds to, these developments requires scrutiny if we are to understand more fully the nature of law's role in contemporary society.

In Part II we look at theories and issues that address questions about the nature of legal systems and legal reasoning. The questions here are sometimes more technical, but arguably no less political or controversial. So the question of law's systemic nature is posed in different ways by legal positivists and those who, by contrast, see a necessary connection between both the form and the content of law, and its valid identification *as* law. Whether legal systems and norms embody and guarantee rationality and values such as dignity, justice and the common good is a contested matter, and – as such – is not only theoretically, but practically, significant. We then address questions about whether law invites and deploys a mode of *reasoning* that is peculiarly its own, characteristically involving the application of rules to cases, or whether and to what extent ethical and political concerns, perspectives and imperatives impact on legal reasoning. Again, the stakes are high, particularly given that there is a common expectation that legal rules, once instituted, are to be largely insulated from disagreements that we might call political or ethical, which might be thought to be more properly debated in the political rather than the legal domain. But if that is the case, is a politics of legal reasoning feasible, and if yes, is it also desirable?

In Part III, 'Advanced Topics', we take up a number of themes and concepts that draw on and extend the analyses of some of the key aspects considered in Parts I and II. Here are also included a number of topics that add new dimensions to the jurisprudential themes covered in the earlier parts which we hope will be of interest to students and teachers alike.

How to use this book

This book is introductory. We expect it to work as a point of departure rather than an end point in itself, particularly since not all that can wisely be covered in such a course of study is covered here. Rather our aim is to engage students new to the subject by providing some initial coverage of themes and concepts we think important, and by provoking them into pursuing further reflections and research on topics raised here, among others. We have, for that reason, not attempted to be comprehensive in our coverage, but to focus on issues and debates, and to connect these to more general themes.

It is intended that the general themes in Parts I and II provide an overview of central aspects of the subject. The advanced topics focus on more specific sets of problems, developing in detail aspects of the main themes as well as adding to these in diverse ways. These sections are also usually pitched at a more advanced level and presuppose that the 'general themes' have already been covered.

Throughout the book we have provided readings that we see as indispensable to the comprehension of the text. These follow each section and include references to further reading which is provided mainly for purposes of further research on the topic. Parts I and II also contain a series of tutorials that might be used as the basis for discussion of issues covered in that part of the book. There are three types of tutorial, each of which is designed to encourage different types of skill in the student. The first type are problem-solving, a form which is familiar to most law students, though perhaps less common in the teaching of jurisprudence. These describe a scenario, often based on actual cases, and ask the student to think through certain issues as they are dramatised in the factual situation. The second type are aimed at developing skills in the critical reading of texts. We have either provided extracts from a text, such as a judgement, or directed the student to a journal article or section from a book, and provided a series of questions that should assist the student in reading and analysing the text. The third type are more open-ended essay-style questions, in response to suggested readings either from this book or other texts. These can provide the basis for classroom discussion, or alternatively students might be asked to prepare presentations based on the questions.

The book can thus be used in a number of different ways. It is intended primarily as a textbook for a basic course on jurisprudence, which could focus on the main themes, allowing the teacher either to address the tutorials and advanced topics included in the book or to introduce their own according to their own interests. The purpose of the book is thus to provide the students with a basic introduction to some central issues in jurisprudence and to encourage them to tackle some of the primary texts in the area. Alternatively, the book may be used in a more advanced course, focusing primarily on the advanced topics, where we have given both an overview of the issues and sufficient guidance that they can go on and read some of the primary texts.

That said, there is of course no correct way to use the book; our main hope is that students find it lively and interesting and that it stimulates them to read more widely in the subject.

Part I

Law and modernity

I   The advent of modernity   9

II   Theorists and critics of modernity   61

III   Tranformations of modern law   89

I

The advent of modernity

1	Overview	11
	The idea of progress	12
	Specialisation of knowledge and the individual	13
	Thinking about modern law	15
2	Social contract theory	17
	The emergence of the sovereign state – Westphalia as marker of transition	17
	Hobbes, theorist of the modern state	19
	John Locke: social contract and the law of private property	24
	Rousseau: law between equality and self-government	28
3	Law and the rise of the market system	35
	The institutional dimension	37
	The market system	39
4	Law and the political	45
	Elements of the modern state	45
	Sovereignty	47
	Holding sovereign power to account	51

Chapter 1

Overview

Modernity provides the context for the jurisprudential themes and concepts we explore in this book. The term 'modernity' denotes a wide range of ways of thinking and acting – in science, law, politics, economics, culture and so on – juxtaposed, essentially, to that which preceded it – the 'pre-modern' – and that which challenges it: the 'anti-modern' and the 'post-modern', for example. The advent of modernity marked an attempt to break with the past: to break from the domination of tradition, superstition and an uncritical conformity to 'the way things are'. It is characterised by a new freedom to contest what had previously been taken as given and unchallengeable, and it led in turn to radical changes in forms of political, social and legal organisation.

Modernity emerges fully in the seventeenth and eighteenth centuries and, despite some key oppositions to it identifiable today, it continues to be an organising category up to our time. Immanuel Kant's famous dictum *sapere aude* ('dare to know') captures something of the revolutionary spirit in the fields of knowledge, science and culture. A new optimism pervading the 'Age of Reason' promoted the idea that the world could be understood by the rigorous application of scientific analysis and experimentation as opposed to referring to religious, magical or mysterious forces. The rules and regularities discoverable by science in nature could in turn be applied to the understanding and eradication of social problems (such as disease, famine or poverty). Hence the idea of modernity applied both to the natural and to what became known as the social sciences. The latter, as they emerged in the course of the eighteenth and nineteenth centuries, were driven by efforts to improve understanding of the regularities of social life and the structures and institutions that influence how people interact in society.

Modernity for our purposes addresses predominantly, though not exclusively, the workings and effects of Western institutions and concepts. These will form the focus of this book. But as we will also see, while these institutions and concepts have been influential globally, such influence has not necessarily been positive. Indeed, in modernity, Western societies have produced harms as well as goods and their institutions have been complicit with many practices that do not meet their own professed ideals. We will return to this observation in due course.

The idea of progress

The engine that drives modernity is the idea of *progress*. Whatever is the state of things just now, it could be better: the natural and social worlds could be better understood, technology could be made to work more efficiently or be put to better use, humans and their institutions could be more free, more equal, more just. The *discrepancy* between how things now are and how they could be if they were made better in the future can be described as a discrepancy between 'social experience and social expectation' (Santos 2002, p 2). The desire to improve social experience by meeting these expectations is the source of an exhilarating energy for making social life better.

This drive for improvement produces a constant tension that lies at the very heart of modernity: a tension, as Santos puts it, between emancipation and regulation. Expectations typically produce demands for emancipation from problems currently being experienced: emancipation, for example, from hunger, emancipation from oppression, emancipation from discrimination. Where people's expectations remain unfulfilled, the discrepancy with experience demands to be addressed through advances in knowledge or superior ways of organising things and people. If such emancipatory aspirations are to be meaningfully met, however, they need to be secured in a reasonably ordered manner over time. This is where regulation comes in: regulation institutes the meeting of expectations in an enduring way across the whole of society. It is, says Santos, 'the set of norms, institutions, and practices that guarantee the stability of expectations' (Santos 2002, p 2).

Consider an example. The experience of great inequalities in society has led to many demands for improvements towards more equal treatment. One such demand for equality concerned citizens voting in state elections: the demand that all adult men should be treated equally before the law, irrespective of how much property they owned or what colour their skin was. If achieved – and this emancipation often took a great deal of time and effort in the face of entrenched hierarchies and interests that did not want things to change in such a way – these equalities were best protected through *legal regulations*: equal rights for all men guaranteed by the law and the courts. But the expectations that the principle of equality could offer did not rest there. It pointed to further discrepancies between experiences of unequal treatment and the ideal of equality. Discrimination on the basis of gender was one such discrepancy. To remove it, regulation was again required. Thus legislation was passed to secure equal treatment of citizens irrespective of gender. And so on: once some measure of equality is achieved expectations may again increase, or the demand for equality be made in different areas of social life. The legal recognition of same-sex marriage in many countries is a recent example of this. Based on a principle of non-discrimination, the recognition of the desire for *emancipation* – freedom from the state deciding which gender a person may marry – has resulted in new regulations being established. In this case the notion of *progress* looks like this: (1) experience of discrimination (same-sex marriage outlawed); (2) demand for emancipation (on the principle of equal treatment for all citizens regardless of gender); and (3) new legal regulation (same-sex marriage legally guaranteed).

So there is a constant *dynamic* or *tension* in modernity between emancipation and regulation. As expectations criticise experience on the basis of certain principles – equality, freedom, justice and so on – they seek predictable protection through regulation. Of course, not just any and certainly not all expectations are met. Which ones are is usually a matter of protracted legal, moral and political struggle and debate. In this respect modernity's notions of possibility and progress include a wide variety of very different emancipatory political movements, from liberalism and libertarianism to socialism and communism. And if these theories conflict, what they share is the same dynamic that fuels modernity's unrelenting drive for improvement.

We can find similar demands for progress across nearly all fields of human endeavour. From the late eighteenth century, developments in science were linked to dramatic changes in the fields of production and the economy, culminating in what became known as the Industrial Revolution which was particularly associated with the rise of capitalism. Driven in part by new scientific inventions, such as the steam engine and the mechanisation of production, the Industrial Revolution was a transformation of methods of production and a near-miraculous improvement in European societies' capacities to produce goods. This impetus is still widely prevalent today, albeit in new forms. In technology, for example, there remains a constant drive to improve reliability, efficiency and speed. People seek faster computers, larger memory storage, smaller phones, lighter tablets. The rate of technological development in computing is exponential and provides perhaps the most striking exemplar of the much noted claim that in modernity (unlike in long stretches of pre-modern history) the world people will die in will differ enormously from the world they were born in. The discrepancy between experience and expectation thus continues to drive demands for new knowledge and better application of it. New technologies emerge – in programming, nanotechnology and the like – to meet the desire for ever-improved communication. Likewise in medicine and biotechnology, scientific discoveries are constantly being sought in the effort to eradicate disease and improve health. Again the idea of progress, the desire continuously to make the future better than the past, drives activities across disparate areas of human experience and enquiry.

Of course one need not be an old-fashioned Luddite to realise that technological 'progress' may be a double-edged sword. The same technology that links computers for purposes of efficient global communication can also be used to knock out air traffic control systems, allow identity theft, or disrupt finance and supply chains, quickly putting the well-being of countless people in jeopardy. The very materials that are used literally to drive the engines of modern life – coal, oil, nuclear fuels – also produce emissions that threaten the earth's environment and the species it sustains. And the same scientific study of radioactivity used to improve diagnostic health techniques, for example, has also been deployed in developing nuclear weapons that could destroy human life on the planet. There is, then, an *ambivalence* about progress in modernity that should not be forgotten or downplayed.

Specialisation of knowledge and the individual

It is in this context that we are going to be exploring many facets of modern law in the chapters that follow. But for now, two other aspects to modernity should be mentioned. First, an increased *specialisation* is observable throughout human life. Second, 'the individual' appears as a category of knowledge and action in a decisively new way. We shall say something about these briefly here, but aspects of both will be taken up in more detail later. (The meaning of the division of labour will also be taken up separately.)

The idea of a 'Renaissance man' – someone who was knowledgeable across the full range of human enquiry, in mathematics, science, art, literature and so on – was made much more difficult as modernity progressed. There is an occasional light-hearted debate about who was the 'last person to know everything', but no one ever suggests this is possible beyond the nineteenth century. This is because in the later course of modernity, new disciplines emerged in which the production of knowledge became increasingly varied and specialised. A quick look at the list of departments in a modern university is an excellent way of seeing how knowledge production and dissemination have been divided up into highly specialised units. Most of these disciplines were inventions of modernity, some of them far more recently than you might think: economics departments, for example, were creations of the nineteenth century; likewise sociology and statistics, with criminology and psychology later still. And so too in medical sciences: the specialisation to be found within faculties of medicine follows the fragmentation of knowledge production into ever more distinct areas, often as a result of the application of new technologies developed elsewhere.

The invention of new branches of knowledge, each with their own modes of enquiry and validation, meant the rise of experts at the expense of generalists. On the one hand, these experts track the developments in modern society associated with the idea of *functional differentiation*. Here we find the increasing differentiation of social systems within society that provide their own standards of operation and action that are not subsumable within one single overarching set of principles. As we proceed, we will see how the legal system comes to be treated in precisely this way: as a domain of knowledge and practice separate from, albeit interrelating with, politics and morality, or from the rationality of economic or aesthetic criteria. In jurisprudence, the emergence of legal positivism, for example, is one symptom of this, as are the development of systems theory and autopoiesis as explanations of how individual social systems perform different and irreducible functions within modern society (see 'advanced' sections below).

On the other hand, such theoretical investigations not only created new knowledge, they created new *subjects* of knowledge. Psychology and radiology, for example, are not only new subjects (meaning new disciplines), but they produce new subjects in the sense that they produce definitions and attributes of people that did not exist before. Among the most startling achievements of this development was the creation in modernity of 'the individual'. This sounds strange, but it is analogous to the idea that the teenager was an invention of the 1950s. Of course there had always been youth who had lived in their teens; but it was only with the films of James Dean, beat poetry and the invention of cool that the category of 'the teenager' came into being, which could then in turn be analysed, demonised, marketised and so on. So too with the individual. There had always been individual people; but the category of 'the individual' was a product of modernity. This new subject of knowledge was produced by the work of numerous new disciplines and was given distinctive features – individuality, uniqueness – rather than a person's life being determined by tradition, status or family or by the dominance of religious authority. From these latter, individuals were emancipated, unless of course, they themselves *chose* to participate in them.

Following the dynamic of emancipation and regulation we just identified, the emancipated individual was to be protected in turn by legal *regulation* – this time in the form of newly conceived individual natural or human rights. Thus individuals were deemed to have rights to freedom of religion and of conscience, the right to private life, freedom of expression and association and so on, which attached to and guaranteed the idea of the priority of the individual. In this way the individual came to be treated as the basic unit of society: society could now be understood to be formed by collections of individuals, rather like atoms making up complex molecules, whose individual worth was guaranteed by the law in the form of individual legal rights.

But again as we saw in several instances earlier, there may be an *ambivalence* to this development in modernity. On the one hand, the individual could in theory do what they wanted to do, and be who they wanted to be. But on the other, the category of 'the individual' was itself a creation of forces, institutions and forms of knowledge over which no one individual could have control. Individuals were *defined*, in other words, by social systems – the legal system, the education system, the economic system – according to *their* criteria (legal personality, examination grades, profit and loss and so on) which any one individual did not and could not create. Moreover, families, religious ties and social classes did not cease to exist, nor did their influence necessarily decline uniformly. Hence the ambivalence: the ideal of the emancipated individual did not describe everyone's experience, especially when the powerful and uneven effects of poverty, gender or ethnicity were taken into account.

Thinking about modern law

So far we have sketched an outline of what modernity is, how it is energised and some ambivalences that appear to accompany it. We will delve deeper into aspects of all these, and more, as we explore our themes.

Of course, from our point of view, we are interested in what roles law and legal institutions have to play in all this. And already we have glimpsed something important in this regard: that when it comes to horizons of equality or justice, legal institutions and ideas have played a key role in modernity because regulation is required to stabilise expectations throughout a society and across time as society and expectations change. If legal regulation provides one of society's main capacities for dealing with progress and change, then understanding exactly what this relationship involves, or should involve, raises many questions that continue to be much contested. For example, one set of questions will include thinking about whether law and legal ideas merely reflect wider social and cultural forces and changes, or whether they inaugurate and direct such forces and changes. Another set of questions will involve thinking about law's relation to progress when societies continue to be divided along lines of wealth and power, gender and race. And another will ask whether legal regulation solves or exacerbates the ambivalences found in modernity, such as the dangers associated with technology or environmental degradation. And so on.

We will endeavour to trace how modern legal institutions work and deal with these kinds of questions by looking in some detail at various aspects of their operation. But one thing is worth keeping in mind throughout. Historically, and today, authors give widely divergent answers to the kinds of questions we will be exploring. This is because there are different ways of *describing* what law and legal institutions are and do, just as there are different ways of *evaluating* what they should or shouldn't do. Interpreting how law operates is deeply contested in part because not all theories (or theorists) see the same things when they observe legal and social institutions and practices. For example, where the same laws and economic arrangements affect different people or groups in different ways, with certain groups appearing to get treated far better than others, some will see a just set of arrangements working fine; others will see injustice in need of rectification. Where some will see a legal system in operation even if the government constantly uses retroactive laws, secret trials and evidence acquired through torture, others will see nothing more than an organised use of power that does not amount to a legal system.

What is visible and what is not is an aspect of the theoretical lenses we use, like putting on different pairs of glasses. And since law operates within a range of other, themselves competing, institutions and social forces – the economy, politics, morality and so on – then as well as understanding the work of legal institutions themselves, it is necessary to understand their relation to these other forms and forces. Yet understandings of these are contested too.

So what are we to do? Our purpose here is to shed as much light as possible on the operation of law and legal institutions by giving an account of key interpretations of these issues, and by identifying and tracing some of the central themes and concepts relevant to our subject matter. But keep in mind the divergences and disagreements among interpretations applies as much to detailed techniques of legal analysis as it does for the grand themes of modernity itself. Jurisprudence involves understanding a range of more or less large-scale contested interpretations, values and descriptions. And so it also involves ascertaining where you stand on them. Thinking about law therefore involves thinking about what such contestations signify, both generally, and individually, to each one of us. Doing so is nothing less than consistent with the individual 'Dare to know' spirit of modernity!

Reading

There are many readings of modernity, but accessible general introductions include Giddens (1990), Bauman (1989, 2000) and Habermas (1990). Legal perspectives engaging broadly with modernity include Unger (1976), Murphy (1997) and Douzinas (2007). Further readings can be found referenced in later sections where specific aspects of law and modernity are taken up in more detail.

A classic statement of the 'Enlightenment project' in philosophy is Kant (1991/1784). For an analysis of the limits of this approach, see Foucault (1984). In terms of the changes brought about in the economy and society more broadly, Karl Polanyi's *The Great Transformation* (1957/1944) remains one of the most powerful accounts of the emergence of the market system and the extraordinary social changes it brought about. In *Law and Revolution* (especially in volume 1) Harold Berman explains the changes in law during this period.

Chapter 2

Social contract theory

The emergence of the sovereign state – Westphalia as marker of transition

If we look at Europe during the feudal period that preceded modernity, we see a very different picture from that which we take for granted today. The concept of political authority lacked the sharp edges that the modern notion of the sovereign state furnishes it with today. For one thing political and religious authority remained largely undifferentiated during the Middle Ages, fused in the encompassing notion of the *respublica Christiana*. But the idea of this all-encompassing Christian empire had neither the hierarchical structure nor the jurisdictional powers we associate with modern political authority centred in the state. In fact authority was dispersed. To the extent that there was rule as we understand it today, it was exercised in cross-cutting and undercutting ways, by monarchs and ecclesiastical authorities, but also by commercial organisations, town councils and guilds. This was a radical form of what we would identify today as legal pluralism. As Harold Berman puts it in his important book *Law and Revolution: The Formation of the Western Legal Tradition*, it was not unusual for 'a serf [to] run to the town court for protection against his master. A vassal might run to the King's court for protection against his lord. A cleric might run to the ecclesiastical court for protection against the King' (p 10). This legal pluralism with its jurisdictional overlap of canon law, feudal law, royal law and merchant law (*lex mercatoria*) was ill-suited to the project of centralising political power and the economic demands of a growing mercantile class for the stability that an expanding capitalist economy required. Thus the creation of formal-rational bodies of law in the form of constitutions and codes, greatly influenced by the reception of Roman law, was crucially linked with the emancipatory projects of the new society (see Weber in chapter 3).

We can contrast this to the way in which *sovereignty* came to be understood in the course of the seventeenth century onwards, where it featured as the central element of how unified state power is exercised internally and externally. Internally, the unitary concept of sovereignty is central to the establishment of a uniform, vertical relationship between the state and its citizens. And it is also key to understanding its external or foreign relations: in the international 'community' the relationship between sovereign

States is horizontal in the sense that there is an assumption that they are formally equal, reciprocally recognised and have a corresponding right of non-intervention (Santos 2002).

To a large extent these developments that are captured by the key concept of sovereignty emerge with and around the Treaty of Westphalia of 1648. It was in fact during the sixteenth and seventeenth centuries that the ecclesiastical-political order began to come apart under the pressures of the Reformation (initially in Germany) and the rise of the Italian city-states. With the Reformation there was both a challenge to the authority of the Catholic Church and its doctrine and a gradual shift from ecclesiastical to secular authority. As the latter developed and independent political entities emerged, a language and a logic of rule of statecraft and of 'reason of State' began to develop – that is the notion of rules as entailing the governing of states as self-contained and independent entities. Although these were processes that lasted a long time, it has become customary to refer to the Treaty of Westphalia, that ended the bloody Thirty Years War, as the significant watershed for this development towards the society of sovereign states.

If Westphalia is the important turning point, it was not necessarily perceived as such at the time (those who met in Westphalia still saw themselves as members of a Christian community, the agreement was expressed in Latin and there was still no talk of 'sovereignty'). It is rather because, in retrospect, the Treaty ushered in a series of fundamental shifts in the institutions and language of politics. It largely brought the church under state control; it abolished any supervisory authority (papal or other) over states and, most significantly, it established state jurisdiction over territory, and an exclusive one at that. States now, through their governing authorities, enacted the law that was binding on their citizens, and they had the monopoly of legitimate violence when it came to reckoning with breaches of the law or conflicts among its citizens.

By way of framing what follows, we can draw again on Santos to see how the activity of regulation in modernity can be broken down into three 'principles or logics . . . that provide meaning and direction to social action'. These are the state, the market and the community. They can be summarised as follows (Santos 2002, p 3):

1 'the principle of the *state* embodies the vertical political obligation between citizens and the state, an obligation that is variously insured . . . by coercion and legitimacy';

2 'the principle of the *market* consists of the horizontal, mutually self-interested obligation among agents of the market';

3 'the principle of *community* entails the horizontal obligation that connects individuals according to criteria of non-state and non-market belongingness'.

In the following sections we will analyse aspects of each of these. We will do so by referring to some key concepts drawn from authors whose influence in modernity has been immense: Hobbes, Locke and Rousseau. Later variations, disagreements and departures from their insights, as well as a troubling of these categories themselves, will be taken up afterwards. In line with the approach taken in this book generally, attention to the historical context will be required to understand the development of the theory.

Hobbes, theorist of the modern state

Few works are as emblematic of the changing nature of sovereignty in this period as Thomas Hobbes's Leviathan. Written in France while Hobbes was in exile from the turmoil of the English civil wars, it was published in 1651, two years after the execution of King Charles I and the declaration of the Republic (which was to last only until 1660 when the monarchy was restored). Hobbes's work gave a rigorous philosophical justification for a strong unitary sovereign state, and its insights remain hugely influential. As Richard Tuck puts it, 'Nowadays, it is generally reckoned to be the masterpiece of English political thought, and a work which more than any other defined the character of modern politics' (Tuck 1996, p ix).

To think about the origin and purpose of the modern sovereign state with Hobbes, we can select two themes. The first concerns the problems of order, peace and security. The second addresses equality, the individual and consent. We will take each in turn.

The problem of order is a problem that faces all societies: how is social order to be established and maintained? For Hobbes, this was no mere philosophical question. As he was writing, England had descended into a state of violent disorder: civil war. Hobbes was writing in a context where it had become apparent that any ultimate authority or any principle of unity had disappeared. With no foundational principles available, the challenge was to imagine how order would be created out of contingency. In Leviathan he sought to solve the question of order and in doing so offered a number of insights that are central to thinking about the authority of the modern state. He employed several theoretical devices to do so including 'the state of nature' and the notion of the 'social contract'.

Consider first the state of nature. Hobbes asks us to imagine what condition the population would be in if there were no state. What is 'man' naturally like without a state, or where (as in civil war) state authority has completely broken down? According to Hobbes this 'state of nature' would be a place of profound insecurity, 'and which is worst of all, continual fear, and danger of violent death'. In this condition, as he famously put it, 'the life of man [is] solitary, poor, nasty, brutish, and short' (Hobbes 1996, p 89). Where every individual was roughly equal in capabilities and vulnerabilities – even the strongest men had to sleep – the condition could be well described as 'a time of Warre, where every man is Enemy to every man . . . and men live without other security, than what their own strength and their own invention shall furnish them withall' (Hobbes 1996, p 89).

This miserable condition of constant insecurity has more than just a physical dimension. There is also, just as importantly for Hobbes, no sense of common standards that can be appealed to in order to ameliorate this warring state. People have no consensus on what counts as right and wrong, and individuals have nothing with which to measure whether either their own or anyone else's behaviour is fair or unfair, appropriate or inappropriate. In the state of nature, anything goes. Hobbes describes this condition as follows:

> To this war of every man against every man, this also is consequent; that nothing can be unjust. The notions of right and wrong, justice and injustice, have there no place. Where there is no common power, there is no law; where no law, no injustice. Force and fraud are in war the two cardinal virtues. Justice and injustice are none

> of the faculties neither of the body nor mind . . . They are qualities that relate to men
> in society, not in solitude. It is consequent also to the same condition that there be
> no propriety, no dominion, no mine and thine distinct; but only that to be every
> man's that he can get, and for so long as he can keep it.
>
> (Hobbes 1996, p 90)

Insecurity, therefore, is not just about the lack of physical integrity. There is a lack of shared criteria for assessing anything, which means there is no guarantee of stability for whatever things one might want to use or acquire, whether it be food, or shelter, or even arms for self-protection. If everyone has a right to whatever they can get hold of in the state of nature, then really such a right amounts to nothing at all. Instead whatever someone has they will have by virtue of possession alone, not because it is exclusively theirs or because they have a secure right to it. In the state of nature there is no property; there is only possession. The reason for this follows from the fact that there are no standards of right and wrong, no measure of justice or injustice. Why not? Because for Hobbes there are no laws, and there are no laws because there is no common *authority* to make laws and apply them to everyone. There are merely individuals with their own interests, and there is only whatever power and force can deliver.

This is then a state of total disorder, where the maxim *homo homini lupus* (man is wolf to man) is the dominant logic. But it is one that individuals (more or less quickly) realise is disastrous because they perceive their condition as one of vulnerability, where even their individual abilities to preserve themselves are constantly threatened. Individuals understand that it would be better to seek peace than to endure such chaos. Applying even minimal reasoning will therefore lead them, Hobbes says, to realise the first 'law of nature; which is to seek peace, and follow it' (Hobbes 1996, p 92). To achieve peace means that everyone must try to act together in such a way that will end the disorder and create some security where none existed before. This then is the second law of nature that reason will lead men to realise:

> That a man be willing, when others are so too, as farforth, as for Peace, and defence
> of himself he shall think it necessary, to lay down this right to all things; and be
> contented with so much liberty against other men, as he would allow other men
> against himself.
>
> (ibid.)

For Hobbes, then, to get out of the condition of the war of all against all requires that each individual renounces their own strength and agrees with everyone else to seek peace. To create and then maintain peace and civil order, it is necessary for them to establish a single source of authority, the sovereign. This sovereign – or Leviathan – would represent everyone, and it would need to be given sufficient power to be strong enough to secure peace and to enforce the law against each individual. This agreement – or covenant, as Hobbes calls it – that creates the sovereign is what has come to be known as the social contract.

Before we go on to see how this works (and Hobbes's version will be different from those given later by Locke and Rousseau), let us pause to note something important about his method. At one point in his account of the state of nature Hobbes imagines an objection: that there 'never was such a time, nor condition of warre as this'; that is, the state of nature is a pure fiction, with no basis in reality at all. With two exceptions, his answer is perhaps surprising: Yes, that's correct, he says: 'I believe it was never generally so, over all the world' (Hobbes 1996, p 89). This means that what Hobbes is giving us here is not intended to be a historically accurate account of the genesis of sovereign authority out of the actually existing chaos of man's natural condition. Rather the state of nature and the social contract are intellectual devices he uses to think about what makes a sovereign state necessary and legitimate. He is providing what may be called a rational reconstruction of political legitimacy, rather than a factually accurate description of how any particular sovereign state came into being. This method of rational recon-struction is one that we will see being taken up by several theorists. (And what about the two 'real-life' exceptions where the description of the state of nature does apply? One is civil war, which is indeed a real enough case of radical disorder and not a product of Hobbes's theoretical imagination. The other exception is, he said, those places that have in fact 'no government at all . . . such as the savage people in many places of America [who] live at this day in that brutish manner' (Hobbes 1996, p 89). In this case, Hobbes, like many theorists before and since, readily adopted the distinction between 'civilised and savage' that would be deployed for centuries in legitimating Western colonial exploitation of those deemed lawless and lesser people.)

For Hobbes, the social contract that creates the state has been well described as a contract of alienation (Loughlin 2000, p 129). Although the multitude of people are the authors of the instituted sovereign authority, they have no ongoing contractual relation-ship to it. To maintain peace, order and security, the people have renounced (or 'alien-ated') once and for all their individual strength, and they now owe complete obedience to the sovereign's superior and indivisible will. If they did not behave in such a way, if they challenged the sovereign's right to rule over them, the danger would be of a descent back into the state of nature and its disorder, as happens in the case of the radical dis-agreements that lead to civil war.

As such this single sovereign authority has a monopoly not only in making laws that apply to everyone in the territory, but a monopoly on the force required to execute these laws. If the social contract gave an important theoretical justification for the legit-imacy of that authority, putting it into practice required the institutionalised organisa-tion of power. Hobbes was very matter of fact about this:

> Covenants being but words, and breath, have no force to oblige, contain, constrain, or protect any man, but what it has from the public sword; that is from the untied hands of that man, or assembly of men that hath sovereignty.
>
> (Hobbes 1996, p 123)

This power of the sword is clearly visible in the famous image that serves as the frontis-piece for Leviathan, where the massive figure of the sovereign wields the sword over his subjects and the land. But this power has come from the people – in the frontispiece image the people make up the body of the sovereign while looking up at it, in awe, at the same time – so that it is in renouncing their power to create the sovereign that the tranquillity of civic order is achieved. Interestingly, the other symbol wielded by the sovereign body on the frontispiece for Leviathan is a crozier. Hobbes had in mind the nefarious effects of religiously motivated civil wars. By embodying civil and religious power, the sovereign is positioned above the church. The powerful sovereign is thus given all powers to regulate individuals' actions, but Hobbes states clearly (planting in this way the seed of liberalism) that it cannot intrude on individuals' interior conscience. In other words, the sovereign regulates the *actions* of its subjects but not their *beliefs*.

It is the sovereign's task to secure the subjects' obedience: 'the use of so much power and strength [must be] conferred upon him, that by terror thereof, he is enabled to conform the wills of them all, to peace at home, and mutual aid against their enemies abroad' (Hobbes 1996, pp 120–121). Creating this overwhelming power is the price subjects paid for the 'peace and defence of them all'. And it is precisely, and for Hobbes not at all paradoxically, with their subjection that they achieve freedom: 'For in the act of our submission, consisteth both our obligation and our liberty' (Hobbes 1996, p 150).

Peace, order and security in civil society can only be achieved for Hobbes under a strong centralised state that brooks no dissent from its subjects. This is, in its most stark form, the 'vertical' relation that Santos identified as the principle of state regulation. And yet Hobbes also describes this powerful Leviathan as 'a mortal god'. This apparently oxymoronic formulation is, however, an entirely apt description of the sovereign state. On earth, it has a god-like power over its subjects. It has been created, like Frankenstein's monster, by humans in a way analogous to how God created man: 'the pacts and covenants by which the parts of this body politic were at first made, set together and united, resemble that *Fiat* [power], or the *Let us make man*, pronounced by God in the Creation' (Hobbes 1996, pp 9–10). It alone has the authority to make law and its laws are commands the subjects must obey on pain of the sanction of the sword. And since there is no contract between the sovereign and the subject, no covenant binds or could bind the sovereign's power, nor are there any laws that could constrain it. As we will see shortly, unlike in Locke's account of the social contract, subjects therefore can never have a legitimate or rightful claim against the sovereign's authority, even if many of them believe the sovereign is abusing its power, simply because that authority is the source of all rights. Of course, a wise sovereign should not act deliberately to harm its subjects, says Hobbes, and the subjects must hope the sovereign will indeed act for the good of them all. But beyond such hope, there is no lawful recourse available to them.

And yet at the same time this awesome power is 'mortal'. It is susceptible to death, to being killed. That this is descriptively true can again be seen in the case of civil war, where the government may be destroyed and there is no single effective authority in place while the war lasts. But the underlying reason for the sovereign's mortality is crucial: the sovereign state is a human creation, a human 'artifice', not something natural or God-given. And what humans create they can also destroy.

The significance of this cannot be overstated. Hobbes's account of the sovereign state sets a challenge to much of what had previously been assumed in political and legal theory in the pre-modern world. If for Aristotle, man was 'by nature a political animal; it is his nature to live in a state', then Hobbes's account is a direct challenge to this: man can live without a state, indeed it is his natural condition to do so, and it is a pretty miserable condition too. And a number of other long-standing political and legal assumptions are fundamentally undermined by this new way of thinking: gone is the 'divine right' of rulers to rule; gone are claims to obedience derived from unquestionable natural or religious authority; and gone is the plurality of competing authorities and jurisdictions we noted earlier. All these are replaced by one humanly made figure, 'this, our artificial man', the sovereign, whose secular commands alone now count as law. And when we recall Hobbes's argument that 'where there is no law there is no injustice' – no standards of right and wrong, or of justice or property – then since that sovereign authority is an artificial construct it means that so too are all those other moral and legal standards. Hence this act of human will – this fiat or Let us make man – puts humans and their creativity centre stage in a dramatically new way. For these reasons, as Loughlin rightly observes, it is 'Hobbes who makes the decisive break with the ancient world' (Loughlin 2000, p 134).

This leaves us to address the second theme we identified: equality, the individual and consent. We can deal with these more quickly, partly because they are implicit in the account we have already given of Hobbes's theory, and partly because they will be taken up in more detail in subsequent sections.

In postulating a state of nature where individuals compete with one another in the war of all against all, Hobbes is clearly emphasizing that individuals exist prior to the state. It is their desire for peace that forms the main motivation for establishing the social contract. It is their self-preservation that provides the purpose of the sovereign state. And it is the protection of individuals and their rights over time that the state alone can secure. As D'Entreves puts it, 'the theory of the social contract, apart from occasional precedents which can be found in ancient writers, is an entirely modern product. It is the distinctive mark of the political theory of individualism' (D'Entreves 1951, pp 55–56).

Such valorisation of the individual is, as we saw earlier, a common theme of modernity and Hobbes is often taken to be one of its most extreme exponents. And this individualism has, in turn, significant implications for an understanding of the state itself. By both historical and contemporary standards Hobbes's is a highly minimal, a highly emaciated, account of the state. There is no talk here of the state as the highest or most perfect form of human association that was so central to those thinkers who followed in the Aristotelian tradition. And there is certainly no sense of the pervasive redistributive tasks so commonly expected and found in contemporary states, with their rights not only to individual liberties, but to healthcare, education, welfare and the like. All these were still some way in the future and were none of Hobbes's concerns. Rather, by providing minimal individual security through the doubling of obligation and liberty, the state thereafter leaves individuals alone to pursue whatever they wish to do – so long as they obey the law.

We must now note the two final aspects of Hobbes's theory. The first is implicit in the very notions of the social contract and individualism he puts forward. It is this: as individuals, all people are equally individuals. This claim sounds straightforward, but in its application it too has a radical quality to it. It is grounded, says Hobbes, in that 'natural equality' whereby 'Nature hath made men so equal in the faculties of body and mind [such that] the difference between man, and man, is not so considerable' (Hobbes 1996, p 87). Never overly optimistic, Hobbes finds that this equality in mind and body is precisely the source of competition and distrust that causes men to be disposed to fight with each other. But the value in the principle of equality is nonetheless one that carries, in a positive way, right through into the establishment of the civil order. For what must be granted to one person must in good logic be granted to all. Indeed Hobbes writes this directly into the terms of the social contract itself: 'That at the entrance into conditions of peace, no man require to reserve himself any right, which he is not content should be reserved to every one of the rest' (Hobbes 1996, p 107). There is a universalism to this position that Hobbes traces back to the Bible's golden rule: 'Whatsoever you require that others should do to you, that do ye to them' (Hobbes 1996, p 92). Equality is a foundational value in this account not only in spiritual terms, but also in a way that differentiates it from much pre-modern thinking: that is, it is now treated as central to the institution, and the legitimacy, of a humanly made state.

The second aspect requires us to note that Hobbes's introduction of a radical form of legitimacy is one that not only challenges views that have gone before, but also sets a possible basis for future progress. That form of legitimacy is the idea that at some point, sovereign authority is a human construct *based on the consent of the people*. Minimal, and final, as this consent is in Hobbes's version, it is nonetheless a hugely powerful idea and one whose energy is still far from spent. When Hobbes wrote with appropriate precision that the sovereign could be 'one man or one assembly of men', this latter notion introduced at least the possibility that the consent of the governed could take the form of representative government. Of course, by modern standards Hobbes was no democrat, and many subsequent theorists have seen in his work a justification for strong-state authoritarianism. Yet it is in the notions of equality and consent that we can find the seeds of something recognizably modern that would be taken up and developed by future thinkers in more progressive ways. There would still be a great deal of resistance to achieving anything like equality and the consent of the governed as operational principles of government, with none more powerful than those to be found in the historic hypocrisies that simultaneously proclaimed equality for all and then denied them for many. But still, the seeds were sown. Their growth, and just as importantly their variation, will be taken up in the following sections.

In his effort to analyse and account for the key features of modern sovereignty, Hobbes's analysis thus contains a number of features that are recognizably modern: individualism, a role for equality and consent in establishing the dominance of secular authority, and the explicit demand for the complete obedience of subjects to the laws created by a single, unlimited sovereign power as the necessary price to be paid for order, peace, liberty and security. His contribution to modern legal theory can hardly be overestimated: the authoritative nature of law, the form of law as sovereign command, the separation between law and morality (in the sense that law does not receive its validity from morality), all classic tenets of legal positivism, are already formulated in deeply insightful ways by Hobbes.

John Locke: social contract and the law of private property

John Locke (1632–1704) is another of the key figures in the social contract tradition. His version of social contract has become a classic and his influence on modern political and legal philosophy is at least as great as that exercised by Thomas Hobbes, providing a reference point for the eighteenth-century revolutions in America (including being an influence for Thomas Jefferson's Declaration of Independence, for example) and France. In a nutshell, Locke's theory of the social contract represents the paradigmatic formulation of modern liberal legal theory.

The starting point of Locke's legal theory is the classic device of the state of nature. Unlike Hobbes, Locke does not assume that the state of nature is necessarily a dangerous, chaotic and lawless place. To the contrary, the state of nature in Locke is already marked by a sociality grounded in incipient forms of ordered relations in the form of natural laws. Human beings are born equally with natural rights (including, crucially, those to life, liberty and property) whose moral status is *antecedent* to the introduction of any positive law. Drawing on Christian theology, Locke postulates that the Earth has been given to all men by God: 'the goods of nature were originally common, both because the Bible says so, and because universal freedom and equality must mean original communism' (Laslett 1988, p 101). And yet this gift comes with a clear imperative: do not let it go to waste, make the most out of it; or, in other words, improve the value of the gift. Nature has thus to be made productive and this entails, among other things, that it ought to be made fruitful through the efforts of 'industrious and rational' individuals (Locke 1988, p 291). A comparison with Hobbes's theory can illustrate this point: human beings in the Hobbesian state of nature are worried about their survival, and they are driven by the passion of fear because they are aware of their vulnerable condition and their potential exposure to the risk of violent death; human beings in Locke's state of nature are motivated, from the very beginning, by productive concerns driven by individual interest. As aptly defined by C.B. Macpherson, Locke's man is the embodiment of 'possessive individualism'.

It is no surprise, then, that the focal point of Locke's theory of the social contract is property. The challenge he faced was however to show how, from an 'original communism' in the state of nature, a civil society where *inequalities* existed could be explained and justified. In the *Second Treatise on Civil Government* (1689), Locke provides a reconstruction of the generation of private property to just those ends. The key opening assumption is self-ownership: each human being owns their own body, and lives originally in an environment (Earth) not owned by anyone because it was given to humanity in common: 'Though the Earth, and all inferior Creatures be common to all Men, yet every Man has a Property in his own Person. This no body has any Right to but himself' (Locke 1988, p 287). Therefore, nature is seen as existing in common and it is to be cultivated and improved, through individual labour and the property each has in this. The historical context provides the background for this conception of property. Locke writes after the so-called 'enclosures', when huge portions of land had been enclosed and transformed into private land in order, it was claimed, to increase their fertility and, as a consequence, their value. Against this background, Locke assumes that things left in common tend either to perish or to remain underdeveloped, while individual interest would drive human beings to increase the value of their property. It is this type of interest that motivates people to improve what they had received in common.

So it is through 'the Labour of his Body, and the Work of his Hands' (Locke 1988, pp 287–288) that property is acquired: 'Whatsoever then he removes out of the State that Nature hath provided, and left it in, he hath mixed his *Labour* with, and joined to it something that is his own, and thereby makes it his *Property*' (Locke 1988, p 288, original emphasis). In other words, this mixing of labour and nature provides the original entitlement over the property of an object. According to Locke, labour is any process of altering a thing from its original indistinct condition in nature and by doing so provides a basis for acquisition of property *before* the social contract. Crucially such acquisition does not depend upon the consent of others. It is a natural process – individuals working on nature – that produces the right to one's own property.

A limit is however imposed on appropriation: one is under an imperative not to take more than one can use. On the one hand, over-production could result in things appropriated going to waste and, on the other, that which exists in common can be appropriated only 'where there is enough, and as good, left in common for others' (Locke 1988, p 291). (This is what Nozick (1974) will call 'Locke's Proviso'.) But instead of treating this as a final limitation on property acquisition, Locke introduces a contractualist device in·order to make property more fruitful and labour more productive. At the following stage of accumulation of property, Locke disentangles labour and property. After the initial appropriation, and despite the notion of natural limits imposed upon it, a silent consensus accrues on the possibility and desirability of unlimited accumulation of wealth. In this way, legal entitlement to property becomes both secure and subject to exchange through contract.

At this stage, two inventions are introduced in order to stabilise this societal development. On the one hand, a social contract (pactum associationis) that formally institutes society is agreed upon by human beings. The main motivation to get out of the state of nature is given by individual interest: it is rational, from the perspective of each individual, to leave the state of nature, where claims based on natural rights might be recognised but not institutionally protected, for a civil state which organises the protection of individual freedom and property. A second contract (pactum subjectionis) is then agreed for the institution of a civil government, tasked with the institutional powers to legislate and execute laws. The purpose of the government is clearly defined from the very beginning: to protect the rights to life, liberty and property. But given that life and liberty are deeply intertwined with ownership of the person, it is possible to sum up the main purpose of the government as being the guardian of private property. It is not by chance that to describe the government's job, Locke resorts to the metaphor of the night guardian. As he famously summed it up: 'The great and chief end therefore, of Mens uniting into Commonwealths, and putting themselves under Government, is the Preservation of their Property' (Locke 1988, pp 350–351).

The second invention, money, allows circulation of property, and hence the development of an exchange economy. This is a key passage in Locke's reasoning because the introduction of money is seen as a neutral act, supported by consensus, to allow for unlimited accumulation. If the problem of over-accumulation in the state of nature was that things might go to waste, and thus God's imperative about improving nature breached, the use of money was a brilliant invention since no matter how much of it one accumulated it would never rot! As Locke puts it, 'and thus came in the use of Money, some lasting thing that Men might keep without spoiling, and that by mutual consent Men would take in exchange for the truly useful' (Locke 1988, pp 300–301). It is of the utmost importance that the establishment of both money and the government are deemed to rely on consent, while the original acquisition of property does not.

This reconstruction of the emergence of money is presented by Locke not as the enabling condition that makes exchange value possible (for more on exchange value, see chapter 5, 'Law, Class and Conflict: Karl Marx'), but as a neutral tool. Locke disentangles labour from money and in this way the original link between labour and property is lost. The outcome is that inequality in property and wealth is justified, at one level, by the recognition of a legal entitlement to property which can be exchanged, and, at another level, through the fiction of a silent consensus with regards to the introduction of exchange value and its unit of measurement, that is, money. Accordingly, the natural limits imposed on the personal labour of an owner can be overcome by allowing the appropriation of the fruits of somebody else's work through exchange: that is, through wage labour.

In contradistinction to the 'original communism' of God's gift to all in common, Locke has arrived at a position where inequalities in wealth can be justified and sustained by the law. And since it is the 'great and chief end' of government to protect property, it does not matter that it is unequally distributed: it is the duty of government to protect, through a system of 'settled and known laws' whatever distribution of property results from market activity. That there may not be 'enough, and as good, left in common for others' is no longer a concern of government and law.

It is important to note that in Locke's theory, once the state is instituted by the social contract, the relation between government and governed is no longer contractual. It is instead best described by using another private law technique, namely trust. This follows from the fact that, in contrast to Hobbes's contract of 'alienation', Locke's social contract is one of *delegation* (Loughlin 2000, p 165). Government is entrusted to carry out the purpose delegated to it by the people – to protect fundamental rights – and to do so with limited means, that is through general legal rules interpreted by impartial officials and enforceable in a predictable and accountable manner. This legal condition is, for Locke, necessary for the secure enjoyment of the rights and liberties of citizens. Good government is thus limited government; a government limited with respect to its purpose and its means. Such are the conditions that make sovereign power accountable through time and under the doctrine of the rule of law.

One other crucial new right for citizens follows from this. Given the limited purpose and means delegated to government by the people, if the government oversteps these limits – if the government in other words breaches the trust placed in it – then citizens have the right to resist its actions. Locke theorises explicitly a right to resistance which grants citizens the possibility to dismiss the government and to form a new one. This, he says carefully, should only be invoked in the most egregious circumstances under which citizens' rights to life, liberty and property are no longer securely protected. Again, the difference with Hobbes's theory of sovereignty is striking. According to the latter, the dissolution of sovereign power brings society back to the state of nature. Given the disastrous conditions this would entail – a descent into civil war, for example – Hobbes believes that to have a government is always better than plunging back to the state of nature. Locke's philosophy does not make any room for an illiberal government. If the government infringes citizens' rights, and in particular if it fails to protect individual property rights, then the citizenry can justifiably revolt against it. There is perhaps no better description of this Lockean theory than the famous call to rebellion in the American colonists' Declaration of Independence against the British government:

> We hold these truths to be self-evident, that all men are created equal, that they are endowed by their Creator with certain unalienable Rights, that among these are Life, Liberty and the pursuit of Happiness. – That to secure these rights, Governments are instituted among Men, deriving their just powers from the consent of the governed, – That whenever any Form of Government becomes destructive of these ends, it is the Right of the People to alter or to abolish it, and to institute new Government.

Let's take stock. As we have seen, Locke's theory of natural rights pre-existing the social contract is deployed to justify a liberal theory of property and the state. In his conception of legal order, government and positive law are instituted as a way of protecting the natural rights human beings enjoy in the state of nature, but which are nonetheless insecure there. Thus they decide to subject themselves to positive law (through the artifice of the social contract) because they understand that a certain amount of interference in their natural liberty is necessary in order to protect their rights. Note that leaving the state of nature does not require any transformation of human beings. They remain self-interested agents even after the creation of civil society and government. In sum, positive law is understood by Locke as an interference upon individual's freedom, but a necessary one. Men have to endure a certain amount of government intrusion in order to see their expectations stabilised and their rights protected. The latter represent a shield for individuals in their relation with government. But should individuals and their property be subject to a 'long train of abuses', citizens' trust may be lost and a right of rebellion justified. Hence Locke believes that only a limited government, that is, a government which enacts the strictly necessary amount of law, is truly legitimate. This is a view of rights that will inform modern conceptions of fundamental and human rights up to the contemporary age.

Rousseau: law between equality and self-government

Jean-Jacques Rousseau, a Francophone philosopher born in Geneva in 1712, is our third classic author writing in the tradition of the social contract. Yet, it will be seen, Rousseau's take on the social contract is highly distinctive, to the point where one could question whether his theory can be seriously deemed a form of contractualism. In fact, his use of the devices of the state of nature and the social contract is geared not towards the construction and the consolidation of a legal order for the protection of people's lives (as it is for Hobbes), or for the protection of property (as it is for Locke), but for the creation of equality and collective self-government.

Rousseau's problem is not the state of nature in itself, given that he does not characterise it as an intrinsically dangerous place or as a realm of fully fledged and harmonic natural rights. Famously, Rousseau opens his masterpiece, *The Social Contract* (1762), by remarking that 'Man was born free, and everywhere he is in chains' (Rousseau 1994, p 45). This means that the natural freedom of the state of nature has been lost in favour of the enchainment of civil society. Why had men lost their freedom in this way? Rousseau believes that this is not the unavoidable fate of a race of human beings prone to evil or just moved by selfish interests. Rousseau's social contract narrative resonates with his predecessors because he shares an individualistic premise based on the strategic rationality of human beings facing the undesirability of the state of nature:

> I make the assumption that there is a point in the development of mankind at which the obstacles to men's self-preservation in the state of nature are too great to be overcome by the strength that any one individual can exert in order to maintain himself in this state. The original state can then subsist no longer, and the human race would perish if it did not change its mode of existence.
>
> (Rousseau 1994, p 54)

Rousseau resorts here to the language of costs and benefits in order to explain why human beings opt for the social contract. The rational actors see it as a beneficial exchange:

> [N]othing is truly renounced by private individuals under the social contract . . . instead of abandoning anything they have simply made a beneficial transfer, exchanging an uncertain and precarious mode of existence for a better and more secure one, natural independence for liberty, the power of hurting others for their own safety.
>
> (Rousseau 1994, p 70)

But it does not take long for the reader to discern that this individualistic language is misleading, employed tactically to enable Rousseau to position himself within the social contract tradition. In fact, another logic is at play in his masterpiece: it is actually through the negation of individual autonomy – that is, through renouncing completely the natural right to freedom – that the social contract is realised. Only by surrendering completely one's autonomy, does the social contract become possible:

> If individuals retained some rights, there being no common superior to give judgment between them and the public, each would make his own judgement on certain points, and would soon aspire to do so on all of them: the state of nature would remain in force, and the association would become, necessarily, either tyrannical or meaningless.
>
> (Rousseau 1994, p 55)

In fact, there is more going on in Rousseau's social contract than the mere deployment of strategic rationality. The move from the state of nature to society is driven not by individual autonomy and private interest, but rather by the general constraint of the common interest. The social contract is seen as the answer to the question of which form of association makes it possible for persons to unite while, at the same time, remaining free by obeying oneself alone. Rousseau's aim is to prove that only a social contract where each gives oneself to all (and therefore to none) can enable a form of association based on the common good. The primacy of the common over the private interest is demonstrated by the transformative aspect of the social contract. This is not an external dynamic – i.e., the simple act of agreeing with some other (or, at least, it is not only that) – but an internal process: a transforming of one's identity. The complete alienation of one's rights to the whole community brings about nothing less than a profound change in the subject, which is necessary in order to overcome Rousseau's social contract and which thus foreshadows a critique of instrumental reasoning and its reductive depiction of social relations.

In contrast to Hobbes and Locke, Rousseau's social contract entails an anthropological mutation. The individual emerges from it radically transformed into a citizen, 'replacing instinct by justice in his behaviour, and conferring on his actions the moral quality that they had lacked before' (Rousseau 1994, p 59). The transformation entails no less than the acquisition of moral status. In light of this consideration, Rousseau's effort aims at transcending, if not utterly dismissing, the liberal version of the social contract: the only way to overcome the corruptive and dysfunctional logic of liberal (economic) autonomy is to build a different social being upon the bases of the primacy of the public interest and a strong and substantial conception of equality. At this point, Rousseau introduces his idea of the general will (*volonté générale*) as a device for overcoming decision-making processes based on individual interests. With the introduction of the notion of the general will it is possible to give an essential definition of the social contract: '*Each of us puts his person and all his power in common under the supreme direction of the general will; and we as a body receive each member as an indivisible part of the whole*' (Rousseau 1994, p 55 [original emphasis]). In order to understand the general will it is useful to compare it with the 'will of all'. The latter is the aggregation of each and every will of the citizens of a community. Wills are determined not by the common interest, but by what is in the individual interest of each one. The outcome of a decision based on the will of all is simply an aggregation of wills which does not take into account the common good. The general will introduces the idea of the common interest as the driving force behind the formation of each and every will. In other words, when deciding on political issues, citizens ought to form their will not according to preferences dictated by their own petty private interests, but according to what is in the interest of all (that is, of the whole community). The general will provides the basis for an ideal of popular sovereignty. In fact, sovereignty, 'being only the exercise of the general will, can never be transferred, and . . . represented except by itself' (Rousseau 1994, p 63). This is because through the general will, the people become the subject and at the same time the object of sovereign decision-making.

Rousseau believes that law plays an essential role in the creation of a political order based on the general will. It is only through lawmaking that people become a sovereign subject and it is only through lawmaking that self-government can be achieved once the object of the law becomes the people itself. Therefore, legislative power 'belongs to the people, and can belong to it alone' (Rousseau 1994, p 91). Also, the law is necessary for realising freedom: people are free only as long as they are following laws that they gave to themselves. Rousseau (unlike Hobbes and Locke) adopts a positive conception of freedom. Freedom is defined as positive because it is not absence of external interference, but autonomous self-government. Given their importance, general laws must have distinctive characters. Rousseau's definition of the law is of great importance for the story of modern law:

> when the people makes a ruling for the whole people it is concerned with itself alone, and the relationship, if created, is between the whole object from one point of view and the whole object from another, the whole remaining undivided. Then the matter on which the ruling is made is general, as is the will that makes it. It is this act that I call a law. When I say that the objects of laws are always general, I mean that the law considers the subjects of the state as a collectivity and actions in the abstract, but never a man as an individual, nor any particular action. Thus the law can rule that privileges will exist, but it cannot bestow them on any person by name.
>
> (Rousseau 1994, p 74)

Accordingly, Rousseau draws a distinction between law and decrees. The former ought to be acts of the general will, therefore its object has to be general, while decrees concern a particular object or individual.

Three further aspects of Rousseau's notion of the social contract confirm the insufficiency of the liberal, contractarian logic for the creation of a society out of the state of nature. First, the figure of the 'Legislator', who is supposed to frame the fundamental laws and submit them for the community's approval, exists outside the reach of social contract: to establish a proper constitution, a legislator external to society is necessary. Although the precise nature of the Legislator is something of a mystery, the combination of its foundational necessity for the social contract together with its essential existence outside that contract represents a denial of the social contract's grounding in individual autonomy. Second, when sovereignty is brought about, its authority has to be expanded and protected. In this sense, Rousseau draws a clear distinction between sovereign power and government. The latter is defined as 'an intermediate body set up between subjects and sovereign to ensure their mutual correspondence, and is entrusted simply with the execution of laws and with the maintenance of liberty, both social and political' (Rousseau 1994, p 92). Given that the government is concerned with executive power, it has to be endowed with strength. However, for this reason, Rousseau suggests that its activities have to be constrained. Rousseau favours a 'limited government', but unlike Locke, he does not support this idea for protecting individual rights. Rather, he believes that limited government is necessary in order to protect the authority of the sovereign body. Third, from his description of the role played by the customs and the morals of the people, it is clear that Rousseau understands the state's laws as reflecting a concrete community ethos. Laws are clearly 'general' in a double sense: (1) because of their general subjects and objects, but also (2) because they have to rest upon the general customs and virtues of citizens. Citizens will have to develop an attachment to the political community because their actions will represent the ultimate bulwark against abusive governmental power.

Positive freedom and substantive equality

To grasp why the synthesis between freedom and substantive equality is Rousseau's driving question requires understanding his criticism of political economy. This is not to say that the relation between freedom and equality is ever fully settled by Rousseau. Recently, Frederick Neuhouser (2013) has put forward a solid argument that equality (and in particular economic equality) has only instrumental value in Rousseau's legal theory, with freedom alone having intrinsic value. While this reading cannot be ruled out, it nevertheless downplays the role that substantive equality has in shaping Rousseau's legal and political philosophy.

To avoid any misunderstanding, two points must be highlighted. Rousseau himself refers to the impossibility of a perfect substantive equality: 'as for equality, the word must not be taken to mean that the degrees of power and wealth should be exactly the same' (Rousseau 1994, p 87). Equality has a significant substantive dimension, but it cannot be measured through some rigorous mathematical weighing. Along these lines, Rousseau also recognises the existence of diverse forms of substantive equality – such as where, in a language later taken up by the social theorist Pierre Bourdieu, symbolic or social capital, rather than material welfare, is at stake. As evident from Rousseau's discussion of the role of private property, for example, equality is directly addressed to the conditions of subsistence, but not just that. Equality in power and education are all immanent to the shaping of a specific type of citizen without whom a truly political order would be impossible.

The second remark, which follows, is that equality plays a guiding role in Rousseau's work. At a critical level, it is the basis upon which Rousseau erects his criticism of modern forms of socialisation. At a normative level, it is the bedrock of his ideal of the legal order:

> instead of destroying natural equality, the fundamental contract substitutes moral and legal equality for whatever degree of physical inequality nature has put among men; they may be unequal in strength or intelligence, but all become equal through agreed convention and by right.
>
> (Rousseau 1994, p 62)

In other words, equality serves a double function in his work: it illuminates the short-comings of the political economy of modern society, and it provides the ground for a more radical type of legislation.

Such emphasis on substantive equality remains largely missing in the tradition of classical liberal philosophy, as it is illustrated most clearly by Locke's theory of property. The radical consequence of the focus on substantive equality takes the form of an alternative view of the relation between society and the legal order. The lesson to learn from this reading of Rousseau's work is that the modern development of society brings about the dominance of particular and selfish interests, blocking any possible reconciliation with more authentic forms of individual and collective participation (i.e., the value of self-government) with claims of equality (i.e., the value of justice). Rousseau's legal philosophy is decidedly anti-liberal because he grasps (whether fully realising it or not) the dilemma of modern liberal society, exposing the inadequacy of its formalistic solution to the problem of equality.

Locke vs Rousseau: the question of property

The best starting point to capture Rousseau's alternative approach to modern law is to look at how property is defined. For it is in this that we can see how Rousseau's legal philosophy derives from his critique of classical political economy (although it is arguable how much Rousseau himself knew modern political economy). In brief, the key contrast is that Locke's liberal legal theory is organised as a device for protecting the right to private property. Of course, Locke's use of property has to be retrieved carefully because the word is often employed in its wide sense to include the idea of self-ownership. As already remarked, in this sense property extends to life and liberty as well as estates or goods.

But in contrast to Locke, Rousseau's legal theory is not conceived as a device for protecting a natural right to property. It is oriented towards the common interest, with private property assuming a derivate form. This contrast is highlighted in their respective treatment of land. There are two aspects to this, both announced in *The Social Contract* where Rousseau discusses the touchstone of property, and most particularly land:

> In general, the following conditions are required in order to justify the right of first occupancy for a given piece of land. First, the land must as yet be uninhabited; secondly, no more must be occupied than is needed for subsistence; and in the third place, possession must be taken not by empty ceremonies but by work and

cultivation, the only mark of ownership which ought, in default of juridical title, to be respected by others.

(Rousseau 1994, pp 60–61)

The first theme is the limitation of private property in accordance with the needs of each, a theme linked, through *A Discourse on Inequality* (originally published in 1755), to the subsistence of each citizen and their family. The criterion of subsistence operates in two directions: it establishes a threshold that cannot be overcome, but it also introduces a minimum standard necessary to achieve independence. Just as in the case of the alienation of freedom, the cession of a minimum quantity of land necessary for subsistence is not valid. This is the basis of a concrete conception of freedom: without a minimum amount of property there is no space for self-government, because relations of domination easily spread across society.

The second main difference is found in the idea of labour as a source of legitimacy for the original acquisition of property. While Locke introduces, after the original appropriation, the conditions of use and improvement that allow him to shift attention to the preservation of land's fertility and then the possibility of appropriating other people's work through contract and money, Rousseau maintains that personal labour remains the legitimating factor for property. The right to property, therefore, comes from one's continuous personal labour in utilizing and maintaining it; it is the 'only mark of ownership'. This ensures that the cycle of production is directly tied to consumption and subsistence and not to accumulation. As emphasised in his *Discourse on Inequality*, the great transformation occurs when men decide to start accumulating resources not for immediate but for future consumption, and instrumental rationality opens up a space for an autonomous form of economic activity.

Contrary to Locke's irenic account of the legitimacy of social inequality, Rousseau locates the seeds of the further corruption of men in the process of social differentiation. Division of labour, uneven distribution of wealth and the rise of a distorted form of pride (*amour propre*) become co-extensive with society. Far from Locke's pacified presentation of the emergence of private property, Rousseau's prose, with its dramatic overtones, identifies property as corrosive and an obstacle to the end of equality:

from the instant one man needed the help of another, and it was found to be useful for one man to have provisions enough for two, equality disappeared, property was introduced, work became necessary, and vast forests were transformed into pleasant fields which had to be watered with the sweat of men, and where slavery and misery were soon to germinate and flourish with crops.

(Rousseau 1984, p 116)

Rousseau offers a historical approach to labour in contrast to Locke's naturalistic approach: labour is conceived as socially constructed from the very beginning. The moment of appropriation, according to Rousseau, takes its meaning vis-à-vis the social context. It is the functional link of appropriation to the common good of society that justifies the connection between the owner and the things that are regarded as being her 'property'.

Rousseau's legal and political philosophy, while controversial, proved to be a constant source of inspiration for democrats and republicans. In particular, his work was hailed as a major point of reference by many French revolutionaries (Furet 1981, p 31). A paradigmatic instantiation of his influence can be seen in Article 6 of the 1789 Declaration of the Rights of Man and Citizen, which states that 'Law is the expression of the general will'. Even more evident were the signs of Rousseau's main legal and political concepts on the Jacobin draft for the Constitution of the Year I (which never entered into force), whose main driving force was to be seen in the role attributed to popular power. Rousseau's theory has remained an unavoidable contribution for all those interested in democratic legal orders.

Reading

Thomas Hobbes's *Leviathan* (1996) is a key text to read, particularly chapters 13–31. The secondary literature on Hobbes is vast, but the work of Quentin Skinner is always insightful (see for example his *Hobbes and Republican Liberty*, 2008). D'Entreves (1951) sets social contract theory helpfully within a historical context. A useful collection of papers on the concept and changing conceptions of sovereignty more generally is Walker (2003b), and the historical essay by Robert Jackson (1999) is particularly useful on Westphalia and the new mapping of sovereignty in Europe.

Locke's *Second Treatise on Civil Government* is the starting point for any engagement with his work. Laslett (1988) provides an excellent 'Introduction' to Locke. For the theory of possessive individualism see C.B. Macpherson (1962). Critiques of Locke's theory of property can be found in Tully (1980), Waldron (1988, ch 6) and Meiksins Wood (2012, ch 7). A well-known contemporary version of Locke's political theory is put forward by Nozick (1974) and one of Locke's theory of property rights by Epstein (1985).

An insightful introduction to Rousseau's social theory is given by Shklar (1969), and an overview of the role of the will in Rousseau's legal theory is available in O'Hagan (2003, pp 122–125). For analyses of equality and inequality in the philosophy of Rousseau see Cohen (2010) and Neuhouser (2013). A useful collection of essays dedicated to Rousseau's conception of law is edited by Brooks (2005). A comparison between Rousseau and Marx is drawn by Della Volpe (1978).

Chapter 3

Law and the rise of the market system

In this section we explore in more detail the economic and social contexts in which the consolidation of capitalism took hold. We will pay particular attention to the legal conditions that facilitated this development, as well as considering some of the social consequences.

At the end of the eighteenth century the Industrial Revolution ushered in an enormous improvement in European societies' capacities to produce goods and, at the same time, arguably the most devastating dislocation ever in the lives of the common people of Europe. And, as we will see, owing to the effects of global imperialist expansion, associated forms of dislocation came to be extended to vast areas of the world. While the prevalence of the market economy and the expansion of the economic system took hold at different times, followed a different pace and took different forms depending on the more local cultural and labour practices in different parts of Europe, the advent of modernity is facilitated and crucially linked with their emergence. This occurs in marked contrast to an earlier pre-modern, pre-capitalist or traditional society. Where pre-modern societies relied on agricultural forms of subsistence and were largely rural, modern society is industrialised and organised around a capitalist economy. If traditional societies were based on face-to-face interaction with family and acquaintances in small, self-contained communities, modern society is based on various forms of mediated communication and the paradigmatic form of economic exchange is with strangers. And if traditional societies structured by beliefs in magic and religious or mystical symbols played an active role in the organisation of social life, modern society is characterised by the declining importance of religion, and the belief that the social and natural world can be demystified through the application of science.

The transition from pre-modern to modern, from feudal to capitalist, was both revolutionary and fraught. On the one hand, markets introduced their own dynamic of bringing people together around new technologies of communication and exchange in a way that directly countered the forms of closure of the traditional societies of feudal Europe, with their limited possibilities of challenging hierarchies and received wisdom. New possibilities of expanded knowledge and a pluralism of value are associated with the emergence of factory towns and urban environments. On the other hand the violent uprooting of life from local contexts shattered people's reliance on the value systems that governed social life, and as people came to commit their work to the factories of the industrial cities there emerged also a crippling dependency on the owners of the mills and the masters of industry under the very real threat of starvation for those who could not find work or were laid off. A new freedom coupled with a new insecurity is constitutive of the new social experience of modernity. These transformations have had a lasting impact, not only on how we live, but also on how we think about ourselves and our relation to the world that we live in. Indeed, it is not surprising that sociology – the science of society – has its origins in the thought of the eighteenth and nineteenth centuries as writers struggled to understand the nature of the social changes that they were living through.

Let us have a closer look at the rise of the market system. The spectacular changes in production and the economy took effect with stark intensity in the period between the 1790s and the 1830s in England and southern Scotland. As far as agricultural production was concerned, the relationship between the landlords and the tenants who worked on the land increasingly took the form of leases whose rents were no longer fixed by custom or law, as they used to be, but became subject to market conditions, unfixed and variable. A new agrarian capitalism developed where tenants became subject to competitive pressures, which meant that they had to increase productivity, rely on agricultural 'improvement' and extract more value out of the wage labourers who worked for them on the farms, to survive in what in effect had become a market in leases. The competition that is thereby introduced allowed what we might call a purely economic form of coercion in Britain; whereas in other parts of the Continent, notably France, the landed classes had to mobilise political and military forms of coercion to police the tenants and sustain the conditions of the mode of agrarian production; in Britain compulsion was locked in place by market imperatives.

The decades between 1790 and 1830 also mark an exceptional migration from the countryside to the factory towns, so that by 1830 the urban population had risen to 40% (compare this with France where 95% of the population lived in rural areas at the same period). As those who could no longer sustain a livelihood in the old communities structured around attachments of 'blood and soil', with their locally limited capacity to produce and trade in goods, flocked to the factory towns, there occurred an unprecedented geographical mobility, the rapid growth of cities and significant changes in the forms of social life. We associate the Industrial Revolution with the extraordinary advancement in technology and the use of machinery, the rise of factory towns, the emergence of slums, the long working hours of children, the increase in population and the concentration of industries. A number of factors contributed to these developments: certainly amongst them was Watt's discovery of the steam engine that drove the machines, the extraordinary new possibilities that came with an intensified division of labour and specialisation in the processes of production, as did the opportunities of innovation and the motive of accumulation of wealth. We will not dwell on these any further at this point. Instead, and in order to understand the magnitude of the increase in productive capacity and the scale of social dislocation, we must go back to look at how the conditions of such a transformation were set first institutionally, and then culturally in terms of the rise of the market mentality. In what follows we will look at both dimensions:

(i)   *Institutionally*, the crucial role that the law played in these developments
(ii) *Culturally*, how a new market mentality is forged creating the new spirit of capitalism

The institutional dimension

We have already seen in John Locke's defence of property that it is developed at least in part in terms of a justification against 'waste'. Enclosing in the name of 'improving' what would otherwise be wasted, Tudor legislation in England removed people's common property in land. Acts of enclosure were passed extinguishing common and customary use rights, depriving people of access to the common land and its resources and thus effectively depriving them of the traditional sources of their means of subsistence. In England the enclosure of six million acres of common land between 1760 and 1830 created dependency of the agricultural population upon money wages. Similarly in Scotland the Highland Clearances in the mid- to late eighteenth and early nineteenth centuries involved the forced eviction of inhabitants of the Highlands and western islands of Scotland, resulted in the destruction of the traditional clan society and began a pattern of rural depopulation of Scotland. The most notorious amongst them took place between 1810 and 1820 and involved the eviction of thousands of families, the burning of their cottages and the establishment of large sheep farms. Out of these processes emerged the new classes of capitalist modernity, organised according to the economic logic of a market in rents and wages, polarised around those who owned the means of production and therefore controlled agricultural and manufacturing industry and those who had no other means to stay alive except their ability to work, but nowhere to commit it except to the owners of capital in exchange for the means of subsistence.

We will need to distinguish two ways in which the process of transformation was institutionalised, both at a political level and at a legal level. On the one hand the transition from feudal to capitalist modes of production was effected politically by the operation of the state, and the deployment of ordinary and sometimes excessive violence. There occurred a political process by which the emerging bourgeoisie gradually enlisted the state apparatus in its service. On the other hand legally it was inextricably linked with the creation of new forms of property rights, the extinguishment of customary rights and perquisites, and the legal regulation of the wage-labour relation. Politically, then, state power is deployed "to hasten, as in a hothouse, the process of transformation of the feudal mode of production into the capitalist mode, and to shorten the transition," as Karl Marx put it (Marx 1865/1990, pp 915–916). At the same time the political process was buttressed and supported by laws that radically reshaped the way in which property relations were organised. Where the independent livelihoods of the rural poor had been based on use rights over land, what was being ushered in was a profound legal transformation where the rural populations, in the words of Edward Thompson, were seeing 'the very roof beams which housed their practical economy . . . being eaten away' as successive legal enactments 'signalled that lawyers had become converted to the notions of absolute property ownership, and that . . . the law abhorred the messy complexities of use-right' (Thompson 1977, pp 240–241). Legal enactments and instruments effectively forced people off the 'common lands' and into wage labour. During this period which is sometimes referred to as the 'pre-history of Capitalism' acts of 'enclosing' were coupled, in England, with the draconian legal prohibition of vagabondage, begging, wandering, etc, and anything that might be perceived as an 'exit opportunity' from wage labour. The Black Act of 1723 created fifty new capital offences and 'signalled the onset of the flood-tide of eighteenth-century retributive justice' (Thompson 1977, pp 206, 223). Supported by subsequent enactments and evolving through strategic judicial interpretation (see Hay 1975), it became a powerful instrument of repression used to punish by example those displaying 'malice to the gentry' and thereby strengthened the resources of stability by seeking to extinguish any expression of popular disaffection.

While it is true that the creation of a market in land, which forced tenants to compete for access, and the creation of market in labour, which forced proletarians to compete for jobs, introduced a form of economic coercion that did not rely on political means, we should not ignore how the institutions of law and state supported and buttressed the new relations of production. The institutional support can be understood both as internal and external. One might think of 'internal' as facilitative, even constitutive of the new forms of exchange that capitalism depends on, where forms of contract and property were transformed to enable forms of capitalist exchange: what could be the object of property was expanded to include labour – one's capacity to work – as were expanded the 'instances' of property, to include for example 'alienability': property became ownership of commodities that could be freely transferred in the marketplace. But law also played the role of external support of the capitalist system, whereby the criminal law, for example, is used to police the consolidation of markets initially through the draconian legislation against foraging, etc (the Black Act, above), the judicial deployment of selective prosecutions to police it, the asymmetry between 'master and servant' (more on this below), and the prohibition of association and combination of workers throughout the nineteenth century. Ellen Meiksins Wood summarises the function of the law in this way:

> the courts would put the proprietor's right to profit above other kinds of right, such as the customary use-rights long enjoyed by non-owners, or the right to subsistence. And the civil authority reacted more violently, especially in the wake of the French Revolution, to protest against unjust prices and market practices. Coercion by the State, in other words, was required to impose the coercion by the market.
>
> (Meiksins Wood 2002, p 62)

Gradually the law came comprehensively to regulate the conditions of labour – including such matters as the length of the working day and the level of wages. There can be little doubt that much legal effort here was directed at facilitating capital accumulation, so that even Adam Smith would comment that 'whenever the legislature attempts to regulate the differences between masters and their workmen, its counsellors are always the masters' (Smith 1976, p 157). The Master and Servant Law of 1823, in fact, entertained no measure of formal equality between the two, providing that a breach of contract on the part of a master constituted a civil offence, while the violation of an agreement by an employee was a criminal offence subject to retribution of up to three months imprisonment with hard labour. (There is evidence to suggest that some 10,000 prosecutions per year occurred under the 1823 Act (see Doogan 2009, p 106).) But the regulation of class relations also took more benevolent forms, as for example with the factory legislation of the mid-nineteenth century that was protective of the workers and in fact achieved a remarkable physical and moral regeneration of labour powers, and to which Marx dedicates a sustained analysis (Marx 1865/1990, pp 406–408). Yet it is not far-fetched to argue that the protective legislation in response to the industrial practices in Britain of the late eighteenth and early nineteenth centuries, which had led to widespread exhaustion and frequent deaths of factory workers, constituted measures taken to secure the reproduction of the labour force.

In these processes we witness the rise and consolidation of *market society*. The institutional changes were closely tied to changes in economic thinking, clearly linked with new figurations of class relations and the rise of the new merchant classes whose power was economic and was exercised in terms of their ability to buy, and who therefore were keen to force their society's vital resources into the sphere of exchange. And yet these developments could not occur without a sea change in the cultural imaginary of the age, which we might identify as the new *market mentality*.

The market system

If Adam Smith was, as Kenneth Galbraith puts it in his discussion of the history of economics, 'the prophet of its achievements and the source of its guiding rules' (Galbraith 1998, p 58), he would not have had much opportunity to witness the massive changes brought about by the Industrial Revolution at the time that he published his most famous treatise *The Wealth of Nations* in 1776. There were certainly in evidence the manufacturing workshops and the mines, but otherwise there were neither the great factories nor the acceleration of production. And yet in prophetic mode, Smith described with fascination the division of labour and the specialisation that gave the capitalist enterprise its extraordinary efficiency. In a famous passage he describes the division of tasks in a factory manufacturing pins: 'One man draws out the wire, another straights it, a third cuts it, a fourth points it, a fifth grinds it at the top for receiving the head; to make the head requires two or three distinct operations.' The unprecedented efficiency and increased productivity that the division of labour was capable of, alongside man's 'natural propensity to truck, barter and exchange one thing for another', were the basis of commercial activity and at the heart of the dynamism of the new system. It was not simply the drive to increase productivity that so impressed Smith, but also, he already noted at this early stage, a crucial ambivalence: the capacity of the new working methods to dominate the lives and mentality of the workers. The fragmentation of their work into simple repetitive tasks brought on a mindlessness and ensured that they lost sight of the connection of their own effort to the final product: a disconnect – or as Marx would describe it, an *alienation* – that in the subsequent history of capitalist production acquires great significance.

Smith would build the 'guiding rules' of the economic science on the basis of these insights. The science was based on an understanding of natural human motivation to maximise utility for oneself and to act out of self-interest. In his famous formulation, 'it is not from the benevolence of the butcher, the brewer or the baker, that we expect our dinner, but from their regard to their own interest. We address ourselves not to their humanity but to their self-love' (bk 1, ch 2). Moreover, the competitive pursuit of self-interest in the marketplace was the source of the public good. The market mechanism delivers the seamless co-ordination of private interests. In Smith it is famously described metaphorically as the invisible hand: 'the individual is in this, as in many other cases, led by an invisible hand to promote an end which was no part of his intention' (bk 4, ch 2).

In the attribution of economic motive to individuals, the argument about the price of mechanism and the connection to value, and in the commitment to free trade, the basis of the market system is laid out in *The Wealth of Nations*. In the picture of the *homo economicus* Smith gives us an original and ingenious coincidence of the maximisation of self-interest and the public good; and in the notion of the invisible hand what results is a spontaneous ordering of preferences and allocation of social value. It is of course only fair to say that in Smith's view, such practices were located only within the economy and did not explain the motivations for virtuous behaviour in morality and politics, far less provide a foundation for social relations generally (see e.g. Veitch 2017). As Polanyi notes, for Smith *wealth* was merely

> an aspect of the life of the community, to the purposes of which it remained subordinate . . . there is no intimation in his work that the economic interests of the capitalists laid down the law to society . . . In [Smith's] view nothing indicates the presence of an economic sphere that might become the source of moral law and political obligation.
>
> (Polanyi 1944, pp 111–112)

Such an amoralistic, essentially anti-Smithian, version of economics was still to come.

Historically, there was of course little that was actually spontaneous about the emergence of market society, the prevalence of the market mentality and the facilitation of capitalist production. While Smith assumed the market mentality ('the propensity to truck, barter and exchange') as axiomatic truth of the human condition, as natural and therefore as expressed throughout social history, in fact 'gain and profit made on exchange never before played an important part in human economy. Though the institution of the market was fairly common since the later Stone Age, its role was no more than incidental to economic life,' wrote Karl Polanyi in his economic history of modernity, *The Great Transformation*, an analysis that remains unsurpassed in its insight that the creation of market society was inextricably linked with the commodification of its main resources: land, labour and money. Polanyi writes about Smith's naturalization of the profit motive that 'in retrospect it can be said that no misreading of the past ever proved so prophetic for the future' (Polanyi 1944, p 43), as market thinking took hold with the expansion of the capitalist economy in Europe.

Max Weber, whose work we will look at more systematically in the next chapter, gives us a painstaking sociological account of the laborious processes though which the market mentality displaced earlier forms to install itself as the central feature of economic thinking. In his first major work written in 1904/5, *The Protestant Ethic and the Spirit of Capitalism*, Weber argues that the Protestant faith, especially Luther's notion of calling and the Calvinist belief in predestination, set the stage for the emergence of the capitalist spirit. Weber's analysis shows that material production was not on the whole governed by what we would call today economic rationality. He takes the example of textile production, a key industry of the eighteenth and nineteenth centuries in Britain and the rest of Europe, which involved until the 1830s the co-existence of industrial production with the labour of individuals working from home, who produced the greater part of the goods. Until the 1830s it was inconceivable that the labour of the home weavers would be put into competition or that it would be geared to delivering maximum profit in a market-'rational' way. As Weber describes the labour of the domestic weavers in *The Protestant Ethic and the Spirit of Capitalism*:

The number of business hours was very moderate, perhaps five to six a day; in the rush season, where there was one, more. Earnings were moderate; enough to lead a respectable life and in good times to put away a little. On the whole relations among competitors were relatively good, with a large degree of agreement on the fundamentals of business. . . .

The form of organisation [of the industry] was traditionalistic if one considers the spirit which animated the entrepreneur: the traditional manner of life, the traditional rate of profit, the traditional amount of work, the traditional manner of regulating the relationships with labour, and the essentially traditional circle of customers . . .

Now at some time this leisureliness was suddenly destroyed, and often without any essential change in the form of organisation, such as the transition to a unified factory, to mechanical weaving, etc. What happened on the contrary was often no more than this: some young man from one of the putting-out families went into the country, carefully chose weavers for his employ, greatly increased the rigour of his supervision of their work, and thus turned them from peasants into labourers. On the other hand he would begin to change his marketing methods by so far as possible going directly to the final consumer . . . and would adapt the quality of the product directly to their needs and wishes. At the same time he began to introduce the principle of low prices and large turnover.

There was repeated what everywhere and always is the result of such a process of rationalization: those who would not follow suit had to go out of business. The idyllic state collapsed under the pressure of a bitter competitive struggle, respectable fortunes were made, and not lent out at interest but reinvested in the business. The old leisurely and comfortable attitude toward life gave way to a hard frugality . . .

The new spirit, the spirit of modern capitalism, had set to work.
(Weber 1930/1905, pp 66–68)

This provides an excellent snapshot of how the 'hard frugality' imposed by the new economic thinking took hold, forcing out the older norms and expectations of the ways of life that EP Thompson referred to as the traditional 'moral economy' and replacing them with those of 'bitter competitive struggle' which resulted in longer working hours for labourers and increased profits for owners.

However, central as these processes were to the development of capitalism, it is equally important to remember that the creation of the labouring class in Europe was coupled with extraction of wealth from the colonies, a coupling that allowed an extraordinary flourishing of capitalism in the metropolis. And while the exploitation of colonies often involved loot and plunder, it also took more systematic form through the legalization of the expropriation and enclosure of colonial lands from indigenous peoples and the exportation of the capitalist system to the periphery.

The relentless pursuit of raw materials, cheap labour and expanding markets required to feed the capitalist profit habit thus saw opportunities being hunted down across the face of the earth. In such activities, private enterprises were able to draw on the administrative, legal and military resources of the imperial state as required.

The bombing of the Chinese by the British navy in the mid-nineteenth century in order to keep open the market for British drug dealers offers a prime example (putting Queen Victoria at the head of a vast international drug cartel of a kind that contemporary Columbian drug lords could only dream of (Galeano 2000, pp 133–135)). Despite the legitimatory exhortations of the '3 Cs' – Commerce, Christianity and Civilization – records of the routine barbarity of colonialism abound. But the excessive violence of such practices should not lead us to forget the 'normal' violence of the everyday exercise of colonial rule.

Although different in several key respects, imperial conquests brought colonised populations into economic relations that in many ways replicated the legalised market system and the experience of labourers in Europe. On the one hand, we again find the commodification of labour, land and money – through public credit and debt systems – protected through private law categories and enacted and enforced by state authority. On the other, we see how private enterprises deployed techniques that radically altered the living conditions of the colonised. By way of example, Harvey notes how 'colonial authorities during the nineteenth century and later' complained that 'the problem in India or Africa is that you can't get the indigenous population to work a "normal" working day, let alone a "normal" working week. They typically work for a bit and then disappear' (Harvey 2010, p 147). Part of the problem was that new – 'modern' – notions of time and time-keeping, in hours and even minutes, that had developed in the factories of the Industrial Revolution, had to be imposed to discipline the indigenous populations. Far from being 'natural', these new temporalities were inventions of modernity that formed part of the 'market forces' of capitalist development.

The general problem in the colonies had been noted by Marx when he described how a Mr Peel, an English colonist seeking to establish a capitalist enterprise in Western Australia, failed in his task: along with means of production,

> Mr. Peel had the foresight to bring with him, besides, 300 persons of the working class, men, women, and children. Once arrived at his destination, "Mr. Peel was left without a servant to make his bed or fetch him water from the river." Unhappy Mr. Peel who provided for everything except the export of English modes of production to Swan River!

In this setting, it became clear, said Marx, that 'capital is not a thing, but a social relation between persons, mediated by things' (Marx 1865/1990, pp 931–933). It was only by the subtle if relentless operation of legally induced dependencies, along with the disciplining of time and people, that 'normal' capitalist relations were introduced. For these reasons, far from being the spontaneous development of a 'free market', Marx reminds us that capital came into the world 'dripping from head to toe, from every pore, with blood and dirt.'

The displacement, dislocation and disciplining of people in modernity was not however exclusively associated with labour becoming commodified and the peasant class turned into proletarians, and this for at least one significant reason: the era of modernity coincided with the massive commodification of *people as property* in the European-run slave trade. Around twelve million African men, women and children were enslaved (over a million dying in transit) in the forced removals carried out over three centuries by Western imperial powers including Britain, Portugal, Spain and latterly the

United States. Slave labour was thus central to the growth and consolidation of colonial economic power. It reached its maximum intensity in the eighteenth century (the 'Age of Enlightenment') supplying mainly South and North America with labour to exploit the manufacture and trade in sugar, tobacco, cotton, etc. As 'unfree' labour, this was not a capitalist mode of production, but it relied no less on legal categories, institutions and enforcement agencies to operate successfully. It was not until the nineteenth century, and in the United States, not until after a civil war in the 1860s that the practice, if not the legacy, was brought to a close.

In his analysis of the rise of capitalism Karl Polanyi sums up the 'Great Transformation' brought on by the installing of the market mentality in society:

> We submit that an avalanche of social dislocation, surpassing by far that of the enclosure period, came down upon England; that this catastrophe was the accompaniment of a vast movement of economic improvement; that an entirely new institutional mechanism was starting to act on western society; that its dangers, that cut to the quick when they first appeared were never nearly overcome.
>
> (Polanyi 1944, p 40)

Of the vast institutional mechanism of Polanyi's quote, our particular interest has been with law. Capitalism, as we know it today, developed during this period in all its revolutionary potential and, during this first period, also without the mechanisms of social protection that came later to soften the effects of exposure to the market system, where even the most basic necessities of life are produced for profitable exchange and where society's most fundamental resources, nature and people's ability to work to produce goods, are also submitted to the same logic of commodification and exchange and the same requirements of competition and profit maximization. The law played a vital role in terms of both sanctioning a regime of property rights that allowed ownership in and alienability of these basic commodities (land and labour) and making exchange possible through the sanction of enforceable contacts. We also saw the crucial role that criminal law played in policing the development of the labour market, by preventing 'exit opportunities' from it and ensuring that propertyless labourers were obliged to sell their labour for a wage in order to stay alive. A deep dependence on the market installs itself for the vast majority of the population, which in turn, as we will see with Marx, creates profits for those who buy their labour.

Marx's argument about the violence of the foundation of capitalism, Polanyi's argument against Smith's projections and Weber's cultural/religious account of the transformation all point ultimately to this: that the processes that effected the transformation of feudalism to capitalism were historically specific and therefore contingent developments. No necessity drove them. Self-interest and the profit motive, the demands of utility-maximisation and accumulation are not the fulfilment of some natural propensity of man nor the answer to some innate logic of social relations. They were developments that were institutionally enabled and policed, and as Weber's account also shows, they cut against the grain of older sensitivities and lifeworlds. Capitalism is the 'late and localized product of specific historical conditions' (Meiksins Wood 2002, p 117), its 'expansionary drive is the product of its own historically specific internal laws of motion. And those laws of motion required vast social transformations and upheavals to set them in train' (Meiksins Wood 2002, p 117).

We looked at the momentous changes in society and in the economy with the creation of the market system . We will close this first section on the advent of modernity by looking at a final dimension of the grand transformation, the political system.

Reading

Two classic texts that described as well as influenced the transformation in the economic system with the advent of modernity are A Smith, *An Inquiry Into the Nature and Causes of the Wealth of Nations* (1814) and K Marx's *Capital* (1865). Karl Polanyi's *The Great Transformation* (1944) is a masterwork in economic history tracing the emergence of market society. Other important historical works include E Hobsbawm, *The Age of Revolution: Europe, 1789–1848* (London: Weidenfeld & Nicholson, 1962); K Galbraith *A History of Economics* (1998); E Thompson, *Whigs and Hunters: The Origin of the Black Act* (London: Allen Lane, Penguin, 1975), as well as his *The Making of the English Working Class* (London: Penguin, 1991 [or. ed. 1963]). Ellen Meiksins Wood's *The Origin of Capitalism* (2002) is a concise and very readable Marxist account of the transition from feudalism to capitalism. Relatedly see M Overton, *Agricultural Revolution in England: The Transformation of the Agrarian Economy 1500–1850* (Cambridge: Cambridge University Press, 1996).

Max Weber's *The Protestant Ethic and the Spirit of Capitalism* (1930/1904) provides a sociological analysis of the transformation with special emphasis on the dimensions of culture and religion.

Douglas Hay's *Albion's Fatal Tree: Crime and Society in Eighteenth-Century England* (1975) provides a fascinating social history of crime and with the legal system that maintained the propertied classes.

On the slave trade see the database at www.slavevoyages.org/, and for a classic reading of slavery in the United States, see Genovese (1988). On legal and political aspects of imperialism see for example Anghie (2005), Mamdani (1996) and on the British Empire, Newsinger (2013).

Chapter 4

Law and the political

In this section we follow through in more detail the developing relations between law and the modern state. We will highlight the following themes: the nature of 'public' political power; sovereignty; the separation of powers; the rule of law; and the role of rights. We trace an ongoing dynamic between the augmentation and centralisation of state sovereign power and the varied attempts to limit it.

Elements of the modern state

According to Quentin Skinner, 'by the beginning of the seventeenth century, the concept of the state – its nature, its powers, its right to command obedience – had come to be regarded as the most important object of analysis in European political thought'. In doing so the modern state had come to represent the unity of the political order, appearing as 'an omnipotent yet impersonal power' (Skinner 1978, pp 358, 349).

Historically, three factors shaped the modern state at its dawn and, at the same time, defined the relation between state and society. First, European societies, which had been put under severe stress and indiscriminate violence by religious conflicts during the sixteenth century, had looked to secular authorities as a necessary means of their own preservation (Koselleck 1988; Loughlin 2010). What became known as the *secularization thesis* amounted to this: the state emerges as a substitute for religion in sustaining the order of society, while its main concepts (sovereignty, separation of powers and so on) nevertheless drew heavily on theological concepts (Schmitt 1985). In the case of France and England, religious wars had clearly played a key role in the consolidation of at least some of the defining traits of those modern states. Pacification was built on the recognition that faith and religion would not count as the defining legitimating factor of the state legal order.

The second factor concerned the capacity to generate the kind of power whose nature we might identify as *public*; power that is general and abstract, in the sense that it is applied uniformly to society, and is thought to be or treated as *qualitatively different* from private forms of power. Hence the state creates institutions and agencies designed to serve the public interest and whose formal status is not directly determined by private law or patrimonial interests (Thornhill 2011, pp 56–61). Unlike feudal arrangements, in the modern state there is a separation between the person and the office. In principle, political and legal power comes to lie in the institution, not in the person. Only in this way does the power created by the state become *autonomous* political power, which is then translated into general and abstract laws applied uniformly across society. These operations required the construction of a series of infrastructures that allowed state power to be exercised in an inclusive manner over society.

The third factor, related to the previous two, concerns the shaping of the relation between society and the state, the private activity of the citizens and the public action of officials. The state's *governing* activity was very much directed at reaching and managing compromises which would hold society together. So although the state, as we have just seen, exercised public power, it was far from being a neutral actor: for the purpose of generating and sustaining societal consensus the state intervenes actively in society. The neo-Marxist theorist Nikos Poulantzas puts it like this: '[the state] is a relationship of forces, or more precisely, the material condensation of such a relationship among classes and class fractions, such as this is expressed within the state in a necessarily specific form' (Poulantzas 1980 pp 128–129). Of course it is difficult to appreciate the meaning of the term 'material condensation' at this stage of the analysis, or what he means by specific form. But we can retain from this the idea of the *active* role of the state, the notion that the state does not supervene on an *already* ordered society but actively shapes it, and that it is not possible to disentangle the development of the modern state from the undergirding development of the production and reproduction of society. In effect, the modern state, by separating the political system from civil society, enabled capitalism to flourish by using public power selectively to allow the accumulation and protection of private wealth.

These three originating factors can help in defining the origins of the modern state and providing reasons for explaining the transition from one form of state into another. It should be remarked that the creation of an autonomous public power, independent from religion, along with the rise of the political economy of capitalist societies and the formation of modern international law, made state law a central element of governance. To the concentration and centralisation of powers corresponded, in the realm of legal theory, the move from a condition of legal pluralism to one where the idea of a unified positive law would offer solid explanatory tools. It is no coincidence that the nineteenth century saw the affirmation, first of the nation as the main collective subject within the state (hence, the expression 'nation-state') and then, in particular in the European continent (France, Germany, Italy and to a lesser extent Spain), of the *Rechtsstaat*, that is, a state based on the rule of law. Given the role of positive law in the definition of this form of state, one can understand why Max Weber defined the state in terms of its 'monopoly' of the exercise of legitimate force within a determined territory.

With modernity, statehood became the paradigmatic form of unity for the polity, displacing other forms of political organisation like cities and city-states, and multinational empires or federations. Modern states now are deemed to have five essential and defining characteristics: (a) they have a *territory*, over which they claim to exercise effective control by the use, if necessary, of coercive force against external and internal threats; (b) they claim that this territorial control is *legitimate*, in that their governing authorities exercise it as a right on some moral-cum-political ground; (c) they claim *universal jurisdiction* within the territory, involving authority to make laws and to try all allegations of crime and legal disputes arising within it; (d) they claim *independence*, on the ground that the people of the state are entitled to a form of government free from external interference by other states; and (e) *recognition* of these claims to territoriality, legitimacy and independence is accorded by other states. In international law, indeed, a state is defined as a territory with a *recognised and effective government*, and each state is entitled to respect under the principle of mutual non-interference. Taken together, these five characteristics accord the state its distinctive modern political/legal form.

Sovereignty

The principle of sovereignty accompanies the rise of the modern state, and its presence is crucial to an understanding of how legal and political powers operate within its realm. While the term was used in medieval times as well, its specific meaning changed with the advent of modernity, so much so that, in the words of Bertrand de Jouvenel, although people in the Middle Ages had 'a very strong sense of that concrete thing, hierarchy, they lacked the idea of that abstract thing, sovereignty' (De Jouvenel 1975, p 171). The concept of sovereignty thus goes hand in hand with the development of modernity – even if its meaning remained the object of much controversy.

Historically, the principle of sovereignty had the function of overcoming the fragmentation of different sources of authority and power as these were exercised variably all across Europe in the form of cities, empires and various feudal formations. In the case of the religious wars which were waged across the continent in the sixteenth and seventeenth centuries, sovereignty allowed a suspension of conflict (or, at times, its violent suppression) through the principle 'cuius regio, eius religio' (literally 'whose realm, his religion') which established that the religion of the ruler would determine that of the rules, and led to a form of accommodation of the Catholic-Protestant conflict in Europe. At the same time such a principle also entailed a separation between the public sphere and the inner consciousness (see Koselleck 1988) since, as Hobbes highlighted, what was demanded of the subjects of a sovereign was not real conversion to state religion, but only the formal recognition, in public, of loyalty towards the sovereign's faith. The so-called libertas philosophandi (what in contemporary terms would be termed freedom of thought) guaranteed at that point in time an inner but significant realm of freedom to the individual. This constitutes the beginning of a process which will bring about civil liberties, and whose story is deeply intertwined with the principle of sovereignty. In fact, modernity will develop, among other things, around the dialectic between the authority of sovereignty and the freedom of the modern individual. The negative force which sets into motion this dialectic lies in the interior freedom of the individual.

In the eighteenth century, Rousseau's work already marks a departure from the basic understanding of sovereignty offered by Hobbes. Like Hobbes, Rousseau conceived sovereignty as inalienable and indivisible, but he introduced an important qualification by making the sovereign body equivalent to the popular body. At this point, the sovereign ceases to be a single concrete person or institution; hence, 'the sovereign' and 'sovereignty' become coincident. Such a theoretical move represents the precondition for the other innovative insight offered by Rousseau's Social Contract, where sovereignty and government are sharply distinguished. Sovereignty is expressed through the general will translated into general laws, while government acts with decrees (Rousseau will add that sovereignty is democratic, while government can be aristocratic). Legislation is abstract and general, while decrees address particular events and people.

It is with the great German philosopher Georg FW Hegel that the philosophical reflection on sovereignty reaches its pinnacle. Taking his cue from Rousseau's general will, Hegel drew a sharp distinction between the person of the sovereign and the principle itself of sovereignty. The sovereign is the symbolic representative of the unity of the political order, while the principle of sovereignty is the logic at work within that political order. More specifically, at the end of a long historical trajectory that began with the religious wars and carried through to the modern revolutions and the rise of civil society, Hegel saw in the principle of sovereignty the mediation between the particularities of civil society, organised around the pursuit of individual interests, and the claim to generality of state law. Note here the difference with Hobbes's theory of sovereignty: the author of *Leviathan* sees in the principle of sovereignty a way of neutralising the conflict immanent to the state of nature. This is obtained by creating an uncontested ultimate authority whose commands make the law of the land. The authority of the sovereign is based on the individuals' rational and selfish calculations. However, such an achievement comes at a high price because the existence of society is sacrificed to the creation of the state as sovereign entity. When the sovereign dissolves or is deposed, society itself disappears and men are thrown back into the state of nature. Contrary to this undifferentiated understanding of the relation between state and society, Hegel sees sovereignty as *mediation* because, *at the same time as* it separates civil society and the state, it maintains them in direct relation. In a famous paragraph from the *Elements of the Philosophy of Right* (#278), Hegel defines sovereignty in the following way:

> The *idealism* which constitutes sovereignty is the same determination as that according to which the so-called *parts* of an animal organism are not parts, but members or organic moments whose isolation and separate existence constitute disease . . . Since sovereignty is the ideality of every particular authority, it is easy to fall into the very common misunderstanding of regarding this ideality as mere power and empty arbitrariness, and of equating sovereignty with despotism. But despotism signifies the condition of lawlessness in general, in which the particular will as such, whether of a monarch or of the people (ochlocracy), counts as law . . ., whereas sovereignty is to be found specifically under lawful and constitutional conditions as the moment of ideality of the particular spheres and functions.
>
> (Hegel 1991, pp 315–316)

Hegel's characterization of sovereignty is extremely important because it does not reduce sovereignty to the expression of an individual will, but it locates the principle in between the differentiated poles of the state, on the one hand, and of civil society, on the other. The 'ideality' to which Hegel refers is not 'mere power and empty arbitrariness' but mediation between generality and particularity. The sovereign is not a despot, and its law, which is the outcome of the mediation between individual and general interest, guarantees that individual freedom finds its place (and limit) within the legal order. In fact, outside the state legal order, the interaction among individual wills generates conflict. But while according to Hobbes this is always conflict among atomistic and abstract individuals (i.e., the fiction of the state of nature), for Hegel this takes the form of a concrete and historical conflict, so that in modern times, it is a conflict which contains an idea of modern freedom as social freedom (that is, a relational freedom). Through the mediation of sovereignty, this conflict is neutralised; its function is to maintain the state and civil society related *and* distinct. Sovereignty is not the negation of law; instead its realisation takes effect 'under lawful and constitutional conditions.'

We can pause here to take stock. 'Sovereignty' is both a political and legal concept and captures something of the relation between the two. But like so many terms that straddle the boundary between law and politics, it is a concept denoting a cluster of related ideas rather than one single clearly defined one. Moreover, in nearly all its clustered elements, it is a contested concept, in the sense that different theoretical approaches dispute over its correct explanation or definition, usually also disagreeing about its practical relevance. Sometimes it is used mainly in a *political* sense, to denote a kind of untrammelled power of rulers over those they rule. Sometimes it is conceived of in *legal* terms, as a kind of supreme normative power or highest possible legal authority. It is not even agreed what kind of entity it primarily applies to. Some treat it as an attribute of a person, or entity or agency within a state, such as an emperor, a king, a dictator or a parliament. Some treat it as an attribute primarily of the state itself – a 'sovereign state' being one that is fully self-governing and independent of external control. Some treat it as mainly belonging to the people of a territory, on the ground that they are ultimate and self-governing masters of the institutions of the state established there. 'We the people' adopt a constitution and establish a state with constituted organs of government, limited by the terms of our grant of power to them. Thereafter, 'we' can exercise our sovereignty only through the constitutionally established organs of government, with their powers divided and limited according to the constitution whereby 'we' established them. Alternatively, but only in accordance with constitutionally prescribed procedures, we can exercise the constitutional power of constitutional amendment.

Yet there were other possible points of attribution of sovereignty apart from 'the people'. One was the English common lawyers' view of the sovereignty of the UK Parliament. This affords a striking instance of the ascription of sovereignty to an entity within a state. Strictly, this is sovereignty of a composite body, namely, 'the Queen in Parliament', which is the monarch acting in procedurally fixed ways along with the two Houses of Parliament – the Lords and the Commons. With the growth and eventual triumph of democracy as the underlying ideology of governance, however, the House of Commons became the predominant element in this composite sovereign. But even then, when a party has a comfortable majority in the House of Commons, its leader, as Prime Minister, can, with the support of a Cabinet, each of whose members is appointed and can be dismissed by that same Prime Minister, acquire a personally predominant position: a highly concentrated form of power at the disposal, temporarily at least, of a single political leader. Hence parliamentary sovereignty meant the legally unlimited power of Parliament to enact any law it chooses, except one that would have the effect of binding later parliaments; but what the law ascribed to Parliament was *politically* exercisable in a much more autocratic way.

The jurisprudential reflection of all this is found in the legal positivism of Jeremy Bentham and John Austin, which exercised so powerful a hold on the British juristic imagination during much of the nineteenth and twentieth centuries. They were building to a great extent on ideas originally advanced by Thomas Hobbes. But while Bentham and Austin rejected the fiction of the state of nature and the social contract as a way out of it, they nonetheless argued for the thesis that law always depends on some sovereign person or assembly of persons whom others in a certain territory do in fact habitually obey, for whatever reason. Laws then are whatever the sovereign issues by way of general commands.

As democratic ideas extended their scope as the ideology of governmental legitimacy, so has the idea of the sovereignty of the people extended its sway. Sovereignty was claimed by (and for) the people who adopted the constitution that determined the way they were to be governed, indeed were to exercise their self-government. Always, of course, there was a vanguard of 'founding fathers', but the constitutions they drafted required, by their own terms, ratification by the people through what were considered appropriate forms of popular legitimation. In such a context, the attribution of sovereignty could not credibly be to any single organ of government within the state, and the concept of the people as itself the sovereign, for all the paradoxical quality in this idea – that in the moment of its exercise, absolute popular sovereignty transforms itself into limited constitutional sovereignty – provided an enduring touchstone for political legitimacy.

An alternative, which may escape the paradox, is to attribute sovereignty to 'the state' itself. The existence of a sovereign in the Austinian sense of the term, where sovereignty is attributed to a person or institution, implies effective governance of some territory and of the people living in it. Where sovereigns of this kind exist, they are holders of a power that is logically independent of any higher power of the same kind. There can, of course, be different sovereigns in different territories. Logically, they must be mutually independent, for if one ruler were in effect the overlord of another, that other would cease to have sovereignty. On this account, mutual independence is a necessary attribute of sovereigns, as is territorial separation.

However, where constitutional government has developed in ways expressive of some conception of popular sovereignty, it is most likely that the constitution does not allow for or constitute any sovereign official or institution – indeed, a constitution such as that of France expressly prohibits this. In polities of this kind, the constitutional framework typically establishes some version of the classical 'separation of powers' (see the next section). At a minimum, executive, legislative and judicial powers are assigned to distinct agencies, with some form of checks and balances among the agencies. In large polities, federal or quasi-federal forms of government may further complicate the constitutional picture, insofar as there are separate states, each with its own internal separation of powers, and a division of competences between the authorities of each state and those of the federal government. In such contexts, there is no single person or institution that exercises an unfettered supreme power; that is, there is no 'sovereign' in the Austinian sense.

But a country under such a constitution – whether it be a unitary state or a federal state – may enjoy as complete legal and political independence from power exercisable by other like entities as a state ruled by a sovereign monarch or dictator or a sovereign parliament. The state or federation may, in that sense, enjoy sovereignty. It is often, indeed usually, the case that the constitution of the state or federation was established by some method of popular approval, expressed through a referendum, a constitutional convention, or the like. It is also normal that the constitution provides for its own amendment by similar processes. Where all this is so, popular sovereignty connects in an obvious way with state sovereignty. The state is sovereign in its external relations with other states. Internally, the power to determine or alter the legal frameworks in which government is carried on belongs to the people acting in constitutionally stipulated ways. Democratic forms of government also involve the will of the people, usually expressed through political parties, to determine or at least strongly influence the course of legislation and the policies pursued by the executive.

Holding sovereign power to account

The emergence of a strong centralised state, which thinkers such as Hobbes and Austin theorised and which monarchs and other rulers regularly tried to make the most of, produced justified fears about unlimited and arbitrary power being exercised over subject populations. In the following sections we consider three related responses to this: the doctrines of the separation of powers, the rule of law and the 'braking' effect that individual rights could have on the exercise of sovereign authority.

The separation of powers

One classic device for containing the threatening power of the state was the principle of the *separation* (or distribution) of *powers*. An early mode of separation of powers, as we have already seen, involved that between religious and secular power, whose impetus created the conditions for an autonomous political sphere. Following this separation, another one, this time *within* political institutions themselves, came to centre stage.

In pre-modern times, countering the concentration of power was seen as a condition of an ideal social order because it was believed that social stability would be obtained in this way. The most common understanding of that organisation of powers was the ideal of the mixed government. Mixed government was a form of government based on status: powers would be distributed according to the different estates of society. Classically, Aristotle had already formalised this doctrine by assuming that the ideal government is the one which contains monarchic, aristocratic and democratic elements. The same principle is behind Polybius's and Livy's appraisal of the Roman republic as the mixed arrangement between the aristocracy and the plebeians, channelled into a constitution with multiple veto points given institutionally to both social groups (McCormick 2011). In this way, all major estates of society (monarchy, nobles, clergy and productive sectors) would be represented by government. In Europe, this was the standard model for governing society until the full development of modern legal orders.

However, already in the works of Locke and Montesquieu, an alternative ideal of government began to take shape. Again, the reason for having powers separated was the protection of individual freedom. Only separated powers would limit that concentration which would make the arbitrary use of power more likely. In light of the construction of centralised state structures, what ought to be divided was not social power, but state functions themselves. With some marginal differences, three main functions were identified and all with reference to the law: making law, implementing law and adjudicating law (a classification which echoes the three main human faculties: thinking, acting and judging). The tasks of the three branches of government were thus these: making law and keeping the executive under scrutiny (the legislature); the pursuit of public policy by executive government in implementation of the law or otherwise within a legal framework (the executive); and impartial adjudication aimed at upholding the law, both in disputes between private persons and in matters involving private persons and public authorities (the judiciary). Maintaining some form of separation between these three branches has thus long been understood to be a necessity for the sake of free (rather than tyrannical) government.

A key aspect of the principle of separation of powers is that these functions shall not only be kept conceptually separate, but they have to be exercised by distinct and at least partially autonomous organs. Only by being distributed to different offices can one branch (or power) limit or control the others. Ideally, the legislative function ought to be attributed to a representative assembly, the executive function to government and public administration, and the judicial function to the judiciary. The latter was identified by Montesquieu's seminal work *The Spirit of Laws* (1748/1989) as the essential tenet for a proper separation of powers. In fact, the legislative and the executive powers could be distributed in a mixed way between the same organs and this would not automatically threaten individual freedom. But the decision on whether the law has been applied correctly and without violating individual rights cannot be left to the organs that are in charge of making the law or implementing it. This would create a clear conflict of interests as those who should be judged would also become the judging body. Therefore, only an autonomous and independent body of judges can adjudicate disputes where the government is involved. It is also usually assumed, even today, that this is a precondition for upholding the rule of law in a legal order.

The principle of separation of powers was codified in classic form by the US Constitution of 1787. The first three articles of that constitution are an illustration of the principle, as each article attributes a function to a specific organ: Article 1 establishes the legislative function of Congress, Article 2 defines the executive function of the President and Article 3 the judicial power of courts. While in later decades, the US Constitution would change towards a more mixed system (the President today exercises many legislative functions), the framers clearly wanted to constitutionalise a strict principle of separation of powers. Even more assertively, Article 16 of the French Declaration went so far as to state that a society 'with no definition of separation of powers, has no constitution at all'. In fact, the revolutionaries made a huge effort to achieve a balanced distribution of functions among different organs and this was the source of severe political frictions, as exemplified by the famous debate over the veto powers to be attributed to the monarchy. It should be added that in both cases (French and American), the main concern of the constitution's drafters was to counter previous absolutist regimes. Hence, separation of powers came to be seen as the main constitutional device for limiting the arbitrary exercise of power.

We can identify different types of *accountability* within the separation of powers model. Government concerns the maintenance of order and the pursuit of some conception of a common good or of the public interest of the state and its citizens. Where the separation of powers is maintained in any of its possible versions, the activities of the executive branch of government and of law-enforcement agencies such as the police are carried out under general rules that are the responsibility of the legislature. The legislature can also hold the executive to account politically. So far as concerns the legality of all exercises of governmental power, the judiciary has a final say upon what are the limits of the law laid down by the legislature or contained in a constitution itself. In short, there are rules that permit official use of force in reasonably defined circumstances, and these rules also prohibit non-official uses of force save in exceptional cases of self-defence.

As we will see in more detail shortly, the 'rule of law' is the ideal according to which all political and governmental power is in fact exercised under rules of law. Yet obviously effective government cannot just be a matter of 'rule following' – it calls for statesmanship and political commitment, and its ends are expressed in political programmes, not legal codes, leaving considerable scope to the discretion and judgement of those exercising the various offices of state. However, a constitution, whether a formally adopted constitutional text or a mixed body of law and custom, typically designates not only the functions of various office holders, but also the method of their election or appointment to office. This enables the exercise of effective checks and balances to prevent the holder of any one of the powers of state from coming, in fact, to enjoy unlimited power rather than the defined, but extensive, power the constitution confers. This means that the legislature, in further empowering the executive or in regulating its powers, will never grant unlimited discretion, and the courts exercise scrutiny of governmental conduct to ensure that limits are respected.

When that is so, it is possible for the conduct of the affairs of state to be genuinely carried on under law. Some, not necessarily perfect or complete, separation of these powers among different persons, offices and institutions has thus become a defining feature of the constitutional state. Democratic forms of election to public office as a member of the legislature or as the chief or a member of the executive government, though not (with a few exceptions) to judicial office, have also come to be a feature of these states. Fully democratic electoral systems, based on 'one person one vote', emerged later than the separation of powers, and would be all but impossible to achieve or sustain in other circumstances.

When coming to terms with these different forms of accountability it is important to understand that this presupposes that law can be considered as a kind of *normative order* – that is, it is concerned with providing or maintaining an authoritative basis for order in human conduct and affairs, through reference to standards of conduct that lay down how people and office holders ought to or must behave and the ways in which they are to be held accountable for their behaviour. Law is thus (in several senses) institutional, for it is made or reformed by legislatures, implemented by executive agencies and law-enforcement officials, and subjected to adjudication by courts. The law of modern states is also *coercive* in character, in that the executive and specialist enforcement agencies of the state can exercise physical force to ensure implementation of judgements by the courts (whether by criminal penalties or civil remedies), authorised – and limited – by laws laid down by legislatures or developed through judicial precedent. State law is thus normative (concerning what ought to be or must be done or omitted) and institutional, as well as coercive.

Finally, where there is a well-functioning separation of powers, it is nonetheless necessary that there is a coherence to the system as a whole. The *system* element depends on the way in which the activities and practices of the institutions and agencies hang together in a relatively coherent way. This depends on the institutions acknowledging a common body of constitutional or sub-constitutional rules and principles that empower each of them to act as they do and that seek to co-ordinate their activity, as well as regulating and empowering conduct of citizens. Where the 'separation of powers' exists the 'rule of law' is possible, in that each of the institutions keeps or is kept to carrying out functions only in accordance with established law, taking action against citizens only when empowered by law and only in case of violation of the law by citizens. In this context a vital role falls to the courts as the final interpreters of the rules that confer legal power and authority on all the institutions, including the courts themselves. All the relevant rules and principles of conduct can thus be seen as systematically interrelated because the courts, especially the highest courts, accept it as obligatory to implement only rules that satisfy common criteria concerning their origin or content. They do so in accordance with a shared interpretation of the relevant criteria (see Part II, section 11).

The rule of law

We have made reference to the 'rule of law' in passing, and it is a concept we will explore in greater depth later. The doctrine of the 'rule of law and not of men' has a lengthy, if not uncontested, pedigree. In this part we outline some of its key aspirational elements as they developed as ways of countering the actual or potential exercise of arbitrary power by the state and doing so in the interests of protecting individual liberties.

In the first place, it is only where officials faithfully observe the constraints laid down in laws and constitutions that the rule of law obtains. Acting without legal warrant or beyond officially granted powers – *ultra vires* – cannot be done with impunity. The rule of law thus promotes a form of accountability, albeit one that is not identical to that achieved through the separation of powers. Central to this is the capacity to challenge governmental actions that affect individuals' interests by demanding a clear legal warrant for official action, or nullification of unwarrantable acts through review by an independent judiciary. This is possible, it is often said, provided there is a legal system composed principally of quite clearly enunciated rules that normally operate only in a prospective manner and which are expressed in terms of general categories. Such rules should also set realistically achievable requirements for conduct, should form overall some coherent pattern, not a chaos of arbitrarily conflicting demands, and should be predictably applied by officials.

The predictability of rule-governed behaviour and application exists in tension with another characteristic of the rule of law, namely that liberty under law requires recognition that law also has an *argumentative* quality. Any legal text may be open to several interpretations in the light of contested principles and values that are taken to underlie this or that rule of law or branch of law. People are entitled to argue for one favoured interpretation against another, and in disputes between citizen and citizen, or citizen and state, each side may seek interpretations favourable to their own view of the matter (and hoped-for outcome). This testing of propositions is also true with respect to the determination of facts, an activity which constitutes much of professional legal work, insofar as the parties have the right to check the reliability of evidence (including the possibility of cross-examining witnesses) and challenge factual claims made by the other party, rather than have one party's account taken as the truth before a court. Recognising the argumentative quality of law is particularly important when one of the parties to a dispute has much more power or resources at its disposal, as when it is an organ of state – a government official or the police, for example – or a major corporation. The ability to test legal and factual claims made by either party, to look at every side of every important matter raised, and not come down at once on the side of power, prejudice or apparent certainty, therefore has a value that must co-exist alongside that of predictability.

With this in mind, the values that the rule of law can be seen to promote are legal certainty, the security of legal expectations and safety of the citizen from arbitrary interference by governments and their agents. Thus where the rule of law is observed, people can have reasonable certainty, in advance, concerning the rules and standards by which their conduct will be judged and the requirements they must satisfy to give legal validity to their transactions. They can then have reasonable security in their expectations of the conduct of others, and in particular of those holding official positions under law. In this context, citizens – and indeed everyone within the jurisdiction – may be thought to gain confidence that their activities will be judged in accordance only with established rules and principles of law. Thus their personal liberty and liberty to conduct private and economic activities are subject to restraint, only by virtue of legal powers clearly vested in persons acting with the authority of the state under the constitution or under legislation as interpreted by the judges in courts of law. Civil liberties in this way depend on respect for the rule of law. Finally, another value – social and political trust – is often seen to be indirectly enhanced by the presence of the rule of law. This is so as the security of expectations allows planning by individuals in the knowledge that other citizens and state officials will act, and be held to account in their actions, in ways that are reasonably foreseeable according to law and not arbitrary or capricious.

Yet if everything is arguable (or even if rather many points are arguable) and open to a decision either way, there may be a degree of scepticism concerning the possibility of a genuine 'rule of law' that does uphold tolerable certainty in human affairs. In particular, there may be concern that decisions on legal points are ultimately a matter of judges' discretion. How the judges decide, on whatever grounds they favour, determines legal outcomes both for individuals and, through the system of judicial precedent, for society at large. A 'rule of laws, not men' might become no better than a rule by one set of men (the judiciary) rather than another (the legislature). In this way, the prized 'separation of powers' may appear as something of a sham, and the autonomy of law and adjudication from politics or arbitrary decision may be revealed as the reality.

One possible manifestation of this scepticism claims there is a false consciousness implicit in (and generated by) theorising about the rule of law and the separation of powers. People may be taught to believe in the virtue of legal certainty and its possible achievement under the rule of law or in a *Rechtsstaat*, a 'law-state'; but the belief is an illusion. They may be comforted by the thought that it is actually achieved in their own state, but the thought is false. It is not true that even when substantive results in lawsuits go against one's own individual interest or class interest at least formal justice is achieved, or that all citizens live under the same rules, and they are fairly enforced. On this view adjudication and enforcement *are* capricious and biased, and cannot be otherwise. Legal uncertainty is pervasive and legal decision-making is done in response to ideology under cover of rule-of-law talk.

We will consider in more detail later the debate between critics who develop this view and those who, like EP Thompson, have found some 'unqualified human good' in the rule of law. But even those who claim the kinds of liberty supposedly upheld by respecting the rule of law are of real value may still acknowledge its insufficiency with respect to the operation of power in society. Equality before the law and liberty under the rule of law are compatible with very great economic and social inequalities and indeed injustices. Where law produces what seem substantively unsatisfactory outcomes for people, the question of trust (or distrust) is posed anew: why should they accept that there is any value at all in the 'majestic equality' of the impartial administration of rules that affect very differently the interests of different individuals and different classes? The possibilities implicit in other forms of holding power to account, such as that to be found in the operation of democratic institutions, may afford one answer to this. But even then, the values associated with the rule of law, and in particular the dynamic between legal certainty and arguability, may still be thought to be worthy of respect.

Rights as restraints

State sovereignty created and concentrated an enormous quantity of power in few institutions. This was the distinctive mark of the institutional organisation of statehood. But, as already mentioned, sovereignty emerged alongside the idea of the modern individual subject. With such a conception of the individual came also a specific view of what the subject of law should be. If the promise of modernity was to bring about order and freedom, then it was necessary to bestow certain legal protections upon the individual in order to allow him/her to enjoy at least a form of negative freedom. Negative freedom may be thought of simply as the absence of any external impediments placed on the individual, so that the subject can act according to his/her own will and without being coerced by authority or anyone else. It is not surprising, then, and as we saw with Locke, that rights were initially conceived as shields against the state which enjoyed the legitimate monopoly of coercive force. Hence, as a way of protecting negative freedom from the significant power concentrated in the sovereign state, individual rights as spheres of protection became progressively the other functional side of sovereignty.

The language of rights was already available at the inception of modernity through the tradition of natural law, from which the conception of natural rights was extracted (Tuck 1979; Tierney 1997). However, rights were not conceived at first as uniformly legally justiciable instruments, but as moral notions inscribed in an objective order of things. In the case of natural rights, they were often conceived as moral properties common to rational persons (and, in the most progressive expressions, to all persons *tout court*). Indeed it is possible to trace back the origins of the discourse of human rights precisely to this tradition of natural law. But it is only with the rise of modernity and the modern understanding of the creation of state institutions that the language and the logic of rights came to penetrate increasingly into both the political and the formal legal order.

Rights represent a very particular way of talking about law and politics. They make a special type of political claim, grounded in a distinctive form of argument. We can turn again to John Locke's conception of natural rights which already contained the basic elements of this type of analysis, grounded as it is in an individual's natural rights. As we have seen, Locke suggested that humans originally lived in a state of nature in which they were free and equal, and in which they possessed or acquired certain natural rights, particularly rights in their own person and to property resultant on their labour. The purpose of agreeing to organised rule through government was that natural rights and liberties could be better protected by the state and so, with the formation of political society natural rights do not disappear, but are now guaranteed by positive law through a process of instituting government by consent. This highlighted the mutual 'co-implication' of rights and the state: that is, in other words, the state's formation (and its ongoing purpose) was defined simultaneously as the duty to secure and protect rights. Hence Locke provided the justification for making natural rights positive (that is, legally protected), and this provided a crucial limitation on the exercise of political power.

At the time, this was a radical way of thinking, and marked a sharp break with classical political thought. Previously, individuals had been regarded as subjects under a duty of obedience to their rulers, and such rulers (as in the case of James I and Charles I, for example) often grounded their right to rule as a 'divine right' that kings had got from God. But on the new account, it was the people who were now to be considered as the holders of inalienable rights, rights that cannot be given or taken away. In this version, natural rights enjoy priority – both in chronological terms and against acts of the state that might interfere with them. As such they have a power or finality to them in that they are not amenable to calculations of utility on behalf of the sovereign in pursuit of particular policies. That is, rights cannot – or at least should not – be subject to a test of whether the consequences of upholding the right are good or bad: if someone has a right, then it should be upheld regardless of the consequences. If someone has a property right, or a right not to be tortured, then that right should not be violated just because the state thinks there may be beneficial consequences in doing so. If a person has such a right, then there are clear limits placed on what can be done by the state. Rights are, to use Ronald Dworkin's analogy, like trumps in a card game: they prevail over political claims framed in consequentialist terms.

But if rights are thought of as ongoing restraints on the exercise of sovereign power, then this should not detract from the revolutionary potential that accompanied their birth. As D'Entreves writes:

> The modern theory of natural law was not, properly speaking, a theory of law at all. It was a theory of rights. A momentous change has taken place under cover of the same verbal expressions . . . On the eve of the American and French Revolutions the theory of natural law had been turned into a theory of natural rights . . . a liberating principle, ready to hand for the use of modern man in his challenge to existing institutions.
>
> (D'Entreves 1951, pp 59–60)

Historically, these two revolutions, the American and the French, occurring in the last quarter of the eighteenth century, were important moments for the codification of individual rights. The French Declaration of the Rights of Man and the Citizen (1791) and the American Declaration of Independence (1776) and eventual enactment of the US Bill of Rights (1789) were documents that marked the moment where rights were slowly but steadily becoming the main building block of modern legal and political orders. What was once mostly constructed around legal rules concerning power structures was progressively being seen as a matter of rights. The main value protected by this first wave of rights was, as we have noted, a form of 'negative freedom'. The logic of this was already recognised in the interpretation of Article 5 of the French Declaration of the Rights of Man: 'Law can only prohibit such actions as are hurtful to society. Nothing may be prevented which is not forbidden by law, and no one may be forced to do anything not provided for by law.' The interpretation of this article has shaped the liberal understanding of modern legal orders, as it postulates that everything that is not explicitly forbidden by law cannot be curtailed, and from which it is often assumed that in the sphere of what is not explicitly prohibited, every social or private action can be interpreted as permitted by law. Of course, this type of freedom was legally endorsed, however, only as long as it was compatible with the fundamental aims of the legal order.

Be that as it may, it is a commonplace to define this first wave of individual rights as 'negative rights' in the sense that they protect this version of negative freedom. Negative rights are rights to which correspond only duties of abstention. Take, for example, the freedom of expression or the freedom of speech. The core duty accompanying these rights does not require imposing positive action on the state, to provide, for example its citizens with channels of expression or communication, access to the media, or opportunities of debate and dissemination of views. What it does is to impose on the state the obligation *to avoid* any interference in the formation and expression of the opinions of its citizens and, at best, to intervene when such freedom is encroaching upon someone else's rights (e.g., their right to privacy). The institutional protection for this kind of negative right came to be entrusted to the judicial bodies. The courtroom was seen as providing an ideal space for staging a confrontation between two parties on the potential violation of a negative right, typically concerning the actions of the state on one hand and the interests of the individual on the other. The question to be debated was whether state action or intervention had violated the negative rights of the individual.

To witness the enduring influence of this notion, we may note that even today, in many jurisdictions, the legitimacy of a state's action is measured against the proportionality of its interference on individual rights. An example of this is provided by the European Court of Human Rights in its case law on Articles 8–11 of the Convention. These cases are always framed in terms of the how far a state can go in limiting the individual freedom of one of its citizens. Yet this was not the only available conception of rights. Already during the two revolutions, several voices pleaded for the recognition of a number of 'positive rights', in particular housing and education (e.g., Thomas Paine, Condorcet). While in the US Bill of Rights only negative rights were included (to the point where even today, in US constitutional law, other socio-economic rights are not constitutionalised), other debates saw demands to formulate and codify rights that required *positive* action by the state, entrusting the realisation of certain positive rights to the legislature. As we will see, it is only at a later stage, mostly in the twentieth century, that the conception of freedom underlying the logic of rights was to be modified according to new fundamental aims of the legal order given expression in the demand for 'positive rights'.

But from their genesis, the early revolutionary constitutions set in place an enduring role for rights that was two-fold: they simultaneously provided a brake on state power, and yet, under the doctrines of the separation of powers and the rule of law, their recognition was guaranteed by the state at the behest of individuals.

Readings on the state

For in-depth treatments of the history of the modern state see Poggi (1990), Tilly (1992), Rokkan (1999). A theoretical analysis of the state is offered by Jessop (2016), which is inspired by Poulantzas (1980). See also Milliband (1977). For an overview of the limits of the state from the perspective of political philosophy see Croce and Salvatore (2015). On the constitutional dimension beyond the state see Teubner (2012).

Readings on sovereignty

Influential contemporary theories of sovereignty are offered by Agamben (1998), Loughlin (2003a) and Grimm (2015). For a recent historical reconstruction of the principle of sovereignty see Tuck (2015). The relationship between sea and land in the definition of sovereignty is reconstructed by Benton (2010). On the limits of sovereignty in contemporary legal orders an essential reference is MacCormick (1999); see also Walker (2003a).

Readings on rights

For a general overview of theories of rights see Campbell (2006). For historical reconstructions of rights see Bobbio (1996) and for a good collection (with commentaries) of classic texts on rights see Waldron (1987). For natural rights see Tuck (1979) and Tierney (1997). An enormously influential take on rights is Dworkin (1977).

II

Theorists and critics of modernity

5   Law, class and conflict: Karl Marx   63

    The function of law   66

    Ideology   67

6   Law, legitimation and rationality: Max Weber   71

    Max Weber: modernity and formal legal rationality   71

    Forms of political authority   73

    Forms of legal rationality   74

    The development of legal modernity   77

    Modern law and the economic system   79

    Weber as theorist and as critic of modernity   81

7   Law, community and social solidarity: Emile Durkheim   83

Chapter 5

Law, class and conflict

Karl Marx

As we discussed earlier in the section on law and the market system, the organisation of industrial production and the advent of capitalism was preceded, and would only have been made possible, by a systematic effort to secure the conditions under which the working population would commit their labour to factory production. Marx called this moment that preceded capitalism 'original accumulation.' Lands were 'enclosed', people were driven off the common lands (e.g., the clearances in Scotland), while forms of nomadic living and of living off the land were outlawed. For Marx, the most acute and historically most influential critic of capitalism, these measures, secured primarily through the medium of law, were the conditions of driving the newly propertyless class into 'wage slavery'. Once these conditions were in place, opportunities to resist the new forms of economic activity became radically limited, and those deprived of any form of property had no option but to submit to the owners of capital, whereby a significant part of the value of their work could now be misappropriated by those who owned the means of production, the bourgeois class, as a matter of 'free' agreement according to the logic of capitalist production.

To understand both the measure and nature of the injustice of the 'misappropriation' of the value of the work of the labouring masses and the role of law in organising its conditions, we need to take a step back and visit some fundamental premises of Marx's theory.

Marx's point of departure is the image of the productive man, who only realises the true nature of the being that he is ('species-being' Marx calls it) through creative labour. As human history is conceived in terms of a continuing process of creation, satisfaction and reproduction of needs (as opposed to animals whose needs are fixed), man interacts with the material world in order to create the means to satisfy those needs, and this interaction between man and society, production, becomes the very foundation of society. Labour underlies man's relation to the material world and his relations to others: since production requires co-operation and interdependence between people, at the basis of social life there is a co-ordination of individual labour, and thus there is no society that is not founded on a definitive set of relations of production. The social nature of the individual is a fundamental premise in Marxist theory, as one only realises one's own creative self through collective action and social interdependence. Marx goes on to examine and denounce the exploitative nature of that interdependence in societies which are organised in class terms. All human history, for Marx, was a history of a succession of forms of class societies, each with its distinctive form of 'relations of production': in slave societies class structure was organised around the institution of ownership of the person (slave), in feudal societies it was arranged through differential status (feudal lord and vassal); in capitalist societies classes polarise around the ownership of the means of production. There is the class of those who own the means of production – the factories, the land, the technology, the raw materials – and then there are those who own nothing except their ability to work, an ability that remains an empty abstraction if denied the means of its realisation. We saw how the stage that Marx called 'original accumulation' above secured the total dependency of the class of labourers exclusively on the class of owners of the factories. This compulsion however finds 'expression' in the language of freedom, one of the many contradictions that Marx was incisive in identifying. The 'will' of those who own the means of production and of those who 'own' their labour power, employers and workers, 'meet' in the contract of employment, understood as a 'free agreement' entered into by both sides to exchange work for a wage. Compulsion is thus expressed as freedom: to enter or to abstain from the contract of employment. This, for Marx, is a key instance of what he describes as *ideology*.

The crux of the injustice that Marx identifies at the heart of capitalism is that under capitalist conditions of production, a minority grouping (the bourgeois ruling class), by virtue of the ownership of the means of production, is able to appropriate a significant part of the value of the work of the majority (the labouring class). Like the political economists before him (Adam Smith, David Ricardo, etc), Marx identifies labour as that which produces and determines value in society. But his revolutionary insight is that part of that value is usurped by the class that did not generate it: he calls it 'surplus value'. Surplus value is the difference between the value of what the product fetches in the market and the value that those who produce the goods (workers) are recompensed for, which is the wage they get and which ensures merely their subsistence. The injustice of the system lies in the fact that those who produce the goods are recompensed for only a part of the value of the goods they produce; the capitalist class appropriates the rest. In fact the more efficient workers are at producing the goods the greater the margin of value appropriated by the owners of production, and in effect paradoxically, the cheaper, therefore, the worker. Under capitalist conditions, surplus value is skimmed off, workers robbed of part of the value of their work, capital 'accumulates' and classes polarise. It is in this way that two fundamental classes emerge and gradually consolidate: a subordinate class that labours and a ruling class that appropriates surplus value. This creates a potentially explosive antagonism between an ever-shrinking minority of property holders (because powerful market players become increasingly powerful at the expense of weaker market players through economies of scale) and an increasingly pauperised working class, caught up in a vicious circle where the more dependent they become, the more expansive the 'reserve army' of the unemployed, and the more able their employers to suppress wages. Capitalism, argues Marx, contains the seeds of its destruction because it harbours this 'contradiction' at its very core.

It is obvious in this analysis that Marx begins with production and treats the economic instance as the fundamental, organising factor of society, on which all else depends. The economy is the *base* of every society, determining its shape and the nature of its institutions – at least 'in the final instance' – in the same way as the foundations of a building, say, determine and delimit the shape of what rests upon them. Marx famously used the metaphor of the 'base' and 'superstructure' to describe the social structure of class society. As the 'base' of society, the economy acts upon the (other) institutions of civil society in a way that can be described as causal (but in a loose sense; not in the sense that any change in the economy directly causes a change in society). He meant that the organisation of our economic activity would determine the type of political, legal, religious, educational, cultural, etc, institutions that we have. Law, located thus amongst the institutions of the superstructure, is very much in keeping with the conditions of the mode of production. Its operation broadly reflects the necessities of the mode of production, and its function is to sustain and regulate capitalist economic and social relations. For example, if the contract is the characteristic form of modern law, it is because the form of the contract governs economic relations – particularly the sale of labour. However, the form of law, which sees the contract as a fair exchange between two equal individuals, masks social inequalities and the fact that contract law systematically reproduces the economic interests of the bourgeoisie. For Marx, then, the form of law was a means of systematically reproducing the interests of a particular social class and masking or repressing the underlying economic inequalities. In this way the institution of law maintains and consolidates power differentials in economic relations.

If the economic base determines in the last instance the kind of institutions we have in the superstructure, the role of the superstructure is not confined to simply reflecting the economic relations of society. Of course, says Marx, the superstructural political institutions that we have will reflect, facilitate rather than impede, economic interests (look, for example, today at the relationship of the City of London and the UK government, the latter's meek attempts to control the former, the bankrolling of the parties by the industrialists, etc); of course the educational institutions we have will reflect and reproduce relations of production (in an education system that discriminates between those who will receive expensive privately funded education and those who will receive education befitting their future role as workers); of course our cultural institutions will reflect and reproduce dominant values; and so on. But that, for Marx, tells only half the story. The other half is how the superstructure works to manage, alleviate and defuse the potentially destructive contradictions that arise because of the injustice of the economic system, and thus how the superstructure helps to alleviate class conflict. Its institutions are crucially implicated in providing legitimation of the capitalist mode of production, and the legitimation they provide is in turn linked to ideology. Ideology works to alleviate contradictions and render the society coherent and seamless. How to best understand this?

Take the example of religion. When Marxists called (the Christian) religion the 'opiate of the people', their argument was that the religious teaching to 'turn the other cheek' to your aggressor, or the promise that it is the meek that will inherit the earth, served to disarm the dispossessed from a claim to justice in the here and now. Or when Marxists denounced the parliamentary system as a 'talking shop' of the bourgeoisie, their argument was that the populace is duped into thinking that they are represented in the processes of democratic will-formation in the legislature, while the real decisions that affect (and devastate) lives are taken behind the closed doors of the boardrooms of the bourgeoisie or (to update Lenin's dictum) of the institutions of global capital, such as the World Bank, the International Monetary Fund (IMF), the World Trade Organization (WTO) and the G20. What we find in these examples is a clear legitimating function of the institutions of the superstructure: religion and politics in these examples function directly to mask, justify or redeem the injustice of capitalist social relations.

The function of law

It is often remarked that when it came to the institution of law, Marx says little directly about it, at least in a systematic way. The primary category of analysis for Marx, as we saw, was social class, and classes were defined and understood in terms of their position in relation to the means of production. But while the *economic* analysis that Marx offers focuses on how the bourgeoisie extracted profits from labour by forcing down the price of labour and maintaining the price of the objects produced through control of supply and demand in the market, there is a *legal* dimension to these processes that is highly significant. The economic *means* of production was thus accompanied by distinctive social *relations* of production, which aimed at the reproduction of the social position and power of the dominant class, significantly, though not exclusively, by means of law.

To explore this dimension we may usefully turn to the work of the Soviet jurist Evgeny Pashukanis, whose account of the relationship of law to the economy through what he identified as the 'commodity form theory of law' has, belatedly, become hugely influential. Pashukanis argued that the form of law, especially the form that the law's basic categories of *legal subject*, *legal relation* and *legal norm* take, directly correlate to market relations of commodity exchange. The formation of capitalist production develops in tandem with bourgeois law, and the form of law coincides with that of commodity exchange. This is important. Pashukanis is in effect arguing that law is not merely an institution in the superstructure reflecting economic relations, but is instead crucially implicated in constituting them. If capitalist relations were structured around owner-ship and the wage relation, it was the legal categories of property (ownership of means of production) and contract (the labour contract) that, so to speak, run alongside the economic forms and allowed the economic system to function as it did. Law was also centrally implicated in the commodification of social life, not merely by extending the category of property right to cover one's very ability to work – for Marx the most *human* of activities, remember – but also by constituting the nodal points of social interaction in terms of contracts, rents, interests, etc. In a capitalist society these were all legally sanctioned and policed. This is where the notion of *commodification* also becomes impor-tant. For the market mechanism to operate, there needs to be an equation of goods in exchange, and thus a common denominator which would allow comparisons needs to be introduced. Equivalence is generalised across spheres of human activity, involving an abstraction from the use value that made those activities meaningful to humans individ-ually and interpersonally. Now the logic of exchange takes over, and with it the hijacking of value by the profit motive. Money, Marx's 'cash nexus', allows the flow of all things in the marketplace as commensurable. It introduces a measure of all things in exchange. There is a loss in this, argued Marx: things are no longer of value for what they are (use value), but for what they are worth in exchange (exchange value). And where the cost is borne most heavily is in relation to that most fundamental of activities, labour. In the process of its double subjection to the logic of exchange value and the material condi-tions of the organisation of factory production, the worker's creative labour becomes nothing but *expendable energy*, abstracted as merely time committed to the factory floor, that can be sold by the worker and bought by the capitalist. Throughout this, it is the legal form, Pashukanis significantly adds, that is implicated in a way that is fundamental.

Let us return to give a summary account of the function of bourgeois law as analysed by Marx. The law enables the market to operate by establishing what it means to own a commodity and the conditions of its exchange. The legal concepts of property and contract are fundamental conditions for giving form to the economic relations of production. What is also of paramount importance is our identity in law as legal subjects. While for Marx our very sense of identity depends on our interaction with others, as legal subjects what ties us together is money and our ability to buy and sell. Law abstracts from social identity those features that are relevant to relations of commodity owners in the market. The legal subject is thus an abstraction from our social situation. We become in law merely bearers of rights and duties which, in liberal law, means that we are commodity owners, free to exchange commodities in the market and free from any interference (from the state primarily). These form part of what Marx identifies as the processes of alienation, which take hold in capitalist societies. Co-operative productive activity is crucially undercut when exchange value stands in for what is of intrinsic value. The early Marx spoke passionately of the commodification of labour as 'reduc[ing] the worker into a fragment of a man, [and] destroy[ing] the fruits of his labour' (Marx 1844, pp 77–87). According to Marx, in the communist world that was to succeed the capitalist one, this form of alienation would disappear alongside the withering away of the capitalist state and its law. Bourgeois law would be replaced by the technical norm, the regulation of things, not the class subjugation of people. We would then, for Marx, recover our true nature, currently obscured by the legal form, the legal description under which we understand ourselves as property owners and commodity exchangers.

Ideology

The notion of legal ideology as used by Marxists is relevant to this function of 'obscuring', to explain how it works, how law operates to prevent visibility of the exploitative nature of social relations. Ideology helps to explain why the 'contradictions' of capitalism do not work to generate 'blockages' in the system or, more simply, why a majority class of progressively dispossessed workers does not rise up to overthrow the exploitative system since, as Marx and Engels famously put it in their 1848 political pamphlet Communist Manifesto, they 'have nothing to lose but their chains'. We saw earlier that if Marx offers a theory of society in which the key determinant of its organisation is its mode of production, the superstructure does not simply passively reflect those economic relations. It also acts back on the base to manage, alleviate and defuse the potentially destructive contradictions that arise there and to help alleviate class conflict. Its institutions are crucially implicated in providing legitimation of the capitalist mode of production, and the legitimation they provide is in turn linked to ideology.

While ideology in common parlance usually means a body of ideas and beliefs, in Marxist terminology it defines a function. This function is to sustain relations of domination by a move at the level of representation. Marx invites us to think about the following questions: Why, given the injustice of a system that is perpetrated by a minority grouping of society (the ruling class) on the majority (the working class), does the system continue its course of reproducing these unjust relations? Is this to do with how real relations are represented and lived? And how is man's relationship to the conditions of his own existence understood by him? He locates ideology as that system of representation that mediates his relationship to the material conditions of his life, that is, in simpler terms, the grid or lens through which man perceives the lived reality of his situation in the social world. Ideology here accounts for a certain misrepresentation, a certain misreading of the conditions that allows the continuation of a system of domination that presents itself as free. As John Thompson has put it:

> the concept of ideology calls our attention to the *ways in which meaning is mobilized* in the service of dominant individuals and groups, that is, the ways in which the meaning constructed and conveyed by symbolic forms serves to establish and sustain structured social relations from which some individuals and groups benefit more than others.
>
> (1984, p 73)

How might 'misrepresentation' work exactly? At the most ordinary level, the superimposition of a framework of general, formal rules upon a sub-terrain of real inequality achieves both the 'mystification' — the cover-up — of the real disparities and also the accentuation of those underlying inequalities. According to the law of contract, as we know, parties to a bargain (whether this has to do with the buying or selling of goods or of labour) approach it on formally equal terms. Thus while a bargain is struck between parties of unequal bargaining power in real terms, legally it appears as an agreement between equals who are as free to reach agreement as they are to abstain. The realities of the vast disparities of bargaining power, or the threat of advancing unemployment (Marx's 'reserve army' of labour power), are all screened off by the apparition of legal equality. The liberal legal order backs and sanctions individual freedom in the market, but this, as Anatole France famously put it, is a freedom that works asymmetrically, in forbidding 'both the rich and poor to sleep under the bridges of Paris.' Equality before the law hides material inequality, the uneven distribution of power and goods. Also, the market operates to give power to the most powerful market player (economies of scale, etc). And yet this privileging of the powerful party is hidden behind a guise of formal equivalence. This concealment is what in Marxist terms is understood as ideology. At the same time as it conceals and abstains from interference, formality boosts capitalist activity that further increases the disparity of wealth and power in society.

Marxists will not deny that coercion to support dominant economic interests often operates 'unmasked', especially when it is 'threatened' by subversive activity. However, such cynical instrumental accounts of law have a limited explanatory power and fail to take account of the vital dimension of legitimation, that is, the importance that power is presented not as brute power but as authority, as justified, fair and creating obligation rather than obliging through force. No order, and in particular not one as unjust as the capitalist order, would be able to sustain itself over time if it did not appear as legitimate. Take an example that Hugh Collins uses in his study of law and Marxism (1982, pp 41–42). Laws that criminalised 'combination' among workers were vital to an early capitalist system that felt the urgent need to protect itself from trade union activity. But such banning needed to present itself as legitimate, and the ideological moment comes with its justification as upholding the equality of the parties to the labour contract; any combination that might allow workers to push for higher wages was thus made to appear unjust, a ganging-up of sorts of one party against the other, irrespective of the fact that the bargaining positions were vastly uneven to begin with. It is in examples like this that we see clearly how a system seeks its justification in justice and equality and is reluctant to rely on brute coercion alone to see through the reproduction of the relations of production.

There are multiple forms through which the ideological 'obscuring' works. Law, argue Marxists, operates ideologically to 'naturalise' concepts like private property and exchange through contract, as if they were essential to our constitution as human beings; to 'mystify' or cover up substantive inequality through formal equality, and powerlessness through equal rights; to 'depoliticise' social struggles, that is, remove their political dimension and make them appear as merely criminal; and present them in a form that depletes them and renders them controllable. Here is Marx in 'The German Ideology':

> The class which has the means of material production at its disposal, has the control at the same time over the means of intellectual production, so that thereby, generally speaking, the ideas of those who lack the means of intellectual production are subject to it.
>
> (1932/1977 p 176)

There is a connection here between material production and the control of intellectual production, but that is not all. From the time of his earliest writings, Marx was keen to expose the subtle ways in which capitalism diffuses resistance and critique through subtle moves and strategies at the level of representation. One of his most famous denunciations is in 'On the Jewish Question' (1843), where he famously draws a distinction between political and human emancipation. He argues that the great political revolutions of the eighteenth century – the French and American – declared political emancipation while leaving the structures of 'private right' intact, notably the regime of property rights, including them as 'rights of man' in the name of which the revolutions were fought. But 'who is "man"?' asks Marx, and 'why are his rights called the rights of man?' He answers: 'No one but the member of civil society, i.e. egoistic man, man separated from other men and the community . . . who sees in other men not the realisation but the limitation of his own freedom' (1843, p 52, 53). In proclaiming and entrenching the rights of 'egoistical' man as the rights of the citizen, the revolutions in fact served to install a system of bourgeois property relations in the name of freedom, and despite the universalism of their declarations and the extension of political rights, left citizens powerless before property owners. For Marx this is 'revolutionary practice in flagrant contradistinction with its theory' (1843, p 54).

Legal ideology, then, functions by presenting contingent arrangements as natural, or by inscribing certain assumptions into the supposed nature of man. Is it really the case, for example, that, as Locke argued, the fact that no one owns me any longer (after the abolition of slavery) means that 'I own myself', or is it not rather that the category of property does not apply in this context? To secure its continuation capitalism must secure that relations of production are reproduced in their current form; that the disempowered remain that; and, thus, that class struggle is prevented from erupting in a way that might challenge the capitalist distribution of advantage through ownership of the means of production. Law, argue Marxists, operates ideologically to 'naturalise' concepts like private property and exchange through contract, to 'mystify' or cover up substantive inequality through formal equality, and powerlessness through equal rights, and to 'depoliticise' social struggles – remove their political dimension and present them in a form that depletes them and renders them controllable. To reproduce itself over time capitalism must secure that relations of production are reproduced in their current form, and that class struggle be prevented from erupting in a way that might challenge the capitalist distribution of advantage through ownership of the means of production. To generate legitimation for the system, the law acts ideologically in a range of ways outlined here. In all these ways the 'critique of ideology' is far-reaching and has informed many critical stances today beyond strictly Marxist positions.

Reading

For an accessible analysis of some of the fundamentals of the theory, see Marx's 'The German Ideology' (Marx 1932). His famous critique of rights and the French and American Declarations are contained in his early 'On the Jewish Question' (Marx 1843) and a discussion of equality in his 'Critique of the Gotha Programme' (in McLellan 1977). His analysis of commodification, use and exchange value and 'original accumulation' are found in his major work of the later period *Capital*, vol. 1.

Marx wrote little directly on law; a useful collection of extracts are collected by Cain and Hunt (1979, esp. pp 52–53, 56–59, 116–117, 132–137, 164–165). In terms of secondary literature on Law and Marxism, for a concise introduction to Marx see Giddens (1971, chs 1–4) and Stone (1985). There is also a useful introduction in Collins (1982) and Cotterrell (1992, pp 106–118). For a recent work discussing the conception of ideology in relation to international law, see Marks (2000, ch 1) and Miéville (2005), and more generally to law, Hirst (1979). In his edited volume, Zizek (1994), especially in chapters 1, 6, 9, 12 and 13, has compiled one of the best collections of writings in the Marxist tradition of ideology.

For other works on law in the Marxist tradition, see especially E Pashukanis's (1978) major work *Law and Marxism* and the very useful introduction by C Arthur. On commodification, reification with special reference to law, see G Lukács 'The Phenomenon of Reification' in Lukács (1971). Althusser (1971) provides one of the most famous, and controversial, accounts of the function of ideology as tied to the material practices of what he identifies as 'ideological State apparatuses'.

Chapter 6

Law, legitimation and rationality

Max Weber

Max Weber: modernity and formal legal rationality

While Marx's thinking about the law tied it intrinsically to class conflict in the economic system and thus at best only recognised a 'relative autonomy' to the institution of law from the capitalist economic system, Max Weber's thinking about society was explicitly, and to a significant effect, centred on the function and nature of law. Furthermore he saw the rise of modernity as tied to changes in rationality, which were expressed most obviously in the institution of law. Weber's main concern was with the question of how particular forms of rationality developed in different areas of social life, including the law, and the extent to which there were common themes or affinities in this process of rationalisation. Weber's central project was thus a historical sociology of the distinctive forms of modern Western rationality. *Rationality* is the organising concept of Weber's sociology, and we will pause to make sense of its significance in the next section.

Max Weber's (1864–1920) influence as a sociologist, philosopher and jurist is staggering. Alongside Marx and Durkheim he is considered one of the founding fathers of the new science of sociology in the nineteenth century. As a philosopher his theorisation of the processes of 'rationalisation' and 'disenchantment' that are associated with the rise of modernity were crucial. Politically he was one of the founders of the Liberal German Democratic Party after the Great War, and he played a key role in the drafting of the democratic Weimar Constitution of 1919.

In drawing out the basic elements of his social theory, we must note that while Weber was often described as engaged in a 'struggle with the ghost of Marx', and while he was in important respects a critic of the 'spirit of capitalism' and the 'disenchantment' that the rationality of modernity had brought to European societies, Weber clearly saw the capitalist economy as only one amongst a range of factors that drove the processes of rationalisation. He wrote an important treatise on the impact of ascetic Protestantism on the development of capitalism; for him the birth of modern capitalism is linked to a number of factors, including the evolution of the shareholding corporation and the emergence of new economic institutions and forms, state-building and state-capacity with the consolidation of the nation-state and modern forms of bureaucracy or political administration, the Industrial Revolution and the uses of technology, and crucially the rule of law. This did not mean that he ignored the relation between economy and society, but rather that he did not see a clear causal relation between developments in the former driving developments in the latter. His sociology of law was an attempt to analyse the distinctive features of modern Western law, by focusing on the conditions that he saw as central to its unique development, and to trace the relationship between the law and the other forms of rational organisation of social life.

What is the meaning of the term 'rational' for Weber? To answer this we must take a few steps back. Weber's 'real achievement', as the German social theorist Niklas Luhmann puts it in his *Sociology of Law*, 'lies in the radical return to a subject-related concept of action. Human action is no longer described with ontic natural characteristics but defined by "meaningful sense", therefore understood as something that has to be identified by the acting subject' (1985, p 16). In this 'radical return' Weber turns the perspective of the social scientist away from objective social laws and structures, away from 'empiricism', and away therefore from the trend to treat social sciences as akin to the natural sciences, and towards the subjective meaning that participants in society give to their action. The actor must relate the meaningful sense of his/her action to that of others in order for them to act in relation to each other. To understand and analyse society the social scientist in turn must try to understand how social actors understand their practices and the meanings they attach to their own actions. It is only in this 'doubling' of understanding that the social scientist can ascribe meaning and detect patterns of social interaction in order to understand social phenomena and how the integration of behaviours depend on 'lasting, learnable and internalisable norms' (Luhmann 1985, p 17). It is this context of how the world is given 'meaningful sense' (see above) by actors acting within it that Weber captures with his term 'rationality', in what we might therefore call an 'interpretative' (or 'hermeneutical') approach.

Now this rationality acquires a specific form for the *modern* individual, and in this the law plays the key role. The individual is assured of expectations about his/her position and results of his/her action that are supported by general rules, because s/he can no longer rely on older forms of trust and personal knowledge of situations and people, as was possible in the more local contexts of pre-modern Europe. Instead the law must now regulate relations amongst 'relative strangers' who rely on the market for their exchanges, in a world that is being revolutionised by capitalism and becoming highly complex. To break the law is no longer a breach of the normative order of the community but incurs compensation for economic damage; the office of the common law judge that used to embody the community's moral sense gives way to the specification and impersonality of the administration of justice; etc. The question of rationalisation is obviously key here, as modern law turns largely away from a clear orientation to value – what we might call its 'substantive content' – and towards formal qualities: conceptual abstraction, generality, neutrality. In this move it cuts itself off from sources of normativity that it previously gave expression to – communal morality, custom, religious authority, and in a significant sense turns upon itself as a differentiated, autonomous system to answer questions of how to support and reproduce the social order. It answers those questions in terms of abstract and general rules of universal applicability: the development of law as a system of norms of its own kind, separate and differentiated from moral, political and religious norms, is the essence of *legal formalism*.

Weber saw modern Western law as having certain distinct features. It was a system of general norms of universal application, organised and backed by the power of the state, applied and interpreted by a specially qualified staff of lawyers. In addition, modern law was relatively independent from politics, although the modern bureaucratic state was itself dependent on a particular legal form. These were not viewed as necessary features of all law, but were understood as the outcome of a particular process of historical development. The study of the form of modern law (as with the study of all other forms of rationality) thus required the development of a particular methodology, focusing on the forms of *legal rationality* and *political authority* and the relationships between them. We shall look at these in the next two sections, before going on to see how Weber used them in his historical sociology of the development of modern law.

But before that a short note on *methodology*: Weber deployed 'ideal types' in his sociology, to describe, amongst other forms, those of law and of political authority or legitimation. These types were not *ideal* in a normative sense; they were identified as ideal to distinguish them from the real in the sense that they were conscious exaggerations of what is encountered in social life. Weber's ideal forms are not encountered in the lived experience of social life in the pure form of their description. Instead, they embody selective principal characteristics of real situations and, as heuristic devices, they enable comparison and therefore the analysis of real social phenomena; in the case before us, of the principal characteristics of specific legal systems and forms of political organisation.

Forms of political authority

In one of the most famous and enduring formulations, Weber defined the state as 'a human community that (successfully) claims the monopoly of the legitimate use of violence within a given territory' (1948a/1919, p 78). The reference of 'legitimate' use (of violence) is to Weber's important organising hypothesis that any political formation could not rely on coercion alone, and that in order to sustain itself over time it would need to appear as justified to those on whom it visited the 'monopoly of violence.' It is this element of legitimation that distinguished authority from the (brute) exercise of power. With the emphasis (always) on the *meaning* that institutions and practices had for those who participated in them, the forms of political authority (or legitimate domination) were analysed in terms of the forms that actors ascribed to political orders. Weber's three-fold classification, again, deploys 'ideal types' as follows:

- *Traditional* domination, which rested on the 'established belief in the sanctity of immemorial traditions and the legitimacy of those exercising authority under them' (Weber 1968, p 215).
- *Charismatic* domination, which rested upon the extraordinary heroism or exemplary character of an individual leader and the order created or revealed by him or her.
- *Legal/rational* domination, which rested on the belief in the legality of a consciously created order and the right to give commands vested in certain persons designated by that order. This is seen as the specifically modern type of administration.

In the case of *traditional* domination, the order appears justified to those who are subject to it because it reflects their shared values, though in societies where it holds sway it is often that domination does not appear as an exercise of authority but is often taken as the natural order of the world, in which case there is no need to justify itself because things could not be otherwise. *Charismatic* domination, unlike the traditional type, is a revolutionary and unstable form of authority. Here authority rests on the charisma of the leader and the 'exceptional sanctity, heroism or exemplary character of an individual person, and of the normative patterns or order revealed or ordained by him' (Weber 1921/1968, p 217). For that reason there is no external limitation of the leader's right to rule, no limit to his/her determination of the content and scope of his/her mission or a questioning of its authenticity. Charismatic authority almost always evolves in the context of boundaries set by traditional or rational-legal authority, but by its nature tends to challenge this authority, and is experienced as a break with the established or accepted order. Charismatic authority is a transient form of authority and eventually succumbs to routinisation, the process by which, as Weber explains, charismatic authority is succeeded by a bureaucracy controlled by a rationally established authority or by a combination of traditional and bureaucratic authority. Finally, *legal/rational* domination is an impersonal form of order where obedience is demanded and given out of respect for the order itself, while the other two depend on the status of an office or the characteristics of certain individuals. In legal domination, legitimation is thus intrinsic to the order. Weber ties this form of domination to the rise of *bureaucracy*. He goes on to argue that, to the extent that legal domination is a rational form of domination, it will tend to have certain characteristics relating to its administrative staff that he famously associates with the structure of bureaucracy: official business is bound by rules; it is carried out within certain demarcated spheres or jurisdictions; it takes place within an official hierarchy of rule and supervision; and it requires some degree of professional training of officials. In addition, in a rational system there is a strict separation between the ownership and the means of administration, with no office being owned by its incumbent. That is to say that there is a separation between the office and the individual, which guarantees the impartiality and technical efficiency of the bureaucracy. Thus 'the purest type of exercise of legal authority is that which employs a bureaucratic administrative staff' (Weber 1968, p 220), for this leads to an increase in the technical knowledge and competency of the administration, which is essential to economic organisation and the organisation of social life under the conditions of the division of labour. In this sense, then, Weber contends that rational bureaucratic organisation is essential to modernity, since it alone is capable of dealing with the problems of distribution of goods and management of the economy, as well as ensuring the continuous regulation of social life.

Forms of legal rationality

In a second hugely influential typology, Weber introduces the (ideal) types of legal rationality in terms of two distinctions: that between the formal and the substantive (or informal); and that between the rational and the irrational. The two dimensions of comparison involve the degree of *rationality* and the degree of *formality*. Rationality measures the generality of the rules employed by the system and the systematic character of the legal order, while formality measures the extent to which criteria of decision are intrinsic to the legal system or instead draw from other sources. Thus the degree of rationality is aimed at the analysis of the internal consistency of a legal system, while the criteria of formality are concerned with the autonomy of the legal system from political institutions, religious authority or communal morality. It must, therefore, be noted that these forms refer to both the internal characteristics of legal systems and the relation between legal systems and other forms of social and political organisation.

Combined, these two sets of distinctions yield a four-fold classification (Table 6.1):

Table 6.1 Ideal types of legal rationality

Substantive-irrational	Formal-irrational
Substantive-rational	Formal-rational

Let us look at each combination in turn.

Formal-irrational

This refers to those types of systems where there is a body of established law, clearly demarcated from other sources of normativity (formality), but where there is no *rational* connection between the sources and specific outcomes. Take the example of forms of sacred or religious law: these are regarded as irrational in the sense that the authority of the law is not related to an internal quality of the rules themselves or their efficacy in organising social life, but is derived wholly from the oracular quality of their source. Thus in the sphere of law-finding, there might be recognised judges who follow certain established procedures for the settling of disputes, but the criteria of decision-making are unknowable. A good example of this type of practice would be the trial by ordeal or battle, which was a highly formalised system but appealed to divine intervention for the determination of guilt. A modern instance of formal irrationality is the institution of the jury, formalised as to the rules of its selection, remit, etc, but irrational because non-transparent regarding the reaching of decisions (which are neither able to be scrutinised nor required to be publicly justified).

Substantive-rational

At the antipode of the formal-irrational we have the substantive-rational type. This refers to those legal systems where there is a rational process for the making and enactment of law, but this draws on set extrinsic or external aims, such as ethical imperatives, religious and utilitarian ends or political purposes. Law is used instrumentally, and its authority depends on the extent to which it is able to fulfil these ends. The legal system in a theocratic regime, colonial administrative systems committed to a 'civilising' mission, or a constitutional system upholding the principles of Islam or furthering the aims of socialism are good examples of the substantive-rational. The substantive element here has to do with the fact that the bodies of norms draw their content and authority from religion, ethics or politics, respectively. One might discern elements of the substantive-rational type, if less straightforwardly, from the welfare systems of Western democracies that rely on state bureaucracies (and therefore rational administration) to promote and further the (substantive ideal of the) welfare of the people.

Substantive-irrational

In these types of systems there may be no formally established body of laws, no established criteria on which decisions are to be made in individual cases, and no clear demarcation between law and other sources of normative demands. There may or may not be recognised judges, and each case will be judged on its own merits. Decisions will commonly have no binding force beyond the particular case to be adjudicated. Examples would include systems where justice is dispensed by committees of elders in small communities, practices that Weber sometimes referred to this as 'khadi-justice' after the practice in certain Muslim courts (Weber 1968, p 845, 976–978), etc. Note, significantly, that the common law, with its analogical reasoning and its inductive method, as well as its origin in community morality, exhibits a strong substantive-irrational dimension in Weber's classification.

Formal-rational

This type refers to systems with a formal process for the enactment of laws, where the laws would be regarded as relatively autonomous from particular social policies or ethical ideals. There would be specialised institutions for the application of the law, and the discretion of judges would be limited. There would be a strong expectation that cases that were alike in their relevant legal characteristics would be treated alike. This requires the development of techniques for determining the relevant legal characteristics of a case and for the identification and application of general rules. Alternatively, it may simply demand the adherence to certain external characteristics of the facts, such as a signature on a deed or the utterance of certain words. Logical formality is in many respects the key to Weber's analysis of modern law, and we shall be examining it at some length below.

In his major work *Economy and Society*, Weber provides us with one of the most concise articulations of formal-rational law:

> First, that every concrete decision be the 'application' of an abstract legal proposition to a concrete fact situation; second, that it must be possible in every concrete case to derive the decision from abstract legal propositions by means of legal logic; third, that the law must actually or virtually constitute a 'gapless' system of legal propositions, or must, at least, be treated as if it were such a gapless system; fourth, that whatever cannot be 'construed' rationally in legal terms is also legally irrelevant; and fifth, that every social action of human beings must always be visualized as either an 'application' or 'execution' of legal propositions, or as an infringement thereof, since the 'gaplessness' of the legal system must result in a gapless legal ordering of all social conduct.
>
> (Weber 1968, pp 657–658)

Before we examine Weber's analysis, let us look at the two typologies together in order to understand both how the law links with politics and how Weber invites us to understand the development of legal modernity. Through these ideal types Weber traces an affinity between the ideal-type formal rational law and the ideal-type legal domination, a relationship that would be confirmed by his historical sociology of Western law. In other words the formal-rational type of law lends itself to be applied by bureaucracies as rule-bound institutions of government. But where there are affinities, there are also tensions between forms of legal and political organisation and the way that the different forms of law could interact with the types of legitimate political domination. For example, while certain forms of law require some sort of extrinsic guarantee for the legal order, as substantive-rational law relies on religious (charismatic) or political ends and authority, formal-rational law claims an intrinsic authority or validity based on the legal form itself. But this means that the question of the legitimacy of the legal system itself can appear as a problem under certain conditions, such as, for example, when legal questions become politicised, where law is required to adjudicate in political disputes, or where policy issues and the pursuit of welfare objectives (concerning housing, health, education, etc) mobilise forms of regulatory law that must in part at least give up the ideals of impartiality and generality if only to reach results. It is in contexts like this that historically, as we shall see, the distinction between law and politics becomes increasingly unstable.

The development of legal modernity

The relationship between forms of law and political organisation becomes clearer if we consider it in the context of Weber's basic outline of a historical sociology of Western law, the central feature of which was the increasing rationalisation of legal thought and the triumph of formal rational law. In this we can illustrate how Weber uses the ideal types as a means of analysing a specific pattern of development, as well as seeing how the development of legal modernity relates to the forms of political organisation.

The broad outline of development of legal modernity is laid out in the following passage from *Economy and Society*:

> From a theoretical point of view, the general development of law and procedure may be viewed as passing through the following stages: first, charismatic legal revelation through 'law prophets'; second, empirical creation and finding of law by legal *honoratiores*, i.e. law creation through cautelary [reasoning on a case-by-case basis] jurisprudence and adherence to precedent; third, imposition of law by secular or theocratic powers; fourth and finally, the systematic elaboration of law and professionalised administration of justice by persons who have received their legal training in a learned and formally logical manner. From this perspective, the formal qualities of the law emerge as follows: arising in primitive legal procedure from a combination of magically conditioned formalism and irrationality conditioned by revelation, they proceed to increasingly specialised juridical and logical rationality and systematisation, sometimes passing through the detour of theocratically or patrimonially conditioned substantive and informal expediency. Finally, they assume, at least from an external viewpoint, an increasingly logical sublimation and deductive rigour and develop an increasingly rational technique in procedure.
>
> (Weber 1968, p 882)

Both strands of development, towards rationality and formality, are evident in the trajectory described above. On the one hand, the increasing rationalisation of law, in the sense of generalisation in its elaboration ('logical sublimation and deductive rigour') and enactment, on the other hand, the increasing formalisation of the law in the sense of its becoming autonomous from systems of religious and political power. At the same time, however, this describes the subjection of political power to the forms of legal rationality, one of the more significant achievements of formal rational law and a characteristic of legal modernity.

These achievements can be broken down into four broad categories.

First, the development of rational law frees the individual from traditional forms of power based in superstition, religion or arbitrary sovereign action, through the development of universalisable norms and the rational administration of justice. The development of modernity thus establishes a particular kind of relationship between formal legal rationality and political power, which is constituted in legal form. This form of legitimacy enables those holding political power to do certain things, in particular when associated with the development of the capacities of rational bureaucratic administration, but (in its formal rational expression) the law now sets limits on arbitrary power.

The second achievement of the creation of a law of general validity and universal application is that it gives people security of expectations. The legal system of the modern nation-state is universal within its territory, superseding all local laws and privileges based on status and special jurisdictions. Formal rational law achieves its ideal expression in the form of a code. Laws must be published in advance in a form that can be understood by all subjects and are merely applied by judges and other legal officials who are formally independent of the sovereign. The actions of the state and its officers are subjected to legal controls, and so become more predictable. Equally, in the area of private law, the protection of private property and the enforcement of contracts become more secure and predictable, allowing the more certain regulation and future planning of economic affairs. By this means the rule of law creates and sustains security in economic, governmental and social life.

Third, there is the development of a sophisticated and specialised type of reasoning that requires that those interpreting and applying the law receive professional training. The idea that the law is both gapless and internally consistent with itself is derived from the reception of Roman law, which took rules that were developed by an inductive process and were context-dependent and generalised them to the level of abstract principles that could be applied deductively, since they were believed to be the highest achievements of reason. Legal problems are thus seen as individuated cases that can be solved in a *systematic* manner by identifying the legally relevant facts and subsuming them within abstract legal norms. Cases are to be solved only by looking at the combination of law and facts, and by excluding consideration of factors such as moral values or social status.

Fourth, as part of a wider process of secularisation, the law is separated from the sphere of ethics. Although this was initially understood in terms of the separation of law and religion, both at the level of the disestablishment of state religion and in terms of the content of individual laws, this has a number of important consequences for our understanding of modernity. Weber traced the reception of Roman law through its transformation into modern or revolutionary natural law, in which the legitimacy of the norms was now to be derived from its inherent principles of 'reason and justice', which allowed it to transcend its origins in princely or priestly power. This, he argued, was the 'only consistent type of legitimacy of a legal order which can remain once religious revelation and the authoritarian sacredness of a tradition and its bearers have lost their force' (Weber 1968, p 867). However, he also pointed out that this form of legitimacy was in tension with the development of a formal rational law whose authority was grounded only in the formal question of the internal *validity* of the norm. The development of legal modernity thus broke the connection between law and reason or justice. Formal positive law need have no particular content and is limited by no other ethical or moral principles. Its positivity meant that for the first time in history legal changes by legislation become an immanent feature of law itself. And it is implicit in both the idea and the historical development of formal rational law that there be some form of specialisation and autonomy from other spheres of values and social life.

It is in connection to this fourth achievement that Weber stressed the importance of technical factors associated with learning and professionalisation that drove the autonomous development of the law. The crucial factor here was the reception of Roman law, initially in the canon law and later as a more abstract system of legal learning, which offered the basis for a universalisation of law that transcended traditional forms and particularistic norms. This had important consequences for the education of lawyers in the early universities. The study of law based on the formal qualities of Roman law became a specialised form of knowledge and encouraged the formation of the legal profession. It also had important consequences for the administration of justice as trained lawyers, whether acting as officials or judges, demanded the rationalisation of law and procedure. This underlines, once again, the close connections that Weber drew between formal rational law – the development of rational administration in the form of bureaucracy – and legal domination.

From this brief account we can see how Weber's conception of formal rational law describes important features of legal modernity. It is tempting to see these achievements as the inevitable result of the unfolding of an immanent process of rationalisation – a march of progress towards better, more rational, law – a temptation that is exacerbated by the language of ideal types and Weber's description of formal rational law as the highest form of rationality. However, it is necessary to ask why this form of law should have developed uniquely in the West, for this was not an inevitable process, even when considered in conjunction with the development of the capitalist economy.

Modern law and the economic system

To begin with, it is important to note that Weber did not see this question as one simply of the relation between law and economy, or between forms of legal and economic thought, although he clearly regarded this relation as being of central importance. Indeed, unlike Marx, he was at pains to deny the existence of a strict correlation or causal relation between the two: changes in external conditions, such as changes in the form of the economy, might have some impact on individual or collective conduct but could not in any sense be regarded as determinants of such conduct. Equally, the law might protect certain economic interests, but it was clear both that these interests might be protected in other ways and that the law also served other interests that could not be reduced to purely economic factors. It is thus important to note that while Weber wished to place the forms of economic organisation at the centre of his sociology, he was also distancing himself in two important respects from Marx's analysis of the development of law and the capitalist economy. First, he was concerned to establish the full range of relations between the economy and other relevant social spheres, without seeing these relationships as being mono-causally determined in any way. Second, in contrast to Marx's class analysis, Weber was concerned with individual activity and orientations towards forms of conduct or ideas as a means of understanding social and economic activities: 'the ability and disposition of men to adopt certain types of practical rational conduct' (Weber 1930, p 26; Ewing 1987). However, unlike many forms of methodological individualism that begin from the assumption of certain natural or intrinsic characteristics, such as self-interest or the ability to reason, for Weber there is no intrinsic quality attaching to human actions or persons, and thus there can be no organising principles beyond the orientation towards certain rationally structured activities. This problematises the idea of rationality, for it is implicit in this view that the world is fundamentally non-rational. This gives his analysis of the rise of formal rational law further distinctive characteristics, notably an emphasis on the contingency of social relations and a degree of scepticism about the capacity of rationality to organise human affairs. The explanation for the rise of formal rational law was sought, then, in the coincidence of, or affinity between, certain interests, combined with an analysis of the intrinsic or internal demands of a developing legal profession.

It is at the juncture of the legal system with the market economy and the state that the 'elective affinities' that Weber saw between formal-rational law, the market system and the bureaucratic state come most evidently to the fore. Weber argued that an economic system of the modern type could not exist without a legal order backed by the state that could guarantee the predictability and stability of economic relations:

> [M]odern economic life by its very nature has destroyed those other associations which used to be the bearers of law and thus of legal guaranties. This has been the result of the development of the market. The universal predominance of the market consociation requires on the one hand a legal system the functioning of which is calculable in accordance with rational rules. On the other hand, the constant expansion of the market consociation has favoured the monopolisation and regulation of all 'legitimate' coercive power by one universal coercive institution through the disintegration of all particular status-determined and other coercive structures which have been resting mainly on economic monopolies.
>
> (Weber 1968, p 337)

In this passage Weber is pointing to the central importance of legal order in supporting the functioning of the market, as well as the way in which economic development created the conditions in which a rational legal system could supersede other forms of social and political organisation. Law functioned to promote the security of the interests of commerce and business and the protection of property. It did so by structuring economic relations in ways that made them more efficient, predictable and enforceable, specifically through the contractual form, but also through the development of devices such as agency and negotiable instruments, which facilitated economic transactions. However, Weber was also at pains to point out that this was not a function of legal rationality as such, for 'the consequences of the purely logical construction often bear very irrational or even unforeseen relations to the expectations of the commercial interests' (Weber 1968, p 855). The formal abstract character of law was also of decisive merit to those with economic power in securing freedom from arbitrary government interference, as it was to those 'who on ideological grounds attempt to break down authoritarian control or to restrain irrational mass emotions for the purpose of opening up individual opportunities and liberating capacities' (Weber 1968, p 813). Once again, however, this was accompanied with a caveat, pointing out that there was no necessary connection between economic freedom of contract and political freedom.

It is in the context of these alignments and affinities between formal-rational law and market freedom that a certain difficulty arises for Weber, that has usually been described as his 'England problem' (this is developed in 1968, pp 814 and 889ff). In short the difficulty is that where Weber sought to establish a positive relationship between the highest form of rationality in legal thought (formal-rational law) and the most advanced type of economic rationality as embodied in capitalism, capitalism developed first in England where no such formal-rational legal system was in evidence. As we have seen, the common law embodied, and continues to embody, a logic of the ('irrational') inductive kind, that moves by tracking commonalities between cases and moves largely through analogy, rather than through deductive reasoning. As a result a number of scholars have concluded that Weber's sociology of law suffers from contradiction. In their responses to Weber's 'England problem' scholars of Weber direct us towards Weber's accounts of alternative sources of stabilisation and securitisation of market expectations tied to the rise of a legal profession that used routine and systematic forms of argumentation, or argue that Weber actually identified formal justice and guaranteed rights, rather than logically formal legal thought, as the features of modern law that directly facilitated the rise of capitalism (see Ewing 1987).

Weber as theorist and as critic of modernity

In summary, then, legal modernity for Weber was characterised by the development of formal rational law, a development that coincided with and contributed to the development of the capitalist economy. The notable achievements of this form of law were to provide a legal form that enabled both the stable and continuous regulation of the economy and social life and the constitutionalisation of political power, through the creation of an autonomous, specialised form of legal reasoning. This released and forged the extraordinary dynamism of the capitalist system, never, for Weber, in a mono-causal way, but certainly in terms of what he described as elective affinities between the two.

And yet, for all his careful dissection of it there is a striking ambivalence in Weber's 'endorsement' of formal rationality. Modernity, for Weber, imposes the 'iron cage' of instrumental rationality. As bureaucracies continue to enhance efficiency, as our technologies continue to deliver efficient outcomes in a world where shared value systems and a shared sense of purpose fade into the background and become a question of individual choice, our societies suffer a loss of meaning, a loss embodied in the increase of our instrumental rationality, a rationality of *means*, and a loss of substantive rationality, or a rationality of *ends*. In this reversal in the relationship of means to ends, where the latter yield to the former, Weber reads a 'disenchantment' of the modern capitalist world.

The notion of disenchantment is most eloquently developed by Weber in one of his most important lectures, 'Science as a Vocation', delivered at Munich University in 1917 and published just after the war and shortly before his death in 1920. He presented disenchantment as a hallmark feature of modern Western society, describing this development, in relation to science, as entailing primarily the conviction that 'there are no mysterious incalculable forces' and that 'one need no longer have recourse to magical means in order to master or implore spirits.'

Here is an extract from the lecture where the notion of disenchantment is directly addressed in a way that captures something of Weber's profound humanism:

> The fate of our times is characterized by rationalization and intellectualization and, above all, by the 'disenchantment of the world.' Precisely the ultimate and most sublime values have retreated from public life either into the transcendental realm of mystic life or into the brotherliness of direct and personal human relations. It is not accidental that our greatest art is intimate and not monumental, nor is it accidental that today only within the smallest and intimate circles, in personal human situations, in pianissimo, that something is pulsating that corresponds to the prophetic pneuma, which in former times swept through the great communities like a firebrand, welding them together. If we attempt to force and to 'invent' a monumental style in art, such miserable monstrosities are produced as the many monuments of the last twenty years. If one tries intellectually to construe new religions without a new and genuine prophecy, then, in an inner sense, something similar will result, but with still worse effects. And academic prophecy, finally, will create only fanatical sects but never a genuine community.

Reading

Weber's major work was carried out between the years of 1904 and 1905 – when he first published the essays that subsequently made up the book *The Protestant Ethic and the Spirit of Capitalism* – and his death in 1920. The bulk of his great synthetic work – *Economy and Society* – was published posthumously in 1921/2, though it was not fully published in English until 1968. Weber provides an excellent short introduction to the questions that animate his sociology in the introduction to *The Protestant Ethic and the Spirit of Capitalism* (1930/1905), pp 13–31).

The classic analysis of Weber's sociology of law based on the ideal types can be found in M Rheinstein (1954, pp xlvii–lxiii). A similar account can be found in Kronman (1983, ch 4). The types of legitimate domination are set out in Weber 1968 ch III (you should read pages 217–226 for an analysis of legal authority). For a general discussion of Weber's theory see Cotterrell (1995), Turner (1996) and Murphy (1997).

Chapter 7

Law, community and social solidarity

Emile Durkheim

We have seen how the geographical mobility that industrial society required uprooted people from traditional communities so that identification with fixed locality was no longer possible. On the other hand, the 'release' from fixed social roles and the erosion of traditional forms of life based on status led to new opportunities to accumulate wealth or develop ways of life or new social identities in the fast-growing modern city. In practice though, the new industrial societies created vast asymmetries in the distribution of wealth, and a labour market to which, under the threat of starvation, the majority of the newly dispossessed were forced to commit their labour. The state and the Market became the two forces and organising principles of the new societies. In Polanyi's words, 'Hobbes's grotesque vision of the State – a human Leviathan whose vast body was made up of an infinite number of human bodies – was dwarfed by the Ricardian construct of the labour market: a flow of human lives the supply of which was regulated by the amount of food put at their disposal' (Polanyi 1957/1944, p 164).

A key problem that emerged in this period was thus the question of social order: what is it that holds society together in the face of the growing social divisions and tensions, the new risks and contingencies of social life ordered by the market, and the spectre of social dislocation where traditional forms of social ordering were being destroyed? How, therefore, in the face of these shifts and new uncertainties, and with the demise of traditional social structures, *was social order possible?* Such questions led in turn to an interest in the social functions of law as an instrument for the production of social order.

The three great social theorists of the period, the 'fathers of sociology' and the new 'science' of society that emerged in the nineteenth century all addressed and answered this question in different ways. We have seen that Marx focused on the theme of social conflict, arguing that the main role played by institutions such as the law was to suppress class conflict and support the dominance of particular class interests, so that social order could be explained in terms of the domination of one class over the other. Weber, by contrast, studied law as a distinctive form of modern rationality, placing special

emphasis on the idea of legitimation, showing how the connection between the form
of law that emerges with capitalism, and the specific type of legitimation it commands,
plays a key role in securing social stability.

We turn now to the third in this trio, the French sociologist and lawyer, Emile
Durkheim (1858–1917). Durkheim stressed the themes of social cohesion and collective belief, arguing that the changing forms of law could be seen as indices of
different types of social solidarity. In this chapter we will focus on Durkheim's
notion of social solidarity, supplementing it with the work of Ferdinand Tönnies.
While the terms Gemeinschaft and Gesellschaft that will be introduced in this section
are Tönnies's, they capture something of the correlation of social and legal orders,
and the distinctiveness of the pre-modern as against modern types that are central
to Durkheim's analysis.

Durkheim's major work was The Division of Labour in Society, first published in 1893.
This book analysed the transformation of the modern world in terms of the development of the division of labour – the extent to which work on particular tasks is subdi-
vided between members of a community, and the subdivision of the labour involved
in the production of particular objects – and its impact on the organisation of social
life. He identified two forms of social solidarity, each of which was associated with
a characteristic form of law. The first – mechanical solidarity – existed in small, unde-
veloped societies, where each clan or social group was a separate economic unit. In
these societies labour was shared and was geared primarily towards the subsistence
and reproduction of that unit. Such groups were characterised by shared beliefs and
values. Law in such societies was repressive – that is to say that it was primarily aimed at
the reinforcement of social solidarity and the punishment or expulsion of those who
threatened collective beliefs. The most prominent type of law to this form of social solidarity was criminal law, as this was used both to protect the community against internal
and external threats and as a means of expressing communal values. The second – organic
solidarity – was typified by modern industrial societies. In these societies there are high
levels of economic interdependence, as individuals typically work at the production
of objects that must be sold to other economic producers and are not producing their
own means of subsistence. However, there are fewer shared beliefs, and Durkheim was
concerned with the pressures that were created towards anomie (normlessness) or social
disorder in such societies. The form of law corresponding to organic solidarity was
restitutive law, which was aimed at the regulation and co-ordination of relations arising
from the division of labour. The most prominent, but not exclusive, type of law was
contract law, governing relations between producers and consumers in the marketplace.
This clearly allowed the maintenance of the market and division of labour, but indicated
a weaker form of social solidarity. For Durkheim, then, law played an important role
in the maintenance of social solidarity, but the way that it did so was fundamentally
different in different types of society.

One can explore the points that Durkheim makes here through the use of an important typology that was introduced by Ferdinand Tönnies. This is the distinction between
Gemeinschaft and Gesellschaft, roughly translatable as 'community' and 'society' respectively
(and thus corresponding in broad terms to mechanical and organic solidarity). With
these terms Tönnies attempted to track the transition between societal change and the
corresponding legal change. While these forms appear very much as ideal types in the

Weberian sense, they each have dominated (as paradigmatic) an epoch in the evolution of our legal tradition.

In the *Gemeinschaft* form of social regulation the emphasis is on law as expressing the will, the internalised norms and traditions of a community, to whom each individual member is part of the social family. In effect there is no clear distinction between what belongs to the private realm and what to the public, what is a legal as opposed to a moral issue, what is properly politics as opposed to justice, religion, morality. The normative order is all-encompassing and unyielding. This form of law is, in Weber's terminology, characteristically substantive. The arbiter of justice does not act under a legal capacity somehow detached from his own moral views, social position and politics. Rather s/he adjudicates on the basis of a justice that is the community's – the sense of which s/he embodies – and s/he does so (again in Weberian terms) irrationally, not by deducing from general premises but in a casuistic, ad hoc, manner, as the case at hand demands.

Gesellschaft law is in many ways the exact opposite of this. We move here from the cohesive community to liberal society and its need to co-ordinate differences in social and professional roles and contributions of labour. Where, in the former, society as a whole imposed the dictates of law, *Gesellschaft* law is geared to individualism. This requires that in the name of protecting the individual, the law must keep society at arm's length. The emphasis is now on the autonomous individual, motivated by self-interest, who enters the public arena to strike deals that will further his/her own interest. The law is there to set up and guarantee that process of exchange as well as the equality of all before it, and in a sense limits itself to the role of passive enforcer of individuals' agreements. To achieve its function this law of liberal society must assume the form of a system of rules that are clear, predictable, general (applying equally to everyone) and self-contained; recourse to outside moral, political or social considerations would undermine legal certainty and moral and political pluralism. The distinction between the two types of law brings into relief competing images of the person. In *Gemeinschaft* law the person is intimately linked with the community to which his/her own sense of identity is intimately tied. In *Gesellschaft* law the person is atomistic, self-determining and limited only by the rights of other individuals; s/he is first and foremost a bearer of rights, that is a cluster of entitlements through which public exchange and public life is possible.

But what is the lever of change between the forms of law? The answer to this depends on the concept of *legitimation*, which addresses these further questions: given that the bottom line of law is that it is a coercive order, is it merely the threat of coercion that motivates people to accept it? Or is there something beyond threat that makes law appear, and makes people act, as if it were binding – which creates an obligation to obey? This matters because, although compliance with the legal order can be secured to a limited extent by coercion, compliance over time may be guaranteed only if the existing order commands the support or loyalty of the mass of the population.

In *Gemeinschaft* law, legitimation is based on shared values and shared understandings. Legal rules (when law takes the form of explicit rules rather than custom) embody shared value commitments. Here society is held together through what Durkheim terms a '*conscience collectif*' or 'collective consciousness', the shared set of beliefs and values which is continually expressed and renewed through the operation of the law. The law is adhered to and respected because the opportunity to question it is absent: the social environment discourages dissent and rewards obedience. But the legitimation reaches deeper than mere external pressure. Allegiance to the rules derives from the fact that the rules give expression to the background common morality, often grounded in religious belief. With no dividing line between that morality and the legal expression of it, adherence to law is inextricably linked to a shared morality. Since it is from this pool of common value that the community draws in order to make sense of the world in the first place, allegiance to law is guaranteed in a strong sense, meaning that any breaches of it require the intervention, in Durkheim's terms, of *repressive* sanctions to maintain social cohesion.

The changes in economic, social and cultural conditions in modernity brought about a change in the legitimation process. The rise of the bourgeoisie in Europe, and the changed economic and social conditions, challenged the status society and subverted the *Gemeinschaft* form of law. As for legitimation, there arose due to the market as facilitator of exchange and of transaction among parties who did not share a world-view, a certain pluralism of values that undercut the sort of allegiance that was possible in *Gemeinschaft*. The logic of legitimation is reversed in *Gesellschaft* law: it no longer draws legitimation from shared substantive values, but instead from its very distance from those values. Communal moral principles that grounded *Gemeinschaft* law are of reduced effectiveness, and religion is relegated to the private realm of individual conscience. *Gesellschaft* law frees itself from the sources from which a challenge to its legitimacy could originate, and appears as a rational system of self-justifying, neutral rules, which are independent of particular religious or moral beliefs. Law stays clear of promoting certain values against others, or certain ends against others, because that is the province of individual freedom of choice. Law merely fixes the formal framework within which individual wills will meet. It fixes common means to diverse ends, guaranteeing formal equivalence, the terms of exchange and the enforceability of the agreement. The legitimacy of law in the liberal era depends upon precisely its withdrawal to the formal side of the social interchange.

In a society where there is very little agreement on substantive issues across the board, it becomes important to agree the rules of disagreement. The law draws its legitimation from merely fixing the framework for settling conflict and abstaining from taking sides, as it were, in that conflict. It merely provides the technical means of compromising between conflicting interests. At the same time it provides institutional backing to a market economy where, in principle, everything is subject to agreement and exchange according to the free will of the parties. Law becomes legitimate in guaranteeing that kind of freedom, and in performing that function brings into play a different kind of solidarity, that which Durkheim calls 'organic'.

So liberal law, *Gesellschaft* law, is a type of law that relies on an image of the person that is not, to begin with, a creature of the community. The person is conceived of as pre-existing it, self-constituting, self-seeking and self-interested; s/he approaches the community in order to strike his/her bargains to realise his/her self-stipulated ends. That is why for Durkheim and Tönnies *contract* is the liberal law's *paradigmatic* form. And it is these changes in *social* conditions that explain why modern normative political philosophy draws so heavily on individualistic assumptions. This is precisely the image of the person as bearer of rights and of society as an association of individual persons that is reflected in the theorists of *social contract* and is one that still pervades liberal political theory. Contract, or agreement between individuals, in this view, dominates the constitution of society and the workings of society, and this crucial legal concept is coupled with those of property and rights. Property in liberal law becomes the inalienable entitlement to enjoy and dispose of objects to an unprecedented degree; unprecedented because any previous system of property circumscribed property more narrowly both as to the kind of things that could be owned (goods, capital, means of production, intellectual products, etc), and as to the incidents of ownership, that is the extent of power over the propertied: alienation, management, dividends, transmissibility. Liberal law thus extended (i) the number of incidents of ownership, that is, the range of entitlements to, dividends from, controls over and management of the propertied thing: in Gesellschaft law, ownership becomes absolute and property is freely disposable; (ii) the range of the kind of thing that may be owned: land and labour crucially, and later image/sound, ideas or knowledge: there is a great increase of what may be propertied: in principle everything becomes exchangeable, alienable, saleable, including, notoriously, labour power; and (iii) the priority and security given to the legal title of the owner against anyone with a different title. The development of a regime of individual property rights is tied to the development of a political economy based on the market and the principles that underlie it.

For Durkheim, then, the form and functions of modern law were to be studied as a means of understanding the nature of the underlying social solidarity. That is why he spoke of the law as 'index' of social solidarity. What makes social order possible under modern conditions of an ever-increasing division of labour in the Gesellschaft type of society is very different to that of the pre-modern type, but still intricately linked to law. But now the law, for Durkheim, has shifted its internal emphasis towards the institutions of private law and the sanction of private agreements (characteristically associated with restitutive rather than repressive sanctions) in the form of contract, which becomes the characteristic of, and the lynchpin of, the emerging form of organic solidarity. In a move that 'frees' social relations from social stratification, from status and from the bonds that it entailed during the ancien régime, the law is severed from a strong collective consciousness in substantive social and political terms, meaning that social order is possible as a new form of interdependence only because pacta sund servanda – that is, that obligations freely assumed, will be met – is guaranteed as the bond that makes society possible. Modern law underwrites this in the form of the protection of individual rights and liberties.

Thus despite the individualism and secularisation to be found in modern societies, there are nonetheless forces that bring people together in relations of interdependence. These forces may be weaker than in earlier, traditional forms of community. But there still remains a form of 'collective consciousness' that transcends individuals and has the function of maintaining and reproducing social solidarity. Indeed, observes Durkheim, it is precisely the shared value of individualism that is, paradoxically, what individuals all have in common. And the values associated with this, such as tolerance towards others' points of view, are visibly reflected in modern law through the protection of such universal rights as freedom of conscience, religion and free speech, as well as, as we have seen, of contract. Thus the role of law for Durkheim, even in complex modern capitalist societies, is to express this collective interest and hence to maintain a new form of social cohesion.

Reading

For a discussion of social solidarity and the division of labour, see Durkheim, *The Division of Labour* (1963/1933), especially chapters 2 and 3. Durkheim's analysis of contract and property is extensively developed in a set of lectures published as *Professional Ethics and Civic Morals* (1992). For one of the best analyses of Durkheim's thinking about law, see Cotterrell (1999), and more generally on his thinking about society see Giddens (1971) and Lukes (1973). Useful summaries and extracts of Durkheim's work are collected in Lukes and Scull (1983).

Durkheim has had a particular impact on criminal law, criminology and the social theory of punishment. Amongst the best analyses here are Garland (1990, chs 2 and 3) and Reiner (1984).

The transformation from *Gemeinschaft* to *Gesellschaft* (and then further to 'regulatory law') are analysed in the much discussed article by Kamenka and Tay (1975). For the classic account of the transition from 'status to contract', see Maine (1861), and for the changes in contract law during this transition see Atiyah's magisterial account (1979).

III

Transformations of modern law

8	The rise and decline of the rule of law	91
	The materialisation of modern law	91
	Law in the welfare state	93
	Beyond the welfare state	97
9	Law and globalisation	100
	Sovereignty after globalisation	103
	Constitutionalism beyond the state	105
	'Unthinking' modern law	107

Chapter 8

The rise and decline of the rule of law

If there were disagreements between Durkheim, Marx and Weber in the analysis of the function of law in modern society and its relation to economic development, there are also certain shared elements. All three recognised that the form of law was changing in response to the social changes that came with the development of the capitalist economy, and the significance of formalism in legal reasoning as being necessary to the securing of a particular kind of stability in legal, social and economic relations. And all recognised the importance of the role of law in reshaping and legitimating the modern state. Yet even as they wrote, the law was changing in response to social and political pressures — in response to what is often described as the 'social question'. In this section we outline some of these changes and the transformations that they brought about to the legal form and the function of law in modern society, notably with the emergence of the welfare state. We will then conclude the section by discussing how modern law is being exposed to a fresh set of pressures with the development of what has come to be known as globalisation.

The materialisation of modern law

Weber's argument, as we saw in the last section, was that modern law was an autonomous and technical discipline which, with the rise of the modern nation-state, had to fulfil the end of legitimising the political system. However, he recognised that there was an inherent tension between law and political power, since the political demand for the implementation of particular policies tended to undermine the formal rationality of the legal system. 'Juridical formalism', in Weber's formulation, 'enables the legal system to operate like a technically rational machine' (1968, p 811) — implementing policy through legislation — but this had the consequence of undermining its capacity to stand opposed to political power. Legal modernity had created a formal rationality without ideals, where the legal profession acted as technicians serving established power and where law was used to promote instrumental ends. Thus:

> [i]nevitably the notion must expand that the law is a rational technical apparatus which is continually transformable in the light of expediential considerations and

> devoid of all sacredness of content. This fate may be obscured by the tendency of acquiescence in the existing law, which is growing in many ways for several reasons, but it cannot really be stayed.
>
> (Weber 1968, p 895)

He identified three developments which were bringing specific pressure to bear on the formal rationality of modern law – what he called the 'materialisation' of formal law. In the first place, he noted the revival and growth of 'particularism' in the law specifically, though not exclusively, in the areas of commercial and labour law. While, as we have seen, the development of modernity had been characterised by the removal of status privileges and jurisdictions and their replacement by norms of general application, writing in the early part of the twentieth century, Weber noted a trend towards the weakening of legal formalism by considerations of substantive expediency specific to certain areas of law. Thus he noted that in the area of commercial transactions the application of the law was coming to be determined by the substantive qualities of a transaction, that is to say the economic purpose of the transaction, rather than the formal properties of the contract. This was accompanied by the development of special tribunals, such as commercial courts, which explicitly sought to develop principles of adjudication that were adapted to the activity that they sought to regulate. The continuation of this trend has been noted by later theorists who have observed, for example, that the outcomes of commercial contractual disputes are more likely to be determined by the relationship between the contracting parties than the letter of the contract, and that the law is used only as final resort (Macaulay 1963; *Social & Legal Studies* 2000). We can also note the continued development of specialised informal dispute settlement institutions, such as tribunals or courts of arbitration, which have their own specialised jurisdiction and rules.

Second, Weber noted the operation of the status demands of lawyers. Legal formalism seeks to minimise the contribution of the lawyer by bowing to the political demand that the law be accessible and intelligible and by attempting to reduce judicial discretion in the interpretation and application of the law. Weber, however, argued that this conflicted with the professional ideology of lawyers, which is based on the claim that the law is a complex science, the understanding of which requires specialised training and knowledge. Indeed he suggests that lawyers have an interest in maintaining the complexity of the law and react to political movements for legal codification, or the simplification of the sources and mode of expression of the law, by seeking to defend their interests and preserve their social status. There is thus a fundamental conflict between professional demands for complexity and political demands for intelligibility, the outcome of which in practice has been the development of increasingly technical and internally differentiated bodies of law.

Third, he noted the impact of social conflict and inequality on the law, as the law was increasingly used as a tool for the management of class conflict. This, he argued, affected the ability of the law to be an abstract and impartial system of adjudication in one of two ways. On the one hand, the existence of social conflict called into question the abstract claims of the law to treat all individuals as equals, which led to political demands for a more social law that would be responsive to certain inequalities. There was thus also a politicising of law – that is to say the use of law as a means of achieving certain policy ends – in order to preserve the legitimacy of political authority. On the other hand, in the process of legal interpretation and application there was an assertion of the need for judicial creativity to supplement the abstract formulation of the law with evidence relating to the meaning and context of certain disputes. Thus lawyers would claim to discover the 'real' intentions of the parties to a contract, rather than looking at its purely formal qualities, and demand the recognition of categories such as 'good faith' or 'fair usage', which would require the judge to be more evaluative rather than merely enforcing the formal terms of an agreement. This reflects an inherent incompatibility between the 'utilitarian' meaning of a proposition and its formal legal meaning as this was governed by the demands of logical consistency. These could only be brought together at the cost of the renunciation of the formal qualities of law, and in particular the idea that the law was complete and 'gapless', in favour of more amorphous and ethical standards of substantive justice.

Although his analysis concentrates mainly on the external pressures that were being placed on the law, it is worth noting that it reflects a general and underlying internal tension in the legal form. This can be seen in the two different aspects of the positivisation of the law – a development that (as we have already noted) Weber regarded as a central achievement of legal modernity. On the one hand, positivisation reflects a fundamental conflict between legal and social fact, which can be traced to the relation between formal and substantive legitimacy in modern natural law. Modern natural law sought to establish the normative legitimacy of the law by codifying the natural qualities of social relations. It thus claimed a direct relation between legal and social fact. However, this form of law is vulnerable to disruption by the evidence of actual social facts or substantive demands made in the name of an ethical claim about legal justice. There is thus a necessary gap between legal and social fact that follows from the failures of social life to correspond to the model of law. Thus while the model of formal law is apparently founded on the premise that legal and social justice are commensurate, the experience of modernity suggests that this is not the case, and the law in practice swings between retreating into formalism and its dissolution in the pursuit of particular substantive ends. That is to say that there is a privileging of either the normative quality of the legal or that of the social, as a result of the unbridgeable gap that has been created between law and society. At the same time, the positivisation of the law results in the specialisation of the legal sphere. This accentuates a fundamental tension between the universalism of the ideology of the legal form and the limited social capacity of the law to resolve social conflicts.

Law in the welfare state

The diverse social developments that Weber identified came together with the emergence of the welfare state in Western nations in the middle decades of the twentieth century. It developed as a response to the devastating effects of the Great Depression and the Roosevelt administration's 'New Deal' in the United States, and later with the post–Second World War concern with justice and equality. This was the case for the victorious Allied nations, where in Britain, for example, the Labour government of 1945 committed itself to an unprecedented programme of building up the education and health systems according to a vision of social democracy, whereby the inability or denial to meet people's basic needs in terms of subsistence, health, education, employment and housing were seen as a violation of their dignity. But it was also the case for the defeated Germany where – perhaps paradoxically for those who today declare their unwillingness to fund it in times of recession – the commitment to the welfare state was tied to the very attempt to rebuild a strong economy. Subsequently, in what proved to be the final step of expansion of welfarism, the 1960s and early 1970s saw popular mobilisations and student/worker upheavals in Europe and America and the demand for the further expansion of social rights and protections. With the market's pretence to be free of power exposed, and with class inequalities and social hierarchies increasingly pronounced, there ensued a legitimation crisis that tried the 'staying power' of liberal capitalism which conceded what came to be known as the 'welfare state compromise'. But by the end of the 1970s, as we will see, the seeds of the 'undoing' of this compromise and the breakdown of the post-war settlement were already visible.

We will say something more about this history, but it is important first to identify the features of the new role for the state that emerged with the development away from the classic model of economic liberalism. The state becomes an interventionist one, it undertakes the macro-management of the economy and is increasingly involved in redressing social inequalities, improving the living and working conditions of workers and extending social rights. In performing the tasks of redistribution of income and resources, regulation and planning ('social engineering'), it changes from the liberal state, the impartial guarantor, to the welfare state.

The hallmark of the welfare state, then, is that it dissolves the strict separation between state and society. In liberal society there were rigid boundaries between various social spheres – the economic, the familial and more generally the private – and the state and its law. The emergent welfare state moves into these spheres in the name of governing and regulating them. In the economic sphere, it supplements the market model with that of a state-regulated capitalism, for example through state demand for unproductive commodities, monopoly regulation and regulation of various forms of economic concentration. In the sphere of labour, the state provides protections for workers in the workplace and against dismissal. In the social sphere, the state provides education (including access to tertiary education on the grounds of intellectual ability, rather than the ability to pay fees) and healthcare (based on medical need, not on the ability to pay) through forms of national insurance. The state also replaces the market on occasions when it redirects capital investment into neglected sectors, or relieves capital of the need to amend certain social costs of production (by providing unemployment compensation or assuming the costs of ecological damage).

But the interventionist role of the state is felt also in the transformations of modern law itself. Take contract law for example. The law of contract reflects this transformation from liberal to post-liberal law as it earlier reflected the shift from *Gemeinschaft* to *Gesellschaft* societies. Contract law was liberal law's paradigmatic form because it expressed the meeting of the wills of individuals, free to enter and shape the agreements. Contract law is now no longer the same. Think of the employment contract and the role of the state as a 'third' party to it: the fixing of the minimum wage, regulating for compulsory maternity and other leave, compensation thresholds and other interferences of all kinds from allocating rights of employment to regulating union membership, to policing the 'fairness' of contracts. In his analysis of contract law Thomas

Wilhelmsson (1995) offers a conception of 'social contract law' as one which takes as its central notion not the freely reached agreement to satisfy individual *desires*, but the notion of (objectively) fair bargaining which satisfies (objective) *needs*. Drawing his examples from Swedish private law, he describes a system where judges have the power to rewrite the contract for the parties and change unfair terms (rather than to declare them simply void), and where state agencies will intervene in negotiations with big companies to set standard terms which are in the public interest and which protect consumers. Unlike 'classical' liberal contract law which is content-neutral, welfarist contract law is content-oriented, with judges looking to interpret the contract in the light of legal policy and social interest. Where classical contract law is conceptualised as the expression of antagonistic tendencies in societies, the contract law of the welfare state may interpret contracts in the light of co-operation. Long-term contracts, especially employment contracts, become the role model of contract law and replace sales of goods. Another typical modern expression of this development is the idea of granting pressure groups, such as consumer organisations, legal standing to challenge companies in the name of 'the public'.

One might extend a similar analysis to property law. Classic *Gesellschaft* notions of ownership comprised the right to possess, to use, to manage and to destroy, the right to the capital, the right to the income of the thing, and an immunity from expropriation. By contrast, a welfarist understanding of property might limit these rights in the name of a common interest, for example in the environment, public access or communal water rights, in such a way that the owner is virtually unable to use the land in a manner geared purely to profit. Societies where the liberal ideas of free ownership still predominate, such as the United States, will typically use forms of restrictions very reluctantly, and in the case of expropriation, grant the full market value as compensation. Societies in which the welfarist argument is predominant will use public law regulations intensively to guarantee that the use of private property is beneficial, or at least not detrimental, to the public.

We have taken these examples from private law as key 'indices' of the paradigmatic change that the regulatory welfare state ushers in. If in the *Gesellschaft* model, as we have seen, individuals could only be held liable for actions that could be attributed to them (criminal law and tort/delict) or transactions they freely entered into (contract), this principle becomes variably displaced or 'supplemented' by another, that of strict liability. Take the example of accidents in the workplace. Factory and construction work, for example, carry risks, and the question of who pays for the cost of injuries is crucial to our industries and economies. If the principles of welfarist legal systems commit to strict liability, and therefore the duty of employers to shoulder the costs of industrial accidents even when no negligence can be proven on their part, it is because it is assumed that those costs should not be borne by those less able to afford them, the workers, and because the social costs of production need to burden also those who most benefit from its organisation.

The more general question of our analysis here can now perhaps be posed in this way: how has the different function that law assumes as an instrument of regulation affected its form, and (in effect) the rule of law? Putting it in very general terms, we could say that the welfare state changed law from formalistic to policy-oriented, and shifted its concern from one with formal justice to one with substantive justice.

We might identify the following features as characteristics (and tensions) in the regulatory-welfarist form of law:

Bureaucracy, justice and instrumentalism

Most writers identify welfare state law with the growth of large state bureaucracies, which are viewed as increasingly expensive and inefficient – more likely to preserve themselves or apply rules in formal and mechanical ways than be sensitive to the needs of individuals. There is an interesting contrast here with Weber's view, which, in describing late-nineteenth-century state bureaucracies, saw not a conflict but a fruitful convergence between bureaucratic structure, the spread of formal rationality and the rule of law. Bureaucracies provided a social and administrative guarantee of formal justice and control of the judiciary. The hierarchy of supervision and division of labour was the most efficient way to handle cases and the uniform and regular application of rules was an effect of the institutional structure. Conversely, however, this guarantee may turn into a threat to the rule of law, for the connection between efficiency and due process is not straightforward. Many contemporary analyses of legal administration have thus focused on the general trend towards mechanical regulation and bureaucratic goal displacement.

The uses of discretion

This second trend associated with the growth of the modern welfare state converges with the first in involving an alleged increase in discretionary powers and a shift away from individual rights-based law to social management. State bureaucracies have increasingly involved themselves in substantive ethical and policy issues associated with welfare interventionism. The expansion of judicial discretion is thus associated with (i) the increasing abstractness or open-endedness of statutory provisions and standards; inherently discretionary concepts such as 'the best interests of the child' replace fault-based legal actions; (ii) an increase in short-term government-of-the-day policy uses of law; and (iii) a blurring of boundaries between broad policy-administrative and narrowly legal aspects of legal administration – such as in the use of law to effect social justice (e.g., equal opportunities legislation). Judges are increasingly expected to adjudicate in fields of expertise – social and economic policy – that are outside their competence. Also, an extended use is made of tribunals and regulatory agencies such as the Equal Opportunities Commission that rely on informal procedures, as do reconciliation procedures in family law.

Weber suggested that the features of law that dominated its liberal era – formality and neutrality – would pervade future development. Neutral rules, Weber thought, were particularly conducive to the workings of bureaucracies and they would persist and expand to new ground without challenge, due to their apparent indispensability to the logic of bureaucratic organisation. While regulatory law has shifted significantly from legislatures to administration, its form remains what Weber predicted it to remain, formal rational. But that, of course, is only part of the story. Let us say that between bureaucratisation and welfarism in law there is both a tension and a convergence. Tension because bureaucratic law is rational law, its form is that of general abstract rules, while welfarist regulation is substantive, particular and casuistic. Convergence because often welfarist concerns key in with bureaucratic ones, for example the welfarist shift away from fault (as socially inappropriate) meets with the efficiency demand of bureaucracy, the speedy processing of cases thus far inhibited by the requirement to explore the *application of complex tort law standards.*

Particularised legislation

The materialisation of law marks the tendency towards particularised legislation: the movement towards breaking up the general categories into sub-categories towards which law applies differentially. The grand category of the legal person gives way to a specification of categories, and the formal equivalence of the legal subject gives way to a proliferation of different legal statuses: consumer (consumer law), worker/trade union member, employee, welfare recipient, business franchisee. In each case the law addresses the legal subject under that more specific description and there is a move from the formal to the material in this. But further: natural and artificial persons, grouped together under liberal law, become differentiated for specific legal purposes, so that, for example, the privacy of the natural person is protected where that of the company is not (access to data, freedom of information).

Erosion of the separation of powers and formal equality

The separation of powers, that other lynchpin of liberal law, is eroded, for example, once courts are called upon to determine whether a government has acted in the public interest. Equally this happens when the legislature delegates responsibility for fixing the terms of what appear as general directives, as the executive state machinery has the resources to do the job better. And it is also true with respect to the increase in specialist tribunals, which signals a move away from general legal categories applied by courts to more informal dispute resolution mechanisms. Finally, formal equality can be undermined once 'reverse discrimination' or 'affirmative action', that is a reverse preference to a disadvantaged group, becomes institutionalised in law in order to redress existing inequalities.

Beyond the welfare state

Transformations in law are unlikely to be total revisions. In the transformation from *Gemeinschaft* to *Gesellschaft* law, elements of the former survived in the latter. The transformation of *Gesellschaft* law to the regulatory-welfarist type meets with a similar inertia. The core of liberal law cannot be easily side-stepped in the name of expediency, of getting things done. Liberal values still inform the way we speak about law and the legitimacy we see in it. On the other hand we expect a responsiveness from law. That is, we expect law to meet social needs and aspirations. And in this, legal action comes to serve as a vehicle by which groups and organisations may participate in the determination of public policy.

This important tension, while still with us in some respect, has also receded to a significant degree. The welfare state and its ideological foundation in social democracy has been on the retreat, at different rates and to different degrees certainly, but retreat nonetheless. And with it, the law of the welfare state entered its own period of crisis. With the rise of the New Right in Europe and the US in the late 1970s and 1980s, the adoption of deregulatory strategies and monetary policies by the Thatcher and Reagan governments initially, and with the gradual prevalence of the Washington consensus globally, there began the 'undoing' of this compromise and the breakdown of the post-war settlement. As Maurice Glasman put it:

> The New Right combined an economic theory which limited welfare, marginalized unions and forbade direct productive interference by the state in the economy with a moral theory that identified the state with oppression and the market with free-dom in the sphere of material distribution.
>
> (1996, p xiii)

Politically speaking, the welfare state compromise appeared to have let both sides down. The Left were (too) quick to protest about the dependency that it created, a tendency encouraged by the practices of the administration of social security law that generate a sense of dependency on the claimant rather than that of entitlement of a social-welfare rights holder. Or more polemically, as Habermas denounced it in his more radical days, the welfarist state had become a 'technocratic administered capitalism' (Habermas 1976). The Right on the other hand discovered that redistribution worked against incen-tives, that unemployment benefits undercut management power by offering the workers 'exit' opportunities from employment, that regulation placed burdens on competitive-ness, and that economic growth could only be achieved through priorities that ran counter to welfarism. In effect business became increasingly unwilling to fund the wel-fare state, an unwillingness that we continue to observe today.

These developments combined with (and combined to precipitate) an extraordi-nary degree of withdrawal (or rolling back) of the state and a newfound freedom for capitalist activity on the global level. On this account, 'globalisation' is a term often used to describe the process of capitalist integration beyond the level of the state, facilitated by new international and regional organisations, international investment treaties and other international instruments. These shifts require that we also adjust our conceptual tools and legal theories to address and understand these changes. The phenomenon of globalisation indeed challenges many of the core assumptions that underpin the account of legal modernity. Thus, for example, where Weber saw legal modernity in the consolidation and singularity of state law, globalisation sees the fragmentation of sovereignty; and where our understanding of legal modernity is based on the generality and universality of state law, globalisation sees the pluralisation and diversity of legal orders. We will take up the question of the extent to which globalisation requires us to revise or replace our understanding of legal modernity more fully in the next chapter. But suffice to note for now that insofar as processes of globalisation operate to put severe pressure on the ideas associated with the public pooling of resources through taxation for the benefit of all citizens based on need and merit; insofar as regional and interna-tional free trade arrangements open up domestic markets in health, education, and even security and policing to market mechanisms; to the extent that the principles of profit and investment opportunity triumph over the principle of solidarity; and to the extent that each of these is put in place through the revalorisation of private law mechanisms at domestic and global levels, then it is clear that in many respects we are witnessing a readjustment of the relationship between capitalism and democracy that sees us moving 'beyond the welfare state' to what Streeck (2014) has called the 'debt state'. As he puts it:

> The democratic state, ruled and (qua *tax state*) resourced by its citizens, becomes a democratic *debt state* as soon as its subsistence depends not only on the financial contributions of its citizens but, to a significant degree, on the confidence of creditors. In contrast to the *Staatsvolk* of the tax state, the *Marktvolk* of the debt state is transnationally integrated. They are bound to national states purely by contractual ties, as investors rather than citizens. Their rights vis-à-vis the state are of a private rather than a public character, deriving not from a constitution but from civil [private] law.
>
> (Streeck 2014, pp 80–81)

Reading

On the shift from the liberal to the regulatory paradigm, see Santos (2002), pp 39–60. In the sphere of contract law, see Atiyah (1979) and, for a normative analysis of the two paradigms, contrast Wilhelmsson (1995) and Collins (1982) on the one hand with Fried (1981) on the other. In Fried's *Contract as Promise* (1981) contract law and the promise principle are contrasted to the socially imposed obligations of compensation, restitution and sharing. Within a school of thought deeply rooted in the liberal paradigm, Fried argues that the idea of obligations created by promises is the fundamental and operative principle of contract. See also generally the symposium on contract law and legal theory in *Social and Legal Studies* (2000).

On the question of crisis that underlies the transformations, see Habermas (1976), Santos (2002) and Glasman (1996). Nelken (1982) looks at the question of 'crisis' in the law. There is also a good discussion of the transformation of formal law in Unger (1976, chs 2 and 3), Cotterrell (1992, ch 5) and Kamenka and Tay (1975). For a discussion of diverse impacts of welfarism on law see the essays by Criller and Morris and McClintock in Adler and Asquith (1981).

For a helpful overview of the welfare state, its history and contemporary transformations, see Garland (2016). Streeck (2014) offers a highly insightful account of the move from the 'tax state' to the 'debt state' and beyond, with particular emphasis on transformations within the European Union. For an innovative account of indebtedness from a Foucauldian perspective, see Lazzarato (2015).

For an introduction to debates on globalisation, see Held and McGrew (2003) and Scholte (2008). For an introduction to globalisation and law see Twining (2000, especially chapters 1, 4 and 7, and (2009), especially chapters 1, 2 and 9.

Chapter 9

Law and globalisation

The literature on globalisation is vast, covering a wide range of subjects often unfamiliar to the legal curriculum. The question of where to start elaborating the relevance of globalisation studies for legal theory can appear quite daunting. It is therefore important to be clear what our purpose is in referring to debates about globalisation. Here, we focus on the key issue of whether the pressures on the nation-state discussed under the rubric of globalisation represent the demise of the paradigm of modernity as we have analysed it thus far. This has important implications for legal theory more generally, given the close relationship outlined above between modernity and contemporary understandings of law. In particular, if modernity is in crisis, this may require us to revisit some core assumptions of current legal thought. We set the context for this discussion by outlining the main contours of the debates on globalisation, before considering in more detail why this has led to claims of epochal change. We then contrast the response that these challenges can be accommodated by adapting existing legal concepts with the argument that we need to transform the basis of existing legal knowledge and conclude by considering some examples of what law, after modernity, might look like.

Debates about globalisation often divide between those who argue that the nation-state is no longer the main organising principle of society, and sceptics, for whom globalisation means very little. One key issue is whether the link between national territory and politics is being undermined, with the state being supplanted at the supra-, sub- and non-state levels as the primary locus of political authority. Claims that technological innovations that compress business time and space have led to the organisation of economic activity on a global scale are met with the response that the global economy is a myth designed to suggest there is no alternative to prevailing neoliberal policies. Some argue that a global culture is being created, evocatively referred to as 'McWorld', while others highlight the still powerful connection between national identity and cultural institutions. These two perspectives on political, economic and cultural globalisation provide helpful tools for engaging with the debates, but they are only a starting point. Moreover, they are far from distinct positions, being connected with varying degrees of complexity. For example, does the development of institutions for regulating the global economy limit the scope for national policy innovation? Are cultural changes driving other forms of globalisation or are they secondary phenomena?

The question that runs through these debates is whether globalisation represents a period of paradigmatic transition. In other words, do the changes discussed above signal the intensification (but continuation) of existing processes, or do they represent a more fundamental rupture with the past? Are forms of knowledge that take the nation-state as the privileged unit of analysis still adequate for understanding ongoing changes? This also engages with claims of modernity's political failure: some see the crises attending globalisation as evidence of the nation-state's inability to deliver its promise of greater emancipation, while others emphasise the resilience of existing institutions. These debates are necessarily linked and give us a flavour of the politics of globalisation. A paradigmatic reading, which advocates a new framework of enquiry, is generally linked to a transformative political strategy that imagines forms of social organisation beyond neoliberalism. A sub-paradigmatic reading tends to assume capitalism's continuation, but seeks to adapt the resources of modernity to manage its excesses.

We can identify three important ways in which globalisation undermines some deep-rooted assumptions of modern legal thought. First, it makes it increasingly difficult for legal study to be contained within the territorial boundaries of national legal systems. To understand the operation of formal state law, we have to take into account the proliferation of supranational sources of law, such as those emanating from the European Union or the World Trade Organization. The obverse of this is that at the international level, sovereignty is undermined by greater acceptance of interference in the internal affairs of states, for example, through the doctrine of humanitarian intervention. Second, while traditional jurisprudence focused exclusively on municipal and public international law, globalisation requires notice of other forms of legal ordering, such as the *sui generis* legal order of the EU. But not all have a formal pedigree. One prominent example is transnational *lex mercatoria*, which regulates interactions between global commercial firms outside official law through practices such as international arbitration. Other types not readily slotted into standard categorisations include Islamic law, which operates across national boundaries, sometimes in opposition to state law. A third challenge addresses how globalisation may be undermining the cultural specificity of law, and asks whether in response, we can construct a theory of law that reaches across legal cultures. In other words, can we develop a conceptual language that can make sense of the relations between, for example, national and supranational, formal and informal, sub-state and non-state contexts?

Globalisation and the reconfigured state

In the modern era, the state has been central to debates in law and politics. The main prize for political parties was to gain control of national legislative and executive institutions, with the power to make national laws and policies seen as the means of implementing their policy agenda. This framework remains influential: much political activity is still directed towards national parliaments and governments, and the study of law largely consists of learning rules of the national legal system where the student resides. However, this traditional focus on the state is coming under pressure from claims that we live in a time of globalisation. In this sense, globalisation stands for the idea that national borders are becoming less important to the conduct of social life. For example, arguments about the emergence of global patterns of economic organisation, or global forms of culture, are advanced to show that we are living in a significantly more inter-connected world, often in relation to the spread of liberal capitalism and Western-style consumerism.

We can identify three ways in which the idea that the nation-state is the sole, or principal, location of political authority is coming under pressure in the global era. First, as noted above, there is relocation of power from the national level to supra-national entities such as the European Union (EU), the World Trade Organization (WTO), the International Monetary Fund (IMF), the World Bank and so on. While the original impetus for these was often framed in relatively narrow terms, such as setting common customs duties, the deliberations of these bodies now affect a wide range of domestic public policy matters, such as agriculture, health, trade, intellectual property rights and social policy. Other developments that should be included here are the rise of regional and international mechanisms supervising the protection of human rights, such as the European Court of Human Rights and, in a different way, the International Criminal Court. The legal instruments issuing from these bodies often have a higher formal status than national laws, and disobedient states can face the threat of sanctions.

Political authority can also be seen to be escaping downwards as well as upwards. Claims for greater devolution of power within existing states are themselves some-thing of a global phenomenon, whether in the UK (in the case of Scotland, Northern Ireland or Wales), Spain (with respect to Catalonia and the Basque Country), Canada, Italy or the former Soviet states. These present a further challenge to the nation-state by redistributing political authority to the subnational level, often constitutionally guaranteed against encroachment from the centre. In contrast to this emphasis on new institutions above or below the state, a third challenge highlights the dispersal of power beyond the state. This argues that political authority is now exercised in multiple settings, for example new forms of decision-making within supranational organisations, networks of international agencies or in the actions of multinational corporations.

As a result, the state is being significantly reconfigured. Some of its former core functions are being performed elsewhere, whether by global regulatory bodies or priva-tised utilities. Those functions it retains are often subject to new restraints, for example that they follow market-based ideas such as efficiency and effectiveness. Some argue that it is important to place these developments in geopolitical context, and that the worldwide trend to adopt neoliberal economic policies, that is reduced taxation, fiscal restraint, deregulation, privatisation, free trade and unrestricted currency flows, nec-essarily leads to a weakened state. The other processes listed above can also be seen to accentuate state weakness: supranational economic and human rights regimes can limit the scope for national policy innovation, while subnational entities have even less power to resist the prevailing global consensus.

Some capture the complexity of contemporary patterns of political authority with the idea of multilayered governance. Where once political activists may have sought to lobby MPs or government ministers, there are now a host of potential actors who may require their attention, whether members of devolved or regional assemblies, Members of the European Parliament (MEPs), non-governmental organisations (NGOs), international agencies, social movements or boards of directors. In some cases, it may be unclear as to who are the responsible actors. The result is to remove the state from any preordained position at the centre of the legal and political universe. As Martin Loughlin has put it, '[t]he success of the modern state over the last two hundred years has been based mainly on its ability to promote economic well-being, to maintain physical security and to foster a distinctive cultural identity of its citizens' (Loughlin 2000, p 145). This account is now being called into question by globalisation.

Sovereignty after globalisation

In an earlier chapter, we characterised sovereignty as a contested concept. If anything, debates over sovereignty have intensified in the context of globalisation. The departure point for these debates is the demise of the nation-state, understood in terms of a homogeneous people exercising self-governance through a single set of public institutions. In this traditional model, sovereignty was seen as an expression of a state's political autonomy. This political autonomy had an internal and external dimension: internal authority over a particular community, and external independence vis-à-vis other states. We can identify two strands of debate that call this account increasingly into question. One addresses principally the first two developments listed above, that is the rise of new sub- and supranational institutions, while the other considers the consequences of globalisation writ large, that is, the rise of the global economy. Each approach brings a quite different perspective to the questions of what sovereignty is, where it resides and how far it has to be reconceptualised as a result of globalisation.

If we take first the new institutional structures that operate across and within borders, some theorists, such as Neil MacCormick, suggest that in an era of multilayered governance, sovereignty may have outlived its usefulness as a concept. Focusing on the development of the EU, MacCormick argues its Member States do not possess unfettered constitutional power to make laws as this can be overridden by EU law. Furthermore, as a result, these states no longer enjoy unrestrained political power in their external relations. However, this does not mean sovereignty has been transferred to the EU, as it does not possess political or legal independence apart from its members. Accordingly, notions of ultimate authority fail to capture the nature of contemporary legal and political relations. Thus as we have seen, MacCormick believes the supposedly sovereign state may well be a transient historical phenomenon, and that we are now in an age of 'post-sovereignty'. This is posited as a preferable framework for the study of law and politics: once we reject the idea of absolute sovereignty, this better tailors discussion about democracy to the reality of a plural legal and political order, for example by acknowledging that sometimes citizens' needs are best met at a smaller level of government, other times at a larger.

Other commentators argue that rather than seeing the appropriate response to globalisation as dispensing with the concept of sovereignty, it is better to consider how it is being transformed (see Walker 2015). They note that despite calls to abandon the language of sovereignty, it persists in political debate, for example, to resist further European integration. Neil Walker describes the present as a period of 'late sovereignty', to signify that we have not achieved a complete conceptual break with the past. For Walker, the key to overcoming the limits of the Westphalian approach is to shift from describing sovereignty as some objective measurement of power to regarding it as a 'claim concerning the existence and character of a supreme ordering power for a particular polity' (Walker 2003b, p 6), whose practical importance depends on its plausibility to key actors in the political system.

The context for Walker's analysis is the growth of non-state entities, such as the EU, as rivals to states in claiming sovereignty. However, what is distinctive about this phase of sovereignty is that these claims are no longer being viewed in absolute terms. This arises because supranational bodies tend not to exercise authority over all matters within a particular territory, but only in respect of certain functions. For example, while the EU claims to be the highest legal authority over matters such as agriculture or fisheries, competences remain with Member States. Accordingly, we can no longer link claims of ultimate authority to territorial exclusivity. Walker argues that this picture of multiple and overlapping – including state and supra-state – claims to authority gives us a better explanation of the emerging global legal configuration. For him, this also has a prescriptive dimension and provides the guiding ethic that law and politics should be based upon the mutual recognition of different authority claims.

Other theorists regard talk of 'post' or 'late' sovereignty as premature. Loughlin finds the original conceptual underpinnings of sovereignty highly relevant today (see Loughlin 2003a). For him, sovereignty expresses a political relationship between rulers and ruled. This relationship combines two facets of sovereignty in the modern state: competence, which refers to its formal legal authority, and capacity, which denotes where political power actually resides. Once this is grasped, he suggests that developments such as the establishment of the EU should not be seen as eroding sovereignty. While Member States may agree to share jurisdictional competence with the EU, this does not amount to a sharing of sovereignty (which in Loughlin's view is conceptually impossible). This is because questions of sovereignty are not determined by new institutional arrangements, but are essentially matters of political capacity. He suggests that the test of continuing sovereignty is whether Member States can withdraw from the EU. Loughlin argues that in the exceptional state of crisis that this scenario envisages, there is little doubt that states retain the right to leave, and for him this shows that they still possess ultimate power and authority. Despite the political and juridical confusion it has engendered, the notification by the United Kingdom to leave the European Union in 2019 appears to give some credence to this analysis. That said, it is equally clear that the relationship between political and legal *competence* in the UK, post-Brexit, and the matter of *capacity*, particularly in economic terms, remains a highly uncertain one.

The debates so far canvassed have focused on public institutional developments, but what of the growth of private political authority beyond the state? An alternative approach is advanced by Saskia Sassen (1996 and 2007) who sees the relevant challenges to sovereignty as grounded in changes in global political economy. In this connection, she posits a 'new geography of power' whose key sites include supranational organisations, but also global capital markets, transnational legal firms, international commercial arbitration, international human rights codes and electronic economic activity. These combine to reconfigure the interface between territory and sovereignty. For example, for some, New York City is a municipality that runs local services such as rubbish collection, while for others it is a centre for international bond agencies, whose credit ratings can veto national economic policies. In this way, the new geography leads to a partial displacement of economic activity from national territory.

Loughlin acknowledges that these developments may present a stronger challenge to sovereignty as capacity because the power ceded to global markets is not readily recoverable by issuing edicts through formal legal authority (Loughlin 2003a). But this raises important questions about the relationship between law and politics: if, as Loughlin suggests, sovereignty ultimately depends on political capacity, is there a point at which the exercise of power by private actors translates into legal competence? Sassen answers this in the affirmative, and highlights new legal regimes that operate outside the public institutional setting, but are located in the activities of multinational corporations. These regimes are important in explaining the rules and procedures that apply, for example, to regulating the internet or intellectual property, or aspects of international trade such as insurance and the maritime industry.

Within the supranational debate, there is a strong tendency to attribute sovereignty to expressions of public power and remove consideration of the private or economic sphere from the discussion. But in the changing landscape of governance painted by globalisation, distinctions such as that between public and private may now appear outmoded and unhelpful. This casts some of the debates outlined above in a different light. If, as Loughlin tells us, sovereignty is an expression of a political relationship, some of the most important relationships in the global age may be those between individuals and the corporations whose decisions affect the quality of their lives in significant ways, or those that arise from the complex interaction between state, supra-state and non-state forms of normative ordering on which the residual effectiveness of state law may now depend. Or if, as Walker tells us, sovereignty is now better understood as a claim, should sovereignty be restricted to those making self-conscious claims, or should we expand it to cover those private actors who remain silent, perhaps because they do not wish to attract unwanted scrutiny to the political authority they exercise? Accordingly, adverting to broader processes of globalisation potentially represents a more radical conceptual rupture with the traditional understandings of sovereignty.

Constitutionalism beyond the state

The diffusion of political authority as a result of globalisation raises important questions about how power is held to account. Traditionally, constitutions have provided the institutional and normative framework for discussing questions of law and politics, and in particular the question of the legitimate exercise of power. In modern times, a constitutionally legitimate regime has come to be understood as one that embodies the values of democracy. As with sovereignty, our conceptual apparatus of constitutionalism initially developed with reference to the nation-state. Thus in its ideal condition, constitutionalism was the means by which a sovereign people within national borders could exercise control over those who governed them, by subjecting politics to the rule of law. But in an age of globalisation, state-centred approaches to constitutionalism may address only part of a broader constellation of political authority. For example, while constitutions safeguard free and fair elections to national parliaments, they generally provide for negligible or no popular participation in decisions of supranational bureaucracies or multinational corporations despite the impact that the decisions of these bodies have on people's lives. Accordingly, globalisation can be seen to provoke a legitimation crisis, as national constitutions can no longer guarantee citizens effective democratic control over their rulers.

There has been considerable interest recently in ideas of constitutionalism beyond the state (Walker 2008). Walker (2003a) argues that constitutionalism – which he sees as the vocabulary for the mutual articulation of law and politics – is intrinsic to the polity understood as the setting for the conduct of politics. In the period of late sovereignty, the polity is not confined to the state, and so we should now associate constitutions with bodies such as the EU or WTO. Walker suggests that we need to understand how some of the traditional functions of national constitutions, such as delineating a formal hierarchy of laws or specifying the rights of citizenship, are now carried out at the supranational level. The extent to which any supranational entity can be characterised in constitutional terms, though, is a matter of degree. In this regard, Walker finds that the EU (where the supremacy of EU law is accepted by Member States) is further down the path of constitutionalisation than the WTO (which has no equivalent doctrine).

Supranational constitutionalism does not simply reproduce national constitutional forms on a broader scale. It is in many respects qualitatively different as these new polities, unlike states, are limited in their jurisdictional scope and do not aspire to provide a comprehensive legal order within hermetically sealed borders. Accordingly, the task of translating state-based constitutional concepts to the supranational level is not straightforward, as the above discussion of the various attempts to adapt sovereignty to the global age demonstrates. However, for Walker the key to accomplishing this is to understand that state constitutional orders have not disappeared, but necessarily exist in relation to non-state sites of constitutionalism, whose purpose is often to influence or direct national legal systems. Accordingly, he suggests we now live in an era of 'constitutional pluralism' (Walker 2002).

For Walker, recovering the language of constitutionalism at the supranational level is important because the often contentious issues which animated traditional constitutionalism, such as the nature of representation and how institutional power should be structured and regulated, remain relevant and important, but have been relocated in the contemporary age. A powerful objection to this project is that it may confer an undeserved legitimacy upon supranational bodies. Given the strong positive connotations of constitutionalism with democracy, to speak, for example, of the WTO as a constitutional entity may suggest a capacity to exert democratic oversight over world trade, which may be absent. Walker's response is that the values and practices of constitutionalism (suitably adapted) are the best available means for engaging in debates over the legitimate exercise of power, and that rather than providing inappropriate closure, they keep dialogue open over how the democratic credentials of the emergent sites of supranational constitutionalism can be improved.

An alternative approach to constitutionalism beyond the state comes under the rubric of 'the new constitutionalism'. According to Stephen Gill, the new constitutionalism is a '"global economic governance project" designed to "lock-in" the power gains of capital on a world scale' (Gill 2000, p 6, 11). The context for this project is the rise of neoliberal economic policies (such as privatisation and low taxation) since the 1980s, which, Gill argues, seek to discipline national governments so that they do not interfere with the free market. New constitutionalism supports this by placing barriers in the way of more redistributive forms of constitutionalism (which might, for example, promote social democratic goals of lowering material inequality) through legal and political measures that are difficult to reverse. Supranational legal forms are also highlighted here, whether it is the WTO imposing sanctions on states that deviate from the global economic consensus, or bilateral treaties that may require domestic constitutional reform in order to be eligible for inward investment. Less formal mechanisms are also important, for example the pressures exerted by corporations on states to lower taxation or reduce domestic regulatory standards if they wish to attract their factories and jobs (resulting in what critics describe as a 'race to the bottom').

The question at the heart of the new constitutionalism is whether economic processes should be regarded as relevant for constitutional analysis. How we answer this has an important implication for how we link constitutionalism and democracy in the global age. In traditional terms, economic actors, like individual persons, were seen as subject to the constitutional jurisdiction of the state. Thus any problems posed to democracy by the growth of private power in the global economy can be addressed by making appropriate adjustments to existing constitutional mechanisms. In this connection, it is argued that developing constitutionalism on a supranational scale may provide the better opportunity for establishing democratic oversight over the forces of the global economy.

But from another point of view, this separation between the economic and the political can no longer be sustained in an era where corporations can be richer and more powerful than many states. For example, comparing annual sales to national gross domestic product (GDP), General Motors has a higher annual turnover than Denmark, and Sony is bigger than Pakistan. If corporations should now be seen as important political actors whose actions and decisions have a direct impact on the lives of millions, this implies that political power (or the polity) not be limited to the public institutional setting of states and supranational organisations. It follows that, according to the new constitutionalism, questions about the location of sovereignty and the exercise and accountability of power now have to consider the relation not just between state and supranational, but also non-state sites of constitutionalism. Moreover, the latter may in practice be the most important, so focusing our attention on the first two sites alone may be of limited utility if our objective is to establish some degree of constitutional regulation over the market. This suggests that it may be necessary to craft innovative solutions, which do not adapt, but replace, current constitutional practices. For some, the only means for effective governance over the global economy is to establish a truly global polity – for example, with global (not international) representative institutions – while for others, the answer lies in bottom-up, not top-down, approaches such as the development of new forms of law and politics in global social movements. What seems clear is that in a time of globalisation many long-standing assumptions about law and politics may have to be revisited and rethought.

'Unthinking' modern law

We turn finally to an important and influential analysis of these issues to be found in the work of the Portuguese theorist Boaventura de Sousa Santos. Santos contends that the problems engendered by modernity cannot be solved within the latter's intellectual and political resources. His primary motivation is to develop an emancipatory

conception of law in response to the political crisis of modernity, ushered in by globalisation. While overtly socio-political, Santos's response to globalisation also addresses
our categories of legal knowledge. For him, the two are deeply connected, as it is only
by 'unthinking' the current basis of legal knowledge that law's emancipatory potential
can be realised.

Santos's theory of law and globalisation is situated within his broader account of
the demise of modernity. As we saw in chapter 1, modernity, for Santos, established a
dynamic tension between regulation (or order) and emancipation (or good order). Its
success was predicated on the promise that a sufficient weight of expectations (of emancipation) could be translated into experiences (emancipatory struggles translated into
new forms of regulation), so that incompatible values, such as equality and freedom,
could be held in balance. This was to be delivered through the nation-state, applying
scientific knowledge through legal instruments. However, he argues that what marks
our time is the wholesale collapse of emancipation into regulation, as, for example, the
welfare state comes under pressure from the global economy in neoliberal mode.

Santos defines globalisation as 'the process by which a given local condition or
entity succeeds in extending its reach over the globe and, by doing so, develops the
capacity to designate a rival social condition or entity as local' (2002, p 178). He distinguishes first between two hegemonic forms of globalisation: 'globalized localism',
which is 'the process by which a given local phenomenon is successfully globalized' – for
example, the spread of US popular culture – and 'localized globalism', which connotes
'the specific impact of transnational practices and imperatives on local conditions that
are thereby de-structured and restructured in order to respond to transnational imperatives' (2002, p 179) – such as the emergence of free trade areas. The core industrialised
countries specialise in exporting to the former, whereas developing peripheral countries
are the prime importers of localised globalisms. Each operates in subparadigmatic mode
as they assume the continued existence of global capitalism. Alongside these, he out-
lines two forms of counter-hegemonic globalisation: subaltern cosmopolitanism, referring to transnational resistance to hegemonic globalisation, for example, the new forms
of political activism under the umbrella of the World Social Forum; and the common
heritage of humankind, which motivates political struggle around issues such as the
depletion of the ozone layer and the proliferation of nuclear weapons. These represent
paradigmatic approaches to globalisation, as they are addressed to audiences that seek
to imagine different forms of social organisation beyond capitalism. Santos is critical of
those approaches to law and globalisation that concentrate solely on hegemonic processes, as this neglects the significance of new forms of law, which are emerging from
daily struggles in diverse settings.

Santos sees the 'globalisation of the legal field' as a constitutive element in these
processes. An important example is the spread of liberal democratic constitutional
reforms to newly established democracies in Central and Eastern Europe and Latin America. While often sponsored by international agencies as the epitome of good governance,
Santos sees these reforms as globalised localisms, elevating Western-style democracy as
the single global model. However, these processes are not just hegemonic in substance,
reinforcing North–South power asymmetries, but also in form through their partial
understanding of legal phenomena. Accompanying these reforms is a series of measures
designed to shore up the rule of law, for example, by providing for the protection of
property rights. Not only is law understood here solely in terms of formal state law, but

also this conception is seen as vital to providing the infrastructure for global capitalist activity.

This brings us to the key point of Santos's critique, namely that the reduction of law to state law is a deeply contingent political product of modernity and which helps explain the latter's emancipatory limits. For Santos, this reduction rests on an artificial distinction between the state and civil society, which obscures the existence of political authority beyond official processes, for example, in the workplace. Moreover, the identification of law solely with the state played a key role in sustaining capitalism. First, autonomous and scientific state law was held up as the instrument for securing societal progress by managing capitalism's worst excesses. But this was also a strategy of depoliticisation, which legitimated the confinement of democratic politics to the state, while excluding them from other sites of social power. So although modernity has, for example, promoted formal democracy in the state, by legislating for equal voting rights among citizens, it has left in place unequal power relations in the workplace.

Santos argues that globalisation makes this limited conception of law implausible when it attempts to describe law as it is and is unacceptable as a vision of what law should be. For him, one feature of the paradigmatic transition is the increasing visibility of forms of law beyond the state. This requires us to widen our knowledge to include, inter alia, the laws generated by transnational corporations, resurgent forms of indigenous law such as the assertion of historic rights by aboriginal peoples, and the broad international human rights regime, which covers the activities of both international agencies and NGOs. The objective is not simply to catalogue different types of law, but also to account for the uneven ways in which they interact with and influence each other – what Santos calls interlegality. In this picture, state law is one of a number of legal orders and not necessarily the most influential – often, for example, operating in the shadow of the (legal) norms of the neoliberal global economy.

Santos thus links this reconceptualisation of law to the political dimension of globalisation. For Santos, the recoupling of law with social power lies at the heart of the counter-hegemonic agenda. This is not just aspirational rhetoric, as his later work discusses the various struggles, whether campaigns against water privatisation in Latin America or the fight for affordable antiretroviral drugs in Africa, which he sees as providing the basis for new international legal regimes. Thus Santos emphasises the need to consider both hegemonic globalisation from above, but also counter-hegemonic globalisation from below. This necessarily changes how we think about state law, as now only one route among many open to legal activists; but to the extent it can be successfully deployed in a broader campaign of resistance, it may retain an emancipatory character. For example, he discusses the transnational coalition for the elimination of sweatshops as an attempt to politicise the law of the workplace in a counter-hegemonic way.

Santos's work provides an ambitious framework for making sense of law and globalisation as part of a broader account of paradigmatic change. His project aims at returning law to its emancipatory potential. This requires us to shift our focus away from traditional state legal forms to the practices of oppressed groups. These new forms of law, found in the interstices of the state and in non-Western settings, may appear alien subjects for legal study to students educated in the Western tradition. But that is precisely his point: that the paradigmatic transition highlights the ways in which old certainties are being undermined, and which require us to 'unthink' many core assumptions of the modernist conception of law.

Reading

For an introduction to the idea of multilayered government, see Ilgen (2003). Loughlin's distinction between right and capacity, or the normative and empirical conceptions of sovereignty, is discussed in Loughlin (2000, ch 10). MacCormick's theory of 'post-sovereignty' is concisely set out in MacCormick (1999, ch 8). For Walker's account of 'late sovereignty', see Walker (2003a) and also the responses by Loughlin (2003a and MacCormick (2004). For an application of the ideas of 'constitutional pluralism' and an elaboration of the constitutional attributes of the EU and the WTO, see Walker (2001), and with respect to global law, Walker (2015). For an application of ideas of the 'new constitutionalism' (Gill 2000) in the context of contemporary investment regimes, see Schneiderman (2008, ch 6) and also Schneiderman (2013).

For an account of paradigmatic and subparadigmatic readings of globalisation, see Santos (2002, pp 172–177). Other aspects of Santos's analysis covered here can be found in more detail in Santos (2002, pp 1–11, 89–98, 177–193 and 465–470). For an account of alternative ways of conceptualising globalisation, drawing on work in the global South, see Santos and Rodríguez-Garavito (2005, ch 1). For a discussion of Santos's theory by Twining, see (2000, ch 8).

General part   **I**

Tutorials

 **TUTORIAL 1**   Sovereignty

Come to class prepared to answer the following questions relating to the history, meaning and contemporary trajectory of the principle of sovereignty.

Reading

- *Jurisprudence*, pp 17-19, Chapter 4.
  Martin Loughlin, *The Idea of Public Law*, Oxford University Press, 2003, pp 72–98.

Questions:

1 What are the origins of modern sovereignty? What are the main differences between pre-modern and modern legal order?

2 Is sovereignty necessarily absolute? Or is it possible to constrain sovereignty?

3 Can a non-state legal order (e.g., the EU) be sovereign?

4 How do you understand the meaning of sovereignty in the age of globalisation?

❖ TUTORIAL 2   Social contract

Reading

- *Jurisprudence*, chapter 2 ('Social Contract Theory')

- Martin Loughlin, *Sword and Scales: An Examination of the Relationship Between Law and Politics*, pp 26–29, 161–175

This tutorial invites us to think about the problems of political power, government and law that inevitably arise whenever there is a state – who should be the rulers, how should they rule, what is the relationship between rulers and the ruled, how society should be organised, and the ultimate question of what is the purpose of having a state.

We look at the answers to these questions given by Hobbes and Locke. The reading from Loughlin analyses these writers and the insights and values they offer in thinking about the relationship between law, rights and political power. It also introduces some criticisms that have been made of their work.

Our overall objective in this tutorial is to strengthen our analysis of some of the central concepts used in contemporary law and politics.

Questions

1   Compare the views of Hobbes and Locke with respect to

   a   How their different views of the state of nature impact on what they believe the state is for.

   b   How they see the purpose of the social contract.

   c   Whether the state is limited in terms of what it can or should do.

   d   What the role of positive law should be and how it relates to individual freedom.

2   To what extent is the idea of the social contract still a useful or persuasive one for understanding the relations between state and citizen, and between law and political power?

Law and general will: Rousseau's social contract

Reading

- *Jurisprudence*, chapter 2 ('Social Contract Theory')

- Jean-Jacques Rousseau, *The Social Contract*, Book I, chapters V–VIII; Book II, chapter VI (any available edition)

In *The Social Contract*, Rousseau develops a theory of political association that would allow individuals to obey only themselves and therefore to remain free. His solution was to imagine a social contract that could be reduced to the following terms: 'Each of us puts his person and all his power in common under the supreme direction of the general will; and we as a body receive each member as an indivisible part of the whole'. This pact not only signals the move from the state of nature to the civil state, but it also brings about a profound change in man: from natural freedom to civil freedom ('which is limited by the general will'). The creation of law is quintessential for realising the change:

> to the acquisition of moral status could be added . . . the acquisition of moral liberty, this being the only thing that makes man truly the master of himself; for to be driven by our appetites alone is slavery, while to obey a law that we have imposed on ourselves is freedom.

Rousseau's theory provides the ground for understanding the legal order in terms of self-government. The tutorial invites reflection on the importance of Rousseau's contribution and the theoretical difficulties that affect a conception of law deeply intertwined with the ideal of positive freedom.

Questions

1 What motivates humans to move from the state of nature to the civil state?

2 What is the difference between the *will of all* and the *general will*?

3 Why is law essential for civil freedom? Contrast Rousseau's answer to Hobbes's and Locke's.

4 Is disobedience of the law ever legitimate according to Rousseau?

5 What is the proper form of the law when adopted according to the general will?

Reading
- *Jurisprudence*, chapter 2 ('Locke' and 'Rousseau')
- John Locke, Two Treatises of Government, *Second Treatise on Civil Government*, chapter V

The aim of this tutorial is to assess the potential tensions between the doctrine of labour-based property and Locke's idea that individuals own their own person. The case of *Moore v the Regents of the University of California* (decided by the Supreme Court of California in 1990) presents an interesting illustration of the tension.

John Moore was diagnosed with 'hairy cell leukemia' after a medical examination at the UCLA Medical Center on October 5, 1976. The researcher, David Golde, took samples of Moore's blood, bone marrow and other bodily fluids to confirm the diagnosis and recommended a splenectomy. Moore signed a standard written consent form, authorising the procedure. The form authorised the hospital to 'dispose of any severed tissue or member by cremation'. Moore's spleen was removed by surgeons at UCLA Medical Center.

Moore's blood profile returned to normal after only a few days, and further examination of his spleen led Golde to discover that Moore's blood cells were unique in that they produced a protein that stimulated the growth of white blood cells, which help to protect the body from infections.

Over the next seven years, Moore continued to visit the UCLA Medical Center. In September 1983, during one of these follow-up visits, Moore was asked to sign a form consenting to the use of his blood for research purposes. The consent form included a portion where the individual was to circle either 'I do' or 'I do not' 'voluntarily grant to the University of California any and all rights I, or my heirs, may have in any cell line or any other potential product which might be developed from the blood and/or bone marrow obtained from me'. Moore refused, against Golde's insistence, an insistence that prompted Moore to seek legal guidance and led to the filing of the lawsuit. In the meantime, Golde and his researchers had obtained a patent for a cell line developed exclusively from Moore's tissue. The patent was assigned to the University of California which then developed commercial products from this cell line. Allegedly, both the University of California and Golde profited from the patent.

In 1984, Moore filed a complaint, alleging among other things causes of action for conversion (wrongful interference with another person's property). Had the Court allowed this action, the practical implication of the strict liability associated with it would have meant that the ownership of the cell line (and all products derived therefrom) would revert to Moore. The trial court (California

Superior Court) dismissed Moore's claim, but the Court of Appeals reversed the decision and held that 'the rights of dominion over one's body, and the interests one has therein, are recognised in many cases. These rights and interests are so akin to property interest that it would be subterfuge to call them anything else.' The Court grounded its judgement on the assumption that given that Moore had not specifically abandoned his spleen by undergoing a splenectomy, he retained a right to the control of his own body and a property interest in his cells.

The patent holders appealed this decision, and the California Supreme Court reversed it, affirming that 'since Moore clearly did not expect to retain possession of his cells following their removal, to sue for their conversion he must have retained an ownership interest in them'. The Court deemed that 'Moore had no property rights in cells taken from his body, but remitted for trial the issue of whether the doctors had been in breach of the duty to obtain Moore's informed consent and of the duty of loyalty to Moore as their patients.' Among the reasons that weighed heavily in the Court's reasoning were policy reasons over the protection of scientific inquiry. The Supreme Court focused on the development of the cell line rather than on the removal of the cells from Moore. It was this focus which led them to decide that Moore could not have a property right in the cell line as he had not intellectually contributed anything to its development. A patent is usually granted to the inventor. The Court considered whether Moore could be regarded as an inventor and decided that he had not done anything to discover his cells' function or to improve their utility, nor had he helped in the research which transformed his tissues into a patentable cell line'; therefore, in absence of any labour put on the discovery, the Court denied to Moore any property-based entitlement.

Questions

1 What is in your view the main justification of property rights?

2 Does Moore's ownership of himself entail property of his cells?

3 Do you find it appropriate to use the language of property rights to describe possession of the human body? What other legal categories might (better) apply to the body and its components?

4 Read Locke's labour theory of property and apply it to the judgement. Which outcome would have been closer to Locke's conception of property?

5 How would you have decided the case?

6 How extended should the legal protection of property be? Should state action as informed by policy considerations be allowed to outweigh property rights?

 ❖ **TUTORIAL 5** Property rights

Reading

- *Jurisprudence*, chapters 2 ('Social Contract') and 3 ('Law and the Rise of the Market System')

Come to class prepared to discuss the following questions:

What is the *justification* for the enclosure of land? How does the law support this justification?

Discuss Locke's thesis that the law take the form of *individual property rights*.

Discuss the following famous quote from Rousseau's *Discourse on Inequality*:

> The first person who, having enclosed a plot of land, took it into his head to say this is mine and found people simple enough to believe him was the true founder of civil society. What crimes, wars, murders, what miseries and horrors would the human race have been spared, had some one pulled up the stakes or filled in the ditch and cried out to his fellow men: "Do not listen to this imposter. You are lost if you forget that the fruits of the earth belong to all and the earth to no one!"

❖ TUTORIAL 6   Understanding legal modernity

Reading

- *Jurisprudence*, chapters 5 ('Law, Class and Conflict: Karl Marx') and 6 ('Law, Legitimation and Rationality: Max Weber')

Responding to pressure from the trade union movement and left-wing political parties, the Ukranian Parliament passed legislation in 1930 to require employers to continue to pay workers who were sick when they were unable to work, for a period of up to two months. The legislation came into force on 1 January 1931.

In February 1931 a dispute arose at the factory of United Washers Ltd, a company that produced components that were essential to the manufacture of domestic appliances. Six workers were sacked after failing to turn up to work for three consecutive days, a situation which the company argued had led to a significant reduction in output. The men argued that they had been sick and unable to work and that they should have received sick pay during their absence. The company responded that the men had been paid for days that they were absent before they were sacked. The case was taken up by the men's trade union which brought a legal action against the company, requiring that the men be reinstated. The court of first instance held that the men should not be reinstated: there was nothing in the legislation that prevented a company from sacking those who were too sick to work, and that they had been paid by the company for the period that they were sick, in accordance with the legislation.

The union appealed the case to the Supreme Court of Ukania, where the five judges delivered the following opinions.

JUDGE ANTONY

The central issue in this case is the wording of the legislation which alone expresses the intention of Parliament. The courts cannot and must not go beyond that wording in the determination of a case, for to do so would undermine the very legitimacy of the legal system. In this case the legislation provides for the protection of employees who are sick, but there is nothing in the legislation to prevent a company from terminating the contract of employment at any point, irrespective of the health of the worker.

JUDGE BELINDA

I am not persuaded by the argument of my brother Judge Antony. The intention of Parliament is expressed in the legislation as a

whole and it is very clear that the spirit or intention of this legislation was to protect workers against just these types of actions by
their employers. The rights given by the statute become meaningless if they can be avoided so easily, and so the legislation must be
interpreted in the light of the intention of Parliament to protect the
security and quality of employment. The legitimacy of the law will
not survive unless it is interpreted in such a way.

JUDGE CHARLES

There is much that is of merit in the argument of Judge Belinda. She
is right to focus on the question of the legitimacy of the law, but unfor-
tunately her argument is purely speculative. The present case cannot
be decided simply on the basis of the narrow interpretation of the legislation. If the courts are to deal with such issues properly they must
be provided with more information about the profitability of washer
manufacture; about time lost through sickness and injury in this sector of the economy; about the income and employability of workers,
skilled and unskilled in this sector; about the attitudes to the law of
all workers and so on. As we know, such information is central to the
management of modern society and the economy, and is the basis for
decision-making by all other organs of government. If the courts continue to confine themselves to the interpretation of the wording of statutes alone, then they run the risk of becoming increasingly irrelevant.

JUDGE DIANA

I am not persuaded that this is a question for the courts at all. It is
clear to me that the legislation has been poorly drafted, in that it
allows employers to act in a way which is clearly contrary to the spirit
of the law. Parliament should, as a matter of urgency, revisit and
amend this statute to close this loophole. This, however, is a political
question, and the courts should not be drawn into such political disputes. The law must stand apart from politics.

JUDGE ERIC

The issue in this case can best be dealt with by placing it in the
context of our existing law concerning the relations between master
and servant. This is an important body of law, which has developed
over centuries, which both expresses and regulates the nature of
the employment relation. New legislation must not be understood
as replacing this traditional law but as merely developing and
extending it to new situations. According to this traditional law,
trust is the fundamental basis of the master–servant relation, and
the courts should move to prevent any action, by either party, which
seeks to undermine this trust. The actions of the employers here do
precisely this and so the men should be reinstated.

Questions

1 How might we categorise these arguments in the light of Weber's typology of legal rationality?

2 The different judgements express different attitudes towards the legitimacy of the legal system. Which of these do you think most accurately expresses the proper basis of legal legitimacy and why?

3 Do these different arguments express differing attitudes towards and understandings of legal modernity?

Reading

- *Jurisprudence*, chapter 9 ('Law and Globalisation')

Washers Unlimited International PLC (WUI) is a multinational corporation based in Ukania. In 1999 they closed all their manufacturing plants in Ukania and opened factories in Ruritania, an ex-Soviet-bloc country that offered cheap labour and low levels of regulation of health and safety. Ruritania is, however, a member of the Council of Europe and a signatory to the European Convention on Human Rights.

In 2013, the nationalist neoliberal party that had been in power in Ruritania lost the general election and was replaced by the Social Democratic Party, which had campaigned on the basis of improving working conditions and limiting the power of foreign corporations in Ruritania. Their first acts on taking power were to introduce a new tax on the profits of foreign corporations and to introduce a new system of health and safety regulation which they promised would be actively enforced. WUI immediately declared that this was unduly restrictive and that they would be investigating ways of closing their factories in Ruritania. As an interim measure they immediately sacked 100 employees who had engaged in a public protest against the employment practices of the company, citing the increased costs of conforming with regulation as the reason for this measure.

Consider the following issues arising from this scenario:

1 The Ruritanian government approaches you for advice on how best to modify the proposed regulatory schema. They understand that regulation might be expensive for business, but they are keen to fulfil their democratic mandate. How might you analyse this situation and advise them?

2 The sacked workers take legal advice. In the absence of any employment rights under Ruritanian law, they decide that they want to bring a legal action against WUI for breaching their right to peaceful protest under the European Convention on Human Rights (ECHR). WUI argue that the ECHR cannot apply against private corporations, and that Ruritanian law is sovereign. The Ruritanian government supports the sacked workers' legal action, arguing that their independence has been undermined by the actions of corporations like WUI.

   a What are the different types of legal order that are involved in this dispute?

b How might a theory of globalisation help us to understand the complexities of this dispute?

c Discuss the theoretical basis for the non-application of human rights to private bodies. Why might this exemption be challenged by the process of globalisation of law?

❖ TUTORIAL 8   The structure of rights

Reading

- *Jurisprudence*, chapter 4 ('Law and the Political')

- Martin Loughlin, *Sword and Scales*, pp 197–214

The expansion of the language of legal rights represents possibly the most successful development of modern law. Almost every legal dispute is today formalised in terms of rights protection or conflict among rights. The aim of this tutorial is to reflect on the history and structure of rights with a view also to discussing their limits.

Questions

1   Article 16 of the French Declaration of Rights of Man and Citizen stated that 'any society in which the guarantee of rights is not assured . . . has no Constitution'. Does this mean that a legal order without rights is inconceivable?

2   Who can be a subject of rights? Do animals have rights? Does the environment have rights? Give *reasoned* answers.

3   Do rights entail the imposition of duties upon others?

4   Are rights valid before the establishment of a sovereign state (i.e., do people have rights before the creation of a legal order)? What would it mean to adjudicate conflicts between individual rights and sovereignty?

5   Do all rights (civil, political, social/economic) share the same structure and protect the same object?

6   Is the foundation of the validity of human rights different from other state rights? Is there a human right to food?

7   What are the consequences of the judicialisation of rights?

Bibliography

Adler, M and Asquith, S (eds), 1981, *Discretion and Welfare*, London: Heinemann.

Agamben, G, 1998, *Homo Sacer*, Stanford: Stanford University Press.

Althusser, L, 1971, 'Ideology and Ideological State Apparatuses', in L Althusser (ed), *Lenin and Philosophy, and Other Essays*, London: New Left Books.

Anghie, A, 2005, *Imperialism, Sovereignty and the Making of International Law*, Cambridge: Cambridge University Press.

Arendt, H, 2012/1950, *The Origins of Totalitarianism*, New York: Shocken Books.

Atiyah, P, 1979, *The Rise and Fall of the Freedom of Contract*, Oxford: Oxford University Press.

Atria, F, 2015, 'Social Rights, Social Contract and Socialism', 24 *Social & Legal Studies* 598–613.

Bauman, Z, 1989, *Modernity and the Holocaust*, Cambridge: Polity.

Bauman, Z, 2000, *Liquid Modernity*, Cambridge: Polity.

Benton, L, 2010, *In Search of Sovereignty*, Cambridge: Cambridge University Press.

Berman, H, 1983, *Law and Revolution: The Formation of the Western Legal Tradition*, Cambridge, MA: Harvard University Press.

Bobbio, N, 1996, *The Age of Rights*, Cambridge: Polity.

Brooks, T (ed), 2005, *Rousseau and Law*, London: Routledge.

Cain, M and Hunt, A, 1979, *Marx and Engels on Law*, London: Academic Press.

Campbell, T, 2006, *Rights: An Introduction*, London: Routledge.

Cohen, J, 2010, *Rousseau: A Free Community of Equals*, Oxford: Oxford University Press.

Collins, H, 1982, *Marxism and Law*, Oxford: Oxford University Press.

Cotterrell, R, 1992, *The Sociology of Law: An Introduction*, 2nd edn, London: Butterworths.

Cotterrell, R, 1995, 'Legality and Legitimacy: The Sociology of Max Weber', in R Cotterrell (ed), *Law's Community*, Oxford: Clarendon.

Cotterrell, R, 1999, *Emile Durkheim: Law in a Moral Domain*, Edinburgh: Edinburgh University Press.

Croce, M and Salvatore, A, 2015, *Undoing Ties*, London: Bloomsbury.

Cutler, AC, 2003, *Private Power and Global Authority*, Cambridge: Cambridge University Press.

De Jouvenel, B, 1975, *Sovereignty: An Inquiry Into the Political Good*, Cambridge: Cambridge University Press.

D'Entreves, AP, 1951, *Natural Law*, London: Hutchinson.

Della Volpe, G, 1978, *Rousseau and Marx*, London: Lawrence and Wishart.

Doogan, K, 2009, *New Capitalism?*, Cambridge: Polity.

Douzinas, C, 2007, *The End of Human Rights*, Oxford: Hart.

Durkheim, E, 1963/1933, *The Division of Labour in Society*, New York: Free Press.

Durkheim, E, 1992, *Professional Ethics and Civic Morals*, London: Routledge.

Dworkin, R, 1977, *Taking Rights Seriously*, Cambridge, MA: Harvard University Press.

Epstein, R, 1985, *Takings*, Cambridge, MA: Harvard University Press.

Ewing, S, 1987, 'Formal Justice and the Spirit of Capitalism: Max Weber's Sociology of Law', 21 *Law & Society Review* 487–512.

Foucault, M, 1984, 'What is Enlightenment?', in P Rabinow (ed), *The Foucault Reader*, Harmondsworth: Penguin.

Fried, C, 1981, *Contract as Promise*, Cambridge, MA: Harvard University Press.

Furet, F, 1981, *Interpreting the French Revolution*, Cambridge: Cambridge University Press.

Galbraith, K, 1998, *A History of Economics*, Harmondsworth: Penguin.

Galeano, E, 2000, *Upside Down*, New York: Picador.

Garland, D, 1990, *Punishment and Modern Society*, Oxford: Oxford University Press.

Garland, D, 2016, *The Welfare State: A Very Short Introduction*, Oxford: Oxford University Press.

Genovese, ED, 1988 [1974], *Roll Jordan Roll: The World the Slaves Made*, New York: Random House.

Giddens, A, 1971, *Capitalism and Modern Social Theory: An Analysis of the Writings of Marx, Durkheim and Weber*, Cambridge: Cambridge University Press.

Giddens, A, 1990, *The Consequences of Modernity*, Stanford: Stanford University Press.

Gill, S, 2000, 'The Constitution of Global Capital', accessed 14 March 2007, www.theglobalsite.ac.uk/press/010gill.pdf.

Glasman, M, 1996, *Unnecessary Suffering: Managing Market Utopia*, London: Verso.

Grimm, D, 2015, *Sovereignty*, New York: Columbia University Press.

Habermas, J, 1976, *Legitimation Crisis*, London: Heinemann.

Habermas, J, 1990, *The Philosophical Discourse of Modernity*, Cambridge, MA: MIT Press.

Harvey, D, 2010, *A Companion to Marx's* Capital, London: Verso.

Hay, D, 1975, *Albion's Fatal Tree: Crime and Society in Eighteenth-Century England*, New York: Pantheon.

Hegel, GFW, 1991, *Elements of the Philosophy of Right*, ed by A Wood, Cambridge: Cambridge University Press.

Held, D, 2002, 'Law of States, Law of Peoples: Three Models of Sovereignty', 8 *Legal Theory* 1–44.

Held, D and McGrew, A, 2003, 'The Great Globalization Debate: An Introduction', in D Held and A McGrew (eds), *The Global Transformations Reader*, 2nd edn, Cambridge: Polity Press.

Hirst, PQ, 1979, *On Law and Ideology*, London: Macmillan.

Hobbes, T, 1996/1651, *Leviathan*, Cambridge: Cambridge University Press.

Horkheimer, M, 1972, *Critical Theory*, New York: Herder & Herder.

Ilgen, TL, 2003, 'Reconfigured Sovereignty in the Age of Globalization', in TL Ilgen (ed), *Reconfigured Sovereignty: Multi-Layered Governance in the Global Age*, Aldershot: Ashgate.

Jackson R, 1999, 'Sovereignty in World Politics: A Glance at the Conceptual and Historical Landscape', 67 *Political Studies* 431–456.

Jessop, B, 2016, *The State*, Cambridge: Polity Press.

Kamenka, E and Tay, A, 1975, 'Beyond Bourgeois Individualism: The Contemporary Crisis in Law and Legal Ideology', in E Kamenka and RS Neale (eds), *Feudalism, Capitalism and Beyond*, London: Edward Arnold.

Kant, I, 1991/1784, 'What Is Enlightenment?', in H Reiss (ed), *Political Writings*, Cambridge: Cambridge University Press.

Kelman, M, 1987, *A Guide to Critical Legal Studies*, Cambridge, MA: Harvard University Press.

Kennedy, D, 2003, 'The Disenchantment of Logically Formal Legal Rationality, or Max Weber's Sociology in the Genealogy of the Contemporary Mode of Western Legal Thought', 55 *Hastings Law Journal* 1031.

Koselleck, R, 1988, *Critique and Crisis*, Boston: MIT Press.

Kronman, A, 1983, *Max Weber*, London: Edward Arnold.

Laslett, P, 1988, 'Introduction', to Locke (1988).

Lazzarato, M, 2015, *Governing by Debt*, Cambridge, MA: The MIT Press.

Lenin, VI, 1917, *The State and Revolution*, various editions.

Locke, J, 1988, in Laslett, P (ed), *Two Treatises of Government*, Cambridge: Cambridge University Press.

Loughlin, M, 2000, *Sword and Scales*, Oxford: Hart Publishing.

Loughlin, M, 2003a, 'Ten Tenets of Sovereignty', in N Walker (ed) *Sovereignty in Transition*, Oxford: Hart Publishing.

Loughlin, M, 2003b, *The Idea of Public Law*, Oxford: Oxford University Press.

Loughlin, M, 2010, *Foundations of Public Law*, Oxford: Oxford University Press.

Luhmann, N, 1985, *A Sociological Theory of Law*, Abingdon: Routledge.

Lukács, G, 1971, 'The Phenomenon of Reification', in G Lukács (ed) *History and Class Consciousness*, London: Merlin Press.

Lukes, S, 1973, *Emile Durkheim. His Life and Work: A Historical and Critical Study*, Harmondsworth: Penguin.

Lukes, S and Scull, A, 1983, *Durkheim and the Law*, Oxford: Robertson.

Macaulay, S, 1963, 'Non-contractual Relations in Business: A Preliminary Study', 28 *American Sociological Review* 55–67.

MacCormick, N, 1999, *Questioning Sovereignty*, Cambridge: Cambridge University Press.

MacCormick, N, 2004, 'Questioning Post-Sovereignty', 29 *European Law Review* 852.

Macpherson, CB, 1962, *The Political Theory of Possessive Individualism*, Oxford: Oxford University Press.

Maine, HS, 1861/1917, *Ancient Law*, London: Dent.

Mamdani, M, 1996, *Citizen and Subject: Contemporary Africa and the Legacy of Late Colonialism*, Princeton: Princeton University Press.

Marks, S, 2000, *The Riddle of All Constitutions*, Oxford: Oxford University Press.

Marx, K, 1843, 'On the Jewish Question', in D McLellan (ed), *Karl Marx: Selected Writings*, 1977, Oxford: Oxford University Press.

Marx, K, 1844, 'Economic and Philosophical Manuscripts', in D McLellan (ed), *Karl Marx: Selected Writings*, 1977, Oxford: Oxford University Press.

Marx, K, 1849, 'Wage Labour and Capital', in D McLellan (ed), *Karl Marx: Selected Writings*, 1977, Oxford: Oxford University Press.

Marx, K, 1851, 'The Eighteenth Brumaire of Louis Bonaparte', in D McLellan (ed), *Karl Marx: Selected Writings*, 1977, Oxford: Oxford University Press.

Marx, K, 1865, *Capital*, vol. 1, many editions, e.g., 1990, Harmondsworth: Penguin.

Marx, K, 1932, 'The German Ideology', in D McLellan (ed), *Karl Marx: Selected Writings*, 1977, Oxford: Oxford University Press.

McCormick, J, 2011, *Machiavellian Democracy*, Cambridge: Cambridge University Press.

McLellan, D (ed), 1977, *Karl Marx. Selected Writings*, Oxford: Oxford University Press.

Meiksins Wood, E, 2002, *The Origin of Capitalism*, London: Verso.

Meiksins Wood, E, 2012, *Liberty and Property*, London: Verso.

Miéville, C, 2005, *Between Equal Rights: A Marxist Theory of International Law*, Leiden: Brill.

Milliband, R, 1977, *Marxism and the State*, Oxford: Oxford University Press.

Montesquieu, CL, 1989/1748, *The Spirit of the Laws*, Cambridge: Cambridge University Press.

Murphy, WT, 1997, *The Oldest Social Science? Configurations of Law and Modernity*, Oxford: Oxford University Press.

Nelken, D, 1982, 'Is there a Crisis in Law and Legal Ideology?', 9 *Journal of Law and Society* 177–189.

Neuhouser, F, 2013, 'Rousseau's Critique of Economic Inequality', 41 *Philosophy and Public Affairs* 193–215.

Newsinger, J, 2013, *The Blood Never Dried: A People's History of the British Empire*, 2nd ed, London: Bookmarks.

Norrie, A (ed), 2000, 'Symposium on Contract Law and Legal Theory', 9 *Social & Legal Studies* 397–447.

Nozick, R, 1974, *Anarchy, State and Utopia*, New York: Basic Books.

O'Hagan, T, 2003, *Rousseau*, London: Routledge.

Pashukanis, EB, 1978, *Law and Marxism: A General Theory*, London: Pluto Press.

Poggi, G, 1990, *The State*, Stanford: Stanford University Press.

Polanyi, K, 1957/1944, *The Great Transformation*, New York: Beacon Press.

Poulantzas, N, 1980, *State, Power, Socialism*, London: Verso.

Reiner, R, 1984, 'Crime, Law and Deviance: The Durkheim Legacy', in S Fenton (ed), *Durkheim and Modern Sociology*, Cambridge: Cambridge University Press.

Rheinstein, M, 1954, 'Introduction', in M Rheinstein (ed), *Max Weber on Law in Economy and Society*, Cambridge, MA: Harvard University Press.

Rokkan, S, 1999, *State Formation, Nation-Building, and Mass Politics in Europe*, Oxford: Oxford University Press.

Rousseau, J-J, 1984, *A Discourse on Inequality*, London: Penguin.

Rousseau, J-J, 1994, *The Social Contract*, Oxford: Oxford University Press.

Santos, de Sousa B, 2002, *Toward a New Legal Common Sense*, 2nd edn, London: Butterworths.

Santos, de Sousa B and Rodríguez-Garavito, CA (eds), 2005, *Law and Globalization From Below: Towards a Cosmopolitan Legality*, Cambridge: Cambridge University Press.

Sassen, S, 1996, *Losing Control? Sovereignty in an Age of Globalization*, New York: Columbia University Press.

Sassen, S, 2007, *A Sociology of Globalization*, New York: W.W. Norton.

Schmitt, C, 1985, *Political Theology*, Chicago: University of Chicago Press.

Schneiderman, D, 2008, *Constitutionalizing Economic Globalization: Investment Rules and Democracy's Promise*, Cambridge: Cambridge University Press.

Schneiderman, D, 2013, *Resisting Economic Globalization: Critical Theory and International Investment Law*, London: Palgrave Macmillan.

Scholte, J-A, 2008, 'Reconstructing Contemporary Democracy', 15 *Indiana Journal of Global Legal Studies* 305.

Shklar, J, 1969, *Men and Citizens: A Study of Rousseau's Social Theory*, Cambridge: Cambridge University Press.

Simmons, J, 1992, *Lockean Theory of Right*, Princeton: Princeton University Press.

Skinner, Q, 1978, *The Foundations of Modern Political Thought*, Cambridge: Cambridge University Press.

Skinner, Q, 2008, *Hobbes and Republican Liberty*, Cambridge: Cambridge University Press.

Smith, A, 1976, *An Inquiry Into the Nature and Causes of the Wealth of Nations* [1776], Oxford: Oxford University Press.

Smith, A, 1978, *Lectures on Jurisprudence* (1762), in RL Meek and DD Raphael (eds), *The Glasgow Edition of the Works and Correspondence of Adam Smith*, vol. V, Oxford: Oxford University Press.

Stone, A, 1985, 'The Place of Law in the Marxian Structure-Superstructure Archetype', 19 *Law and Society Review* 39–67.

Streeck, W, 2014, *Buying Time: The Delayed Crisis of Democratic Capitalism*, London: Verso.

Swedberg, R, 2000, *Max Weber and the Idea of Economic Sociology*, Princeton: Princeton University Press.

Teubner, G, 2012, *Constitutional Fragments*, Oxford: Oxford University Press.

Thompson, EP, 1971, 'The Moral Economy of the English Crowd in the Eighteenth Century', 50 *Past and Present* 76–136.

Thompson, EP, 1977, *Whigs and Hunters*, Harmondsworth: Penguin.

Thompson, J, 1984, *Studies in the Theory of Ideology*, Cambridge: Polity Press.

Thornhill, C, 2011, *A Sociology of Constitutions*, Cambridge: Cambridge University Press.

Tierney, B, 1997, *The Idea of Natural Rights*, Emory: Eerdmans Publishing.

Tilly, C, 1992, *Coercion, Capital and European States (990–1990)*, Oxford: Blackwell.

Tuck, R, 1979, *Natural Rights Theories*, Cambridge: Cambridge University Press.

Tuck, R, 1996, 'Introduction', to Hobbes (1996).

Tuck, R, 2015, *The Sleeping Sovereign*, Cambridge: Cambridge University Press.

Tully, J, 1980, *A Discourse on Property: John Locke and His Adversaries*, Cambridge: Cambridge University Press.

Turner, B, 1996, *For Weber: Essays on the Sociology of Fate*, London: Sage.

Twining, W, 2000, *Globalisation & Legal Theory*, London: Butterworths.

Twining, W, 2009, *General Jurisprudence: Understanding Law From a Global Perspective*, Cambridge: Cambridge University Press.

Unger, RM, 1976, *Law in Modern Society*, New York: The Free Press.

Veitch, S, 2017, 'The Sense of Obligation', 8(3) *Jurisprudence* 415–434.

Waldron, J, 1987, *Nonsense Upon Stilts: Bentham, Burke and Marx on the Rights of Man*, London: Methuen.

Waldron, J, 1988, *The Right to Private Property*, Oxford: Oxford University Press.

Walker, N, 2001, 'The EU and the WTO: Constitutionalism in a New Key', in G De Burca and J Scott J (eds), *The EU and the WTO: Legal and Constitutional Aspects*, Oxford: Hart.

Walker, N, 2002, 'The Idea of Constitutional Pluralism', 65 *Modern Law Review* 317–53.

Walker, N, 2003a, 'Late Sovereignty in the European Union', in Walker (2003b).

Walker, N (ed), 2003b, *Sovereignty in Transition*, Oxford: Hart.

Walker, N, 2008, 'Taking Constitutionalism Beyond the State', 56 *Political Studies* 519.

Walker, N, 2015, *Intimations of Global Law*, Cambridge: Cambridge University Press.

Weber, M, 1930, *The Protestant Ethic and the Spirit of Capitalism* (1905), London: Allen & Unwin.

Weber, M, 1948a, 'Politics as a Vocation' (1919), in HH Gerth and CW Mills (eds), *From Max Weber: Essays in Sociology*, London: Routledge & Kegan Paul.

Weber, M, 1948b, 'Science as a Vocation' (1917), in HH Gerth and CW Mills (eds), *From Max Weber: Essays in Sociology*, London: Routledge & Kegan Paul.

Weber, M, 1968, *Economy and Society, An Outline of Interpretive Sociology* (1921/22), 2 vols, Berkeley: University of California Press.

Wilhelmsson, T, 1995, *Social Contract Law and European Integration*, Aldershot: Dartmouth.

Yack, B, 2001, 'Popular Sovereignty and Nationalism', 29 *Political Theory* 517–536.

Zizek, S, 1994, *Mapping Ideology*, London: Verso.

Part II

Legal system and legal reasoning

I Legality and validity   131

II Theories of legal reasoning   161

I

Legality and validity

10 The differentiation of law and morality   133
11 Identifying valid law: the positivist thesis   137
    Hart's concept of law   137
    Kelsen's 'pure' theory of law   140
12 The challenge of natural law   144
    The question of form   144
    The question of content   151

Chapter 10

The differentiation of law and morality

One way to understand the advent and development of modern law, as was analysed in Part I, is as a process of differentiation, where secular authority was separated from religious authority, and where the principles of national state jurisdiction ensured that (increasingly) democratic legislatures enacted, and State bureaucracies implemented, positive legislation over the territories of nation-states. The idea of differentiation denotes the gradual emergence and establishment of separate normative orders, of morality, law, politics, religion, etc. The separation meant that religious doctrine was no longer a source of law, or individual faith a criterion for holding public office of participating in the public sphere, but that faith could be seen as a private matter (freedom of religion). It meant that comprehensive world-views gradually gave way to a relative plurality of value commitments, recognised and protected as a matter of individual right. And that justice came increasingly to withdraw to the formal side of social interchange (equality of all before the law) rather than embodying any comprehensive doctrine to be enforced through the law.

At a conceptual level, these developments raise a general concern about the relationship between law and other kinds of values. Can law be understood without including any necessary reference to those values that it may seem desirable for law to embody, notably morality and justice? Is it possible, in other words, and is it desirable, to identify valid law without reference to other kinds of normative or evaluative standards?

The tradition of *legal positivism* gives an affirmative answer to these questions. Legal positivism emerges as a distinct approach to legal analysis in the work of Jeremy Bentham and John Austin, English jurists writing in the late eighteenth and early nineteenth centuries, and it received great impetus in the work of two twentieth-century legal philosophers, Hans Kelsen and H.L.A. Hart. These authors differ in their approaches, yet they all see as important the need to identify valid law without reference to questions of moral values. They argue that what the law is, and what it ought to be, are different questions and require different kinds of answer. As Austin famously put it, '[t]he existence of law is one thing, its merit and demerit another. Whether it be or be not is one enquiry; whether it be or be not conformable to an assumed standard, is a different enquiry' (Austin 1954/1832, p 157).

There is in much jurisprudential writing a problematic tendency to abstract such statements and the dilemmas behind them from the historical contexts within which they arose. This impoverishes our understanding of these debates and consequently the complexity of the answers. Legal positivism arose under specific historical conditions as a response to highly charged contestations of political authority. For example, Hobbes's profound statement of sovereignty as *juris-diction* (i.e., the Leviathan's absolute power to pronounce the law for the subjects), a high moment of *positivism*, is published in the midst of political turmoil in England soon after the execution of Charles I. Locke's theory of the *natural right* of property both inspired and found its way into the constitutional thinking of the protagonists of the American revolution, which asserted the rights of American property owners against the juris-diction of the British Crown. The Reformation itself had had a massive impact on the tradition of natural law thinking as developed from Aristotle through the writings of Thomas Aquinas, emphasising the cultivation of moral wisdom (*phronesis* in Aristotle, *prudentia* in Aquinas) which very much relied on natural law as the expression of practical reason in human affairs (more on this soon). Against this 'substitution' of (human) reason (*ratio*) for God's will (*voluntas*), Luther will insist that each individual has responsibility for him- or herself to comprehend God's will.

This is not to say that an understanding of the rival schools of thought is inextricably tied to the histories of its founding statements or the historical conflicts that underlay them. But it is to insist that theories of positivism and natural law embody and express traditions of thought from which they cannot be severed without loss of meaning. In our discussion of Max Weber, we saw that he characterised the common law as (predominantly) of the 'substantive-irrational type': it moved 'irrationally' by way of analogy from case to case (and not deductively – 'rationally' – through subsumption to rule) and it was 'substantive' to the extent that it drew heavily on communal values and morals. The remedies it provided did so on a case-by-case basis, resistant to generalising classification and categorisation. It is against the grain of this legal corpus of dispersed instances that Blackstone writes the *Commentaries* in the stated effort to bring systematicity to the law, clarifying, classifying and ordering the heterogeneous material. A presupposition of such ordering is that there are certain principles of reason that might allow the material to be collected in a coherent way. The *Commentaries*, as an example of eighteenth-century natural law scholarship, are an effort to make of the law a rational whole, on the assumption that natural reason found expression in the legal materials and it was a question of merely bringing that coherence to the surface. Note how deep the tension runs, and how it is played out, in early modern English legal history. On the one hand we have the natural law's elevation of principles and reasons above the heterogeneity of common law remedies, as the essence of legal thought, buttressed by the natural rights thinking in the tradition Locke represents, where natural law is the law that embodies the natural rights of man. On the other hand we have a positivism that eschews such principled reconstructions, and sees law as coincident with the will of the lawmaker, in the tradition that *auctoritas, non veritas, facet legem* ('authority, not truth, makes law').

An important parallel of the tension and dilemmas surrounding codification we find on the Continent in the development of what came to be known as the *Historical School* of jurisprudence. At the beginning of the nineteenth century the towering figure of Friedrich von Savigny wrote powerfully about the law as embodiment of the living culture of the people. 'Law,' he wrote, 'has no self-dependent existence . . . its essence is the life of man himself' (1831, p 46). And while Savigny did not oppose codification as such, he emphasised the danger of its capturing, stilling and eventually stultifying the live expression of the collective animus of the people as it is realised in the spontaneous development of the law.

The possibility of 'value-free' analysis was influential across diverse areas of intellectual enquiry throughout the nineteenth century in the emerging social sciences. It had philosophical roots in David Hume's observations that, first, there is a crucial difference between factual statements (that such and such is the case) and evaluative statements (that such and such *ought* to be the case), and second, that the latter cannot be logically derived from the former. For Hume, descriptive (factual) accuracy should not be conflated with (evaluative) desirability: 'The anatomist', he wrote, 'ought never to emulate the painter' (Hume 1978/1739, p 620). Taking the lead from Hume's insight, legal positivists sought to clarify our understanding of law – a description of what the law *is* – by freeing it from value judgements about what it ought to be.

Yet if this 'analytical jurisprudence' sought clarity, it did not disavow the very real importance to society of pursuing moral and political values, such as justice and equality and so on. In fact, the major legal positivist authors wrote a great deal about what such values were and how they may be best pursued, including through legal means. But this kind of enquiry, they maintained, was separate from the problem of identifying valid law. Moreover (and it sounds rather odd at first hearing), for legal positivists there were good *evaluative* reasons for pursuing a non-evaluative theory of law. If we could describe accurately which laws were in force in any given jurisdiction then we could make a clear and coherent assessment of them as a matter of independent critical evaluation. A legal system whose legislation was, for example, racially discriminatory would still contain valid laws (assuming they were procedurally enacted properly), even though many citizens and observers would consider them politically and morally abhorrent. To mix the undesirability of these laws from a political or moral point of view with the question of whether they were legally valid fused two different things: what the law is (here and now) and what it ought to be if it were more just and equal. And it was important to make this point not just for analytical reasons but because legal reform itself depended upon being able to give an accurate description of what the law is and how it is changed, in order to be able in turn to make it better. The anatomist, Hume concluded, is not expected to be creative like the painter is, yet he 'is admirably fitted to give advice to a painter . . . We must have an exact knowledge of the parts, their situation and connexion, before we can design with any elegance or correctness' (ibid, p 621). Hence conflating legal validity with moral or political judgement simply muddied the waters of analysis and potential reform.

It is important to realise that as an analytical project, legal positivism is not appropriately comparable with what is commonly called the 'natural law' tradition; it is far narrower and technical in scope, while the latter is much wider in ambition and resources, and the question of legal validity is only a very small component of a far richer exploration of human values over times and contexts. Within its narrower ambit, nevertheless, legal positivism's analytical approach with its descriptive successes and the merits of its method of 'value-free' analysis, has been, and to an extent remains, highly influential.

In the following sections we set out some of the key ideas of Hart and Kelsen and consider some differences between the two. The lens through which we look at their theories here is specifically as part of a thematic concern with the role of political and moral values in the law. (We return to different aspects of their work later.) In the subsequent sections we explore prominent criticisms of the work of the legal positivists in what regards their theses both about the form and the content of law, and the key positivist contention that the question of morality is incidental to (rather than necessary to) the understanding of law's form and content.

Chapter 11

Identifying valid law

The positivist thesis

Hart's concept of law

Sympathetic to Bentham's and Austin's legal positivism, Hart nonetheless identified a number of problems in their analyses. For Austin, law 'properly so called', is the command of a sovereign backed by the threat of a sanction. He defined the sovereign as 'a determinate human superior, not in the habit of obedience to a like superior, [which] receive[s] habitual obedience from the bulk of a given society' (Austin 1954/1832, p 166). This 'command theory' of law, as Hart saw it, may well resemble common perceptions of the criminal law, but it was inadequate as a full description of law. One of the main reasons why is that there are different *kinds* of laws, many of which do not operate as commands at all, but rather involve the conferring of powers. These powers may be found in the domain of public law, such as with jurisdictional powers – laws, for example, establishing or varying the jurisdiction of courts or tribunals – as well as in the myriad private law powers to make contracts or wills or establish corporations. In all such cases, and they are very many, it is not accurate, said Hart, to describe the relevant laws as commands. Nor is it appropriate to see their use as involving the threat of sanctions. For Hart, an alternative understanding was required if the legal positivist tradition was to remain persuasive.

This new understanding involved shifting attention from commands to *rules*. For Hart, a legal system was best understood as the 'union of primary and secondary rules' (see Hart 1961, ch V). Primary rules imposed obligations – tax law, for example, or the law of negligence imposed on citizens legal obligations: duties to do, or refrain from doing, certain actions. These laws came in the form of rules, not commands. Importantly, there is something about the quality of rules that makes them different from commands: a robber in the street, argued Hart, may demand that you hand over your money. You may feel obliged to do so. But it would be wrong to say that you had 'an obligation' to do so. What a 'tax demand' did, by contrast, was precisely to impose obligations to pay money, and these obligations had their source in legal rules established by legislation. You may or may not feel obliged to pay your taxes. But that was different from saying you had an established legal obligation to do so. Primary legal rules of this sort were therefore duty-imposing rules: rules that established binding legal obligations.

But as we have already noted, not all legal rules are of this kind. There were also, Hart argued, secondary rules. They were 'on a different level from the primary rules, for they are all *about* such rules' (Hart 1961, p 92, original emphasis). The importance of these rules lay in their relation to primary rules in such a way that established a legal *system*. According to Hart, there are three types of secondary rules. First, there were those power-conferring rules that established who, or which institutions, had the legal authority to *decide legal disputes* and impose penalties for breach of obligations. They also established the procedures that were to be followed to make such judgements. These Hart called rules of *adjudication*. They allowed for a certain efficiency in the processing of legal disputes by identifying authoritative bodies and procedures to determine legal outcomes.

Second, there were those power-conferring rules that established who, or which institutions, and according to what procedures, were legally authorised to make changes to legal rules. These were secondary rules of *change*. In the most obvious sense, such rules established the conditions according to which new primary rules could be introduced or older rules amended. Think of the many levels at which rules of change are prescribed by our legal systems: at the level of 'constitutional amendment', i.e., the conditions under which the constitution can be revised; at the level of making changes to legislation; at the level of the powers that are conferred on local government to vary legal standards with respect to areas within their jurisdictional competence; etc. But rules of change are not limited to State authorities; they are also conferred on individuals. Here secondary rules of change are those that confer powers in private law that allow individuals to change their legal position or status in prescribed ways: the power to change your legal status by way of marriage; the power to assume an obligation through contract; the power to establish a corporation; and so on. These may in turn create new (to you) primary legal obligations, but they require powers being conferred, as Hart said, at a different level from such primary rules.

The third type of secondary rule is the rule of *recognition*. At its most simple, it is 'a rule for conclusive identification of the primary rules of obligation' (Hart 1961, p 92). In complex legal systems there may be, says Hart, a number of such rules and they may take different forms. But what they have in common is that characteristic of establishing definite criteria to *identify* valid law. It is the rule of recognition, or in a complex setting, an 'ultimate rule of recognition' that does this. The content of such an ultimate rule will vary from jurisdiction to jurisdiction: in the United Kingdom, for example, Hart noted that the ultimate rule of recognition was '[w]hatever the Queen in Parliament enacts is law.' In addition to providing criteria for recognising valid law, this rule also introduces the key idea that all the rules together, primary and secondary, form a legal *system*: 'the rules are now not just a discrete unconnected set but are, in a simple way, unified' (Hart 1961, p 93).

It is in this sense that a legal system is best understood as 'the union of primary and secondary rules'. But it is of course also necessary that the rules of the legal system, and especially the rules of obligation, are generally effective; most of the people most of the time must act in accordance with legal rules and be liable to sanction where they do not. This is a necessary *condition* for the existence of a legal system. But this fact of efficacy is not the reason for the validity of its rules. That requires that the rule of recognition, which provides the criteria of validity for all the other rules, be accepted as a common standard at least by the *officials* of the system. Rules, said Hart, had two aspects: an 'external' aspect, where rules were essentially predictions of how people would behave (for example, when the traffic light is at red we can predict that drivers will stop), and an 'internal' aspect where, seen from the *participants'* point of view, rules provided *reasons* for people to act in certain ways (the red traffic light is the internalised reason why drivers stop). In complex societies, said Hart, most of the people need not accept legal rules from the internal point of view. Instead, '[t]he rule of recognition, if it is to exist at all, exists only as a shared social rule *accepted qs a binding common standard of behaviour* by those whose official power as a "legal power" is dependent ultimately upon that very rule' (MacCormick 2008, p 34, original emphasis). The ultimate rule of recognition in a legal system is not itself a legal rule, but a conventional rule: 'It "exists" . . . by the custom and usage of those bound by it' (ibid, p 137). And so it is, concludes Hart, that the ultimate rule of recognition 'can neither be valid nor invalid but is simply accepted as appropriate for use in this way' (Hart 1961, pp 105–106).

Part of the significance of Hart's legal positivist approach lies in its description of legal validity as having no *necessary* connection to political or moral values. One legal system may, for example, impose the death penalty, another not; one may allow discrimination on the grounds of race or gender, another declare these as illegal. In all, or any, such cases, the question of legal validity does not depend on its correlation to particular political or moral values. It is, rather, answerable by reference to the system's ultimate rule of recognition which is itself ultimately a matter of officials' practice.

Hart does note that all societies will normally have certain basic rules and values enshrined in their law: rules against violence, theft, fraud and so on. He describes these as a 'minimum content of natural law' contained in all legal systems (Hart 1958, pp 78–81). For Hart, facts grounded in human nature make it necessary for all legal systems to provide a bare minimum of protection. Human vulnerability entails that law must enact a restriction on the free use of violence and the use of aggression; limited altruism requires systems of mutual forbearance; limited resources require some system of property; limited understanding and strength of will require some form of sanctions. These truisms about human nature, claims Hart, makes it a 'natural necessity' that law embody the minimum forms of protection for persons, property and promises. In *Law, Liberty, and Morality* he goes as far as to say, 'it is indeed arguable that a human society in which [such values] are not recognised at all in its morality is neither an empirical nor a logical possibility' (1963, p 70). And he will also argue for a set of moral and political values that he espouses as desirable in a decent society and which the content of its laws would ideally reflect. But such desirability, and the contingency of laws enshrining certain values, should still not be confused with a description of what constitutes validity in a legal system. Here a certain 'anatomist's' realism – recall Hume – must prevail. Even politically and morally atrocious governments can make and enforce valid laws that cause great harm to a great many of those subjected to them. Even there, argues, Hart, '[the] society in which this was so might be deplorably sheeplike; the sheep might end in the slaughter-house. But there is little reason for thinking that it could not exist or for denying it the title of a legal system' (Hart 1961, p 114).

We will return later in this section to collect certain criticisms of such an approach. But for now we can note one insight offered by MacCormick in the course of his sympathetic treatment of Hart's work. MacCormick observed that '[p]erhaps everywhere there is a line to be drawn between "law" and "politics", but one of the more obvious facts of cross-cultural comparison is that it gets drawn differently in different places' (MacCormick 2008, p 8). For all that Hart's concept of law was intended as generally applicable, it inevitably bears the hallmark of its time: 'it is clearly recognisable as the work of an English lawyer of the twentieth century' (ibid). In that time, and indeed for some time before, matters of political and social justice belonged entirely in the realm of the 'political nation'. It was here, according to MacCormick, that questions of entitlement and rights were argued over and settled, and the outcomes of these conclusions, where appropriate, enacted into law. In such a system, legal officials were expected to apply the law declared by the political system, and for this they needed clear criteria – rules of recognition – for what counted as legally valid and binding rules and what did not. The political morality of these rules was not something officials, and in particular judges, was required to engage with.

Even without comparing different types of legal and constitutional traditions and practices, it is clear, says MacCormick, that the British understanding Hart imbibed and described as to where the line between law and politics is drawn has itself changed markedly in recent decades. Two factors stand out. One involves the large-scale impact of supra-state entities (in particular the law and policies of the European Union) and the simultaneous effects of internal devolutionary adjustments (a Scottish Parliament, and Assemblies in Wales and Northern Ireland). The other is the incorporation of the European Convention on Human Rights into domestic law which has, among other things, offered a vast new area of interpretative leeway to determining the content of the law and resulted in an increasingly direct role of the judiciary in what were formerly taken to be within the exclusive domain of the 'political nation'. These, combined with the fragmentations and re-combinations of sovereignty, the pluralisation of legal orders and the existence of competing and overlapping jurisdictions have together made the legal landscape quite different from when Hart's work was developed. On the one hand, such developments make far more complex the problems of identifying valid legal rules according to an ultimate rule of recognition that would provide unity for a single UK legal system. But more importantly they have challenged the very notion of the autonomy of law where (as we saw above) the politicisation of law and the legalisation of politics mark a clear shift in where it is appropriate to draw the line between law and politics. Together these make much more problematic the descriptive endeavours of a legal positivist approach that would seek to maintain a conceptual separation between law and political and moral values.

Kelsen's 'pure' theory of law

The question of the autonomy of legal validity from political and moral values is addressed in a second version of legal positivism, which developed by Austrian jurist Hans Kelsen. Following again Hume's insight on the underivability of normative ('ought') statements from factual ones, Kelsen argued that the validity of norms could only be derived from other norms, not from factual statements about the way the world is or human beings are. With respect to law, therefore, Kelsen noted that '[it] is a peculiarity of law to regulate its own creation' (Kelsen 1957, p 365). Yet his approach differed from Hart's in important ways as we will now see.

According to Kelsen, there is a science of legal norms. 'Its exclusive purpose is to know and to describe its object' (Kelsen 1967, p 1). Its object is positive law. The proper method for analysing legal norms must be objective; it cannot, he argues, refer to other, subjective, criteria: whether the law is good, fair or just, for example. Legal science thus offers a 'pure theory of law', purified from these other, subjective, 'alien elements'. It is in this sense that jurisprudence is 'value free'.

Kelsen distinguishes between the subjective and objective meaning of acts. For example, you might write down a wish-list of who you want to benefit from the things belonging to you when you die, and sign your name at the end. The existence of this piece of paper and what it means to you can be distinguished from its objective legal meaning. If your legal system recognises such an act as sufficient to create a will, there now exists a legally valid document, the content of which creates certain legal rights and obligations that can be legally enforced, if need be by a court of law, on your death. Contrarily, you may perform exactly the same act – producing a piece of paper with your wish-list and signature – but if the law of your country requires your signature to be witnessed, then that piece of paper fails to create a legally valid document: its objective meaning (in this instance that the signed document creates no enforceable legal rights and obligations) is quite different, despite your subjective act being the same. The law, for Kelsen, therefore provides a 'scheme of interpretation' which confers objective legal meaning on actions: 'The judgment that an act of human behaviour, performed in time and space, is "legal" (or "illegal") is the result of a specific, namely normative, inter-pretation' (Kelsen 1967, p 4). It is that normative schema specific to law – the norms of positive law – that is the object of legal science, and, says Kelsen, we can and should analyse it without reference to questions of moral or political worth.

Legal norms confer objective meaning on human actions. But what makes these legal norms valid? That is, what makes them binding in such a way that 'an individual ought to behave in the manner determined by the norm'? (Kelsen 1967, p 193). Con-sider an example we used earlier: there is a letter from the tax office notifying you that you are liable to pay the amount of tax calculated by them. What makes this tax demand legally valid? For Kelsen, like Hart, this legal obligation imposed upon you is valid because of a superior norm, say the legislation which sets out the basis of particular taxes and how to assess them. This legislation will, in turn, be valid because of its source; as a duly enacted act of parliament. And what makes this act of parliament valid? This will be referred again to a higher norm, in this case most likely a constitution which stipu-lates the validity of parliamentary enactments as law. If we persist in such questioning we may trace the validity of the constitution back, says Kelsen, to a 'historically first' or original constitution. The matter then comes to a head: if there is no constitution prior to this one – that is, no higher constitutional or legal norm to which it can refer for its validity – then what makes it valid? This is where Hart and Kelsen differ. Hart, it will be recalled, had turned at this point to the conventional practices of officials and their 'internal point of view' on the rule of recognition. But Kelsen's answer is that every legal order must at this stage refer to a 'basic norm' – in German *Grundnorm* – which alone can infuse the whole legal order with validity.

What is this basic norm? For Kelsen it is a logical presupposition: 'that one ought to behave as the constitution prescribes.' It is therefore not a legal act, nor a matter of will: it is a matter of thought only – it has to be presupposed. But why does it have to be presupposed, and what purpose does it serve?

It has to be presupposed, argues Kelsen, because once we trace back the authority of legal norms to the historically first constitution, we cannot refer to another, higher, posited norm. We have, so to speak, run out of (positive, posited) legally authorised norms by reaching the historically first constitution. But given the conceptual gulf between facts and norms, no factual statement can provide validity to this constitution. We just have to assume it as valid in the following terms: 'Coercive acts *ought* to be performed under the conditions and in the manner which the historically first constitution, and the norms created according to it, prescribe' (Kelsen 1967, p 201, emphasis added). Only this presupposition can, as a matter of thought, answer the question of how legal validity is *possible*. It alone can answer the ultimate question of 'why the norms of this legal order ought to be obeyed and applied' (p 212). As MacCormick sums up, 'no positive, laid-down rule could confer upon constitution-makers the authority to do so. Everyone just has to act as if they had such authority' (MacCormick 2007, p 45).

As to its purpose, 'the basic norm constitutes the unity of the multiplicity . . . of all norms belonging to the same legal order' (p 205). In other words, the validity of a divergent range of legal norms is traceable through a hierarchy of legal authorisations which reaches its grounding in the basic norm. Where a particular claim cannot be so traced – like the demand of the robber for your money, or an unsigned wish-list – then it falls outside the validity-conferring system. Such a demand or wish authorises no legal official to act in accordance with it. It is in this sense then that Kelsen writes,

> The function of this basic norm is to found the objective validity of a positive legal order, that is, to interpret the subjective meaning of the acts of human beings by which the norms of an effective coercive order are created, as their objective meaning.
>
> (Kelsen 1967, p 202)

We should note two points from this conclusion. First, Kelsen is clear that as a 'coercive order', law must be *effective*: 'a minimum of effectiveness is a condition of validity' (Kelsen 1967, p 11). By effectiveness, Kelsen means two things: one, that legal norms are 'applied by the legal organs (particularly the law courts), which means, that the sanction in a concrete case is ordered and executed'; and two, that by and large individuals obey these norms: 'they behave in a way which avoids the sanction' (ibid). It is important to distinguish carefully between efficacy as a *condition* for validity, and the *reason* for the validity of a legal norm. The former is a *fact* (people, including officials, by and large *are obeying* the law), but as a fact it cannot be the reason for validity of legal norms. That reason, which alone creates objectively binding norms that people *ought* to follow, can only be another norm, whose validity is ultimately traceable, as we have seen, to the basic norm.

The second point is that legal validity is in no sense dependent upon any link to political or moral *values*. Again, that is not to say that we ought not to strive to make law fair or just or reasonable. As Kelsen notes, 'If the idea of justice has any function at all, it is to be a model for making good law and a criterion for distinguishing good from bad law' (Kelsen 1957, p 295). The problem is, however, that reasonable people (not to mention unreasonable people) disagree on what justice requires. Such 'subjectivity' – that justice depends on the point of view, interests or preferences of people – cannot be the source of objective legal meaning. Good law and bad law are still both law, and only the pure theory of law, freed from the subjective matter of what counts as 'good' or 'bad', can describe the objective existence of legally valid norms. But the consequence of such a view is stark: '*Any* kind of content might be law' (Kelsen 1967, p 198, emphasis added).

For the remainder of this chapter we will revisit two fundamental tenets of positivist thought that we have discussed above from the point of view of objections and counter-theses that can be described as deriving from Natural Law theory. The positivist theses that we have explored relate to the content and the form of law. In respect of the *content* of legal norms the positivists maintained that whether they be considered as just or unjust is entirely separable from their validity. In respect of form, they argued that law exists in the form of rules that are laid down, *posited*, as a matter of social fact.

Chapter 12

The challenge of natural law

The question of form

Why does form matter? Why does it matter – morally and politically – that the law appear in the form of rules? The most straightforward answer is given by the ideal of the rule of law. In our society, democratic liberty is best expressed by subjecting the exercise of government to the law. What is the meaning of the 'rule of law'? As Neil MacCormick puts it,

> [i]t is that stance in legal politics according to which matters of legal regulation or controversy ought to, so far as possible, be conducted in accordance with predetermined rules of considerable generality and clarity in which legal relations comprise rights, duties, powers and immunities reasonably clearly defined by reference to such rules and in which acts of government however desirable teleologically must be subordinated to respect for such rules and rights.
>
> (1989, p 184)

There appear to be two general sorts of reasons for maintaining the rule of law. First, there are *reasons of fairness*. The legal regulation of social relations is to take place through general rules applied in an impartial fashion to all persons alike and known in advance. The rules are to be applied by impartial specialists in law according to the internal logic and validity of the system and excluding any personal or non-legal considerations. Hence generality and reference to formal sources guarantee certain fundamental notions of fairness. The rule of law means (1) equality of legal subjects before the law in that individual cases are dealt with in terms of their facts alone and no one may be exempt; (2) government accountability and hence control of arbitrary action (including the actions of judges) – the doctrine of separation of powers means that judges should merely apply rules, not create them; and (3) since legal systems involve coercion and stigmatisation, the rule of law attempts to make coercion 'the friend of freedom' by regulating its use. We can consider all these as aspects of the phrase 'government of law not men'.

Second, there are what may be called *instrumental reasons*. The rule of law offers an efficient technique of social management in governing a pluralist market society where no underlying consensus of values can be presumed and there are conflicts of interests. The uniformity and predictability of law facilitates personal and commercial planning, entrepreneurial initiative in the market and in private spheres of action. Clear and technically authorised general rules are the perfect instrument for pursuing social and individual goals, whatever they may be. Weber thought of the rule of law in the shape of general formal and abstract rules as being instrumental in the rise of capitalism, and Marxist writers, as we saw, who also saw it as inextricably connected with capitalist society, argued that is offered legitimation to an unjust social order.

Fuller and the 'inner morality of law'

All this may appear as fairly uncontroversial. The idea that law should be given the form of general, clear and prospective rules does not appear as a reason to divide positivists and natural lawyers. We will begin to appreciate the nature of the disagreement when we look at one of the most interesting jurisprudential defences of the rule of law by the influential American legal theorist Lon Fuller, writing in the 1950s and 1960s. Fuller elevates the core features of the rule of law to nothing less than what he calls the 'inner morality of law'. Legality, for Fuller, is the 'enterprise of subjecting human conduct to the governance of rules' (Fuller 1969, p 106). This inner morality offers some fundamental constraints simply through law's formal features.

What are the features of this inner morality? What are the characteristics of legality? Fuller sets out the eight necessary features. These eight features must, in some degree, all be present in a legal system as a whole. Legality is an art and we must balance them against each other so that we get the best mix. But the condition of something being called a legal system is that this mix is present.

1   There must be rules: This is interpreted as the demand for generality. There must be rules of some kind and their essential feature is that they must be general in scope.
2   Promulgation: The demand that the law be made public, not kept secret. Citizens are not likely to know the content of all the laws, but they must be able to find out.
3   No retroactivity: Rules must be prospective. That is, in order to govern human behaviour they must be set out in advance in order that citizens are able to decide whether to conform to them or not. The basic human right of no punishment without a law expresses this principle.
4   Clarity: Rules must so far as possible be clear in order that they may be understood and followed. While some interpretative leeway is inevitable, and some flexibility of standards desirable, rules that are deliberately unclear contradict the possibility of ordering human conduct according to them.
5   No contradiction in laws: Rules that demand competing actions give no clear guidance as to what behaviour is expected by the law.
6   Laws must not require the impossible: Laws that demand behaviour over which citizens have no possible control cannot allow them to subject their conduct to rules.
7   Constancy: Laws must not keep changing rapidly if they are to produce stable expectations of what the law requires of its citizens, though of course this does not mean that they cannot change incrementally in order to meet the needs of a changing society.

8   Congruence between official action and declared rules: What officials do must be in accordance with the laws set out in advance, otherwise what the rules required and their application would differ in such a way as to leave citizens subject to the arbitrary powers of those in authority.

In defining the conditions under which the ideal of the rule of law can be realised, Fuller borrows from the German sociologist Georg Simmel the idea that

> there is a kind of *reciprocity* between government and the citizen with the respect to the observance of rules. Government says to the citizen in effect, "These are the rules we expect you to follow. If you follow them, you have our assurance that they are the rules that will be applied to your conduct." When this bond of reciprocity is finally and completely ruptured by government, nothing is left on which to ground the citizen's duty to observe the rules.
>
> (Fuller 1969, pp 39–40, emphasis added)

For Fuller the instantiation of each principle is required in a legal order in order that law's fundamental purpose, namely the subjection of human conduct to the governance of rules, be fulfilled. These principles are intrinsic to what it means to have law at all. At the same time they are the necessary and sufficient condition for the possibility of bringing about 'reciprocity' between government and citizen. That is law's achievement, and in bringing it about (as distinct from merely instituted power) it acquires a 'moral' dimension. That is why Fuller speaks of an 'inner morality of law'.

We need to take this more gradually. For Fuller the purpose of legality is to prevent our being governed by arbitrary will. What this means is that law is there to prevent our domination by the arbitrary will of officials and others who claim to know what is best for us. It is there to open up, and to preserve, free communication between people. That is why, for Fuller, the proper way of 'putting ourselves under the governance of rules' is through legality, understood as a complex ideal embracing standards for assessing and criticising decisions *that purport to be legal*. Where this ideal exists, according to Fuller, official action is enmeshed in and restrained by the web of rules, and no power is immune from criticism or completely free to follow its own bent, however well intentioned. That is why law is to be seen as intrinsically involving a procedural *inner morality* that comprises the eight principles we examined above.

While the ideal of reciprocity requires a firm commitment to the fulfilment of all eight principles of legality, this does not mean – with the exception of publicity – that they can all equally be fully realised on all occasions. Fuller uses the language of 'aspiration' to account for this. According to him, one might usefully distinguish between a 'morality of aspiration' and a 'morality of duty'. Aspiration sets the standards of excellence towards which any practice (including the practice of lawmaking) must strive; 'duty' sets the minimum threshold below which any realisation of that aspiration cannot fall without giving the lie to the aspiration. Fuller's lawmaker Rex should strive to realise clarity in the knowledge that it cannot fully be achieved in the writing of all laws; what he cannot do however without giving the lie to the practice of lawmaking is fall below the threshold ('duty') where his laws are incomprehensible to the citizens. Similarly with the other requirements of legality, laws do change over time and constancy is sacrificed in that measure; principles of strict liability do in some sense demand the impossible in holding actors liable for consequences that they may have done everything in their power to prevent; and sometimes in the case of common law judgements, which change or 'develop' the law, the principle of non-retroactivity may appear to be compromised (see, for example, the 'marital rape' cases, *Stallard v HMA* in Scotland or R v R in England).

Hart famously objected to Fuller identifying the requirements that make legality possible as a 'morality'. For Hart this had been a purely formal account of the rule of law that has no necessary moral dimension as such. After all, couldn't even a fascist, or racist, or other totalitarian government meet these ideals without sacrificing its programme? For Hart this supposed 'inner morality' is perfectly compatible with the pursuit of immoral ends. If principles that ensure the effectiveness or efficiency of a particular practice are identified as an 'inner morality' then we would be able to speak of the 'inner morality of poisoning' and other absurdities. Efficiency, for Hart, should not be confused with morality.

But Fuller's point is a deeper one. His contention is that before you make that argument about law you have to know the point of law; or rather, that any argument about the law must be sensitive to its purpose. If you see law as a social technique for the ordering of society then Hart's objection that collapses 'inner morality' into efficiency may have some bite. For then, law is seen as nothing more than a neutral technique for managing a society, and with the separation of means and ends, perhaps the question of efficiency does indeed become something distinct from moral value. But law is not just a technique. If, like Fuller, you see law as committed to the moral purpose of bringing about reciprocity, then the means of achieving it (clarity, prospectivity, etc) acquire a moral dimension of their own: they are all aspects of what makes possible that reciprocity.

Fuller follows Aristotle here, for whom the conditions of excellence of a practice are internal to the practice. The practice of law is the 'enterprise of subjecting oneself to the governance of rules' and thereby eliminating the arbitrary from everyday life. The principles of law are instances of precisely that enterprise that comes replete with value. Although pertaining to the form of law (general, clear, prospective, etc), the eight principles that make law possible, make possible the rational enterprise of bringing about the principle of reciprocity upon which legal order and with it the principles of a well-run society rest.

Although the important work of John Finnis will be discussed in greater depth in the next section, one might already in this discussion of legality and form borrow an important insight from him. It has to do with the notion of *practical reasonableness*. One thing, he claims, which any healthy community requires, is some common authority. Unless we all in common accede to the authority of some common code of conduct we cannot live together in community at all. And the implementation of any common code of conduct requires the institutionalisation of some agency or agencies, which adjudicate upon breaches of the common code. The more complex a political society becomes, the more rich and varied are the opportunities it presents for diverse manifestations of the good. But the more that is so, the more we face problems of co-ordination with each other. Hence the more sophisticated are the common public agencies we need for adjudication, administration, enforcement and amendment or enrichment of our common and authoritative code of social conduct. The achievement of co-ordination, which is the achievement of law, becomes in this way of thinking a means of human flourishing – the achievement of moral good. Law is both part of the procedure for arriving at things and part of the good itself. We will discuss the idea of the 'good' below. For now suffice it to note how Finnis's argument about practical reason lends further credence to Fuller's view that law requires reciprocity and connection. It is more than a neutral means of organising a society; rather, it is something that is a moral enterprise in itself. That way of living is in itself morally good for us. It is in this way that the rule of law becomes itself a shared interaction that both protects and enriches us.

Waldron and the 'procedural' defence of the rule of law

In one of the more recent engagements with, and critique of, the legal positivist position, Jeremy Waldron updates and renews Fuller's critique in ways that have important bearing on how we think about what it means to be governed by law as opposed to other forms of rule and discipline. According to the legal positivist approach, argues Waldron, the rule of law (or what we may also call the principles of legality) is 'simply one of a number of ideals (such as justice, liberty, or equality) that we apply to the law, rather than anything more intimately connected with the very idea of law itself' (Waldron 2008, p 59). On this account, it is possible, as we have just seen, to establish what the law is independently of political or moral values. Waldron argues that this view is incorrect. Instead, he says, 'we cannot really grasp the concept of law without *at the same time* understanding the values comprised in the Rule of Law' (Waldron 2008, p 10, emphasis added). Identifying valid law cannot therefore be done first, and then the question of the values of the rule of law be analysed and applied (or not, as the case may be) separately. The rule of law, writes Waldron, 'is an ideal designed to correct dangers of abuse that arise in general when political power is exercised, not dangers of abuse that arise from law in particular' (Waldron 2008, p 11). Choosing *law* as the way of checking or organising the exercise of political power – that is choosing 'governance through *law*' rather than through management or decree – means that law itself is 'prescribed as the remedy, rather than identified as the problem that a separate ideal – the Rule of Law – seeks to remedy' (Waldron 2008, p 11). The rule of law is not then an optional add-on to the question of legal validity, but is inextricably connected to what it means to be able to identify valid law at all.

To defend this approach, Waldron argues that we need to pay particular attention to the '*procedural* and *argumentative* aspects of legal practice' (Waldron 2008, p 5, emphasis added) that together connect what most people regard as the basic aspects of the rule of law with a richer account of the law's role in protecting and enhancing underlying values of human dignity and responsibility. To understand this better Waldron offers an analogy with the use of the term 'democracy'. The former East Germany called itself the German Democratic Republic. Yet what it was and what it called itself were two different things: no one, least of all its citizens, was taken in by the label 'democratic'. In order to *be* a democracy, certain standards have to be met, for example regularly held free and fair elections. In other words, there are certain conditions that provide independent criteria for identification of that practice as a democracy, regardless as to how it is self-described.

Is the same true of the use of the terms law and legal system? Are there criteria that must be met independently for their application to be legitimate? Waldron argues that there are, and is critical of legal positivists for being far too casual, too generous, in employing the term law to refer to any system of centralised order whose rules need only be efficacious and identifiable (in Hart's case, for example, by reference to an elite's rule of recognition). For Waldron, to qualify for the designation law, or legal system, requires something more than merely what legal positivists would have us believe, because 'to describe an exercise of power as an instance of law-making or law-application is already to dignify it with a certain *character*' (Waldron 2008, p 12, emphasis added). Such 'character' may or may not be actually present in a centrally organised order. So, just as a state that calls itself democratic may in fact not be, '[n]ot every system of command and control that calls itself a legal system is a legal system' (Waldron 2008, pp 13–14). We must go beyond the claims of legal positivists by understanding the *inseparability* of principles of legality and the existence of that which we dignify with the title law.

What then are the special features that are required to achieve the character of law and legal system? Waldron argues that there are five. First, there must be courts. By courts we understand not just institutions that apply the law to individual cases, but something much richer than this. Courts are bodies that apply the law in a particular way, providing an impartial third party to adjudicate between litigants. But most importantly, they do so under certain *procedural* conditions. For example, they hear and allow submissions from both sides, and they offer the opportunity for challenges to evidence and interpretation to both sides according to predetermined rules of evidence and procedure. Moreover, the examination and testing of the case are done in 'open court', and the reasons given for a decision likewise made publicly available. When we read about states where the rule of law is deemed under threat, a common reason for that threat is precisely because of a breakdown in or failure to instantiate those procedural guarantees that we associate with the existence of courts; for example, secret decisions of unknown officials where one party may not be able to find out what the evidence and rules being applied are. In such cases, we may not only criticise the fairness of the process, but ask whether the rulings of such bodies should be dignified with the title of legal at all.

The second characteristic identifies the need for 'general public norms'. The generality of norms was a factor we considered earlier when we looked at Fuller's work, and Waldron shares his insights here, noting that law's generality makes an important contribution to instantiating the 'principles of impersonality and equality' (Waldron 2008, p 25) that are central to a conception of law. Waldron also gives special emphasis to the value of 'publicity'. Where it is lacking, for example where the creation and application of secret or unknowable directives are being used to discipline citizens, this might well involve the exercise of centrally organised power, but that is no reason for calling such an exercise of power law. For Waldron, unlike the mere coercing of human behaviour, or the herding of animals, people who are governed by law require to be made publicly aware of, or at least capable of finding out with assistance, the normative rules that apply to them. Only if this is the case are they being treated as responsible agents capable of understanding these rules *as* normative demands (things they ought to do but may not) and making decisions according to this knowledge. Taken together then, the first and second characteristics of law and legality combine firstly to respect people's 'dignity as beings capable of explaining themselves' and secondly to be 'respectful of persons as agents; it respects the dignity of voluntary action and rational self control' (Waldron 2008, p 28).

Waldron describes the 'positivity of law' as the third essential characteristic, but takes it to have more significance than that described by the legal positivists. Both share the idea that human law is posited (positive) law, and thus understand that as a 'mode of governance' it is made by people rather than discovered through some mystical or transcendental insights. But buried at the heart of this observation is something more fundamental. That law is humanly made means that it can change, by human means. That it could be different from what it is now means that the very 'idea of law, therefore, conveys an elementary sense of freedom, a sense that we are free to have whatever laws we like' (Waldron 2008, p 31). Of course, there may be many obstacles in the way of achieving this, some of which may be desirable, some not. But again where the rule of law is under threat, and where the exercise of power takes a non-legal form, it is precisely this very elementary aspect of freedom that is often denied.

Fourth, Waldron identifies another aspect to 'publicness' in these terms: the fact that the law 'presents itself in a certain way – as standing in the name of the public and as oriented to the public good . . . [is] one of its defining characteristics' (Waldron 2008, pp 31–32, emphasis added). The matter of 'presentation' is important here, since any particular legal system or set of laws may not in fact deliver something that seems good for all. But that failure is different, says Waldron, from failing aspirationally to try to achieve or aim at the common good. We should not dignify as 'law' a set of orders or commands that simply seek to promote the interests of a few and which explicitly disavow the general and equal application of norms to all in the name of all. To qualify for the label of law, legal institutions and laws must therefore 'orient themselves in their public presence to the good of the community – in other words, to issues of justice and the common good that transcend the self-interest of the powerful' (Waldron 2008, p 31). Comparing Hart's claim, we might say that where many people in a society are treated in a sheep-like manner, and the sheep 'end in the slaughter-house' there is, on this principle, *every* reason for 'denying it the title of a legal system'.

The final characteristic Waldron calls 'systematicity'. Again this is a richer notion than that offered by the legal positivists' account of system validity. It invokes the sense in which the positive rules of the system all cohere. This is most commonly achieved through demanding a coherence of values that underpin the particular rules. It is perhaps most evident in common law judging (and we will turn to this with respect to judicial reasoning in later sections, and especially in the work of Dworkin and MacCormick), but it applies to legislation too. In positing new laws, legislation too should be understood as fitting into an ongoing body of law that has coherence as a whole, often explicitly provided by tests of constitutionality. Systematicity in this sense is not just a matter of identifying valid law – though it also involves this – but includes a more profound value: 'It means that law can present itself to its subjects as a unified enterprise of governance that one can make sense of' (Waldron 2008, p 35).

For Waldron, having law, as opposed to other means of governing, requires seeing law as a common 'public resource', and while this requires a certain predictability it is, just as importantly, a resource for argumentation and contestation. This requires the procedurally guaranteed opportunity to debate the meaning not only of what the law ought to be but what the law actually is and requires. This 'arguable' character of law, as MacCormick calls it, is central to what we understand as legal practice, typified in the testing of arguments for and against particular propositions of law by advocates in court.

And it is centrally in debates in legal argument over what the quality of coherence – or systematicity in this expanded sense – means that legal institutions again uphold the rationality and dignity of those subject to it. Legal positivists overlook this larger sense and so offer an impoverished account of law. This is the case not merely with respect to an aspirational quality, but to something that is descriptively essential to what it means to have governance through law at all: as Waldron puts it, '[c]ourts, hearings and arguments are aspects of law which are not optional extras; they are integral parts of how law works and they are indispensable to the package of law's respect for human agency' (Waldron 2008, p 60).

These five characteristics show, says Waldron, that a non-evaluative account of legal validity is descriptively wrong. To have valid law and a valid legal system requires knowing that governance through law means something different than just the deployment of centrally organised power. It means the working presence of procedural and institutional elements that the legal positivist account does not provide. It means understanding the congruence between these elements and legal validity in such a way that is not optional. In precisely the same way that holding regular free and fair elections is a non-optional requirement for having a democracy, the *concept* of law and ideal of the *rule* of law must be understood together and simultaneously, not separately and sequentially.

The question of content

Radbruch and 'intolerable injustice'

In the final part of our discussion, the problem of identifying valid law turns directly to the question of the substantive *content* of the law. Most concisely, we can ask, is Kelsen correct to say that *any* kind of content can be law?

One of the most important negative answers to this question was given by the twentieth-century German legal theorist Gustav Radbruch. In response to the Nazi atrocities from 1933 to 1945, Radbruch offered an analysis that was profoundly critical of legal positivism's claims. His views influenced not only fellow legal theorists but also lawyers and judges among whose tasks was to argue and decide cases which had to assess the validity or otherwise of Nazi-period enactments. Was it possible that a policy of mass extermination was also legal? Could those who were involved in the perpetration of mass slaughter defend their actions against accusers by saying that what they did was legally authorised at the time they did it? Did the legal positivist understanding that 'a law is a law' mean that there was nothing more to be said about the legal validity of such acts than that while they might be humanly abominable, they were nonetheless still lawful? Radbruch did not think so, and the German Federal Constitutional Court has endorsed his analysis in its own reasoning.

There is one kind of reason here that appears in an argument of an immediate post-war German prosecutor reported by Radbruch. The case concerned the prosecution of a man, Puttfarken, who had, as a clerk in the Justice Department during the Nazi period, informed on another man (Gottig) to the authorities for writing on a wall that 'Hitler is a mass murderer and to blame for the war'. Puttfarken's denouncement had led to Gottig's trial, conviction and execution. Standing trial himself now, as an accomplice to murder, could Puttfarken claim that what he had done was legal at the time? The prosecutor comments:

> Anyone who informed on another during these years had to know – and did in fact know – that he was delivering up the accused to arbitrary power, not consigning him to a lawful procedure with legal guarantees for determining the truth and arriving at a just decision.
>
> (quoted in Radbruch 2006/1946, p 2)

This clearly resonates with Waldron's claim that the rule of law, and indeed, the law itself, requires certain procedural guarantees in order to qualify as legal. Where these disappear to be replaced by exercises of force, such as in Nazi Germany, then we are entitled, as the prosecutor urges, to no longer call this a legal system.

Puttfarken was found guilty, and the problems of how to deal with informants, and indeed with the judges who had acted on the information in sentencing to death those like Gottig, was one that surfaced in a number of instances. But important as these were, they were of course not the worst of the atrocities associated with Nazi rule. The extermination of millions of Jews and others by the regime raised profound questions about the defensibility of actions under the supposed imprimatur of the state and its law. It was here that Radbruch's analysis about the *content* of law became most important.

Radbruch's 'formula', as it has become known, states that 'extreme injustice is no law': 'Where there is not even an attempt at justice, where equality, the core of justice, is deliberately betrayed in the issuance of positive law, then the statute is not merely "flawed law", it lacks completely the very nature of law.' In light of this, the Nazi state did not create bad, albeit still valid, law. In Radbruch's view it did not create law at all: 'it never attained the dignity of valid law' (Radbruch 2006/1946, p 7). As lawyers say in other contexts, it was void *ab initio*.

This is the core of the claim that political and moral values – centrally, justice and equality – *do* limit what counts as valid law. In the task of identifying valid law, for Radbruch there are certain contents that simply *cannot* be law.

Radbruch is careful to acknowledge that there are often complaints that positive law produces injustices or perceived immoralities, and that these complaints are often valid. And as a lawyer he maintains that in the vast majority of these cases, the validity of the positive law must still prevail, for reasons including the need to stabilise legal expectations. 'Any statute is better than no statute at all,' he argues, 'since it at least creates legal certainty' (Radbruch 2006/1946, p 6). But this cannot be conclusive of the matter of legal validity as such. There are other cases where 'the conflict between statute and justice reaches such an intolerable degree, [that] the statute, as "flawed law", must yield to justice' (Radbruch 2006/1946, p 7). Such cases of 'extreme injustice' cross the threshold of 'intolerability' in such a way that even instances of 'appropriately enacted and socially effective norms lose their legal character' (Alexy 1999, p 17). Such enactments may be collectively organised forms of action which sanction conformity, but because of their content they are not merely politically or morally repugnant, they are legally invalid. These exercises of power, such as those carried out by the Nazis, might in fact 'serve as a basis for the "must" of compulsion, but [they] never serve as basis for the "ought" of obligation or for legal validity' (Radbruch 2006/1946, p 6). There is a limit in precisely that respect, which consists in the political-moral threshold test for validity.

But is what counts as 'extreme injustice' not liable to be open to dispute? Radbruch acknowledges that it may be, and that no clear defining line can be drawn here between extreme ('intolerable') and merely 'tolerable' injustice. But this does not of itself invalidate the formula, since the fact that one cannot identify a clear line does not mean that you cannot identify instances of extreme injustice. There can be little controversy over the fact that, as the Federal Constitutional Court expressed it, 'the attempt to destroy physically and materially certain parts of one's population, including women and children, in accordance with "racial" criteria' constitutes 'extreme injustice' (Alexy 1999, p 33). That, at least, is a clear case.

This example, says Robert Alexy, is decisive and shows that there is indeed a necessary connection between legal validity and moral and political values. And it is underpinned by the fact that, besides being socially effective and requiring procedural techniques for establishing how to make or change law, there is something more fundamental about law that necessarily determines the limits of its content.

This is what Alexy calls law's 'claim to correctness'. Imagine, he says, a new constitution being enacted by a state in which the majority is suppressed by the minority, and whose opening line is this: 'X is a sovereign, federal and unjust republic.' There seems to be something intuitively wrong with this. It is not simply that it is unconventional or that it might be politically imprudent. Nor even that it is morally problematic. There is a deeper flaw that is signalled by it seeming 'somehow crazy' (Alexy 1999, p 28). The reason for its absurdity lies in the fact that it contains a profound *contradiction* because 'a claim to correctness is necessarily bound up with the act of giving a constitution, and in such cases it is above all a claim to justice' (Alexy 1999, p 29). There is a 'performative contradiction' in the constitutional provision in that a constitution or law that explicitly states its own injustice contradicts what we implicitly understand constitutions and laws to be. Constitutions and laws claim, at least implicitly, to be correct or right – not wrong or unjust. It is this claim, concludes Alexy, that 'determines the character of law. It excludes understanding law as a mere command of the powerful' (Alexy 1999, p 28).

Radbruch's formula was deployed in post-war legal reasoning to invalidate many Nazi-era enactments. It also resurfaced in legal argument after the fall of the Berlin Wall in 1989. Several former East German soldiers were prosecuted for shooting those trying to cross the wall from East to West Berlin. Their defence was that their acts were legally authorised at the time. The Federal Court of Justice used Radbruch's 'intolerability' thesis in deciding that the acts were 'an offence to a higher order of law [and] manifested a patently gross offence to the fundamental tenets of justice and humanity', and so concluded that the 'border law' the soldiers sought to rely on in their defence had 'from the outset no validity.'

Finnis, the common good and the 'focal meaning' of law

This point about 'a higher order of law' is one that has a profound resonance throughout the natural law tradition. The idea that there are values, grasped through the exercise of reason, that transcend any particular state's laws, and that these values hold good independently of whether any state in fact recognises them, has been an important motivator of political ideas and practices, as well as in defences and critiques of the law. That their claimed reasonableness and universality has meant different things over time has also, perhaps ironically, been an essential part of the tradition. In their conservative mode, for example, they have at certain periods defended as natural the status quo of slavery and patriarchy; in their revolutionary mode – as natural or inalienable rights – they have inspired the overthrow of governments. And in their recent instantiation as 'universal human rights' they have held government acts up to scrutiny in light of principles deemed essential to what it means to be human. And it is the relation between funda-mental values and positive law that has always, according to John Finnis, been at the heart of answers to the central questions posed by natural law theories:

> How and why can law . . . give its subjects sound reason for acting in accordance with it? How can a rule's, or a judgment's, or an institution's legal ("formal" or "sys-tem") validity, or its facticity as a social phenomenon, make it authoritative in its subject's deliberations?
>
> (Finnis 2007, s 1)

In light of this, it is specifically with respect to the validity of legal norms in the face of political and moral injustice that Radbruch's formula extends a tradition going back to St Thomas Aquinas and beyond which finds expression in the Latin phrase 'lex iniustia non est lex'. This should not, argues Finnis, be taken to mean that 'an unjust law is not a law' in any simplistic sense. Rather it means that an unjust law is 'not straightforwardly or unqualifiedly a law'. That is, in noting that it is an unjust law, it is still recognised there is law but only in a distorted sense, in the same way we might say that 'an invalid argu-ment is no argument' or a 'disloyal friend is not a friend' (Finnis 2007). In declaring a particular instance of law as being a distortion in this respect, there may be occasions where legal validity still overrides moral or political objections to its injustice, and where the proper question becomes: should, in conscience, this valid law still be obeyed? But there may be other instances, such as those Radbruch's formula identifies in the case of Nazi atrocities, where we say more than this: that in the 'extreme injustice' of its content, the law fails to create legal obligations since the enactment itself fails to be legally valid.

For Finnis, although the law can be seen as a system, it is not from its pedigree that it gets its normativity, but from its function of bringing about the common good. Finnis follows Aristotle in arguing that men and women are inclined towards leading 'flourishing lives' (eudaimonia in Aristotle) in realising values or goods that are basic for them, and whose realisation can only be achieved in common with others. The latter is what led Aristotle to identify the city (the polis) as the context of human flourishing, and Finnis to talk about community. What are these basic goods? Finnis lists seven: life, knowledge, play, aesthetic experience, friendship, practical reasonableness and religion (Finnis 1980, pp 85–90). The basic goods are goods in themselves; they are objectively good, and self-evident: they furnish the basis of moral justification; they are not them-selves in need of further justification. The fact that these goods furnish intelligible ends for human life presenting problems of balancing between the requirements they present in concrete situations for each individual, and problems of coordinating amongst individuals who are all pursuing their own instantiations of these goods presents us with the need of law. For Finnis, law, as a form of practical reasoning, advances the common good by instantiating the basic goods.

On the one hand, legal reasoning, as a form of practical reason, expresses and sub-stantiates the basic goods. Reasonable and sociable beings must recognise their need for community with others as the necessary context for pursuing the good. The creation of a condition in which all members of a community have full opportunity to participate in the good (to use their practical reasonableness in realising other goods) is the realisation of a good shared by all members of the community. Law facilitates this pursuit.

The second thing that has to be remembered in Finnis's analysis is his emphasis that what any healthy community requires is some common authority. As was noted earlier, unless we all in common accede to the authority of some common code of conduct we cannot live together in community at all. And the implementation of any common code of conduct requires the institutionalisation of some agency or agencies, which adjudicate upon breaches of the common code. The more complex a political society becomes, the more rich and varied are the opportunities it presents for diverse manifestations of the good. But the more that is so, the more we face problems of co-ordination, each with another. Hence the more sophisticated are the common pub-lic agencies we need for adjudication, administration, enforcement and amendment or enrichment of our common and authoritative code of social conduct.

This links to another significant point about legal reasoning. Finnis employs Aqui-nas's idea of *determinatio* (as adapted from Aristotle) to express how the very abstract requirements of the good acquire specific form and present us with concrete moral imperatives. The flourishing of life, of knowledge, and so on, as basic goods, is pitched at too abstract a level to give guidance in practical dilemmas, which require the mediation of practical reason and, paradigmatically in this context, of legal reason. As occupying the middle space between what drives human endeavour (common goods) and concrete situations calling for regulation, legal reasoning, for Finnis, establishes itself, necessarily, as a species of practical reason and this, again necessarily, ties it to morality.

Clear analytical thinking, object positivists, demands that we separate the 'is' and the 'ought', questions of what the law is from questions of what it ought to be. A defi-nition of law, they say, must deploy criteria proper for description, not evaluation. The primary task is to identify the law; to evaluate or criticise it comes as a second step. Finnis presents a powerful methodological objection to this fundamental thesis as the basis of his own defence of natural law at the beginning of his *Natural Law and Natural Rights* (1980).

> A theorist wishes to describe, say, law as a social institution. But the conceptions of law (and of jus, lex, droit, nomos, . . .) which people have entertained, and have used to shape their own conduct, are quite varied. The subject-matter of the theo-rist's description does not come neatly demarcated from other features of social life and practice. . . . Can the theorist do more, then, than list these varying conceptions and practices and their corresponding labels? How does the theorist decide what is to count as law for the purposes of his description?
>
> (Finnis 1980, p 4)

Finnis takes Kelsen to task. He finds in Kelsen 'no critical attention to the methodological problem of *selecting* concepts for the purposes of a value-free or descriptive' theory of law (Finnis, 1980, p 5, emphasis added). What he *does* find, however, is awareness *that point or function* is intrinsic to the descriptive understanding of the subject matter. So Kelsen defines law as a specific social technique; for Kelsen law is 'the social technique which consists in bringing about the desired social conduct of men through the threat of a measure of coercion which is to be applied in case of contrary conduct' (Finnis, 1980, p 5).

'But how does Kelsen propose to justify the definition itself?' asks Finnis. He quotes Kelsen:

> 'What could the social order of a negro tribe under the leadership of a despotic chieftain – an order likewise called "law" – have in common with the constitution of the Swiss republic? *[Let us interject to ask: Who is doing this calling, this naming? Whose willingness so to refer to the tribe's social order (in language expressing distinctions which the despotic chieftain and his subjects do not care to make) is thus being made decisive?]* Yet there is a common element that fully justifies this terminology ... for the word refers to that specific social technique which, despite the vast differences ... is yet essentially the same for all these peoples differing so much in time, in place, and in culture.'
>
> (Finnis 1980, pp 5–6)

How revealing this interjection of Finnis's! It confronts Kelsen with the objection that he has in fact *chosen* to include the chieftain's despotic regime under the extension of the concept law because he treats 'the technique that brings about a specific social conduct' (see above) as *decisive*. Finnis builds up his objection more gradually:

> What could be simpler? One [Kelsen] takes the word 'law'. Ignoring a wide range of meanings and reference (as in 'law of nature', 'moral law', 'sociological law', 'international law', 'ecclesiastical law', 'law of grammar'), and further ignoring alternative ways of referring to, e.g., the 'negro tribe's' social order', one looks at the range of subject-matter signified by the word in the usage which one has (without explanation) selected. One looks for 'a common element'. This one thing common is the criterion of the 'essence' of law, and thus the one feature used to characterize and to explain descriptively the whole subject-matter. There is thus one concept, which can be predicated equally and in the same sense (i.e. univocally) of everything which, in a pre-theoretical usage (which the theorist allows to determine his theoretical usage), somebody was willing to call 'law'.
>
> (Finnis 1980, p 6)

'Pre-theoretical' is a term that matters here, because (for the positivist) it captures the first 'descriptive' moment of gathering the instances of law, as if such gathering is possible without a principle of selection and based only on the semantic descriptor 'law'. The business of theorising law (for the positivist) comes then at a second step, after the work that 'a flatly univocal meaning of theoretical terms [here 'law']' has led the search for a lowest common denominator or highest common factor or for the 'one thing common'. To contest this, Finnis adopts from Aristotle the notion of 'focal meaning'. Every attempt, he says, to define an institution must elevate certain criteria as significant, and this choice necessarily carries an element of evaluation. 'From what viewpoint, and relative to what concerns, are importance and significance to be assessed?' Instances of law do not carry identifying labels that would allow their 'pre-theoretical' aggregation. Theoretical engagement always furnishes the criterion of selection. And that criterion has to do with what one theorises as the relevant key value (focal meaning) of the institution.

Take another example, one on which Aristotle insisted, that of friendship. There are more or less peripheral cases (business friendship, friendship of convenience, cupboard love, casual and play relations, etc). On the one hand, there is no point in denying that the peripheral cases are instances of friendship. Indeed, the study of them is illuminated by thinking of them as watered-down versions of the central cases, or sometimes as exploitations of human attitudes shaped by reference to the central case. But they are that, peripheral, because they are relatively problematic instantiations of what is the significant thing about friendship – what one can credibly theorise as its constitutive value and necessary underpinning: loyalty. Peripheral cases of friendship are peripheral because they are remoter approximations of loyalty. And, arguably, beyond a certain point they can no longer be seen even as peripheral in the way that someone who claims to be another's 'disloyal friend', we might argue, misunderstands the meaning of friendship. There is a clear parallel here between the theorisation of friendship and of law: the identification of instances of either require a theorisation (neither are 'pre-theoretical') of what criteria are elevated as significant to the identification of a practice as friendship or as law.

Here is Finnis:

> Practical philosophy is a disciplined and critical reflection on the goods that can be realized in human action and the requirements of practical reasonableness. So when we say that descriptive theorists (whose purposes are not practical) must proceed, in their indispensable selection and formation of concepts, by adopting a practical point of view, we mean that they must assess importance or significance in similarities and differences within their subject-matter by asking what would be considered important or significant in that field by those whose concerns, decisions, and activities create or constitute the subject-matter.
>
> (Finnis 1980, p 10)

He will relate this 'long march through the working or implicit methodology of contemporary analytical jurisprudence' eventually to the hermeneutic method of Max Weber, who

> arrive[d] at the conclusion more rapidly (though on the basis of a much wider social science): namely, that the evaluations of the theorist himself are an indispensable and decisive component in the selection or formation of any concepts for use in description of such aspects of human affairs as law or legal order. For theorists cannot identify the central case of that practical viewpoint which they use to identify the central case of their subject-matter, unless they decide what the requirements of practical reasonableness really are, in relation to this whole aspect of human affairs and concerns. In relation to law, the most important things for the theorist to know and describe are the things which, in the judgment of the theorist, make it important from a practical viewpoint to have law – the things which it is, therefore, important in practice to 'see to' when ordering human affairs. And when these 'important things' are (in some or even in many societies) in fact missing, or debased, or exploited or otherwise deficient, then the most important things for the theorist to describe are those aspects of the situation that manifest this absence, debasement, exploitation, or deficiency.
>
> (Finnis 1980, p 16)

He asks:

> Does this mean that descriptive jurisprudence (and social science as a whole) is
> inevitably subject to every theorist's conceptions and prejudices about what is good
> and practically reasonable? Yes and no. 'Yes', in so far as there is no escaping the
> theoretical requirement that a judgment of significance and importance must be
> made if theory is to be more than a vast rubbish heap of miscellaneous facts
> described in a multitude of incommensurable terminologies.
>
> (Finnis 1980, p 17)

And he concludes:

> The descriptions are not deduced from the evaluations; but without the evaluations
> one cannot determine what descriptions are really illuminating and significant.

Let us conclude this discussion of the separation of law from morals with a discussion
of the famous case of *Airedale National Health Service Trust v Bland* ([1993] 2 WLR 316). The
facts are well known. Anthony Bland had suffered severe injury in the Hillsborough
Stadium disaster. He never recovered consciousness and remained in a persistent vegetative state (PVS). Medical experts judged that he had no prospect of recovery or
improvement. The Trust applied for a declaration to remove all of the treatment,
including feeding, which was keeping him alive. The House of Lords granted the
declaration.

Clearly in this case several stark and central issues of morality are at play. Is the outcome morally justified? Is it justified by the state of the law? Is it worse to kill than it is
to let die? How are we to assess the boundary between life and death? Are either of these
distinctions morally significant? Is quality of life an issue with which the courts should
concern themselves in these cases? The Lords struggled with these issues: witness Lord
Browne-Wilkinson's agonising over the decision (as quoted in Finnis 1993, p 329):

> The conclusion I have reached will appear to some to be almost irrational. How can
> it be lawful to allow a patient to die slowly, though painlessly, over a period of weeks
> from lack of food but unlawful to produce his immediate death by a lethal injection,
> thus saving his family from yet another ordeal . . .? I find it difficult to find a moral
> answer to that question. But it is undoubtedly the law.

But if analytical clarity is our priority, Finnis would insist, how do the positivist judges
in *Bland* purport seriously to maintain the distinction between an ethical response and
'what is undoubtedly the law'? Is it really rational to distinguish between two courses of
action (one 'legal', the other 'illegal') that are undertaken by the same actor (the medical
profession) with the same intention (to bring about the termination of Bland's life), and
having the same result (the termination of Bland's life) because one is performed
through a commission of an act (e.g, by lethal injection) and the other the omission of
an act (withdrawing life-sustaining treatment)? Finnis is of course arguing that a 'basic
good', life, should under no rationale – moral or legal – be terminated; we may agree
or disagree on the ethics of that. But has he perhaps pointed out in the 'irrationality' of
that distinction a certain irrationality of a legal decision – Lord Browne-Wilkinson's

'what is undoubtedly the law' – that is at pains to keep itself pure of ethics, establishing its credentials on what is properly legal alone?

Reading

The theory of legal positivism has generated a large literature, both favourable and critical. The most important starting points for further reading are the main twentieth-century proponents Hart (1961), Kelsen (1957, 1967, 1992) and Raz (1980). For the most concise account of legal positivism, see Hart (1958). A helpful summary (esp. ss 1, 2 and 4) of legal positivism is available at http://plato.stanford.edu/entries/legal-positivism/. A sympathetic treatment of Hart's work is provided by MacCormick (2008). Lacey's biography of Hart (2004) situates his work within the jurisprudential debates and social milieu of the period. Tur and Twining (1986) provide an important engagement with Kelsen's work, as do Paulson and Paulson (1998). On John Austin's 'command theory of Law' (1995/1832), see also Schauer (2015). On the positivist/natural law divide that has dominated analytical jurisprudence, see, in particular, Dworkin (1977).

For Hart's engagement with Dworkin, see his 1979 lecture (published in Hart 2016). For a contextualisation of the sociological significance of questions about the nature of legal validity to the rise of legal modernity, see Part I.

D' Entrèves (1965), Stone (1965) and Finnis (1980) offer perhaps the best introductions, from quite different perspectives, to natural law thinking. Finnis (2007) is an excellent short introduction. For Finnis's definition of law, see (1980, pp 276–90). His methodological stance on the evaluation and description of law, and focal meaning, is developed in chapter 1 of Finnis (1980). For the discussion of *Bland*, see Finnis (1993), and for a concise account of the relation of natural law to ethics, see Finnis (1999). Finnis's work has now been collected in a series of five volumes (Finnis 2011). See especially volume IV.

Alexy (1999) provides a succinct analysis of Radbruch's theory as well as engaging directly with a range of legal positivist critiques of his views. For a useful biography of Fuller, see Summers (1984). The 'Hart-Fuller' debate can be found here: H.L.A. Hart (1958) [on the 'informer', see esp. pp 615–621] and Lon L. Fuller (1958) [see esp. Section 5]. David Dyzenhaus, 'The Grudge Informer Case Revisited', *NYU Law Review* (2008, pp 1000–1034), provides an extensive re-appraisal of the debate – [on the 'informer', see esp. pp 615–621]; Lon L. Fuller, 'Positivism and Fidelity to Law – A Reply to Professor Hart', p 71; *Harvard Law Review*, p 630 (1958) [see esp. Section 5]. For an application of Fuller's theory to 'wicked legal systems', see Dyzenhaus (2010) for apartheid South Africa, and for a recent restatement, see Rundle (2012). On the rule of law more generally, see Bingham (2011) and Gowder (2016).

II

Theories of legal reasoning

13 Formalism and rule-scepticism   167

   The promise of formalism   167

   The challenge of American legal realism   173

14 The turn to interpretation   182

   Hart and the 'open texture' of legal
      language   182

   MacCormick and the limits of discretion   184

   Dworkin, justification and integrity   188

15 The politics of legal reasoning   193

   Critical legal theory   193

   The U.S. critical legal studies movement   194

   Feminist critiques of adjudication   198

Introduction

Consider the following scenario. A woman gives birth to conjoined twins. Unless some attempt is made to separate the twins, both, according to medical opinion, will die a short time after birth. The couple has travelled from the island of Gozo, off Malta, to Manchester seeking medical assistance unavailable in Malta. While medical intervention to separate them is possible, and while it might keep one twin alive, the other would necessarily die. Of the two, the weaker twin, Mary, was only alive due to the supply of oxygenated blood from her sister, Jodie, without which she would have died anyway and could not have been resuscitated. The parents, guided by their religious beliefs, are opposed to any medical intervention, refusing to contemplate, let alone authorise, that one of their children should die to let the other survive. The doctors, on the other hand, are under a professional duty to try to save life and a legal duty to act in the best interests of the children. But what are the best interests of the children, in the *plural*, when one can live at the expense, and only at the expense, of the other? In the face of the parents' unwillingness to have them undergo an operation, the doctors apply to a court to have the legal authority granted to them to go ahead with the operation. How should the court decide? Can they decide on the basis of moral beliefs about life? Are these to play any role at all? Is the cost of treatment a relevant factor at all to be considered? Or must they follow existing legal rules? But what happens in a situation where there are, or seem to be, no pre-existing rules?

The judges of the Court of Appeal, in this case, after agonising over it, decided in favour of lawful separation but on the basis of very different lines of reasoning. The surgical operation was performed and, as expected, Mary died and Jodie lived.

Take a second case. Five days after the 2001 UK *Anti-terrorist Act* came into force, eight men were taken from their homes in the early hours to high-security prisons where they were detained as category A prisoners. They were immediately locked up in solitary cells for 22–23 hours a day; and for some it took about three months just to get access for family visits and telephone calls. The men were not taken to a police station for questioning and were not questioned by anyone, they did not have any allegations put to them and they were not told the reasons for their internment. Over the following few months another nine people were rounded up, and all seventeen were kept in conditions not dissimilar to Camp Delta, at Guantanamo Bay. The Court of Appeal having allowed the detention on grounds that 'the emergency which the government believes to exist justifies the taking of action which would not otherwise be acceptable', a challenge to the detention finally reached the House of Lords before a Bench of nine judges. The judges had to decide whether the 2001 Act, which gave the government the power to detain indefinitely non-nationals, was lawful; in other words whether the UK government could lawfully derogate from its obligations under the **Human Rights Act 1998** that forbids indefinite detention. The detainees argued that there was no 'national emergency threatening the life of the nation' such that would allow the derogation, and that the detention provisions discriminated against them on 'grounds of national origin'. While the court upheld the challenge on the basis that it was indeed discriminatory and disproportionate, the majority also conceded that it was not for the court to decide whether there was an emergency, and deferred to the government to determine the matter. It is worth quoting here the Attorney-General's submission as summarised by Lord Bingham in his opinion:

> [I]t is for Parliament and the executive to assess the threat facing the nation, so it [is] for these bodies and not the courts to judge the response necessary to protect the security of the public. These [are] matters of a political character calling for an exercise of political and not judicial judgement.

The aim of this part of the book is to describe the kind of arguments that are employed in legal reasoning, and the normative theories behind them, which focus on what kinds of arguments are *appropriate* to legal reasoning.

Of course, we cannot argue about what kinds of arguments are appropriate in legal reasoning unless we have an idea of what law is. If, for example, we think that all that law is a system of rules, then we might argue that legal argumentation involves merely the 'mechanical' application of those rules to cases that fall within their ambit. But then we might find it difficult to explain what it is that makes some cases so hard, and why it is that top lawyers and judges routinely disagree about what the law requires. If, alternatively, we believe that law is to be understood as an argumentative practice that necessarily engages questions of morality and politics, then that belief will incline us to reach very different conclusions about how legal argumentation is to be best understood and carried out. Or again, if we treat law as essentially an open-ended practice, where policies of 'social engineering' or conserving the status quo are the determining factors, then we will have a different view of the nature and purpose of adjudication. And so on.

We will look in this part at how theorists and judges approach and answer these questions in different ways, and what they say about the nature of legal reasoning, the nature of law and the connection between the two. If legal argument is about justifying the application of the law in terms of principles and values, then the judges may be right in engaging with moral and political justifications, or wrong to artificially exclude them. Conversely, we may be unwilling to grant judges the power to invoke moral and political argument without understanding how their reasoning may be influenced by factors they do not explicitly engage with – their professional or class background, or issues of gender or political bias.

How we answer the more general and abstract questions on the nature of law and legal reasoning bears directly on what we argue is the right solution in each and every case in law. It is in this sense that practices of adjudication and reasoning with law, their underlying features, rationality or biases, are absolutely central to an understanding of the operation of law, and are therefore in need of closer, critical, examination.

As lawyers and students of law we do of course look to the law for answers. It is not, so the assumption goes, for us as lawyers to look to politics, religion and other normative orders, or to look into our conscience to find the right legal answer. And to look to the law means fundamentally to look to the sources of law. There are a number of sources of law, including in some cases custom, in some others international treaties that are binding and generate obligations, in some cases even authoritative writings like those of Blackstone or Hume. But in most cases, as far as the common law is concerned the main sources of law are statute, the laws enacted in our parliaments, and precedent, prior binding decisions of our courts. Where the sources provide contrasting determinations, there are rules that tell us how to sort out the clash: more recent law repeals older law, constitutional law prevails over ordinary law and so on. All these sources exist as a matter of fact: they are enacted as laws, decided as cases, agreed as treaties, observed as custom. So if clear rules originating in the sources of law provide the solutions to questions of law and, in cases where these solutions conflict, provide solutions for that conflict in terms of formal tests (of repeal and constitutionality), what is there to disagree about in legal argument and how (and why) do morality and politics bear on legal argument? Is it not the case that while they do of course inform the kinds of debates we have over what law we want to enact, after that discussion is over and a decision is made (typically in our parliaments), the political disagreement ends at the point at which the law comes into being?

It is no less than the key organising principle of our constitutional systems, the separation of powers, that is at stake here. If political disagreements of the kind that are proper to Parliament, as the democratic forum, are not contained there but instead 'spill over' into arguments in courts, then the separation between the political enactment of law (in Parliament) and its legal application (in courts) is compromised. The fundamental principle of the rule of law, as we will see, is also jeopardised. Is this 'spill-over' or continuity between political and legal argument something that can and should be avoided, or might there be reasons why we might welcome it?

These are difficult but unavoidable questions, questions that frame the practice of legal reasoning even when they are not always at the forefront of our engagement with the law when we read, interpret and apply it. So before we move to these deeper questions that frame and inform the practice of legal reasoning, whether it is undertaken by judges, other state officials, teachers and students of law, or lay persons as they reason about their rights and duties under the law, let us distinguish analytically, in the way it is ordinarily done, between two moments of legal reasoning – that of reasoning about 'facts' and that of reasoning about 'rules'.

It is of course often the case that what gives rise to a dispute is a disagreement over facts. 'Fact-finding' impacts on legal reasoning, and gives rise to difficult questions over the processes and instruments we have in law for establishing what can be taken as evidence that a fact has occurred, what counts as proving that it has, according to what principles of admissibility and what standards of proof, and distribution of 'burdens' – what party, that is, carries the 'onus' of proving what. While much of this belongs to the branch of law called 'evidence' and will not be directly of concern to us here, it also of course impacts directly on what comes into view as the 'factual situation' that calls for legal response. To that extent it is of direct relevance to legal reasoning and we will discuss issues of 'fact-finding' in this part of the book. But legal reasoning is of course also crucially concerned with the 'rules', how one reasons from the 'rules' that the sources of law provide, and how to understand the interface between the two: reasoning about facts and reasoning about rules.

When it comes to understanding the 'rules' and how to deal with cases where they are not clear, judges often resort to certain 'rules of thumb': the 'literal rule', the 'golden rule' and the 'mischief rule'. The first of these prescribes that judges first of all opt for the 'literal' meaning of a rule, and it involves judges taking to the dictionary to resolve ambiguities of terms. If this exercise at retrieving the 'literal' or 'ordinary meaning' of the rule yields unreasonable results, then the 'golden rule' tells them to deviate from it or, in extreme cases, to ignore it; then the 'mischief rule' is meant to kick in and direct the judge to identify the 'mischief' that the rule was enacted to rectify, or to give effect to the law in the light of the purpose that guided its enactment.

For all their wide use these rules are obviously of limited value, either circular or, ultimately, question-begging. Only briefly, the 'golden rule' begs the question what counts as 'unreasonable' enough to trump the 'literal' interpretation; the 'literal' rule, in turn, misses the basic insight that what is the 'ordinary' meaning of any statement can only count as that given a context, and that the meaning of any statement that may be deemed 'ordinary' in some contexts is only relevant in those contexts. The 'purposive' rule either states the obvious – that a rule is enacted for a purpose which should inform its meaning – or points to very difficult questions over the 'original' intention of legislators or 'teleological' approaches to law, that a simple reference to 'purpose' merely elides. It is remarkable then that, as Francis Bennion puts it:

> Consult even the latest edition of almost any other book on statutory interpretation and you will find the same old parrot cry trotted out: 'the interpretative criteria consist of the literal rule, the mischief rule and the golden rule, and the court chooses between them.' It amounts to a serious breakdown in communication.
>
> (Bennion 2001, p 2)

He concludes:

> There is no golden rule. Nor is there a mischief rule, or a literal rule, or any other cure-all rule of thumb. Instead there are a thousand and one interpretative criteria. Fortunately, not all of these present themselves in any one case; but those that do yield factors that the interpreter must figuratively weigh and balance. That is the nearest we can get to a golden rule, and it is not very near.
>
> (Bennion 2002, pp 3–4)

In what follows we will look at theories of law and legal reasoning that have provided very different answers to the question of how one deals with 'hard' cases in law and in fact how the very distinction between hard and easy cases is drawn. It is these kinds of questions that theories of legal reasoning are concerned with, and to which we will now turn.

Chapter 13

Formalism and rule-scepticism

The promise of formalism

Formalism in an extreme form presents a picture in which law is and *should be* an entirely self-determining system, where judges are never faced with choices or alternative interpretations of a kind that would be resolvable only through extra-legal considerations, such as moral or political values. For a formalist, therefore, such considerations never enter into the determination of legal outcomes.

Many lawyers and statesmen in nineteenth-century Europe took the project of constructing such systems as a serious ambition. On the Continent, the great codes in Germany (the BGB) and in France (the Code Civil) brought together what was to be called the 'jurisprudence of legal concepts' – abstract, conceptual and logical legal scholarship in the exegetical tradition – and a revival of Roman law. (The work of German sociologist Max Weber analysed the historical development of this.) In Britain, Jeremy Bentham argued the case for codification as part of his general attempt to reform the law in an enlightened, liberal fashion. In both cases, codifying the law was seen as a safeguard against arbitrariness in the courts and interference by the executive in the legal process. The idea of the importance of the separation of powers and the ideal of a democratic society resulted in a picture of the law which saw judges as mere executors of the legislature's will, applying the law mechanically. The image of law that emerges as particularly powerful in the nineteenth century, both in codified legal systems on the Continent and among common lawyers, might be summarised as follows: the more nearly we could come to constructing a legal system of clear and coherent rules, containing precise and 'scientifically' analysed terms, elaborated out of perfectly analysed and synthesised concepts, the concepts being unvaryingly used in the same sense throughout the whole body of law, the more we may succeed in producing a gapless, highly formalised and thus properly rational system of law, capable of guaranteeing 'the rule of law'.

It is above all the idea of a self-contained system of norms that defines the aspiration of formalism: a system, we might describe it, that already contains the answers to legal questions within it. It might be worth repeating here Max Weber's concise definition of formalism (from Part I) and relating it to Roberto Unger's, to whose critique of formalism we will return later.

For Weber formalism (or the 'formal-rational' type of law) means that:

> First, that every concrete decision be the 'application' of an abstract legal proposi-
> tion to a concrete fact situation; second, that it must be possible in every concrete
> case to derive the decision from abstract legal propositions by means of legal logic;
> third, that the law must actually or virtually constitute a 'gapless' system of legal
> propositions, or must, at least, be treated as if it were such a gapless system;
> fourth, that whatever cannot be 'construed' rationally in legal terms is also legally
> irrelevant; and fifth, that every social action of human beings must always be visu-
> alized as either an 'application' or 'execution' of legal propositions, or as an
> infringement thereof, since the 'gaplessness' of the legal system must result in a
> gapless legal ordering of all social conduct.
>
> (Weber 1921/1978, pp 657–658)

And for Unger:

> Formalism is a commitment to, and therefore also a belief in the possibility of, a
> method of legal justification that contrasts with open-ended disputes about the
> basic terms of social life, disputes that people call ideological, philosophical or
> visionary. Such conflicts fall far short of the closely guarded canon of inference that
> the formalist claims for legal analysis. . . .
>
> A second distinctive formalist thesis is that only through such a restrained,
> relatively apolitical method of analysis is legal doctrine possible. . . . Doctrine can
> exist, according to the formalist view, because of a contrast between the more
> determinate rationality of legal analysis and the less determinate rationality of ide-
> ological contests.
>
> (Unger 1983, pp 1–2)

Legal reasoning and the pure theory of law

In our discussion of legal validity above, we discussed Hans Kelsen's important statement of the 'pure theory of law'. We can see formalism as an expression, in legal
reasoning, of Kelsen's aspiration to set out a pure science of law. The making of judicial
decisions that apply to individual cases is, for Kelsen, the making of individual legal
norms. Nothing significant separates norm-creation from norm-application, and both
fall under the sign of validity. For Kelsen, the application of law is a moment of *juris-diction*
(the stating of the law) by officials of the legal system authorised to do so. What does
this mean? It means that in reaching the individual decision – that passes a sentence
on a wrongdoer, or that deems a specific contract void, or that annuls a marriage or
that allocates custody for child, *whatever* the content of a decision may be – the official
of the system follows precisely the same logic of authorisation that has guided the
production of norms in general: the logic, that is, of validity. The production of
the individual legal norm is authorised by a superior norm that establishes the
jurisdiction of the court and provides for the content of a judgement in terms of the
abstract norm that is given concrete expression in the case at hand, in the same way
as the norm-creating capacity of a governmental agency is authorised by the statutes

that set it up and determine its powers. And this, again, occurs in the same way as the enactment of statutes by parliaments is authorised and circumscribed by constitutional norms. It is the same logic of validation at work, of an inferior norm by a superior norm, simply at different points of the scale; or more accurately in Kelsen's terms, of the hierarchy of norms.

Here is Kelsen, describing how the objective meaning of law attaches to the subjective behaviour of individuals, in the Pure Theory of Law (1967/1934):

> [Let us] analyse any condition of things such as is law – . . . [e.g.] a judicial ruling. We can distinguish two elements. The one is a sensible act in time and place, an external process, generally a human behaviour; the other is a significance attached to or immanent in this act or process, a specific meaning. . . . A man, clothed in a gown, speaks certain words from an elevated position to a person standing in front of him. This external process *means* a judicial sentence. . . . These external circumstances, since they are sensible, temporospatial events, are in every case a piece of nature and as such causally determined . . . indeed not legal matter at all. That which makes the process into a legal (or illegal) act is not its factuality, nor its natural, causal existence, but the objective significance that is bound up with it, its meaning.
>
> (Pure Theory of Law, p 478)

And Kelsen will conclude:

> The Pure Theory of Law, as a specific science of law, considers legal norms not as natural realities, not as fact in consciousness, but as meaning-contents. And it considers facts only as the content of legal norms, that is only as determined by the norms. Its problem is to discover the specific principles of a sphere of meaning.
>
> (Pure Theory of Law, p 478)

What Kelsen is offering here is a radical account of the self-containment of law, which, as we saw, is the essence of formalism. Law comes about as a separate sphere of meaning by vesting events in the world with the objective meaning of law, that is, for Kelsen, through the prism of validity. Why does the behaviour of the 'man, clothed in a gown' *mean* the passing of a sentence? Because the law lends it objective significance through rules that determine the conditions under which it is validated as a legal act. It is then bound up with the notion of jurisdiction, and the chains of authorisation link the speech act of the judge back to the body of law of which it is an instantiation. The judge thus speaks the law. And his voice is the voice of the law, not of his personal conscience, not of morals, or religion. That is why Kelsen writes:

> What is here chiefly important is to liberate law from the association which has traditionally been made for it – its association with morals. This is not of course to question the requirement that law ought to be moral. That requirement is self-evident. What is questioned is simply the view that law, as such, is a part of morals and that therefore every law, as law, is in some sense and in some measure moral.
>
> (Pure Theory of Law, p 478)

Formalism and deduction

The promotion of the values of objectivity, impartiality and neutrality are all linked to the formalist concern with determinate rule application. Neil MacCormick has vividly portrayed this:

> A system of positive law, especially the law of a modern state, comprises an attempt to concretize broad principles of conduct in the form of relatively stable, clear, detailed and objectively comprehensible rules, and to provide an interpersonally trustworthy and acceptable process for putting these rules into effect. That process is especially visible in cases where there is some interpersonal dispute or where social order or justice have been held to require the organization of public agencies to police and enforce observance of rules that might not otherwise be voluntarily obeyed. In these situations, the private complainer or public rule-enforcer must bring forward some assertions about the state of facts in the world, and attempt to show how that state of facts would call for intervention on the ground of some rule that applies to the asserted facts. Accordingly, the logic of rule-application is the central logic of the law within the modern paradigm of legal rationality under the 'rule of law'.
>
> (MacCormick 1994, pp ix–x)

Put at its simplest, the model at work here, says MacCormick, can be written as the following formula:

R + F = C or 'Rules plus facts yields conclusion'

or, in perhaps its more familiar depiction, as the separation between a major premise containing the rule and a minor premise containing the facts. According to this formulation:

(1) $X_1, X_2, X_3, X_4 \ldots X_n \rightarrow P$

(2) $X_1, X_2, X_3, X_4 \ldots X_n$
_____

(3)   P

Statement (1) is called the major premise of the syllogism and it appends the 'operative facts' to a sanction. These operative facts are the necessary and sufficient conditions for the legal sanction to take effect. Necessary because they all have to be met; sufficient because the law requires no further condition except these. Think of all the conditions, for example, that the law stipulates in order for a will to be valid. These will pertain both to the mental state of the testator and to external, objective conditions (the existence of witnesses, for example). These will be stated in the major premise exhaustively, $(X_1, \ldots, X_n)$ and the law's 'sanction' (P) (the creation of a valid will) will be conditional on their all being fulfilled.

Statement (2) is called the 'minor premise' of the syllogism, and it concerns establishing that the required conditions stipulated in the major premise have in fact occurred as a matter of empirical evidence. To establish the minor premise litigants and the court will engage in 'fact-finding', in establishing what happened as a matter of fact.

If there is established a coincidence between statement (1) and statement (2), if, that is, all operative facts stipulated by the law in the major premise are established as a matter of fact in the minor premise, then the 'sanction' of the law, (P), follows as a matter of logic. No further legal argument is required. The subsumption of S (2) under S (1) yields the legal outcome as a matter of course. *Modus ponens*, this method of reasoning that relies on deduction, is at the heart of the formalist picture of law. The material or relevant facts as established through the use of rules of evidence are then subsumed under the rule. Legal formalism argues that establishing legal conclusions is therefore a process of rational justification, not one of evaluative or subjective judgement. This is important since it limits the discretion of judges and also provides for certainty, predictability and objectivity in the law.

The legal rule that is laid out in the major premise S (1) may have as its source either a statutory provision or a rule based on a binding precedent. It may also have as source custom, an international treaty or institutional writings. Whatever the source of S (1), the formalist aspiration that one can discover the law simply by subsuming facts to laws rather than through any creative intervention does not come undone due to possible difficulties in establishing the content of S (1). Such difficulties, of establishing the exact content of the major premise, become clearly evident when it is the outcome of a previous judicial decision, where the 'rule' that informs the decision and which it establishes as binding for the future, does not appear in a clear-cut and unambiguous statement. Not every word uttered by the judges in the previous case is relevant or binding; instead the *ratio decidendi* of the precedent case will need to be identified, separated off from what are mere *obiter dicta* of a case, and established by being stated in the form of a rule. Of course, there is no agreed statement of what the *ratio* is or how to find it in any given case. But that, argues MacCormick, is not a reason to doubt the possibility of extracting it from a decision. 'When a Court gives a ruling on a point of law which it conceives to be necessary to its justification of its particular decision, it would seem not unreasonable to regard that ruling as the *ratio* of the case' (1978, p 83).

Formalism, as we have sketched it, assumes a connection of legal reasoning with deductive logic. Here is an example of deductive logic in practice, exemplified in the form of syllogistic reasoning used in the presentation of legal determination. In *Daniels* the plaintiffs, having suffered poisoning from drinking a lemonade heavily contaminated with carbolic acid, sued the manufacturer for damages in compensation for their illness, treatment expenses and loss of earnings while ill. Here is the syllogistic translation:

(i) In any case if goods sold by one person to another have defects unfitting them for their only proper use but not apparent on ordinary examination, then the goods sold are not of merchantable quality.

(ii) In the instant case, goods sold by one person to another had defects unfitting them for their only proper use but not apparent on ordinary examination.

(iii) Therefore in the instant case the goods sold are not of merchantable quality.

(MacCormick 1994, p 22)

As we saw, sentences (i) and (ii) here are the 'premises', while (iii) is the 'conclusion' of this argument: (i) is the 'major premise', the Rule; (ii) is the 'minor premise', the Fact; (iii) the Conclusion. Together this constitutes the argument form called a 'syllogism'. The argument is a deductive argument, where the conclusion is deduced from the premises. The important thing about syllogistic deduction is that the validity of the argument depends purely on its logical form. So long as the premises are true, the conclusion must also be true; one could not assert the premises and deny the conclusion without self-contradiction. The form of this deductive argument can be expressed formulaically as follows:

All M are P	e.g., famously:	All men are mortal
S is M		Socrates is a man
S is P		Socrates is mortal

In legal rules, the major premise usually takes the form of a conditional statement: an 'if – then' sentence. For example: 'if a person agrees to do any act which tends to corrupt public morals, [then] that person is guilty of a crime at common law'; or 'if ["where"] the seller sells goods in the course of a business, [then] there is an implied condition that the goods supplied under the contract are of merchantable quality' (Sale of Goods Act 1979, s 14(2)2). In order for the syllogism to work, as we discussed at some length above, the material facts of the present case must match the 'operative' facts as stipulated in the major premise. In this way the conclusion – the 'then' component of the sentence – comes into effect as a legally – and logically – justified conclusion. While judges will seldom literally use logical formulae in their judgements, this itself does not negate the 'essential truth', says MacCormick, of the form R + F = C in legal reasoning.

We have sketched a view of formalism as embodying a vision of legal rationality operating in the sphere of legal adjudication. Law is understood as a system of known general rules – presumed to be clear and, ideally, capable of a purely literal interpretation – that are deductively applied by judges to factual circumstances to yield a conclusion. Correspondingly, the facts of cases must be presentable in readily identifiable typical situations, admitting of simple and uncontroversial application of legal rules. In these circumstances, the legal conclusion necessarily follows and is justified according to the operation of logic. According to MacCormick, so far as legal systems include rules that are mandatory to apply in every case to which they clearly refer, observance of the requirements of deductive logic is a necessary element in legal justification.

Formalism and the rule of law

There is both a descriptive and a normative side to the formalist theory and ideal. Formalism is a theory about how law *does* contain within its formal, systematic structure all answers to the questions that can be posed in law and legal argument, and at the same time claims that this containment is a good thing, in that it separates off questions of what law is from what one might see as questions of justice or of politics. That does not mean that the formalist would not wish law to be just. It simply means that whether it is just or not does not impact on its being law, and that keeping those two questions distinct is a good thing for the reasons that we saw Hart arguing the case earlier. The emphasis, with formalism, is on the dynamics, we might say, of that containment of all legal answers within the body of law. The more we succeed in this, the more the law will comprise a set of general – and logically consistent – rules capable of being 'deductively' applied to every relevant case of proven facts. The more this is so, the more certain, predictable and uniform will be the law.

Formalism is a realisation of the rule of law ideal in which

> government in all its actions is bound by rules fixed and announced beforehand – rules that make it possible to foresee with fair certainty how the authority will use its coercive powers in given circumstances and to plan one's individual affairs on the basis of that knowledge.
>
> (Hayek 1944, p 54)

With this statement, it is important to note the political stance of the formalist position. That is, legal formalism is not just a theory about how judges do or should decide cases that come before them; it is also an approach that seeks to uphold and promote certain political and moral ends too. This may seem paradoxical. Yet, a belief in the virtues of formalism is bound up with taking a specific stance on the doctrine of the rule of law, the separation of powers, personal, political and economic autonomy, and judicial accountability in the political system (see Part I).

The challenge of American legal realism

The attack on formalism

The formalist image of law has never gone unchallenged, and the earlier part of the twentieth century saw throughout the Western world various forms of what may even be called a 'revolt' against formalism. This was not simply a revolt against an idealised deductive model of rule application, but was critical of even the more nuanced forms of formal justification. This critique was frequently associated with new approaches in the sociology of law and 'sociological jurisprudence', involving people such as Roscoe Pound in the US, François Gény in France, and Rudolf von Jhering, Eugen Ehrlich and various proponents of *Freirechtsfindung* ('Free law-finding') in Germany.

The American Legal Realists comprised a loose grouping of legal academics and practitioners (such as Llewellyn, Frank, Oliphant, Holmes, Rodell, etc). They were not concerned to offer a theory of law or even a theory of legal reasoning. They were concerned with changing legal education, legal practice and court processes, so as to bring into the open the policy issues involved in lawmaking by judges. This was seen as important first, for the training of lawyers and judges; second, for an improvement in the predictability of judicial decisions; and third, for the flexibility that judges should show in updating the law to deal with changing social conditions. The ideas of these thinkers were influenced by pragmatism in philosophy (John Dewey and William James) and by a belief in the role that scientific experts could play. They were not rigorous philosophers or social scientists, but they had a profound effect on American legal education and practice and a delayed and patchy influence in Britain.

The critique took the form of arguing that formalistic interpretation was not in fact the only available (or commonly used) approach to legal doctrines and codes, and arguing that formalism involved ignoring the social interests on which law was truly based and by reference to which it ought to be interpreted and developed. The revolt against formalism was particularly vigorous in the US in the 1920s and 1930s, at the time of the early conflict between Roosevelt's 'New Deal' and the conservative constitutional activism engaged in by the US Supreme Court judges who would systematically strike down redistributive policies on constitutional grounds. The most typical example of this was the Supreme Court's 1905 decision in *Lochner v NewYork* (198 US 483 (1905)) that came to define an era of Supreme Court constitutional jurisprudence ('Lochnerism'). *Lochner* was a labour law case that concerned the introduction of protective measures by the government that limited (on health and safety grounds) the hours that employees (in bakeries) were allowed to work to 10 hours per day or 60 hours per week. The major-ity held that the New York law violated the due process clause of the US Constitution, constituting an 'unreasonable, unnecessary and arbitrary interference with the right and liberty of the individual to contract.' In other words, the question the Court answered in the affirmative was whether the US Constitution's protection of liberty forbade laws aimed at labour protection and the placing of limits on the operation of the free market. Vigorous theoretical debate ensued, over formalism and the relation of law to politics, and gradually, over the next few decades there arose something akin to a 'movement' in legal theory that came to be known as 'legal realism' – the doctrines of its main propo-nents amounting to various forms of more or less extreme scepticism about all aspects of legal formalism.

The sceptical attack on formalism over whether rules are capable of determining outcomes was coupled with a strong political programme of 'social engineering', that is the idea that law can be used as an instrument of policy and a belief that scientific expertise can make a real difference to how societies can be 'run' with the help of the law. What brings together the two aspects – the critique and the programme – is a new agenda to study 'law in action', not, that is, as it is presented 'in the books' as containing certain constitutionally unchallengeable, because a-contextual, commitments to the protection of liberty and property, but as institutionally embedded and harnessed to the pursuit of social and welfare aims. For Roscoe Pound the Anglo-American common law system is characterised by an 'individualist spirit agrees ill with a collectivist age', and which arouses resentment by turning great social and economic issues into private legal disputes, encouraging 'petty tinkering where comprehensive reforms are needed' (1960, p 185).

An influential account of the 'common points of departure' of the main Realist scholars is provided by Karl Llewellyn (1931, pp 55–57) and include the conception of 'law in flux', and the judicial creation of law; the interpretation of law as relevant to its purpose and assessment as to its effect; the notion of society in flux, where the rate of change is faster than the law, therefore the need for law to keep up; a 'distrust in tra-ditional legal rules and concepts insofar as they purport to *describe* what either courts or people are actually doing'; and an insistence on evaluating the law in terms of its effects.

The 'Path of Law': law as prophecy

Some of these theses are already present in the much earlier address by Oliver Wendell Holmes, 'The Path of the Law' (1897), that remains one of the seminal pieces of legal writing. In this piece, Holmes, a forerunner of the American Legal Realists, argued that the reality of legal decision-making should not be concealed by the pretence that law is a system of known rules applied by a judge to produce logical outcomes – the 'myth of legal certainty'. The life of law, Holmes stated, is not logic, but experience:

> the felt necessities of the time, the prevalent moral and political theories, intuitions
> of public policy, avowed or unconscious, even the prejudices which judges share

with their fellow-men, have a good deal more to do than the syllogism in determining the rules by which men should be governed.

(Holmes 1897)

'The Path of the Law' contains a number of surprising claims, perhaps none of them generating such controversy as Holmes's invitation to the student of law to adopt the 'bad man's point of view':

> If you want to know the law and nothing else, you must look at it as a *bad man*, who cares only for the material consequences which such knowledge enables him to predict, not as a good one, who finds his reasons for conduct, whether inside the law or outside of it, in the vaguer sanctions of conscience. . . . Take the fundamental question, 'what constitutes the law?' You will find some text writers telling you that it is something different from what is decided by the courts of Massachusetts or England, that it is a system of reason, that it is a deduction from principles of ethics or admitted axioms or what not, which may or may not coincide with the decisions. But if we take the view of our friend the bad man we shall find that he does not care two straws for the axioms or deductions, but that he does want to know what the Massachusetts or English courts are likely to do in fact. I am much of his mind. The prophecies of what the courts will do in fact, and nothing more pretentious, are what I mean by the law.

(Holmes 1897, pp 460–461)

The object of the study of law, then, is for Holmes nothing but 'prediction', or as he puts it 'prophecy':

> [A] legal duty so called is nothing but a prediction that if a man does or omits certain things he will be made to suffer in this or that way by judgement of the court; and so of a legal right. The number of our predictions when generalized and reduced to a system is not unmanageably large.

(Holmes 1897, pp 458–459)

Elsewhere he says:

> I wish, if I can, to lay down some first principles for the study of this body of dogma or systematized prediction which we call the law, for men who want to use it as the instrument of their business to enable them to prophesy in their turn.

(Holmes 1897, pp 458–459)

He takes the example of contract to illustrate the point:

> Nowhere is the confusion between legal and moral ideas more manifest than in the law of contract. Among other things, here again the so called primary rights and duties are invested with a mystic significance beyond what can be assigned and explained. The duty to keep a contract at common law means a prediction that you must pay damages if you do not keep it, – and nothing else.

(Holmes 1897, pp 458–459)

For Holmes it is 'experience', not 'logic', that dictates outcomes. It is in this respect, he says, that 'a second fallacy' comes in:

> The fallacy to which I refer is the notion that the only force at work in the develop-
> ment of the law is logic. . . . The danger of which I speak is not the admission that
> the principles governing other phenomena also govern the law, but the notion that
> a given system, ours, for instance, can be worked out like mathematics from some
> general axioms of conduct. . . . This mode of thinking is entirely natural. The train-
> ing of lawyers is training in logic. The processes of analogy, discrimination, and
> deduction are those in which they are most at home. The language of judicial deci-
> sion is mainly the language of logic. And the logical method and form flatter that
> longing for certainty and for repose which is in every human mind. But certainty
> generally is illusion, and repose is not the destiny of man. Behind the logical form
> lies a judgment as to the relative worth and importance of competing legislative
> grounds, often an inarticulate and unconscious judgment, it is true, and yet the very
> root and nerve of the whole proceeding. You can give any conclusion a logical form.
>
> (Holmes 1897, pp 458–459)

'I cannot but believe,' says Holmes,

> that if the training of lawyers led them habitually to consider more definitely and
> explicitly the social advantage on which the rule they lay down must be justified,
> they sometimes would hesitate where now they are confident, and see that really
> they were taking sides upon debatable and often burning questions. So much for the
> fallacy of logical form.
>
> (Holmes 1897, pp 458–459)

Rule-scepticism

Two of the forms of Realist scepticism that have attracted much attention will be outlined here: rule-scepticism – the doctrine that rules do not and cannot play the determi-
native part in legal decision-making that formalism credits to them; and fact-scepticism – the
idea that 'facts' are not so much independent entities that legal processes discover, but
rather propositions about a supposed reality that is generated by legal processes.

The reality is, it is argued, that judges typically cannot decide cases simply by following rules and precedents because these rules are never totally determinate. Again,
Holmes stated the position unambiguously: 'no case can be settled by general propositions . . . I will admit any general proposition you like and decide the case either way'
(Holmes et al., 1953, p 243).

According to an early helpful analysis of rule-scepticism provided by Wilfred Rumble (1968), judges face interpretative choices for a number of reasons including, though
not limited to, the following:

- The ambiguity of legal language means cases and statutes are open to different interpretations.
- The avalanche of precedents: You can find a precedent for either side and for almost any view.

- Multiplicity of techniques for describing what a precedent established. How is the *ratio decidendi* determined?
- How broad is the scope of a given precedent? How do you decide between broad and narrow implications? How can you tell in an unprecedented situation whether an old rule was supposed to cover it or not?
- The potential for distinguishing: no two cases are ever identical. Which are the important differences of law or fact for the purposes of decision?
- The potential for comparison: cases that once might have seemed quite separate may come to seem similar in some important respect.

Thus rule sceptics find various ambiguities both in statutory interpretation and in the use of precedent. Laws do not take the form of clear, general, unambiguous rules, but are radically indeterminate. The idea of treating like cases alike poses radical problems about likeness and difference. Consequently, there is always room for some factor other than the legal rule that conditions the decision – factors ranging from the influence of prejudice to attention to policy. Such factors may operate randomly or they may offer alternative regularities and predictabilities of law that do not derive from the rules as such.

Realist critiques may thus take different forms. At the level of legal denunciation, realism seeks to unmask hypocrisy and double standards by showing that formalism licenses prejudice and arbitrary decision-making cloaked in the form of authority and judicial deference to the rules. At another level, it involves the more everyday observation that predicting judicial outcomes may depend more on knowing about factors that have nothing to do with the rules as such ('Know your court', as lawyers often say).

In any case, the Realists argued, when judges consider a case, they do not work 'forward' from general rules but backwards from the type of outcome that seems appropriate. So any syllogistic logic manifest in the final presentation of a judicial opinion can be contrasted to the logic by which the decision was actually reached.

The issue raised then, in mainstream jurisprudence at least, has been understood primarily in terms of the questions it raises about judicial decision-making. Judicial creativity is seen as a challenge to the doctrine of the separation of powers and hence the rule of law ideal. Rule-scepticism clearly presents a problem for any theory that claims law can be described purely as a system of rules. Yet in response it might be argued that the Realists conflated, on the one hand, the process of thinking about or reaching a decision (the 'discovery' of the decision) with, on the other hand, the way in which it is justified. Drawing an analogy with the physical sciences, 'discovery' is identified as the moment when a judge has an idea about what the outcome should be, a process that may well be non-syllogistic, involving hunches, personal views and possibly extra-legal considerations, including views about policy (just as great scientific discoveries may be unpredictable and inspirational – in 'eureka' fashion). But such insights have to be tested to see if they fall within the relevant sphere of legal truth, and only if they do can they be justified. Syllogistic reasoning only comes in at the second stage of testing and presenting the rationale. Jurisprudence is interested only in the justification process. So long as a decision may be justified by reference to an existing rule of law, then the judiciary has not exceeded their constitutional powers. But arguably this merely postpones the problem. Is this justificatory reasoning itself rational and determinate? The Realist criticisms apply here too.

Fact-scepticism

It has been argued that not only formalists, but also rule sceptics, ignored the difficulties associated with facts in adjudication. The facts are an essential element in the application of the law, but to what extent is it the case that courts – judges, or lawyers, or juries – actually get at, or even can get at, the 'truth'? Much of a court's, and thus the lawyers', time is spent on ascertaining or arguing over the facts, yet this has often been neglected when considering processes of justification in legal decision-making. Among Realists, it is the 'fact sceptics' who turned their attention to such matters.

They argued that we should look at the challenges that come from the world of the lower courts. From this perspective, the grand debates about legal interpretation appear remote and academic. This 'appeal court jurisprudence' concentrated on prestigious and intellectually stimulating 'hard cases', but thereby ignored many salient if more mundane aspects of the everyday life of the courts. So Jerome Frank, writing in the 1940s–1950s, chastised his fellow legal Realists: rule sceptics concentrated on a very limited aspect of the law in action, whereas most cases were decided on their facts. Like his fellow sceptics, he was extremely dubious about the predictability of legal outcomes. Moreover, the possibility existed that the facts as found by judge and jury did not correspond to actual facts.

At its simplest, Frank's scepticism can be understood in terms of the psychology of fact-finding. Witnesses' observations and memory may be extremely hazy, but they will be pressed to produce clear and confident statements in court. Pre-trial interviews with lawyers may even amount to a form of witness coaching in which the witness gets an idea of which version of the facts would best suit prosecution or defence stories. Then, under cross-examination they will be subject to many techniques of double-checking and discrediting. By the end of this process, which began in uncertainty in the first place, we may be many degrees from the truth. Ironically, even witnesses who are sure of the truth, and tell it as they saw it, may be 'bad' witnesses. In jury trials these psychological problems are compounded by the jury's complex reactions to witnesses and their capacity to be swayed by the oratory of the lawyers. Yet the jury is supposed to be the 'master of facts'. Even judges in this setting may be less than rational in their reactions and their influence on juries is not inconsiderable. This aspect of Frank's position has been developed subsequently by social psychologists' studies.

To counter such psychological instabilities of truth-finding, Frank called upon the expertise of psychology itself. Experts could be brought in to examine witnesses for the accuracy of their perceptual apparatus and their propensity to lie (with reference to standards of reliability and credibility). Juries should be abolished altogether but, failing that, there should be training in jury duties at school, and jury experts to accompany and advise the jury in the court. The confusing and emotional panoply of costumes and ritual should be eliminated. And judges should undergo psychoanalysis to control their projective tendencies.

Frank focused primarily on the adversarial process, which he likened to a trial by combat with each side's champions trying to do down the others – a 'fight' method of proof. While this may have made sense in the past, when we believed that God was on the side of justice and truth, it is not appropriate to the age of secular rationalism. Instead he proposed an inquisitorial system, which would include better training of legal officials, impartial government officials to dig up all the facts, specialisation of judges and state administrators to deal with the complex facts of modern society, and increasing use of expert witnesses.

Today, Frank's belief in the value of scientific expertise, free proof and managerial legal officials may seem naive, costly and politically worrying. But Frank's basic points have had considerable influence in disturbing the formalist presumption that 'law' divides neatly from 'facts' and that the jury can easily master them. Put polemically, the present system of proof seems self-contradictory. On the one hand, it is based on a presumption that ordinary people can assess and make inferences from the facts as disclosed. On the other hand, legal methods of getting at facts are far from everyday standards of perception or making sense of the world (and, for many, should be). Whether or not legal proof and procedure is as incoherent as Frank would argue, legal virtue and legal vice – confusion and protection, ordeal and ideal – are often embedded in the same legal rules and procedures.

The faith in science

With the knowledge provided by the social sciences, including what we might call today socio-legal studies, it would be possible for the law to be deployed rationally in the pursuit of specific goals: social protection, social inclusion, crime control and the multitude of other policy aims that drive regulatory states in the efforts to enhance social welfare.

It is worth quoting from 'The Path of the Law' at some length here, from a passage of Holmes where the faith that law can learn from science (and the opposition to its learning from its history!) is unequivocally expressed:

> For the rational study of the law the black-letter man may be the man of the present, but the man of the future is the man of statistics and the master of economics. It is revolting to have no better reason for a rule of law than that so it was laid down in the time of Henry IV. It is still more revolting if the grounds upon which it was laid down have vanished long since, and the rule simply persists from blind imitation of the past.
>
> What have we better than a blind guess to show that the criminal law in its present form does more good than harm? I do not stop to refer to the effect which it has had in degrading prisoners and in plunging them further into crime, or to the question whether fine and imprisonment do not fall more heavily on a criminal's wife and children than on himself. I have in mind more far-reaching questions. Does punishment deter? Do we deal with criminals on proper principles?
>
> I look forward to a time when the part played by history in the explanation of dogma shall be very small, and instead of ingenious research we shall spend our energy on a study of the ends sought to be attained and the reasons for desiring them. As a step toward that ideal it seems to me that every lawyer ought to seek an understanding of economics. The present divorce between the schools of political economy and law seems to me an evidence of how much progress in philosophical study still remains to be made.
>
> (The path of the law, p 474)

This conception of law as an applied science 'imported, on the one hand, consideration of the ends to be served by the legal order, or in other words the policies and values that it connotes, and on the other hand, examination of its technical efficiency and more especially its effects' (Yntema 1960, pp 322–323).

Finally, the Realists argued that judges were faced with crucial policy questions. Formalism was being used as a cloak for hiding innovations and policy decisions, even, conservatively, to deny the need for change. Remember their commitment was to a form of legal scholarship that would provide guidance for 'social planning and perspective' in the wake of the catastrophe of the 1929 Wall Street stock market crash and the ensuing depression. Recognising that law had become a policy battleground, Realists espoused judges openly taking a stand. Thus they supported the adoption of a form of explicit 'substantive rationality' (see Weber, 1921/1978, pp 657–658) in the search for just and appropriate solutions to particular cases or types of case. Taking a stance was unavoidable, and the judges' cloaking of their decisions behind the façade of legal neutrality was merely an ideological move hiding their endorsement of the status quo. As Joseph Singer (1988, p 482) puts it well:

> [American] legal realists criticized the idea of a self-regulating market system which was immune from state involvement or control. They challenged the [traditional] distinction between public and private spheres. The realists asserted that state and society could not be completely separated either logically or experientially. Once the state had been created, it altered (or was intended to alter) the distribution of power and wealth in society. [E]ven by failing to intervene in 'private' transactions, the state effectively altered contract relations; it delegated to the more powerful party the freedom to exercise her superior power or knowledge over the weaker party. Thus, the state determined the distribution of power and wealth in society both when it acted to limit freedom and when it failed to limit the freedom of some to dominate others.
>
> From this perspective, a free market system could not be distinguished in a significant sense from a regulatory system. All market systems distribute power, and thus constitute regulatory systems. The rules in force have the effect of privileging the interests of some persons over the interests of others. It is impossible for a legal system not to so distribute power and wealth. Any definition of property and contract rights necessarily requires the state.

However, Realist arguments about policy should not be interpreted too contextually, as a specific response to the idiosyncratic developments of the American legal system. Rather, they reveal one of the underlying tensions between the 'justice' and 'instrumental' aspects of modern law. Since policies are by definition oriented to factors outside the legal system (the *social* rather than *systemic* context), how far can a theory of legal interpretation require that judges have to blind themselves to such goals? If the law is deliberately framed with a view to social policy, it seems bizarre to restrict the ways in which such considerations may enter into the application of law.

Realism has had an enormous impact on subsequent arguments about law and legal reasoning. It has inspired the growth of socio-legal studies that attempt to look at the range of non-rule factors influencing the legal process, and to examine the internal perspective of the judicial community. In its more radical Marxist versions – or in Critical Legal Studies (CLS), as we shall see shortly – the Realist strain is taken to mean not only that the rule of law in its formalist guise is unattainable, but that it is an important myth legitimating an inherently oppressive system, a symbolic/ideational device to make injustice seem morally acceptable to its victims.

Reading

For a short and clear defence of the rule-based account of legal reasoning, read Neil MacCormick's 'Foreword' to MacCormick (1994), and for his reconstruction of *Daniels* in terms of a series of purely deductive syllogisms, see chapter 2 – 'Deductive Justification' – of that book.

With regard to the formalist analysis of the application of statutes, see MacCormick and Summers (1991, ch 13, pp 511–525). For an analysis of formalist reasoning from case law, see MacCormick (1994, pp 19–29).

For Kelsen's exceptional, if demanding, analysis of the pure science of law, as an account of the systematicity of law and its containment within the formal structure, see Kelsen (1967).

For a defence of formalism as a normative ideal, see Hayek (1944), in particular chapter 6.

For an early, highly influential piece and a classic text in the Realist tradition, read Holmes (1897). Cotterrell (2003) in *The Politics of Jurisprudence*, 2nd edn, chapter 6, provides an excellent discussion of 'sociological jurisprudence' as expounded by Roscoe Pound and the points of convergence and divergence with the American Legal Realists. See in particular the section on 'Llewellyn's Constructive Doctrinal Realism' (pp 187ff). For Llewellyn's answer to Pound, see Karl N Llewellyn, 1931, 'Some Realism About Realism: Responding to Dean Pound', 44.8 *Harvard Law Review* 1222–1264. See also Karl N Llewellyn, 1930, *The Bramble Bush: Some Lectures on Law and Its Study*.

For comprehensive historical accounts of currents in American legal history, see Horwitz (1992) and Duxbury (1995).

For Frank's account of fact-scepticism, see Frank (1949a) especially pages 418–423 and Frank (1949b) 'Introduction'. See also Jackson (1995) for an updated and illuminating account of the 'psychology of fact-finding', issues of reliability of witnessing, advocacy techniques of cross-examination, and the construction of narratives. For further development of these issues, see the Advanced section on trials and fact-finding.

For Hart's critique of American Legal Realism, see Hart (1983) and (1961, ch 7).

Chapter 14

The turn to interpretation

Hart and the 'open texture' of legal language

In his article, 'The Legal Nightmare and the Noble Dream', H.L.A. Hart (1983) responded to the Realist picture by presenting a dichotomy between formalism or 'absolutism' (the 'noble dream') and the picture of total legal anarchy he attributes to rule sceptics. In *The Concept of Law* (1961), while making certain concessions to Realism, Hart suggested that Realists were 'disappointed absolutists', who have grossly exaggerated interpretative leeway because they secretly sought a utopian version of the rule of law ideal.

Hart argues that while the vast majority of cases where legal rules are applied are straightforward, easy cases, there is inevitably an element of judicial discretion in legal reasoning because of the necessarily 'open texture' of law. Drawing on the philosophy of Wittgenstein, he argues that the indeterminacy of natural language makes it impossible for meaning to be somehow 'stilled' and contained in determinate form in rules. Words and phrases may have a 'core' of settled meaning, but there is always a 'penumbra' of doubt and this always leaves room for interpretation and disagreement. Second, there exists a relative ignorance of fact. We cannot predict what 'fact situations' the future may generate and, in that sense, how our attempts to capture future eventualities through general categories today may be challenged. We cannot predict whether our current legal designations will be adequate in the future, although it is precisely future behaviour and situations that we are forever at present trying to regulate. Third, there exists an indeterminacy of legal aim in the legislative process: rules cannot, nor should they, aim to cover all eventualities. Such openness is not a weakness, but may be considered desirable, since it allows the law to be developed to meet changing or unforeseen circumstances. Moreover, the law uses general standards, which themselves necessarily introduce indeterminacy (or at the very least an under-determinacy): standards such as 'reasonableness' ('the reasonable man test', 'reasonable foreseeability', etc), 'proximity' (in negligence), 'fairness', 'good faith', 'equitable', and so on, all inevitably allow for leeway in interpretation. These legal standards are not formal rules in the way that we would think of arithmetic rules – they are open to, and demand, interpretation in the instant case.

In addition to this, we know that valid rules or principles in our law come into conflict with each other: the right, for example, to free speech claimed by a newspaper publishing details of a celebrity's private life may conflict with that celebrity's right to privacy. Often in these cases there is no simple way of rendering the legal rule as clearly as the formalist position might claim; interpretation – or a balancing of the competing valid rights claims – is required.

Finally, it will also be the case that in legal systems based on precedent, the assessment of the *ratio decidendi* of a precedent case is itself a source of indeterminacy. Even in a single judgement, or especially in an appeal court decision where there may be different majority opinions to analyse, there will be room for interpretation in ascertaining what the rule is. This difficulty is magnified where there exists, as often there will, a series of cases in a particular area of law, many of which may be treated as providing potential precedents, and at least some of which may themselves conflict.

Against both the formalists and, as we have seen, the Realists, Hart argues that legal rules cannot function as simple predictions of what judges will do, since they are rules of adjudication. Thus in Hart's view, formalism and rule-scepticism (the claim, as we have just seen, that rules do not and cannot do the work legal formalists say they do) are both exaggerations. Rules can have a clear meaning in legal cases and here formal interpretation works unproblematically. In fact, arguably much of our dealing with the law corresponds to this paradigm.

But where, for any number of the reasons mentioned, the law is not clear, says Hart, there are inevitably going to be hard cases. Here the judge must use his or her discretion to adapt the pre-existing rules to new cases as they arise. Since the law as established does not supply a clear answer to the case at hand, necessarily the judge must work out a basis for the decision by reference to substantive (and therefore not simply formal, deductive) extra-legal moral or political considerations. Yet while in such 'hard' cases judges may have strong discretion, it is never total discretion. No matter how the judge reaches his or her decision as a matter of thinking the problem through, they must publicly give reasons for their decision in the form of arguments about justice, social policy, morality, and so on and show how these arguments are best weighed up in justifying the decision which they give.

On this view then, law is a system of rules supplemented by law-creating exercises of judicial discretion, where adjudication is best thought of as being a middle way between purely formal legal rationality and overstress on substantive rationality after the style of the Realists.

But if it is the case that there are these systematic sources of indeterminacy (of the kind both Hart and the Realists drew attention to), and if it is also true that judges – at least in 'hard' cases – have a great deal of discretion in deciding, would this not be a cause for concern? Would this not tend to undermine the values of judicial objectivity and neutrality, and the predictability offered by the formalist approach? Are there no more substantive constraints on how judges reason, or no more to say on how these substantive constraints might operate when we think about how we expect judges to justify their decisions?

We know that lawyers do argue about the meaning or the application of a particular rule of law, and that sometimes even our most senior judges, often by writing dissenting opinions, disagree about what a legal rule requires or how it applies to the facts of the case before them. Given this, we might ask two sorts of questions. First, are there any common types of reasons why reasonable disagreement about the meaning and application of law occurs in a legal system? If so, what are these factors, and how should we understand the role they play? Second, given the fact of disagreement, does this mean that formalism as an approach to legal interpretation is neither in practice, nor even as an ideal, defensible; or, to put it even more strongly – is legal formalism at the end of the day simply a myth? And if it is, what interests would be served by promoting such a myth? Alternatively, is legal formalism – as an approach to how legal decisions are justified – true, but only to an extent, and in practice in need of being supplemented by a range of other justificatory techniques? If so, what are these techniques and how should we understand how they operate?

MacCormick and the limits of discretion

Drawing on and expanding Hart's theory, Neil MacCormick attempts to develop an account of adjudication, which shows clearly what substantive constraints exist in legal reasoning and how they work. As we have already seen, he seeks to show the – very important – place of established valid legal rules as normally applicable by simple deduction or 'subsumption' in clear cases. Now we can turn to how the underlying logic of legal argumentation in its non-deductive phases or elements works. Picking up on the insights of Hart on the open texture of law, MacCormick offers an 'extended formalism' in which the analysis of legal reasoning is true to both common law reasoning and the justificatory arguments that constrain freewheeling substantive reasoning. This is an account that, he argues, is based on what judges actually do in practice. It is, in other words, a descriptive account. But it is a normative one too: that is, it is one that argues that the forms of justification he identifies in judicial decision-making should be looked on as good practice.

Before looking further it may be helpful to clarify three types of problems judges or lawyers will encounter in interpreting legal rules. These are problems of relevancy, problems of interpretation and problems of classification.

- Relevancy refers to the question: what is the relevant legal rule? Can it be properly established that the case as averred can be warranted by reference to a valid rule?
- Interpretation refers to the problem: given that there is a relevant legal rule, how should it be interpreted?
- Classification refers to whether or not the case as averred can be properly classified as of the type which would fall under – be subsumed under – the relevant legal rule.

In easy cases, where the rule can be established and interpreted clearly and the facts classified without difficulty, the case can be subsumed as an instance of the rule and the legal ruling can be established uncontroversially. Hard cases, by contrast, are those in which problems of any of the three types identified may arise individually or in combination, and so raise the question of how the judge should act to apply his or her discretion where the relevant ruling is not immediately obvious. Problems of relevancy might mean that we identify a 'gap' in the law, or a clash of laws, or a lack of 'fit', or that we allow analogy to do too much work in establishing similarity between cases even where the latter may be somewhat strained. Problems of classification might mean that the case before the judge may not be immediately subsumed under a single legal rule. Problems of interpretation may arise where there is some doubt or contest over whether a condition stipulated in the major premise can be interpreted to include the instance within its ambit. How, then, is the ruling to be given in the case at hand?

In response to these problems, MacCormick identifies a number of constraints in legal reasoning – conditions that any suggested ruling must meet to qualify as a legal ruling. The first is 'universalisability', which, he argues, is and should be a part of all judicial decision-making. Indeed, he says, it is of the essence of justification as such. That is, to give an adequately justified decision, a judge must make a ruling that deals with the particular case before the court as an instance of a general or universal class. MacCormick suggests that what judges do is to consider whether a proposed decision is capable of universal application. For example, in *Donoghue v Stevenson*, the issue of liability was not simply about this specific manufacturer's negligence towards Mrs Donoghue. Rather, as Lord Tomlin put it (quoted in MacCormick 1978, p 57):

> I think that if the appellant is to succeed it must be on the proposition that every manufacturer or repairer of any article is under a duty to everyone who may thereafter legitimately use the article . . . It is logically impossible to stop short of this point.

The stress on 'every manufacturer', 'any article', 'everyone' in this passage exemplifies the criterion of universalisability and, MacCormick argues, it is necessary for this to be met if a decision is to be properly justified. Putting the argument that justification is not based on the merits of the particular case, but rather on a universal or general treatment of it, he concludes:

> I cannot for the life of me understand how there can be such a thing as a good reason for deciding any single case which is not a good generic reason for deciding cases of the particular type in view, that is to say, the 'merits' of any individual case are the merits of the type of case to which the individual case belongs.
> (MacCormick 1978, p 97)

Universalisability is an extension of the requirement of formal justice. This requires us to treat like cases alike and different cases differently. Justification through universalisation is therefore linked to doing justice to all members of a class in the same way. MacCormick describes this as follows:

> One who has to do justice among other persons, and one who seeks this or that as a matter of justice, is committed at least to the principle that like cases are to be treated alike and differences of treatment to be grounded in difference of relevant factors in a situation. In so far as we have reason to wish that our public agencies act in relation to citizens in a rationally comprehensible and predictable way, we have reason to wish that they act in accordance with this conception of formal justice.
> (MacCormick 1979, p 110)

Formal justice therefore requires that for a decision to be justified, it must treat the instant case in the same way as any other similar case. If there are sufficient relevant differences, then distinguishing this case from another can be justified.

While applying these criteria may be sufficient to dispose of the case at hand, it may be that two competing understandings of the law can be found to be both universalisable and justified by reference to formal justice (treating like cases alike). Thus, for example, in *Donoghue v Stevenson*, both the majority and minority opinions – the one holding manufacturers liable according to the principle of negligence, the other denying it by reference to the lack of a contract – may be justified in precisely these ways.

In order to test the competing propositions of law, the next step, for MacCormick, is one where universalisability combines with consequentialist calculations.

> Among the consequences of a ruling [are included] both (i) the logical implications of the ruling, viewed by reference to the range of hypothetical cases it covers; and (ii) the results of practical outcomes which will or may ensue given the existence of a rule showing those logical implications.
>
> (MacCormick 1979, p 116)

Here, what is properly to be evaluated is not the individual ad hoc decision between parties; it is, instead, the consequences of the ruling about the point(s) in issue which matter. What will be the case if this or that among the rival propositions of law proposed by rival parties prevails? How do such consequences square with justice, common sense, public policy, and so on? Consequentialism may commonly be seen in legal judgements in the form of 'floodgates' arguments, suggesting according to this rationale why liability should not be extended. But those are by no means the sole instances, and in fact MacCormick here would include criteria of value ranging from 'justice' to 'common sense', 'public benefit' and 'convenience'.

What does this (unusual) combination of the arguments from universalisability and consequences achieve? It is a combination that for MacCormick, as we saw, brings substantive reasoning in law, involving argumentation about consequences, under the sign and constraint of formal justice which requires universalisability of the grounds of decision. The explicit or implicit (universalised) ruling by the court on the question before it ought therefore to be tested and justified in terms of the court's evaluation of its consequences. These is something important at this juncture about how the ruling captures and expresses the 'generic category' at stake. In a famous commentary, Julius Stone puts the point in terms of the following query:

> *Donoghue v Stevenson*, standing alone, could yield logically a range of propositions . . . concerned with any combination of the following facts:
>
> 1) *the presence* of dead snails, or any snails, or any foreign body, or any unexpected quality
> 2) *in* opaque bottles of beverage, *or* in any bottles, *or* in any chattels for human consumption, *or* in any objects whatsoever
> 3) *caused by the negligence of the defendant* who is the manufacturer [of beverages], *or* any manufacturer, *or* any person working on the object, *or* anyone dealing with the object
> 4) *[Etc]*
>
> (Stone 1946, p 187, quoted in MacCormick 1978, pp 117–118)

Stone tracks a large number of such possibilities of determining the *ratio* of the case across a range of categories, but enough has been said to appreciate the problem that such a proliferation reveals: that universalisation itself does not settle the question of the relevant general category, in other words, of the preferred level of generality at which to pitch the solution. It is at this point that it makes sense to read MacCormick's argument about consequences, as the consequences that follow from suggesting a ruling at the appropriate level of generality. Different consequences accrue from different levels of generalisation: *Donoghue v Stevenson* would hardly have had the effect it had, nor would the dissenting judges have worried about 'opening the floodgates', if its *ratio* had involved compensation for injuries resulting from decomposing snails, or had it been confined to manufacturers of opaque bottles of beverage.

But if a decision is justifiable on the basis of consequentialist argument, does it follow that judges can act on the basis of any ruling whatever, which they represent as having advantageous or highly acceptable consequences? Are there no other constraints beyond those already identified? MacCormick argues that there are two other important constraints.

The requirement of *consistency* in law: rulings must not be inconsistent with pre-existing laws, in the sense of not directly contradicting some binding or authoritative rule. If we discover, that is, that the candidate ruling that has met the criteria of 'universalis-ability' and has the most desirable consequences, contradicts nonetheless a valid rule of the legal system, then it fails as a legal solution and must be ruled out of the competition. If that were not so, the idea of legal systems as being or including systems of valid, binding rules would be necessarily false.

The requirement of *coherence* in law is similar to consistency, yet there is an important difference between them. While consistency is a negative property, consisting in the absence of contradictions, coherence is a positive property. To fulfil its requirements, judges must decide cases only in accordance with rulings that are in keeping with the existing body of law and supported by it. And this is primarily achieved by reliance on principles in legal argument. The ruling in a hard case must be shown to be justifiable by reference to some legal principle, and thus 'coherent' with already settled law. While consistency is an either/or quality, coherence is a matter of degree. For MacCormick,

> general principles are to be understood as expressing values which are held to be significant in and for the legal system. They are broad normative generalisations under which more concrete rules and rulings of the system can be subsumed. Hence 'coherence' is secured by observance of general principles in legal argumentation, to the extent that sets of rules are made to make sense by being geared together to the pursuance of some supposed value or values.
>
> (MacCormick 1981, pp 118–119)

Another important aspect of 'coherence' is manifested in argument by analogy. Arguments from analogy are not formally valid in any sense. Rather they work by being more or less persuasive. In cases that are partially similar and partially different, an analogy may support without compelling the decision in the case.

Judges use analogies reasonably often. And while they do not count as a formal justification, they can often have a direct impact on how the judge treats the case and the light in which s/he expects others to see it. For example, in the case of In re A (Conjoined

Twins), the case that provides the fact situation described in the first paragraph of this part, Lord Justice Ward wrote:

> In my judgment, parents who are placed on the horns of such a terrible dilemma simply have to choose the lesser of their inevitable loss. If a family at the gates of a concentration camp were told they might free one of their children but if no choice were made both would die, compassionate parents with equal love for their twins would elect to save the stronger and see the weak one destined for death pass through the gates.
>
> (Re A Children 1009–1010)

To summarise, MacCormick finds that judges and lawyers use – and can be expected to use – certain kinds of argument that on the one hand go beyond deductive reasoning, yet on the other work to constrain how they may justify their decisions. In this sense where judges do have to make value choices in interpreting the law, particularly in hard cases, these choices are limited by systemic or substantive constraints (see MacCormick 1993, p 18). As such, legal reasoning is best thought of as centrally about rule application and where the formal application is contested, one that remains nonetheless a process of rational justification.

Dworkin, justification and integrity

Dworkin on 'hard' cases

Since his earliest writings, Ronald Dworkin has consistently maintained that every judicial decision requires discretion understood as the exercise of judgement, as interpretation, and yet none requires discretion of an unrestricted type. Dworkin's attack on formalism – and its core concept of law as a system of rules – is a powerful one and is oriented to its delimitation of the category of hard cases. We neither discover the right legal answer by looking up the right rule, says Dworkin, nor do we 'hit upon' a hard case when we have merely 'run out of rules' in some sense – because, for example, there is a 'gap' in the law, or because of the 'open texture' of the rules (see Hart, above). Because how would we know that we have run out of rules? Dworkin's examples (*Riggs v Palmer, MacPherson v Buick, Brown v Board of Education*; for these examples, see Dworkin 1986, ch 1) are highly convincing attempts to force the 'rules + discretion' model into impasses, because in none of these cases is it obvious that we have indeed 'run out of rules'. In the case of *Riggs*, that Dworkin famously popularised, the prospective benefactor of a will murdered the testator in an attempt to prevent him from changing the will. The formal conditions for the validity of the will did not include a disqualification for murderous legatees. How then, asks Dworkin, might the formalists account for what made this a hard case in the absence of any dispute over the existence (empirical) or meaning (semantic) of the Wills Act that the judges were called to make their decision on? This was a case where the formalist model gave a clear answer, and yet judges argued passionately about whether it was in fact the right legal answer. Their disagreement, for Dworkin, captures precisely what the 'stuff' of law as an argumentative practice is about. For Dworkin, the judges sought the right legal answer by constructing a justification (that subsumed the rule under it) in terms of discussing principles embodied in the law. Hard cases in effect are not hard for the reasons formalists would have it: either because of problems of the correct application of the rule or because, in line with how we have described the formalist position, of semantic ambiguities in the language of the specific rules. Hard cases cannot be 'read off' rules in this way. Discerning and arguing a hard case involves a theoretical disagreement about law, involving principles, standards and purposes embodied in the law; in effect, Dworkin sees hard cases not as pathologies that call for a more or less arbitrary decision to be made, but as pivotal, pointing to the law's essential contestability that calls for decisions that are, as he will call them later, always interpretive.

Let us take things more gradually. The theories of Hart and MacCormick, while accepting some of the Realist claims, maintain that law provides rational constraints to substantive reasoning and that these constraints have to do with the predominantly formalist nature of legal reasoning. It involves a supposition that judges should always seek to make rulings on disputed points of law, should do so consistently with the pre-established law, and should aim at coherence with established law through seeking always to make their judgements conform to legal principles. Such principles, they argue, stand in a rational, justificatory relationship to the valid rules of law. Dworkin criticises these views because of their acceptance of discretion, judicial lawmaking and retrospectivity. If their view of law-as-a-system-of-rules is correct, according to Dworkin, then rules have an all-or-nothing quality and so, once they run out, there is nothing left in law to appeal to. This gives judges a kind of strong discretion that is indeed unrestricted by law, given that law comes only in the form of rules, and hard cases that require discretion are hard precisely because there is no rule governing the case. The rules have in a crucial sense 'run out'. (Compare Hart's presentation of and attack on the Realists.) For Dworkin this inevitable concession is unacceptable. It is unacceptable descriptively, because that is not how judges understand the exercise of legal judgement; if they struggle and agonise over the answer in a hard case, it is not because they think that there is no law to be found covering it and that they therefore need to decide it purely in political or ethical terms. No, it is still the exercise of legal judgement that they are involved in. But formalism (and 'extended' formalism) has it wrong prescriptively too, for Dworkin, because it is an unacceptable violation of the values of law and democracy, as they find expression in the rule of law ideal, to concede that judges should in hard cases usurp the role of the legislator.

The discretion that judges have in a legal system, says Dworkin, is only discretion in the 'weak sense', but this is not MacCormick's 'weak sense', which for Dworkin is still a strong discretion, weakened only in that it is 'rationally' constrained. For Dworkin, the discretion that judges have is, and should be, weak in a different sense. Of course as an exercise of judgement, its outcome is never determinable in advance. But this does not mean that there are not right and wrong ways to exercise judgement. He gives the example of an army officer who is given the instruction 'to choose five men' for a mission. The strong discretion he is given in that instruction differs crucially from the weak discretion he would have been given had the instruction been: 'choose the five best men for the mission'. Obviously the latter instruction gives the officer discretion too, but it consists not in the freedom of choice, but in the exercise of informed judgement as to what 'best' means in terms of the requirements of the mission. It is this kind of discretion that judges are given. For Dworkin there are always relevant legal standards that will inform the outcome even though, unlike the case of merely deductive reasoning from rules, how to apply them is not always clear and always requires the exercise of judgement. This is difficult to do and often controversial, but there is ultimately a right answer. The judge's task is not to legislate new law. It is to apply existing law. The crucial point is that existing law contains more than the positive rules of law.

In his major work, *Law's Empire* (1986), the insight is integrated in a theory of law as interpretive practice. Much has been made of the differences between earlier approaches and that of this book, and although it is fair to say that emphases have been shifted, the later work integrates the earlier insights in a theory of law-as-interpretation, fundamentally enriched by the notion that the law is a practice and that it occurs in a community of interpreters. With this move Dworkin shifts the understanding of the nature of law from text to practice, from settled fact to ongoing revision. In contrast to the concept of law as a matter of past official decisions (positivism), for Dworkin, law is an interpretive concept, the meaning of every law an exercise in interpretation, the very distinction between a hard and an easy case always an interpretive choice. This exercise in interpretation is impossible unless we appreciate that law is a practice and involves us as participants in arguing its meaning. Borrowing from the hermeneutical tradition, Dworkin claims that an understanding of a social practice requires turning to the meaning it has for participants. The meaning of the law, as is the case with every practice and concept, can only be retrieved from within a shared context, a shared form of life, a community. As a community of interpreters of the meaning of our legal practice, we share a context of its possible meanings. We can begin to appreciate its demands not because we hold fast to some rigid list of rules, but because we can take the 'internal' point of view of the participant and interpret its point or purpose and how that might inform what it requires of us in each case. So arguing for the best among possible understandings involves us participants in an argument over the purpose or point of the practice. To discover what the law requires, each and every time, we must attempt to see the institution in its best light and to understand its requirements in the light of what would most fully realise its implied purpose. This exercise in (what Dworkin calls) 'constructive interpretation' must be performed on objective grounds; not, that is, by imposing upon the practice outside moral or personal purposes, but by retrieving purpose from within the practice, as it is intelligible to the people participating in it.

The 'right answer': law as integrity

This is as true of all social practices as it is for law. Interpretation is always justification for Dworkin: one understands a practice – here legal practice – by justifying what it is about; but this imputation of justificatory principle or purpose needs to be one that is already embodied in the practice, one that we retrieve from the best understanding of the practice, not that we impose on it. We may, for example, find that the best justification for awarding damages for delicts is the fair distribution of risks or even the protection of vulnerable members of society. But if that is not what makes sense of the practice of awarding compensation in our legal system, because, for example, the justification for holding people responsible has to do with whether they could have foreseen the injury rather than whether they can pay for it, then however attractive one might find one's own justification, it is not the principle or justification that can be read off the practice; it is imposed, not retrieved. And therefore it does not 'see' the practice under scrutiny in its best light because it does not fit the practice, but instead reconstructs it as something different. The enterprise of 'constructive interpretation' carries great complexity into legal practice and the business of reaching decisions in law. Competing interpretations in law are different rationalisations of the history of the practice competing on the terrain of 'fit'. Justifications command certain 'fits', 'fits' delimit certain justifications. It is a kind of reflexive equilibrium between the two that will allow the best balance of the two – a balancing undertaken against the background of the whole body of the law – to read as the legally right answer.

The 'right answer', for Dworkin, is an answer where weight matters. And what weight means, in this respect, is the gravitational pull of principles that need to be deployed to rationalise rules and decisions into coherence. The judge who is guided by integrity will decide on the morally most attractive principle, that is, a principle that best fits, or carries the most weight within that order, having been entrenched in previous decisions. What does this mean in practice? Take an example: someone is before the court having successfully incited a crowd to perform an illegal act. Can we extend criminal liability to her? Perhaps the 'morally most attractive' justification, the principle that the interpreter of law most values, is that all speech needs to be immune to prosecution; our political activist should be let off. But testing it against the legal practice of his community, the interpreter may find that it is not the case that this principle 'fits' the practice. The law curtails all kinds of speech acts: from threats to forms of advertising. On the other hand the justification might be over-inclusive; perhaps one should limit it to cases of 'political speech', arguing that the best reading of our legal practice demands that political speech acts be protected. In that case, perhaps, the requirement of 'fit' has been met, although it may also, perhaps, now stumble on something different: does the act in question, the incitement of the crowd, fall under the protected category, that is, is it an instance of 'political speech' or has the better 'fit' rendered the justification under-inclusive?

Dworkin calls his prescription for the right answer in law 'integrity'. Integrity means consistency in principle with past decisions and requires retrieving that principle in precedent as the justification that best fits the institutional record. Dworkin tellingly contrasts integrity to pragmatism, which is the name he gives to his main theoretical adversaries, the CLS movement. A pragmatist's recourse to political principles only serves his/her own pursuit of an ideal. There is no commitment to working out common schemes of principle embodied in the law; principles are imputed strategically in order for 'judges [and lay participants] to make whatever decisions seem best for the community's future' (Dworkin 1986, p 95). Unlike pragmatism, '[i]ntegrity demands that the public standards of the community be both made and seen, so far as this is possible, to express a single, coherent scheme of justice and fairness in the right relation' (ibid, p 219). Although every decision about what the law is can be debated as to what the principle to be read into text and precedent ought to be, integrity, unlike pragmatism, does not leave the question open. It insists, as we said, that the operative principle should fit the most coherent scheme of justice that can be envisaged for the past history of legal decisions and morally justifies that practice. Integrity demands that the rationalising principle of the decision at hand be part of a pattern that coheres as a whole and shows it in its best light.

To bring the connection between interpretation and coherence forcefully home, Dworkin uses the metaphor of the chain novel in which judges assume the roles of the consecutive co-authors. In adding his/her chapter to the novel, the author must both assure it reads as a whole as well as the best in its genre; in the same way the judge, if his/her decision is to respect law as integrity, will reconstruct the practice as a meaningful whole, thus sustaining the unity of community by giving coherence to the understanding of its practice of law in which people argue their conceptions of what justice requires. This is for Dworkin, aspirationally, what law is about and he entrusts the momentous task to his imaginary judge Hercules. Although every decision about what the law is can be debated as to what the principle to be read into text and precedent ought to be, integrity does not leave the question open, but provides Hercules with a guiding ideal that will yield the answer; it insists that the operative principle should fit into the most coherent scheme of justice that can be envisaged for the past history of legal decisions. Integrity demands that the rationalising principle of the decision at hand be part of a pattern that coheres as a whole. And that is the crux of Dworkin's restatement of the right answer thesis. Integrity yields the right answer as *mandated* by the law (rather than mere judicial preference) and thus sustains the rule of law ideal.

Reading

For a fascinating account of how analogy works in the common law, with specific reference to the notion of dangerousness in delict as a moving classification system, see Levi (1948, sections I and II, pp 501–519).

The 'conjoined twins' case provides the focus of several essays in Bankowski and MacLean (2006), which also deals in greater depth with issues of universality and particularity in legal reasoning.

For a concise summary of MacCormick's analysis, see MacCormick (1979). For fuller treatment, see MacCormick (1978, 1994 2nd edn, chs 5–9, especially ch 5 on 'second-order justification'). For MacCormick's later restatement of his theory of legal reasoning, see his *Rhetoric and the Rule of Law* (2005).

For a further discussion of Hart on discretion, look at his 'lost essay' (Hart 2013) and the papers discussing it in the 2013 *Harvard Law Review*, especially those by Lacey (2013) and Shaw (2013).

The concept of 'integrity' is developed in Dworkin (1986, ch 7), where it is usefully contrasted with other prevalent views on legal interpretation. For a concise summary of his theory of legal interpretation, see Dworkin (1990).

Dworkin (1985) is a valuable collection of a series of important analyses and interventions.

For a critical application of the theory of integrity in the context of South African apartheid law, see Christodoulidis (2004).

For Dworkin's attack on law-as-system-of-rules, see Dworkin (1977). For his use of the above cases to 'test' the formalist model, see Dworkin (1986, ch 1). Dworkin's formulation of 'rights as trumps' was developed in Dworkin (1977), but downplayed in his later work.

Although *Law's Empire* (1986) remains Dworkin's most important statement of his theory of law, he has developed key ideas further in (2000) and (2006) but particularly in (2011), where his theory of law gives up something of its distinctive commitment to the criterion of 'fit' and of coherence, and takes its place in a broader, integrated theory of value, where political, moral and legal thinking are conceived of as mutually supporting.

Chapter 15

The politics of legal reasoning

Critical legal theory

Critical theory has its roots in Western Marxism, and in particular what was discussed earlier in the book under the rubric of the Marxist critique of 'ideology'. Consequently one needs to turn again to Marx and the processes of production and social reproduction to identify the *object* and *locus* of critique. For Marx, basic categories of the operation of the economy and the material reproduction of society are expressions of capitalist relations. They are *mediated* through the basic categories of private law that give them expression as acts of freedom and autonomous agency. Earlier we looked at how, in the process, key features of the material organisation of society were thereby distorted, misrepresented or elided in the process of giving them expression. It was through this misrepresentation, it was argued, that the capitalist system *extracts allegiance* from those who are ruled over and who find their life chances diminished in the process. If critical theory is to address – let alone reverse – the condition of domination and exploitation, it must look at the ways in which meaning is constructed, and, as far as the legal discourse is concerned, at the way in which legal concepts organise and disguise capitalist distributions.

What is shared across the wide range of critical theory is both an emphasis on the political significance of theorising and its use as a means of empowerment and emancipation. *Critique* reads a transformative intent into theory: deeply sceptical of tradition and received wisdom, the emphasis of critical theory is to disturb and dislodge often hidden assumptions, prejudices and settled understandings about how things are. It is, crucially, a public philosophy of *engagement* rather than an academic discipline withdrawn from the contestations and dynamics of political society.

One might discern therefore certain common themes and tenets shared across the range of critical scholarship and intervention. These constitute fundamental insights of critical theory as captured variously by thinkers in the tradition, and we highlight them here with emphasis on the critique of juridical reason and its critical deployment. They will be taken up in the following two sections as we delve deeper into two important moments of critical legal thinking: the American Critical Legal Studies movement and the feminist critiques of legal reasoning.

The first thing to note is that critical theory always arises from and is situated within specific contexts of action and specific sets of social relations and institutional arrangements. Theory is here a form of public engagement, not an isolated academic discipline. It is very much undertaken as intervention in public life and as such situates itself within particular historical coordinates, arrangements, dynamics and conflicts. And that also means that it intervenes in terms that engage with specific imaginaries, with their vocabularies and rules of signification.

At the same time, critical theory must gain some distance from the ways in which the meaning of identity and action is formed in those situations and entertained by the participants. Compulsion cannot be shaken off unless it is seen for what it is, and it cannot be seen for what it is if it is assumed to be a *necessary* feature of social life. For example, if people assume that there (objectively) is less work available, then they will accept badly paid and demeaning work; if they assume that it is the natural prerogative of managers to set the terms of working relationships they will not organise to control the workplace democratically; where it is assumed that the economy will collapse unless certain profit margins are guaranteed to entrepreneurs then any move to reverse the asymmetries of power and wealth in society are seen as potentially destructive; etc. In all these situations the task of critical theory is to show that where arrangements are presented in terms of necessity, there is in fact *contingency*, and that things could be otherwise. This is both key to critical thinking and one of its steepest requirements. Where founding assumptions carry a certain self-evidence into the imaginary constitution of society, as inscribed in language and as mobilising specific systems of signification and material support, critical theory demands the recognition of the contingency of those foundations, and that is often a difficult theoretical task indeed to shake the self-evidence with which the dominant set of ideas vests its grounds.

In doing so, critical theory exploits contradictions which as we saw in discussing Marxism are inherent in a system that must organise its injustice in the guise of justice. The term can be extended to include inconsistencies, silences and exclusions, the discrepancies between what the capitalist system promises and what it is *capable* of delivering. Capable is an important word here; unlike 'likely' it carries a structural limitation. For example a capitalist labour market cannot deliver on the promise of full employment because a market – in 'optimising' supply and demand – requires a structural element of unemployment to maintain itself *as* a market. The object of critique is to expose such contradictions, between the equality that law promises and the vast inequality in the material distributions of wealth, between the promise of access to justice, to work, to healthcare, etc, and the reality of dispossession, between the promise of equal opportunity and the reality of discrimination on grounds of gender, race, etc. Where contradictions have been tracked, *ideology critique* aims to expose them as the *systematic* expression of dominant interests – whether these are class interests or whether they pertain to gender or race or underlie other forms of oppression – and invites people to *act* on them.

The U.S. critical legal studies movement

In 1976, a new academic movement emerged when a group of scholars formed a network called the 'Conference on Critical Legal Studies'. Despite considerable opposition in the legal academy, the group's influence grew, drawing together a variety of left-wing radical stances towards law into an umbrella movement and giving an institutional unity to those who opposed 'legal orthodoxy'. Picking up the radical moment in American Legal Realism (above), the CLS movement argue that taking legal doctrine seriously means revealing rather than concealing contrary aspects of law (even teaching law through them). With the Realists they argue against formalism that rules do not fix unambiguous meanings; the text of law can be 'deconstructed', they argue, to reveal its inherent ambiguities (see Advanced section on 'law and deconstruction'). Emphasising 'contradictions' means highlighting the choices and possibilities present in law that allow legal scholars, practitioners and judges to tap the resources the law itself makes available in order to argue the case for those who find themselves systematically disempowered by the way legal orthodoxy operates. This ties in with the CLS's second objective – to explore, criticise and eventually reverse the manner in which legal doctrine, legal education and the practices of legal institutions entrench advantage, disempower the vulnerable and sustain the status quo of a pervasive system of oppressive relations in society.

Although it would be wrong to see the CLS movement as a 'monolithic' movement, it is also not untrue to the variety it harbours to discern certain common themes. The first has to do with the claim that the law is riddled with real (not apparent) contradictions. The second has to do with how power operates in law to conceal these. Both of these moments – the tensions in law and the importance of power and hierarchy – are evident in the way CLS analyses law by stressing the various paired master oppositions that resolve cases in opposite and incompatible ways: mechanically applied rules/ situation-sensitive ad hoc standards, values as subjective/values as objective, human action is willed/human action is determined by environment, private/public, individual/ group, law/policy, reason/fiat, freedom/coercion. Such pairs are hierarchically structured in that one side of the opposition is dominant, the other subordinate and supplementary. The dominant side sustains the status quo; the subordinate, in exceptional cases, allows us to question it.

Take the example of contract law and the analysis offered by one of the leading figures in the CLS movement, Roberto Unger. Unger contends that the history of contract law and what is passed down as its doctrinal systematisation is inherently indeterminate: it can be read in different ways depending on the principle we impute each time. Depending on whether we read contract law through the prism of 'individualism' or of 'community' we will 'rationalise' it in competing ways, by imputing alternately the principle of freedom of contract and the counter-principle of fairness of contract. Both readings are possible because both will yield coherent accounts of precedent, even if the aspiration of community, and the principle of fairness it informs, will fit less well, or will strain to make sense of some of that history. As 'suppressed' principle or 'counter-principle', nonetheless, it contains the potential for fresh legal interpretations of the law of contract, more attractive for the value it expresses.

Unger's argument runs something like this:

1   For every rule, there is an exception.
2   The rule represents the dominant principle; the exception stands for a counter-principle, subordinate but still present in law.
3   Different social visions are in contest in law – individualism vs altruism – and these underlie the rule/dominant principle and the exception/counter-principle.

Applied schematically to the law of contract these yield the following threefold pairing of oppositions (Table 15.1):

Table 15.1 Pairing of oppositions

Rule	Exception
Pacta sunt servanda	Except when contract is void or voidable
[contractual obligations must be upheld]	
Principle	**Counter-principle**
Freedom of contract: both as to contractual partner(s) and terms	Fairness of contract: agreements are struck down where:
	(i) terms are unfair
	(ii) communal aspects of social life are subverted
	(iii) parties acted unconscionably
Value	**Counter-value**
Individualism/Autonomy	Solidarity, protection of the vulnerable, community values

This is of necessity schematic. However, the basic point, as emphasised by Unger, is that the possibility is present in law to argue a case as falling under the rule (*pacta sunt servanda*) or the exception (doctrine of duress, undue influence, unreasonable terms, impossibility, unconscionability, protection of good faith and reliance on less formal representations, etc); that this opposition at the level of doctrinal interpretation reflects a deeper opposition of competing principles; and that in that opposition of principles a further deeper and legally irresolvable opposition is in turn played out, between two politically irreconcilable value systems – liberal individualism and socialism. The point is not merely that the law provides a wealth of possibilities for lawyers to argue any case either way, but that in fact our legal system acts both as passive enforcer of private transactions and in a paternalistic, active role as protector of vulnerable parties against economic predators. The law does not contain 'right answers' waiting to be discovered. Instead, the law's oppositions correspond to competing normative visions of human association present within law and that the presence of such clashing perspectives should be discussed openly, not least because the suppressed side of law's oppositions are taken to be the more politically progressive. Thus law is to be taken seriously as a means of effecting radical social transformation.

In subsequent work Unger (1987b) has spoken of the need to institutionalise further categories of rights, including 'solidarity rights'. Although very little is said about the precise content of these rights, one can assume on the basis of Unger's other writings that the content would be retrieved through playing up principles already present – if suppressed – in existing law. The mechanism and logic of this has been elaborated above. In 'Legal Analysis as Institutional Imagination' (1996), he renewed his call for a 'selective probing of institutions' through the 'dialectical exercise of mapping and criticism'. Unger's suggestion in all of this is for an interpretative method of reasoning that draws on and exploits strategically existing, if latent, institutional possibilities. In the case of solidarity rights, reconstruction would proceed from the protection of solidarity in existing law – of contract and delict basically – such as the protection of reliance and the protection of the disadvantaged party, general clauses of good faith and of abuse of rights, and so on, 'by which private law supports communal relations while continuing to represent society as a world of strangers' (Unger 1987b, p 537).

Drawing on Unger's work, Hugh Collins describes a further model for deploying legal analysis in what he describes as a horizontal rather than the above vertical manner (Collins 1987b). According to the orthodox view of how law functions in society, one can discern broadly three spheres of social life with law applying differently to each. There is the sphere of public life, and here our public law provides citizens with robust protection (in the form of civil rights) against the might wielded by the State and organises the democratic system by guaranteeing political rights. Here the law acknowledges a certain asymmetry in the relations of citizen to State and thus affords the vulnerable party protection and guarantees. The second sphere is that of exchange and work. In this sphere liberal law typically treats parties as equal, providing the language and the categories to sanction their dealings with each other, but remaining neutral in the process. Finally there is the third sphere, the sacrosanct private sphere of family and intimacy in which the law intervenes minimally in order to maintain it free of State intervention and secure privacy understood as negative freedom.

There are good, political reasons, claims the CLS movement, why this frozen picture of social life needs to be challenged as maintaining oppression rather than guaranteeing freedom, entrenching advantage rather than opportunity. Family relations, if not put under legal scrutiny, are free to harbour abuse, patriarchal privilege, domestic violence, violation of trust. The sphere of work and exchange is emphatically not a sphere where equal parties strike their deals, but instead where corporate giants manipulate individual workers and where economic predators prey on vulnerabilities of contractual partners.

The CLS agenda for radical political change to counter advantage uses law to renegotiate the boundaries between spheres, and manipulate the fragilities and porous nature of those boundaries to stir up social change. More precisely, the horizontal application of 'deviationist doctrine' here, of critical legal doctrine, depends again on tracing the paired opposition of principle and counter-principle within each sphere and arguing the case for treating the counter-principle as significant. What gives particular credence to this argumentative strategy is that what counts as counter-principle in one sphere is indeed dominant in another. For example, while in the sphere of public life we may have freedom to expose corrupt authority and to associate to pursue our claims, the very same rights are denied in the sphere of exchange. The very same activities draw very different legal responses in the sphere of work where 'whistle-blowing' against corrupt employers is rarely protected and forms of picketing are often criminalised. But the logic of this differential legal response is completely flawed and self-contradictory. The sphere of work and exchange is not a sphere of equality; corporations act increasingly in corrupt ways and their activities need to be exposed to scrutiny, particularly in an era where there are corporate actors who indeed wield much greater power than even nation-states do; employees are one of the most vulnerable categories in the face of ruthless new management techniques, managerial prerogative, the proliferation of forms of under-employment and the threat of unemployment. So why not use the resources the legal system affords us in the form, here, of the protection of rights, and cross the boundaries between spheres, the autonomy of which is becoming increasingly unconvincing, imaginatively to deploy legal argumentation to any particular area of social life?

Unger's work is suggestive and radical, as both to its vision for the possibilities of legal analysis and its careful mapping of the ways in which the logic of law can be deployed to stretch those limits. Against an understanding of law as striving for the right answer on the basis of imputation of the one best principle, like Dworkin, Unger propounds the possibility of political choice through the imputation of 'counter-principle'. Hence the debate between Dworkin and Unger (a debate that however has never taken a direct or explicit form) is best understood against a background of political theory. The critical scholar is attempting to feed the possibility of transformative political action into law. If law is indeterminate and has to be 'rationalised' each time, then it is a malleable vessel for political vision. What legal answer we see as appropriate is relevant to our politics. What reason is 'right' depends on our political choice of what political principle underlying it is right. Dworkin's project is motivated by a typically liberal concern to keep law clean of politics. He professes a theory that will elevate choices from the battleground of politics to the legal forum of principle (see Dworkin 1985). On Dworkin's account of it, law provides the politically neutral means of mediating between politically competing positions, so that what one perceives as the right answer in law does not necessarily identify with what one conceives to be politically desirable. The CLS movement on the other hand not only views it as impossible to avoid political choices in legal debate, but sees the liberal attempt to elevate law above politics as itself not a neutral but a political move.

Feminist critiques of adjudication

Initial challenges

Some of the most consistently challenging critiques of legal reasoning over the last few decades have come from feminist writers. These critiques are inspired not just by academic analysis, but by an understanding of the very real and detrimental effects of law and its reasoning processes on women's lives. The history of law in westernised societies is the history of laws written by men. It would not be at all surprising, then, that women's voices and status have been excluded or denigrated, and that processes of legal reasoning have been profoundly implicated in this. While there is a range of divergent positions within feminist analysis, certain strands have emerged that may be considered as critiques – on the one hand of the substance of law, and on the other of the form of law itself.

For many feminist writers, notably those writing earlier in the feminist tradition, the aim was to establish formal legal equality between men and women as a matter of the substantive content of the law. Such work inspired – and continues to inspire – much thinking behind anti-discrimination legislation and its application, whose intention is to ensure that men and women have formally equal standing and rights in law. Prominently, for example, in the arena of employment law, women struggled to establish the principle of equal pay for equal work and equal access to employment opportunities, pensions and so on, which could be established in legislation that enshrined the universal principle of non-discrimination on the basis of sex. From this perspective, laws that directly discriminated against women undermined equality under the rule of law. If law's self-image valorised its fairness and impartiality, then those same standards demanded that men and women be treated equally in the eyes of the law. In other words, the principle of formal equality among all citizens should be given full, not partial, effect. Sometimes referred to as 'liberal feminism', this approach argued that women's freedom to participate as equals in society meant holding law to its self-professed standards. Hence already-existing principles of law and legal reasoning could be used to develop full and equal rights for women, in both legislation and adjudication.

This belief in the law's ability to include women, where once they had been excluded, came to be seen as having a number of shortcomings. That is, despite claims to formal equality having been heard, legal interpretation nonetheless still drew on a male perspective in the definition or application of general categories. On this account, the interpretation of equal rights or standards contained within them biases that meant women continued to be discriminated against. So, for example, with regard to the criminal law defences of provocation or self-defence, the application of the relevant law to cases that did not fit the (masculine) image of an immediate retaliation worked to exclude situations where women responded to male abuse over a long period of time. And, in anti-discrimination law itself, women, in order to find an appropriate comparator against which the question of discrimination could be addressed, had always to compare themselves to a man in the equivalent situation. Hidden here was that the male standard was always assumed to be the norm, and it was deviation from that which was written through the law's assumptions about equality. The general point here is summed up by Naffine (1990, pp 136–137):

> while the law may appear to offer roughly equal rights to men and women, in truth the law organises around a particular individual who is both male and masculine. The legal person is still very much a man, not a woman, and the law still reserves another place for women: as the other of the man of law.

Conventional techniques of legal reasoning meant that even where equality was announced in law, the question 'Equal to what?' tended to be answered by treating male standards as the unproblematised and universal ones. As Naffine (p 144) continues, the underlying question was really this: 'Why can't a woman be more like a man?' In deciding what aspects of the broader social understandings of roles, relationships and expectations were highlighted or downplayed, judges (who are overwhelmingly male) filled in, more or less consciously, the content of abstract legal categories such as legal personality or formal equality by importing male assumptions of these to inform the law's response, while simultaneously legitimating them as expressing equality. In so doing, women's experiences were devalued, or failed to register, in giving content to the law.

Critiquing the *form* of legal reasoning

These insights raised deeper problems with the liberal feminist approach, which went to the very form of law and legal reasoning itself. The values associated with the formalist position – objectivity, neutrality, universality, formal justice – have all been subjected to criticism by feminist authors. Why would these values be seen as such a cause for concern? The essence of the argument is that while these values purport to treat people equally, they nonetheless operate to do precisely the opposite. There are two kinds of arguments here.

The first is that the very idea of trying to be objective, impartial, neutral and so on in fact embodies a male perspective on social relations. There are two divergent interpretations of how this impacts on legal reasoning. One argues that men and women have different styles of reasoning. Drawing on analyses of moral reasoning, psychologist Carol Gilligan (1982) found that men tended to emphasise abstract, individualistic and universal or rule-driven approaches to moral problems, while women emphasised connectedness and more particularised or contextualised reasoning. The former she associated with an ethic of justice, the latter with an ethic of care. Moreover, Gilligan noted, the 'justice' style of reasoning was traditionally seen as more 'developed' or 'advanced', and hence the notions of objectivity and impartiality given priority, ahead of those associated with 'care'. Thought of in the legal context, it might be seen that the values of legal formalism replicate such a hierarchy, and in so doing implicitly embody a more male-centred account of what is deemed the most appropriate, 'just', way of approaching legal interpretation. In all this, women's essential experiences could be downplayed, and their 'different voices' excluded from processes of understanding and reasoning.

Such an interpretation has been widely criticised with regard to law and social relations generally. According to Catharine MacKinnon, a feminist legal author, this approach 'essentialises' what is really a matter of contingent power between the sexes, not one of natural differences. Caring, suggests MacKinnon, is just what men want women to do. Rather, she argues, it is not difference but dominance that explains sexual relations in contemporary society. While, as we have seen, treating men and women equally means using the male as comparison, different treatment, she argues, is not the result of real differences, but of domination through social practices writ large. Moreover, where exceptions have been made in attempts to recognise 'difference', these are open to the charge of further entrenching male stereotypes and power. Thus even where supposedly well-intentioned judges sought to protect women's differences, 'as a result of their very womanhood', the results could be a form of paternalism that undermined any putative freedom. MacKinnon gives a particularly graphic example of this: where a court decided that it was legitimate to exclude women from a contact job in an all-male prison because they might be raped by inmates, MacKinnon suggests the court took 'the viewpoint of the reasonable rapist on women's employment opportunities' (1989, p 226).

MacKinnon's critique is that the values associated with legal formalism – objectivity, neutrality, impartiality – are themselves suspect since they constitute the basic ways of organising social power to the detriment of women. Central to these are the State – its legislative and adjudication processes – and the doctrine of the rule of law itself when thought of in these terms:

> The state is male in the feminist sense: the law sees and treats women the way men see and treat women. The liberal state coercively and authoritatively constitutes the social order in the interests of men – through its legitimating norms, forms, relation to society, and substantive policies.
>
> (ibid, pp 161–162)

The notion of objectivity, for example, so central to the formalist account, does the work in fact of objectifying – that is, turning into objects – women. Hence for MacKinnon,

'Formally the state is male in that its objectivity is its norm . . . The state is male juris-prudentially in that it adopts the standpoint of male power on the relation between law and society' (ibid, pp 162–163).

As such, understandings of legal interpretation must pay more attention to the form of law, and not just its substantive content; or, rather, it must pay attention to the way in which the power of law's form operates to determine its content. And this is true across the whole range of legal regulation: as Finley argues,

> Legal reasoning and its language are patriarchal . . . Privileged white men are the norm for equality law; they are the norm for assessing the reasonable person in tort law; the way men would react is the norm for self-defense law; and the male worker is the prototype for labor law.
>
> (Finley 1989, p 893)

It is significant that Finley emphasises the linguistic element in legal reasoning since it shows up both the power of language to normalise social relations of inequality, but also, importantly, its limits; that is, that merely changing to non-sexist language in the law – the reasonable person, rather than the reasonable man in negligence, for example – will not necessarily lead to gender equality where underlying structures of inequality remain unaddressed. It is these observations that point to the intimate links between legal language, formalist values and social domination. As Finley puts it,

> Universal and objective thinking is male language because intellectually, econom-ically, and politically privileged men have had the power to ignore other perspec-tives and thus to come to think of their situation as the norm, their reality as reality, and their views as objective. Disempowered, marginalized groups are far less likely to mistake their situation, experience, and views as universal.
>
> (ibid, pp 893–894)

Questions remain, however, about the extent to which it is persuasive to treat all women's experience as uniform, and whether such accounts tend to downplay other social dynamics such as race, class or culture, across which women's experiences may differ greatly (Fraser 1995, pp 68–93).

Comparing approaches

Let us return to some of the aspects of legal reasoning as identified by MacCormick, earlier, and consider them now in the context of feminist critiques. It will be recalled that MacCormick considered three central problems associated with legal reasoning: those of relevancy, interpretation and classification. Now, each of these is open to evalu-ation according to different ways of thinking about how gender bias may be involved.

First, relevancy: what is the relevant legal rule? This is one of the key areas in which contestation has occurred. Let us take one example: the question of whether the princi-ple of equal pay for equal work should apply to domestic labour – labour that continues to be carried out predominantly by women. By excluding such work from being recog-nised within the field of paid employment (and hence attracting the benefits or obliga-tions that may go with it), women's work is devalued in line with what Fraser (1995, p 78) sees more generally as a gendered social hierarchy: gender, she writes, 'structures the fundamental division of labour between paid "productive" labour and unpaid "reproductive" labour, assigning women primary responsibility for the latter'. When considered in addition to discrimination existing across the field of paid employment itself, the result, she concludes, 'is a political-economic structure that generates gender-specific modes of exploitation, marginalisation, and deprivation' (ibid). At this most basic level – the production and reproduction of social goods – the question of relevancy clearly plays a crucial role in being able to recognise and respond to – or, as is more often the case, failing to recognise and respond to – the structured injustices of contemporary gender relations. Establishing the 'relevancy' of a particular law to a particular harm is therefore a crucial way of asserting the applicability of hitherto ignored claims.

Interpretation refers to the problem: given there is a relevant legal rule, how should it be interpreted? Again, here we encounter a whole range of interpretative matters, which can be opened to challenge by feminist encounters with the law. In particular, we might note how certain binary oppositions (or 'dualisms'; see Olsen 1990) operate to construct and naturalise the assumptions within which interpretation takes place. The distinction between public and private is one such opposition, and has a substantial history in legal thought and feminist critiques of it. Here, it has been argued, much of women's experience has been traditionally placed in the 'private' realm into which general legal norms have been only reluctantly applied in order, in theory, that the State respect as fully as possible the autonomy of individuals in their private lives. The effect of this, however, is often to normalise the violence or abuse that may occur in the domestic setting, actions that again impact primarily on women and which would be less likely to be countenanced if they happened 'publicly'. As Lacey points out,

> the practical consequence of non-regulation is the consolidation of the status quo: the de facto support of pre-existing power relations and distributions of goods within the 'private' sphere . . . the ideology of the public/private dichotomy allows government to clean its hands of any responsibility for the state of the 'private' world and depoliticises the disadvantages which inevitably spill over the alleged divide by affecting the position of the 'privately' disadvantaged in the 'public' world.
> (Lacey 1998, p 77)

Although challenging this distinction has been fruitful in raising consciousness – according to the slogan 'the personal is political' – and exposing the failures of legal interpretation to live up to its professed standards, it has also been seen more recently as being descriptively inaccurate and normatively questionable. As legal norms – such as in family or social security law – increasingly regulate or intervene in areas traditionally seen as private, the distinction between the two becomes less clear. Moreover, as Lacey points out, there is an important difference between saying that the 'private' realm should be repoliticised, and that it should be legally regulated. Yet despite this, the language and stereotypical associations of the public/private distinction may still operate in an ideological way. Lacey's analysis shows how generally, as well as in the context of legal interpretation, 'what happens in this kind of rhetoric is that the labels "public" and "private" are used in question-begging ways which suppress the normative arguments which they actually presuppose. This means that the debate sounds commonsensical rather than politically controversial' (Lacey 1998, p 78). It is the importance of that last observation – that what appears as 'common sense' in legal reasoning is itself the result of contingent political victories – that holds the key to understanding the importance of conflicts over interpretation, especially to the extent that these are involved in continuing sexual discrimination.

Finally, classification refers to whether the case can be properly classified under the relevant legal rule. One of the most controversial examples of this concerns the debate over pornography. Should pornography be classified as an actionable harm perpetrated by men against women, or rather as an exercise in free speech or expression and thus be protected by the law? As MacKinnon puts it, 'as a social process and as a form of "speech", pornography amounts to terrorism and promotes not freedom but silence. It promotes freedom for men and enslavement and silence for women' (MacKinnon 1987, pp 129–130). The classification of it under the protection of free speech laws merely confirms her observation that the State and its laws are complicit in the reproduction of domination and sexual violence against women. Contrarily, it has been argued that the rights to freedom of speech and expression should be held as paramount, policed only and at the fringes, by obscenity laws. Here, problems of classification clearly refer not to some internal logic of the law or working through of the law's principles, but to how we should understand harm in the context of expressions or violations of sexuality and the extent to which objective, neutral or impartial accounts of this are possible or indeed desirable, since the very assumptions they make may be part of the problem.

In all these examples, it is clear that attention needs to be paid to the ways in which interpretative leeway and/or the claimed 'naturalness', impartiality or objectivity of legal reasoning may operate to obscure and legitimise gender divisions in the law. This may be referred to as part of the law's ideological role. But it should not be inferred from this that such interpretive leeway is either haphazard or that its assumptions are set in stone. Rather, the types of arguments presented here suggest that gender discrimination is more or less clearly patterned, that legal categories and interpretive modes of reasoning are implicated in this, but that these forms of exploitation can, and should, be challenged through more creative forms of legal intervention.

Reading

For a useful introduction to critical theory, with a special emphasis on the Frankfurt School', see Bronner's 'short introduction'(2017) and the work of Jay (1996). For a historical account of critical legal theory in Europe see Christodoulidis and Van der Walt (2018).

Critical legal analysis in the US has been developed in a number of fields of law: Karl Klare in labour law, Duncan Kennedy in torts, David Kennedy in international law, Roberto Unger in private law, etc. See Kennedy (1976) and (1997) for Duncan Kennedy's distinctive contribution to the Critical Legal Studies movement and Klare (1977) for a critical-theoretical reading of US labour protection. For Roberto Unger's critique of 'formalism' and 'objectivism', see Unger (1983), pp 5–14. For a comprehensive introduction to the emergence of the CLS movement in its various strands, see Kelman (1987). For an accessible summary, see Altman (1993, ch 1).

For a general overview of feminist critiques of adjudication, Olsen (1995) provides a helpful starting point. For interesting collections of feminist engagements with the law, see Munro and Stychin (2007) and Davies and Munro (2016). Important studies have been carried out across a variety of doctrinal branches of law, for example, Buss and Manji (2005), Cowan and Hunter (2007) and Crawford et al (2017).

Hunter et al (2010) provide an innovative recent engagement with legal doctrine. The 'Feminist Judgements Project' 'set out to write alternative feminist judgments in significant legal cases', thereby 'inaugurat[ing] a new form of critical legal scholarship, one which seeks to demonstrate in a sustained and disciplined way how judgments could have been written and cases could have been decided differently' (Hunter et al 2010, p 4). The project has inspired similar work in several jurisdictions, including Australia, the United States and Northern Ireland.

General part **II**

Tutorials

❖ TUTORIAL 1   Legality and the rule of law

Reading

- *Jurisprudence*, chapter 12 ('The Challenge of Natural Law')

For the purposes of the tutorial you should be ready to explain and evaluate Lon Fuller's approach to law. Consider in particular the following questions:

1 What does Fuller mean by saying these principles constitute an 'inner morality of law'? Summarise briefly the purpose of Fuller's 'eight principles of legality'. Are any of the eight ways of making law more important or persuasive than others?

2 Do the eight principles of legality constrain in any way the substantive content of laws? If so, what examples can you think of?

3 Is H.L.A. Hart correct in his criticism of Fuller that they are 'perfectly compatible with the pursuit of immoral ends'? Why/why not?

4 What values do you believe the doctrine of the rule of law upholds? How are these the same or different from Fuller's eight principles of legality?

5 Fuller states that 'there is a kind of reciprocity between government and the citizen with respect to the observance of rules' (Fuller 1969, p 39). In light of his 'principles of legality', how do you understand Fuller's claim? (Select two or three principles by way of example.) Do you find Fuller's analysis persuasive? Why/why not?

6 Jeremy Waldron claims that the concept of law and the rule of law are inseparable. What does he mean by this?

7 Waldron argues that the five 'elementary requirements for a system of rule to qualify as a legal system' support the values of human dignity, reason and responsibility. How do they do so?

8 Why does Waldron see the 'culture of argument' as so central to what we understand as law? Is he, in your view, correct?

9 In light of the arguments put forward by Fuller, Waldron, and/or Radbruch, is the legal positivist claim as expressed by Kelsen – that 'any kind of content might be law' – a persuasive one?

❖ TUTORIAL 2 — Law, power and the rule of law

Reading

- *Jurisprudence*, chapter 15 ('The Politics of Legal Reasoning')

According to Roberto Unger, the idea of constraining power by an impersonal rule of law in liberal societies rests on two assumptions both of which, he says, turn out to be fictitious: first that the 'most significant sorts of power can be concentrated in government', the second that 'power can be effectively constrained by rules' (Unger 1976, pp 178–179). How do you understand these criticisms of the modern idea of rule of law? To what extent are they correct?

❖ TUTORIAL 3   Identifying valid law: legal positivism

Reading

- *Jurisprudence*, chapter 11 ('Identifying Valid Law')

- Lon Fuller, 'The Problem of the Grudge Informer', in Fuller (1969) *The Morality of Law*, pp 245–253.

- David Dyzenhaus, 2008, 'The Grudge Informer Case Revisited', *NYU Law Review* pp 1000–1034, provides an extensive re-appraisal of the debate – available at www.nyulawreview.org/sites/default/files/pdf/NYULawReview-83-4-Dyzenhaus.pdf

Questions

1 Why do we need a theory of legal validity?

2 Explain the account of legal validity given by (a) Hart and (b) Kelsen. What is the difference between the two? What is the 'ultimate rule of recognition' in the UK? What is the 'basic norm'?

3 Read Lon Fuller's 'The Problem of the Grudge Informer' and, in light of the theorists studied, answer the question that Fuller asks at the end of the piece.

❖ TUTORIAL 4   Identifying valid law: natural law

Reading

*   *Jurisprudence*, chapters 11 ('Identifying Valid Law') and 12 ('The Challenge of Natural Law')

The oppressive government of the state of Ukania was toppled by a democratic revolution in 1997. The new government seeks to act in line with sound constitutional and legal principles such as might be found in European Conventions. One of these principles is that there should be no punishment without a law, while another is that no law is to be retrospective in its effect. The new constitution states that those suspected of gross violations of human rights must be brought to trial. It also states that citizens have the right to have justiciable disputes settled by a court of law.

In its final days the old Parliament passed an Act, it was claimed for reasons of maintaining peace and stability in the transition to the new regime, which gave immunity from criminal and civil liability to all functionaries of the former government.

Three cases are now being brought before the courts.

1   Two victims of torture are bringing a civil suit for damages against their torturer.

2   A prosecutor has decided to bring to trial the former head of the security services and the former Home Secretary for conspiracy to murder eighty-three political opponents who died as a result of security operations.

3   A former border guard is being prosecuted, despite his claim merely to have been following legitimate orders, for shooting two people who tried to escape the country.

You are the Minister of Justice and have been asked by the Cabinet for your opinion on these cases.

❖ TUTORIAL 5   Law and morality

Reading

- *Jurisprudence*, chapter 12 ('The Challenge of Natural Law')

Whether we think it a law or not we still have to decide what to do. Saying it is immoral and therefore not a law would have the same practical effect as saying it is a law but immoral and therefore we must not obey it. Does the distinction matter?

Reflect on the following thesis:

> The strict separation between law and morality cannot be upheld: An unjust law is not valid law. Or at least there is a threshold beyond which a law is too evil to count as law. Those who enforced the apartheid regime in South Africa, the soldiers who shot at Germans trying to flee East Berlin during the Cold War, the officials of the Nazi regime *cannot* claim to have acted according to the law. Some acts – including torture and genocide – should be punished regardless of any prior prohibition.

Questions

1 In your opinion, is this argument persuasive in demonstrating that the definition of law necessarily imports value judgements?

2 A member of the British armed forces has objected to going to fight in the Iraq war because he believed it to be illegal on the grounds that it violated the fundamental value of law that it should protect human life. He is now being court-martialled for disobeying orders. He has asked you for your advice as to whether there are any jurisprudential grounds for supporting his defence. What do you advise?

Interpreting or making the law? [1]

Reading

* *Jurisprudence*, chapters 13 ('Identifying Valid Law'), 14 ('The Turn to Interpretation') and 15 ('The Politics of Legal Reasoning')

In 1989, in Edinburgh, J.D. Stallard was charged with raping his wife in the matrimonial home while they were living together there. He took a plea to the relevancy of the charge, relying on Hume's statement (see below) that a husband cannot rape his wife because she has 'surrendered her person' to him. The plea was repelled at a preliminary diet, and the appellant appealed to the High Court.

Here are the facts:

> (2) [Y]ou being married to Evelyn Stewart or Stallard, care of Police Office, Bridge of Allan, and while residing with her at said house at . . . Stirling, did on 25th August 1988 at said house
>
> (a) assault said Evelyn Stewart or Stallard and did strike her on the face and punch her on the leg, to her injury;
>
> (b) order said Evelyn Stewart or Stallard to a bedroom within said house, there order her to remove her clothing and threaten to rip said clothing from her body if she refused, and she having removed her clothing you did assault her, place and lock a set of handcuffs on her wrists, order her to lie on a bed, lie on top of her, threaten her with violence if she screamed for help, have sexual intercourse with her against her will and thereafter kneel by her and emit semen on her face and did rape her; and
>
> (c) further assault said Evelyn Stewart or Stallard, tie her body and legs to said bed with ropes, force a sock or similar object into her mouth and place Sellotape over her mouth and face, and all this you did to her severe injury.

On 21st February 1989 the accused lodged a minute under s 76 of the **Criminal Procedure (Scotland) Act 1975** seeking a preliminary diet on the following ground:

> That the said Johnston David Stallard wishes to take objection to the relevancy of the indictment and more particularly objects that the charge (2)(b) is irrelevant insofar as it alleges that the accused committed the crime of rape upon his wife while they were residing together.

On 3rd March 1989 a preliminary diet was held in the High Court at Edinburgh before Lord Mayfield, when the plea to relevancy was repelled. The accused then appealed to the High Court.

Read the following extract from *HMA v Stallard* from the decision on appeal (emphases added):

LORD JUSTICE GENERAL (EMSLIE)

There is no doubt that if it was the law of Scotland that a husband is not amenable to a charge of raping his wife, the rule rests solely upon the sentence in Hume which was simply adopted and repeated in different language by the later commentators and writers on the criminal law. The statement in Hume that 'a man cannot himself commit a rape on his wife' appears in a passage in relation to a discourse on art and part of rape against a background of abduction. All who assist are involved in the same guilt as the actor.

'This is true without exception even of the husband of the woman; who, though he cannot himself commit a rape on his own wife, who has surrendered her person to him in that sort, may however be accessory to that crime . . . committed on her by another.' . . . The view expressed by Hume and echoed by, inter alios, Burnett, was taken from Hale's *Historia Placitorum Coronae* published in England in 1736 in which he said this [vol 1, p 629]:

'But the husband cannot be guilty of a rape committed by himself upon his lawful wife, for by their mutual matrimonial consent and contract the wife hath given up herself in this kind unto her husband, which she cannot retract.'

The first question accordingly comes to be whether, even in the eighteenth and early nineteenth centuries, the reason given for the husband's supposed immunity for the commission upon his wife of acts which would constitute the crime of rape was a sound one. That reason was, according to Hume, that the wife had 'surrendered her person' to her husband 'in that sort'. This is the first opportunity which the court in Scotland has had to consider whether Hume's statement of the law was sound when it was written and whether it is sound today. It was not necessary in HM Advocate v Duffy or in HM Advocate v Paxton for the court to consider whether Hume's view was and is a sound one in any circumstances during the subsistence of a marriage, but we must do so now. In our opinion, the soundness of Hume's view, and its application in the late twentieth century, depends entirely upon the reason which is said to justify it. Our first observation is that if what Hume meant was that by marriage a wife expressly or impliedly consented to sexual intercourse with her husband as a normal incident of marriage, the reason given affords no justification for his statement of the law because rape has always been essentially a crime of violence and indeed no more than an aggravated assault. Even in Hume's time there was no immunity for a husband who assaulted his wife even if the assault contained elements of the grossest indecency. If, on the other hand, Hume meant that by marriage a wife consented to intercourse against her will and obtained by force, *we take leave to doubt whether this was ever contemplated by the common law* which was derived from the canon law, regulating the relationship of husband and wife. We say no more on this matter which was not the subject of debate before us, because we are satisfied that the Solicitor-General was well founded in his contention that whether or not the reason for the husband's immunity given by Hume was a good one in the eighteenth and early nineteenth centuries, it has since disappeared altogether. *What Hume meant to encompass in the concept of a wife's 'surrender of her person' to her husband 'in that sort', the concept is to be understood against the background of the status of women and the position of a married woman at the time when he wrote.* Then, no doubt, a married woman could be said to have subjected herself to her husband's dominion in all things. She was required to obey him in all things. Leaving out of account the absence of rights of property, a wife's freedoms were virtually non-existent, and she had in particular no right whatever to interfere in her husband's control over the lives and upbringing of any children of the marriage. By the second half of the twentieth century, however, the status of women, and the status of a married woman, in our law have changed quite dramatically. A husband and wife are now for all practical purposes equal partners in marriage and both husband and wife are tutors and curators of their children. A wife is not obliged to obey her husband in all things nor to suffer excessive sexual demands on the part of her husband. She may rely on such demands as evidence of unreasonable behaviour for the purposes of divorce. *A live system of law will always have regard to changing circumstances to test the justification for any exception to the application of a general rule.* Nowadays, it cannot seriously be maintained that by marriage a wife submits herself irrevocably to sexual intercourse in all circumstances. It cannot be affirmed nowadays, whatever the position may have been in earlier centuries, that it is an incident of modern marriage that a wife consents to intercourse in all circumstances, including sexual intercourse obtained only by force. There is no doubt that a wife does not consent to assault upon her person and there is no plausible justification for saying today that she nevertheless is to be taken to consent to intercourse by assault.

This development of the law since Hume's time immediately prompts the question: is revocation of a wife's implied consent to intercourse, which is revocable, only capable of being established by the act of separation? In our opinion the answer to that question must be no. Revocation of a consent which is revocable must depend on the circumstances. Where there is no separation this may be harder to prove but the critical question in any case must simply be whether or not consent has been withheld. *The fiction of implied consent has no useful purpose to serve today in the law of rape in Scotland.* The reason given by Hume for the husband's immunity from prosecution upon a charge of rape of his wife, if it ever was a good reason, no longer applies today. There is now, accordingly, no justification for the supposed immunity of a husband. Logically the only question is whether or not as matter of fact the wife consented to the acts complained of, and we affirm the decision of the trial judge that charge (2)(b) is a relevant charge against the appellant to go to trial.

Questions

1   What *kind* of argument is the Lord Justice General relying on in the above quote? Is it an argument from principle? Is it an interpretation of existing law or does it involve a change of the law?

2   How might the theories of Hart and/or Dworkin help us to make sense of the legal reasoning in this case? Is the rule of law – or any aspect of it – sacrificed in the process?

Part 2

Read the Lord Advocate's Reference No 1 of 2001. It is reported at 2002 SLT 466 and 2002 SCCR 435.

The case was a Reference following the acquittal of an Aberdeen law student on a rape charge.

1   Summarise the arguments of *either* the Lord Justice General *or* Lady Cosgrove *and* the dissenting opinion of Lord McLuskey.

2   Explain the point of disagreement and the legal arguments used to support the opposite opinions.

3   How do the judges view their role here? Do they view it as applying or as creating the law? What do you think is their proper role?

4   Compare with the reasoning in *Stallard*. What, if any, similar issues arise?

Part 3

Read Lindsay Farmer's 'The Genius of Our Law' in 55 *Modern Law Review* 25. (Farmer 1992).

1   What does it say about the judges' 'practical legal approach' and does it help us understand the development of Scots Law as a 'living body of law'?

2   In your opinion is it correct to sacrifice 'abstract legal rules' in the name of this more pragmatic approach?

Reading

- *Jurisprudence*, chapters 13 ('Identifying Valid Law'), 14 ('The Turn to Interpretation') and 15 ('The Politics of Legal Reasoning')

Donoghue v Stevenson is one of the most famous common law cases. Read the following extracts of the opinions:

LORD BUCKMASTER

My Lords, the facts of this case are simple. On August 26, 1928, the appellant drank a bottle of ginger-beer, manufactured by the respondent, which a friend had bought from a retailer and given to her. The bottle contained the decomposed remains of a snail which were not, and could not be, detected until the greater part of the contents of the bottle had been consumed. As a result she alleged, and at this stage her allegations must be accepted as true, that she suffered from shock and severe gastro-enteritis. She accordingly instituted the proceedings against the manufacturer which have given rise to this appeal.

The law applicable is the common law, and, though its principles are capable of application to meet new conditions not contemplated when the law was laid down, these principles cannot be changed nor can additions be made to them because any particular meritorious case seems outside their ambit.

LORD ATKIN

The liability for negligence, whether you style it such or treat it as in other systems as a species of 'culpa,' is no doubt based upon a general public sentiment of moral wrongdoing for which the offender must pay. But acts or omissions which any moral code would censure cannot in a practical world be treated so as to give a right to every person injured by them to demand relief. In this way rules of law arise which limit the range of complainants and the extent of their remedy. The rule that you are to love your neighbour becomes in law, you must not injure your neighbour; and the lawyer's question, Who is my neighbour? receives a restricted reply. You must take reasonable care to avoid acts or omissions which you can reasonably foresee would be likely to injure your neighbour. Who, then, in law is my neighbour? The answer seems to be – persons who are so closely and directly affected by my act that I ought reasonably to have them in contemplation as being so affected when I am directing my mind to the acts or omissions which are called in question.

It will be found, I think, on examination that there is no case in which the circumstances have been such as I have just suggested where the liability has been negatived. There are numerous cases, where the relations were much more remote, where the duty has been held not to exist. There are also dicta in such cases which go further than was necessary for the determination of the particular issues, which have caused the difficulty experienced by the Courts below. I venture to say that in the branch of the law which deals with civil wrongs, dependent in England at any rate entirely upon the application by judges of general principles also formulated by judges, it is of particular importance to guard against the danger of stating propositions of law in wider terms than is necessary, lest essential factors be omitted in the wider survey and the inherent adaptability of English law be unduly restricted. For this reason it is very necessary in considering reported cases in the law of torts that the actual decision alone should carry authority, proper weight, of course, being given to the dicta of the judges.

. . .

I have already pointed out that this distinction is unfounded in fact, for in Elliott v. Hall (4), as in Hawkins v. Smith (5) (the defective sack), the defendant exercised no control over the article and the accident did not occur on his premises. With all respect, I think that the judgments in the case err by seeking to confine the law to rigid and exclusive categories, and by not giving sufficient attention to the general principle which governs the whole law of negligence in the duty owed to those who will be immediately injured by lack of care.

LORD TOMLIN

My Lords, I have had an opportunity of considering the opinion (which I have already read) prepared by my noble and learned friend, Lord Buckmaster. As the reasoning of that opinion and the conclusions reached therein accord in every respect with my own views, I propose to say only a few words.

First, I think that if the appellant is to succeed it must be upon the proposition that every manufacturer or repairer of any article is under a duty to every one who may thereafter legitimately use the article to exercise due care in the manufacture or repair. It is logically impossible to stop short of this point. There can be no distinction between food and any other article. Moreover, the fact that an article of food is sent out in a sealed container can have no relevancy on the question of duty; it is only a factor which may render it easier to bring negligence home to the manufacturer.

The alarming consequences of accepting the validity of this proposition were pointed out by the defendant's counsel, who said: 'For example, every one of the sufferers by such an accident as that which recently happened on the Versailles Railway might have his action against the manufacturer of the defective axle.'

LORD MACMILLAN

What, then, are the circumstances which give rise to this duty to take care? In the daily contacts of social and business life human beings are thrown into, or place themselves in, an infinite variety of relations with their fellows; and the law can refer only to the standards of the reasonable man in order to determine whether any particular relation gives rise to a duty to take care as between those who stand in that relation to each other. The grounds of action may be as various and manifold as human errancy; and the conception of legal responsibility may develop in adaptation to altering social conditions and standards. The criterion of judgment must adjust and adapt itself to the changing circumstances of life. The categories of negligence are never closed. The cardinal principle of liability is that the party complained of should owe to the party complaining a duty to take care, and that the party complaining should be able to prove that he has suffered damage in consequence of a breach of that duty. Where there is room for diversity of view, it is in determining what circumstances will establish such a relationship between the parties as to give rise, on the one side, to a duty to take care, and on the other side to a right to have care taken.

I am happy to think that in their relation to the practical problem of everyday life which this appeal presents the legal systems of the two countries are in no way at variance, and that the principles of both alike are sufficiently consonant with justice and common sense to admit of the claim which appellant seeks to establish.

Questions
1   [General:]
   - Is the 'neighbour principle' a legal or a moral principle?
   - If, as Lord Atkin asserts, it is indeed 'found . . . on examination that there is no case in which the circumstances have been such as I have just suggested where the liability has been negatived', then in what sense is *Donoghue* a hard case?

2   [In relation to MacCormick:]
   - Is it any of the business of the courts to decide cases on the basis of consequences they may have?
   - Discuss the role of coherence in law on the basis of the arguments made by the judges in this case.

3 [In relation to Dworkin:]
   - How would integrity's balance of 'fit' and 'justification' require Hercules to decide the case?

4 [In relation to the CLS:]
   - Discuss the contention that *Donoghue* exhibits nothing else but an early expression of a *politics* of legal reasoning in the judges' conviction that values of social solidarity should inform all social interaction.

❖ TUTORIAL 8   Discrimination and legal reasoning

Reading
* *Jurisprudence*, chapters 14 ('The Turn to Interpretation') and 15 ('The Politics of Legal Reasoning')

Part 1
Read the paper by Ronald Dworkin: 'Bakke's Case: Are Quotas Unfair?' (Dworkin 1985, ch 14).

Questions
1   Summarise and explain the structure of Dworkin's argument.

2   In your opinion does Dworkin resolve the clash between the protection of individual rights and the pursuit of the common good in a satisfactory way?

Part 2
Consider the following scenario:

The medical school of Aberlour University in Scotland is concerned about the make-up of its student population. Measured against the overall population, too many of its students are female (75%), and they do not attract enough ethnic minority students or students from state schools. Recent research shows that state school students perform better at university than public school pupils with the same grades. As a result, the medical school introduces a quota in favour of state school pupils to address the imbalance. Since, statistically, most minority ethnic students are also state-school educated, the medical school hopes that as an indirect result, this policy will also increase the number of minority ethnic students.

John is a black African student, who studied at Fettes, an expensive private school in Edinburgh. His application to the university is rejected in favour of a lesser-qualified female student who studied at a Scottish state school.

Questions
1   Do you think that the introduction of the quota achieves a proper balance between the right to education and other social and political demands?

2   Do you think that John has been treated fairly?

3   In your view how might Dworkin answer this problem? How might Unger? Which approach do you find most persuasive?

❖ **TUTORIAL 9** Legal reasoning and the scope of interpretation: Hart and Dworkin

Reading

- *Jurisprudence*, chapters 13 ('Identifying Valid Law') and 14 ('The Turn to Interpretation')

Questions

1 All legal systems, argues Hart, 'compromise between two social needs: the need for *certain* rules, which can . . . safely be applied without weighing up social issues, and the need to *leave open for later settlement* issues which can only be properly appreciated and settled when they arise in a concrete case' (Hart 1961, p 127, emphasis added).

a   Do you agree?

b   In your opinion can these two 'social needs' be reconciled?

c   Is this a result of the 'open texture' of the law?

d   Discuss this statement with reference to Dworkin.

2 'Law's attitude is constructive: it aims, in the interpretive spirit, to lay principle over practice to show the best route to a better future, keeping the right faith with the past' (Dworkin 1986).

a   Do the terms 'best', 'better' and 'right' in the above quote introduce an irreducibly 'subjective' element to legal reasoning?

b   Discuss the contention that Dworkin's theory is a robust defence of the rule of law.

❖ TUTORIAL 10   Essay questions on legal reasoning

Reading

* *Jurisprudence*, chapters 13 ('Identifying Valid Law'), 14 ('The Turn to Interpretation') and 15 ('The Politics of Legal Reasoning')

Questions

1 'To regard the jury simply as a judicial institution would be taking too narrow a view of the matter for great though its influence on the outcome of lawsuits is, influence on the fate of society is much greater still. The jury above all is a political institution and it is from this point of view that it must always be judged.'

(De Tocqueville, *Democracy in America*)

In your opinion is a compromise possible between the role of the jury in deciding on the truth of the matter and its role as a 'political institution'?

2 '[J]udges ought to strive to give the real reasons for their decision. It is my firm conviction that where courts of law have denied a remedy for the cost of bringing up an unwanted child the real reasons have been grounds of distributive justice. That is, of course, a moral theory. It may be objected that the House must act like a court of law and not like a court of morals. That would only be partly right. The court must apply positive law. But judges' sense of the moral answer to a question, or the justice of the case, has been one of the great shaping forces of the common law. What may count in a situation of difficulty and uncertainty is not the subjective view of the judge but what he reasonably believes that the ordinary citizen would regard as right.'

(*McFarlane and Another v Tayside Health Board* [1999]
4 All ER 961, per Lord Steyn at pp 977–978)

Discuss.

3 'A law of society prescribes what we may or may not do. It *can* be broken – indeed if we could not break it there would be no need to have it.'

Discuss.

4 If law is indeed a matter of rules, *why does it matter* that the great majority of judges are male, white, upper class and educated in private schools?

5 'Legal reasoning is an inherently repressive form of interpretive thought which limits our comprehension of the social world and its possibilities.'

Discuss.

6 'The intellectual core of the [formalist] ideology is the distinction between law and policy. Teachers convince students that legal reasoning exists, by bullying them into accepting as valid in particular cases arguments about legal correctness that are circular, question-begging, incoherent, or so vague as to be meaningless.'

(Kelman 1987)

Discuss.

Bibliography

Alexy, R, 1999, *A Defence of Radbruch's Formula*. In Dyzenhaus, D (ed) *Recrafting the Rule of Law: The Limits of Legal Order*. London: Bloomsbury Publishing, 1999.

Altman, A, 1993, *Critical Legal Studies*, Berkeley: University of California Press.

Austin, J, 1995/1832, *The Province of Jurisprudence Determined*, Cambridge: Cambridge University Press.

Bankowski, Z and MacLean, J (eds), 2006, *The Universal and the Particular in Legal Reasoning*, Aldershot: Ashgate.

Bennion, F, 2001, *Understanding Common Law Legislation*, Oxford: Oxford University Press.

Bennion, F, 2002, *Statutory Interpretation*, 4th edn, London: Butterworths.

Bingham, T, 2011, *The Rule of Law*, Harmondsworth: Penguin.

Blackstone, W, 1830, *Commentaries on the Laws of England*, vol. 2. Collins & Hannay.

Bronner, SE, 2017, *Critical Theory: A Very Short Introduction*, Oxford: Oxford University Press.

Buss, D and Manji, A (eds), 2005, *International Law: Modern Feminist Approaches*, Oxford: Hart.

Christodoulidis, E, Dukes, R and Goldoni, M, forthcoming, *Handbook in Critical Legal Theory*, London: Edward Elgar.

Christodoulidis, E, 1996, 'The Inertia of Institutional Imagination: A Reply to Roberto Unger', 59 *Modern Law Review* 377.

Christodoulidis, E, 2004, 'End of History Jurisprudence: Dworkin in South Africa', *Acta Juridica* 64.

Christodoulidis, E and Van der Walt, 2018, forthcoming, 'Critical Legal Theory', in *Oxford Handbook of Historical Legal Research*.

Collins, H, 1986, *The Law of Contract*, London: Weidenfeld and Nicolson.

Collins, H, 1987a, 'The Decline of Privacy in Private Law', 14 *JLS* 91.

Collins, H, 1987b, 'Roberto Unger and the Critical Legal Studies Movement', 14 *JLS* 387.

Cotterrell, R, 2003, *The Politics of Jurisprudence*, 2nd edn, London: Butterworths.

Cowan, S and Hunter, R (eds), 2007, *Choice and Consent: Feminist Engagements With Law and Subjectivity*, London: Routledge-Cavendish.

Crawford, BJ et al (eds), 2017, *Feminist Judgments: Rewritten Tax Opinions*, Cambridge: Cambridge University Press.

Cross, R, 1995, *Statutory Interpretation*, 5th edn, London: Butterworths.

Cross, R and Harris, JW, 1991, *Precedent in English Law*, 4th edn, Oxford: Clarendon.

Davies, M and Munro, V (eds), 2016, *The Ashgate Research Companion to Feminist Legal Theory*, Abingdon: Routledge.

d'Entrèves, AP, 1965, *Natural Law: An Historical Survey*, New York, Harper.

Detmold, M, 1984, *The Unity of Law and Morality*, London: Routledge & Kegan Paul.

Douglas, H et al (eds), 2014, *Australian Feminist Judgments: Righting and Rewriting Law*, Oxford: Hart.

Douzinas, C and Perrin, C, 2011, *Critical Legal Theory*, New York: Routledge.

Duxbury, N, 1995, *Patterns of American Jurisprudence*, Oxford: Clarendon.

Dworkin, R, 1977, 'The Model of Rules', extracted in R Dworkin (ed), *The Philosophy of Law*, Oxford: Oxford University Press, and expanded in chapters 2 and 3 of *Taking Rights Seriously*, Cambridge, MA: Harvard University Press.

Dworkin, R (ed), 1977, *The Philosophy of Law*, Oxford: Oxford University Press.

Dworkin, R, 1985, *A Matter of Principle*, Cambridge MA: Harvard University Press.

Dworkin, R, 1986, *Law's Empire*, London: Fontana.

Dworkin, R, 1990, 'Law, Philosophy and Interpretation [the Kobe lecture for Legal and Social Philosophy]', *ARSP* 1.

Dworkin, R, 2000, *Sovereign Virtue*, Cambridge, MA: Harvard University Press.

Dworkin, R, 2006, *Justice in Robes*, Cambridge, MA: Harvard University Press.

Dworkin, R, 2011, *Justice for Hedgehogs*, Cambridge, MA: Harvard University Press.

Dyzenhaus, D, 1991, *Hard Cases in Wicked Legal Systems: Pathologies of Legality*, Oxford: Oxford University Press. New revised edition, 2010.

Dyzenhaus, D, 2008, 'The Grudge Informer Case Revisited', *NYU Law Review* 1000–1034.

Enright, M et al (eds), 2017, *Northern/Irish Feminist Judgments*, London: Bloomsbury.

Finley, L, 1989, 'Breaking Women's Silence in Law: The Dilemma of the Gendered Nature of Legal Reasoning', 64 *Notre Dame LR* 886.

Finnis, J, 1980, *Natural Law and Natural Rights*, Oxford: Clarendon.

Finnis, J, 1993, 'Bland: Crossing the Rubicon', 109 *LQR* 329.

Finnis, J, 1999, 'Natural Law and the Ethics of Discourse', 12 *Ratio Juris* 354.

Finnis, J, 2011, *The Collected Essays of John Finnis*, vols I–V, Oxford: Oxford University Press.

Finnis, J, 'Natural law theories.' *Entry in the Stanford Encyclopaedia of Philosophy*

Frank, J, 1949a, *Courts on Trial: Myth and Reality in American Justice*, Princeton: Princeton University Press.

Frank, J, 1949b, *Law and the Modern Mind*, London: Stevens.

Fraser, N, 1995, 'From Redistribution to Recognition? Dilemmas of Justice in a "Post-Socialist" Age', 212 *New Left Review* 63.

Fuller, LL, 1958, 'Positivism and Fidelity to Law: A Reply to Professor Hart', *Harvard Law Review* 630–672.

Fuller, LL, 1969, *The Morality of Law*, New Haven, CT: Yale University Press.

George, R (ed), 1994, *Natural Law Theory*, Oxford: Clarendon.

Gilligan, C, 1982, *In a Different Voice*, Cambridge, MA: Harvard University Press.

Gowder, P, 2016, *The Rule of Law in the Real World*, Cambridge: Cambridge University Press.

Griffith, JAG, 1977, *The Politics of the Judiciary*, London: Fontana.

Hale, R, 1923, 'Coercion and Distribution in a Supposedly Non-Coercive State', 38 *Political Science Quarterly* 470.

Hale, R, 1943, 'Bargaining, Duress, and Economic Liberty', 43 *Columbia Law Review* 603.

Hart, HLA, 1958, 'Positivism and the Separation of Law and Morals', *Harvard Law Review* 593–629.

Hart, HLA, 1961, *The Concept of Law*, Oxford: Clarendon.

Hart, HLA, 1963, *Law, Liberty, and Morality*, Stanford: Stanford University Press.

Hart, HLA, 1983, *Essays in jurisprudence and philosophy*, Oxford: Oxford University Press.

Hart, HLA, 2013, 'Discretion', 127 *Harvard Law Review* 652.

Hart, HLA, 2016, 'The New Challenge to Legal Positivism (1979)', 36(3) *OJLS* 459–475.

Hayek, FA, 1944, *The Road to Serfdom*, London: Routledge & Kegan Paul.

Holmes, OW, 1897, 'The Path of the Law', 10 *Harvard Law Review* 457.

Holmes, OW, Laski, HJ, Frankfurter, F, and Howe, MDW, (1953), *Holmes-Laski Letters*, Cambridge, MA: Harvard University Press, 243.

Hume 1978/1739, *A Treatise of Human Nature*, Oxford: Clarendon.

Horwitz, M, 1992, *The Transformation of American Law, 1870–1960: The Crisis of Legal Orthodoxy*, New York: Oxford University Press.

Hunter, R, McGlynn, C and Rackley, E (eds), 2010, *Feminist Judgments: From Theory to Practice*, Oxford: Hart.

Jackson, B, 1995, *Making Sense in Law*, Liverpool: DC Publications.

Jay, M, 1996, *The Dialectical Imagination: A History of the Frankfurt School and the Institute of Social Research, 1923–1950*, vol. 10, Berkeley: University of California Press.

Kelman, M, 1987, *A Guide to Critical Legal Studies*, Cambridge, MA: Harvard University Press.

Kelsen, H, 1957, *What is Justice: Law and Politics in the Mirror of Science*, Berkeley: University of California Press.

Kelsen, H, 1967/1934, *Pure Theory of Law*, trans M Knight, Berkeley: University of California Press.

Kennedy, D, 1976, 'Form and Substance in Private Law Adjudication', 89 *Harvard Law Review* 1685.

Kennedy, D, 1997, *A Critique of Adjudication [fin de siècle]*, Cambridge, MA: Harvard University Press.

Klare, KE, 1977, 'Judicial Deradicalization of the Wagner Act and the Origins of Modern Legal Consciousness, 1937–1941', 62 *Minnesota Law Review* 265.

Lacey, N, 1998, *Unspeakable Subjects: Feminist Essays in Legal and Social Theory*, Oxford: Hart.

Lacey, N, 2004, *A Life of HLA Hart: The Nightmare and the Noble Dream*, Oxford: Oxford University Press.

Lacey, N, 2013, 'The Path Not Taken: HLA Hart's Harvard Essay on Discretion', 127 *Harvard Law Review* 636.

Levi, E, 1948, 'An Introduction to Legal Reasoning', 15 *University of Chicago LR* 501.

Levit, N and Verchick, R, 2016, *Feminist Legal Theory*, 2nd ed, New York: New York University Press.

Llewellyn, KN, 1931, 'Some Realism About Realism: Responding to Dean Pound', 44.8 *Harvard Law Review* 1222–1264.

MacCormick, N, 1978, *Legal Reasoning and Legal Theory*, Oxford: Clarendon.

MacCormick, N, 1979, 'The Artificial Reason and Judgement of Law', *Rechtstheorie* 105.

MacCormick, N, 1981, *H.L.A. Hart*, London: Arnold.

MacCormick, N, 1989, 'The Ethics of Legalism', *Ratio Juris* 184.

MacCormick, N, 1993, 'Argument and Interpretation in Law', *Ratio Juris* 16.

MacCormick, N, 1994, *Legal Reasoning and Legal Theory*, 2nd edn, Oxford: Clarendon.

MacCormick, N, 1994, 'On the Separation of Law and Morality', in R George (ed), *Natural Law Theory*, Oxford: Clarendon.

MacCormick, N, 2005, *Rhetoric and the Rule of Law: A Theory of Legal Reasoning*, Oxford: Oxford University Press.

MacCormick, N, 2008, *Practical Reason in Law and Morality*, Oxford: Oxford University Press.

MacCormick, N and Summers, R, 1991, *Interpreting Statutes*, Aldershot: Dartmouth.

MacKinnon, CA, 1987, *Feminism Unmodified: Discourses on Life and Law*, Cambridge, MA: Harvard University Press.

MacKinnon, CA, 1989, *Toward a Feminist Theory of the State*, Cambridge, MA: Harvard University Press.

McLeod, I, 2005, *Legal Method*, 4th edn, Basingstoke: Palgrave Macmillan.

Munro, V and Stychin, C (eds), 2007, *Sexuality and the Law: Feminist Engagements*, London: Routledge-Cavendish.

Naffine, N, 1990, *Law and the Sexes*, London and Sydney: Allen & Unwin.

Olsen, F, 1990, 'Feminism and Critical Legal Theory: An American Perspective', 18 *International Journal of the Sociology of Law* 199–215.

Olsen, F, 1995, *Feminist Legal Theory: Foundations and Outlooks*, New York: New York University Press.

Paulson, SL and Litschewski Paulson, B (eds), 1998, *Normativity and Norms: Critical Perspectives on Kelsenian Themes*, Oxford: Oxford University Press.

Pound, R, 1960, 'The Causes of Popular Dissatisfaction With the Administration of Justice', reprinted in R Henson (ed), *Landmarks of Law*, New York: Harper.

Radbruch, G, 2006, 'Statutory lawlessness and supra-statutory law (1946)', 26.1 *Oxford Journal of Legal Studies* 1–11.

Raz, J, 1980, *The Concept of a Legal System*, Oxford: Oxford University Press.

Rumble, WE, 1968, *American Legal Realism*, Ithaca and New York: Cornell University Press.

Rundle, K, 2012, *Forms Liberate: Reclaiming the Jurisprudence of Lon L Fuller*, London: Bloomsbury Publishing.

Savigny, FC von, 1975/1831, *Of the Vocation of Our Age for Legislation and Jurisprudence*, New York: Arno Press.

Schauer, F, 2015, *The Force of Law*, Cambridge, MA: Harvard University Press.

Shaw, GC, 2013, 'HLA Hart's Lost Essay: Discretion and the Legal Process School', 127 *Harvard Law Review* 666.

Singer, J, 1988, 'Legal Realism Now', 76 *California Law Review* 465.

Stanchi, KM et al (eds), 2016, *Feminist Judgments: Rewritten Opinions of the United States Supreme Court*, Cambridge: Cambridge University Press.

Stone, J, 1965, *Human Law and Human Justice*, Stanford: Stanford University Press.

Stone, J, 1946, *The Province and Function of Law: Law as Logic, Justice and Social Control*. Sydney: Associated General Publications Pty.

Summers, RS, 1984, *Lon L. Fuller*, vol. 4, Stanford: Stanford University Press.

Tur, R, and Twining, W, 1986, *Essays on Kelsen*, Oxford: Clarendon.

Twining, W, 1984, 'Some Scepticism About Scepticisms', 1 *Journal of Law and Society*, 137–171.

Waldron, J, 2008–2009, 'The Concept of the Rule of Law', 43 *Georgia Law Review* 1.

Unger, RM, 1983, *The Critical Legal Studies Movement*, Cambridge, MA: Harvard University Press.

Unger, RM, 1987a, *Social Theory: Its Situation and Its Task*. Volume 1 of *Politics: A Work in Constructive Social Theory*, Cambridge, MA: Cambridge University Press.

Unger, RM, 1987b, *False Necessity: Anti-Necessitarian Social Theory in the Service of Radical Democracy*. Volume 2 of *Politics: A Work in Constructive Social Theory*. Cambridge, MA: Cambridge University Press.

Unger, RM, 1996, 'Legal Analysis as Institutional Imagination', 59 *Modern Law Review* 1.

Weber, M, 1921/1978, *Economy and Society: An Outline of Interpretive Sociology*, vol. 1. Berkeley: University of California Press.

Yntema, H, 1960, 'American Legal Realism in Retrospect', 14 *Vanderbilt Law Review* 317.

Cases

Brown v Board of Education 347 US 483 (1954).
Daniels & Daniels v R White & Sons [1938] 4 All ER 258.
Donoghue v Stevenson [1932] UKHL 100.
In re A (Conjoined Twins) [2000] 4 All ER 961.
Lochner v New York 198 US 483 (1905).
MacPherson v Buick 111 NE 1050 (NY 1916).
Riggs v Palmer 115 NY 506 (1889).

Part III

Advanced topics

1 Theories of justice 229

   Utilitarianism versus libertarianism 230

   Liberalism: Rawls's justice as fairness 234

   Socialism 237

2 Global justice 244

   The central issue and some terminology 244

   Content and scope of justice 244

   The conservative view 246

   The progressive view 247

   The way forward 248

3 Transitional jurisprudence
and historic injustices 251

   The rule of law in political transitions 251

   Addressing colonialism: judging in an
unjust society 257

4 Trials, facts and narratives 265

   The legacy of fact-scepticism 265

   Trials and perceptions of fact: language
and narrative in the courtroom 268

   Trials, regulation and justice 270

5 Displacing the juridical: Foucault on
power and discipline 274

   Power and the law 275

Discipline   275

Biopower   277

Governmentality   278

A theory of legal modernity?   279

6 Legal pluralism   282

Classical and contemporary legal
pluralism   283

Strong and weak legal pluralism,
and the position of the state   284

Empirical, conceptual and political
approaches to legal pluralism   286

Future directions in legal pluralism   287

7 Legal institutionalism   290

8 Law and deconstruction   299

9 Juridification   312

The meaning and scope of juridification   312

Habermas on juridification   313

Juridification and the 'regulatory
trilemma'   315

Juridification as depoliticisation   317

A fifth epoch?   318

10 Autopoietic law   321

The concept of autopoiesis   321

An inventory of concepts   322

The coding of social systems   324

Society, sub-systems and the law   325

How does 'the law think'?   327

Chapter 1

Theories of justice

Few topics appear so central to thinking about the relationship between law and politics than the matter of justice. Yet according to David Hume, if there were adequate resources to satisfy people's needs and wants – such as there is with the abundant air we breathe – then the problems of justice would largely not exist. But where resources appear relatively scarce, says Hume, human conventions of justice have developed to organise entitlements and distribution. Political questions then arise as to which principles ought to guide such organisation. Should people be left alone to determine their own sense of justice, individually or within particular groups? Or does some institution, such as the State, need to intervene to provide a common standard for all? If so, what would such a common standard require? Perhaps that people be treated equally? But given that people are not in fact equal – in abilities, say: they may be sick, or be children, or be unable to work – does justice require not equal but different treatment in recognition of these facts? And should people get what they need, or what they deserve, or what would be fair?

The proliferation of such questions signals that not only are the answers likely to be many and contested, but also that there is a wide range of contested questions too. For example, should all relations be considered as amenable to applying principles of justice: parenting, say, or the treatment of animals? Do citizens of one state owe duties of justice to citizens of another? Should law always be used to establish and regulate matters of justice? Can law do justice to justice? Or should talk about 'justice' even be superseded by alternative approaches? For is it not the case that ideas, and practices of proclaimed justice, have readily co-existed with the reality of extensive exploitation and discrimination: against women, racial groups, the poor and so on? Or is this observation precisely why we need to work harder at the problems – to do justice better?

In thinking about the relationship between law and politics, there are different senses in which we speak about justice. For example, *formal* justice is embodied in the principle of treating like cases alike and different cases differently. This is a central element of legal reasoning, including reasoning from precedent, and was taken up in more detail in Part II. There are related aspects of *procedural* justice that are concerned with how institutions go about, or ought to go about, processing legal claims in a procedurally fair manner. (This was an essential element in Waldron's account of law and legality that we outlined in ch 12, Part II.) There is also a subset of instances where societies are called upon to 'do justice to the past' – commonly now identified as problems of *transitional justice* – where societies that have gone through major political and social upheaval are faced with special problems associated with coming to terms with acts of injustice perpetrated by predecessor regimes. Where there have been extensive human rights abuses, for example, questions of *corrective*, *retributive* and *restorative* justice often come to the fore in conflicting ways in assessing how best to deal with these abuses.

In this Advanced Topic, however, we will concentrate on questions of *distributive* justice. This concerns the just distribution of goods, benefits and burdens in a society. We will look at four approaches to distributive justice that have been influential in how modern societies organise themselves with respect to what they think are justice's best guiding principles. These are utilitarianism, libertarianism, liberalism and socialism. We will assess some of their central ideas, though we necessarily have to be selective. (For fuller engagement with the topic, the further reading should be a starting point.) But we should note one thing at the outset: these are *normative* theories; not in the sense that they are concerned with describing legal rules which govern actions, but rather in the sense that they provide arguments concerning why the view they promote *ought* to be adopted. These theories conflict – hence their *political* nature – and you should consider which, if any, you find more persuasive and why.

Utilitarianism versus libertarianism

A *utilitarian* approach to justice seeks to maximise average welfare in a society. Jeremy Bentham and John Stuart Mill were two of the most prominent advocates of this approach. The most famous expression of it sees the goal of increasing overall utility as being to achieve 'the greatest happiness of the greatest number'. It is a *consequentialist* theory: it tests for justice by reference to consequences. There are two main variations. Act utilitarianism considers whether any proposed *action* will result in increasing the average welfare. Rule utilitarianism asks what *rule* is best instituted to increase such welfare. It is in assessing the outcomes of putting the proposed act, or rule, into effect that the morally best or just thing to do becomes clear. The outcome is not just because it was the right act to do or rule to follow: it was the right thing to do or rule to follow because the consequences were perceived to maximise average welfare, to produce the 'greatest happiness of the greatest number'.

Hypothetical examples are often used to make this approach clear. Here are two. A person is detained because police have reasonable grounds to suspect that he has planted a powerful bomb somewhere in a densely populated city. If such a device goes off it is likely to result in mass injury and deaths. The detainee refuses to speak. Is it justifiable to torture him to try to find out where the bomb is? Is it, in other words, permissible, as a matter of justice, to commit harm against one person rather than risk harm to a greater number?

From the point of view of *act* utilitarianism, we are essentially only concerned with the justice – that is, the consequences – of the act in this instance. From the point of view of *rule* utilitarianism, we are concerned with the consequences – or justice – of instituting a rule that would authorise such behaviour. In either case note what we must do in our deliberation: we must add up the pros and cons of the consequences of allowing or not allowing such an act or instituting the rule. We assess the possible harms and benefits and then, as it were, put them on a set of scales in order to determine what act or rule would maximise overall welfare. Reading off the result from the scales we find out what justice requires. In this example, there might seem something intuitively plausible about the idea that justice demands acting in such a way as to minimise the aggregate harms when we weigh the harm done to the detainee against the potential harms done to a large number of innocents. Surely a greater injustice is allowed by failing to act in such a way that protects many innocents from harm?

But is this utilitarian approach the correct way of reasoning? Consider what is negated should torture be permitted: factually, an innocent person might be being tortured – the detainee may be genuinely innocent because of a case of mistaken identity. This possibility is one reason why, in law, a presumption of innocence operates according to which everyone is presumed innocent until proven guilty in a court of law. Moreover, even on consequentialist grounds, applying torture is commonly seen to be less a reliable way of procuring evidence than it is a measure of how much pain a person can withstand. Does torture, that is, even get at the truth? And if the person is willing to plant a bomb on this scale are they likely to confess the truth? And so on. But perhaps the key, non-consequentialist objection to utilitarian reasoning here is that a decent society respects the 'inalienable' human right not to be tortured regardless of the nature of the circumstances. Prohibitions on torture, or on 'cruel, inhuman and degrading treatment', signal that 'To treat a person inhumanly is to treat him in a way that no human should ever be treated' (Waldron 2005, p 1745) On this view, we should in no circumstances even carry out a utilitarian calculation about outcomes: it is wrong to torture *regardless* of the consequences.

Consider then another scenario: a member of your country's air force is shot down while on a reconnaissance mission over a country with whom there are hostile relations. The enemy captors have reasonable grounds to believe that he has knowledge of imminent air strikes, likely to result in major civilian casualties. But he refuses to tell them what he knows about where the strikes are likely to be aimed. Is it justifiable to torture him to try to find out the location of the strikes? Would it be legitimate, as Harvard Law Professor Alan Dershowitz has suggested in the context of detainees held by American forces, to use 'a sterilized needle inserted under the fingernails to produce unbearable pain' (quoted in Waldron 2005, p 1685) in order to get the information and so help to save lives? Should the utilitarian calculation of harms and benefits allow such treatment? Even in the extreme circumstances of war, the international standard on the treatment of prisoners of war declares that it should not. Article 17 of the 1949 Third Geneva Convention states that 'No physical or mental torture, nor any other form of coercion, may be inflicted on prisoners of war to secure from them information of any kind whatever.' On this widely respected view, utilitarian calculations about claimed increases in aggregate welfare are *never* to be entered into: detainee's rights, to use Ronald Dworkin's metaphor, automatically trump any claims about possible consequences.

Consider now two additional concerns with a utilitarian approach to justice. First, to what extent is it possible to measure utility? That is, how can we assess what people's pain and pleasure consists in, in order then that we can calculate how it can be increased? What if people have different understandings or experiences of what for them counts as pleasure or pain? Moreover, are all desirable values – dignity, say, or liberty – reducible to one single measure – 'happiness' – in order that they can be weighed together and a clear solution reached? What our first two examples show is that in some, extremely

important, cases we may be either unable or unwilling to make a commensurating calculation with values at all since it belittles notions of dignity or liberty to reduce them
to a process of measuring 'more or less' happiness. This was a point noted by the Enlightenment philosopher Immanuel Kant, whose work represents a strong challenge to utilitarianism. Dignity, he argued, is not something on which a price can be put and thus
measured against other values, in the way that we might calculate a market price on the
value of cars or computers. He argued that

> In the kingdom of ends everything has either a price or a dignity. What has a price
> can be replaced by something else as its equivalent; what on the other hand is
> above all price and therefore admits of *no equivalent* has a dignity.
>
> (Kant 1993/1785, p 40, emphasis added)

The difficulty of reducing a plurality of values to one single measure – the problem
of the commensurability of values – therefore poses an important challenge to utilitarian
thinking.

A second concern is with trying to figure out what in fact the consequences of
any act – or, in the case of rule utilitarianism, what the consequences of instituting a
particular rule – are going to be. Even if we were to assume that it is possible to compare competing values by weighing them on the scales of pleasure and pain, there may
be conflicting ways of assessing which of the consequences matters most in the process of weighing. Consider another example. You are well-off and live comfortably in
a wealthy suburb in a country which nonetheless has widespread unemployment,
poverty and homelessness which afflict a majority of the population. The government
has failed to remedy these problems. Is it justifiable for those with no shelter and little
source of sustenance to enter properties in your neighbourhood and take what they
need to live? On one reading of utilitarianism a net increase in aggregate welfare
would suggest a positive answer to this. Protecting your property rights, and others
similarly fortunate, seems to result in the consequence of failing to provide for the
majority basic requirements for food and shelter and hence lowers the overall happiness of the society. Wouldn't the aggregate welfare of the society be increased – and
therefore justice be better served – by letting a redistribution of property occur? But
then another consequence of this may be that it leads to a state of anarchy, where no
one, even when they managed to acquire for themselves food and shelter, would have
any security in preserving it. As in Hobbes's state of nature, there would be no property, only possessions, and even those would be limited to what people just happened
to be able to hold on to. The problem of weighing up, according to a single measuring
scale, all these different possible consequences appears to be a further difficulty for the
utilitarian approach.

Using the same example and applying non-consequentialist reasoning – of the type
we touched on in our first two examples – you might argue that your property rights should
take precedence over the claimed needs of those who have no food or shelter. This would
hold that it is wrong to deprive you of the property you had lawfully acquired, and, just
like in our first two examples, that this should hold true regardless of the consequences.
In other words, the protection of property rights should take priority over a wel-
fare-maximising redistribution, even at the cost of failing to meet the basic needs of the
majority. But is this really what justice requires?

One of the most trenchant critiques of the utilitarian position comes in the form of an affirmative answer to this question. It is perhaps best exemplified in the work of Robert Nozick, who defends a libertarian account of justice. Briefly stated, Nozick argues that 'Individuals have rights, and there are things no person or group may do to them (without violating their rights)' (Nozick 1974, p ix). In our example, where you have acquired property, in wealth, land or goods, say, then it is unjust for others – including the government – to deprive you of that property unless you volunteer to do so. To coerce you into giving it up – for example through a system of compulsory taxation – is a violation of your rights and your freedom to do with it what you will.

To defend this position Nozick offers us an 'entitlement' theory of justice. He illustrates it with a story of Wilt Chamberlain, an outstanding basketball player who draws huge crowds to games. Suppose that in his contract with the club there is a clause that Wilt will receive 25 cents from the price of each ticket. The fans flock to see him, happy to pay the admission price knowing of Wilt's contractual provision. By the end of the season, Wilt ends up $250,000 richer. Assuming for the sake of argument that everyone started with an equal amount of money, it is now clear that Wilt is far richer than everyone else. Nozick asks: is this new distribution unjust? Or, conversely, would it not be unjust to deprive Wilt of any of the money he has gained from the voluntary transactions of the fans? Nozick argues that it would. He says that redistribution according to some preset pattern, of equality say, signals a violation in one of two senses: 'To maintain a pattern one must either continually interfere to stop people from transferring resources as they wish to, or continually (or periodically) interfere to take from some persons resources that others for some reason chose to transfer to them' (p 163). Either way, people's rights, and their liberty, would be violated.

At the heart of Nozick's theory is, therefore, the claim that 'Whatever arises from a just situation by just steps is itself just' (p 151). Three principles of 'justice in holdings' underscore this: first, 'A person who acquires a holding in accordance with the principle of justice in acquisition is entitled to that holding'; second, 'A person who acquires a holding in accordance with the principle of justice in transfer, from someone else entitled to that holding, is entitled to the holding'; and third, where holdings have not been acquired according to the first two principles – they may have been attained by deception or coercion – then the 'principle of rectification of injustice' requires that they be returned to the rightful owner. In the case of Wilt Chamberlain then, even though we have gone from a position of equality to an unequal distribution of wealth, assuming that everyone had acquired their money justly and that there has been no fraudulent activity, this resultant inequality is nonetheless just: the voluntary transfer of justly held property. Where a person, or a group, or even – perhaps especially – a government interferes with this process of just acquisition and transfer, it exceeds what is morally legitimate.

Drawing on the work of John Locke, Nozick argues that people have a right of self-ownership and so what they acquire through their own work is theirs as of right. For someone else to deprive them of this is not only to violate their justly acquired rights: it is 'to make them a part-owner of you; it gives them a property right in you' (p 172, original emphasis). The redistribution of wealth by the state outside the three principles of justice is therefore morally wrong. It is in this sense that Nozick concludes that the state's 'Taxation on earnings from labor is on a par with forced labor' (p 169). Accordingly, only a 'minimal' state is justified according to Nozick. This 'nightwatchman' state will be limited to certain core functions such as the 'protection against force, theft, fraud, [and] enforcement of contracts' (p ix). Beyond this no consequentialist reasoning can be invoked without, as we have seen, violating individual rights.

But returning to our earlier example, what about the claims of those without food or shelter that justice demands some fulfilment of their basic needs? On the libertarian account respect for individual rights, and indeed for individuals themselves, means not imposing any 'patterned', or 'end-state', redistribution when the cost is the violation of these rights. Even so, 'Isn't justice to be tempered with compassion?' asks Nozick. The answer is emphatic: 'Not by the guns of the state' (p 348). Voluntary transfer of private property to those in need is legitimate; charity for the needy, in other words, is fine – forced 'giving' is not. As G.A. Cohen puts it, with a jaundiced eye,

> If children are undernourished in our society, we are not allowed to tax millionaires
> in order to finance a subsidy on the price of milk to poor families, for we would be
> violating the rights, and the 'dignity' of the millionaires.
>
> (Cohen 1995, p 31)

We will return shortly to some criticisms of this account. To the extent that it is, as we have noted, one that is highly critical of utilitarianism in offering a defence of (a certain conception of) liberty, we turn now to another approach to justice that also extols the virtue of liberty but which does not do so at the expense of denying the value of *equality* in the sense of what Nozick called patterned distribution.

Liberalism: Rawls's justice as fairness

John Rawls's important book, *A Theory of Justice*, was published in 1971. It is often said by academic writers that political philosophy had been in the doldrums until rejuvenated by this work. This is patently false. Depression-era and post–Second World War reconstruction had seen a massive deployment of intellectual and material resources in attempts to build rights-respecting welfare states. These gave practical effect to philosophically grounded projects with enduring, if now sometimes waning, effects. To be blind to this academically seems to say more about the academic political philosophy community than it does anything else. Nonetheless, Rawls's work has been more widely influential and has become a standard reference point for contemporary debates on justice.

For Rawls,

> justice is the first virtue of social institutions . . . [and] the primary subject of justice
> is the *basic structure of society*, or more exactly, the way in which the major social
> institutions distribute fundamental rights and duties and determine the division of
> advantages from social cooperation.
>
> (Rawls 1971, pp 3, 6, emphasis added)

The basic structure includes 'the political constitution, the legally recognized forms of property, and the organization of the economy, and the nature of the family' (Rawls 1993, p 258). Given that individuals' views on what counts as good and valuable for them may reasonably differ, how should we best decide on the content to be given to the basic structure?

Rawls's answer is that we should endorse justice as fairness. Drawing on the social contract tradition, he suggests that we imagine a hypothetical situation – what he calls the 'original position' – through which we can debate and seek agreement on what he calls a 'first fundamental question about political justice in a democratic society, namely what is the most appropriate conception of justice for specifying the fair terms of social cooperation between citizens regarded as free and equal' (1993, p 3). We can use the original position as a technique of representation to work out how best to 'realize the values of liberty and equality' (p 5). To do so we should imagine ourselves, in the hypothetical situation, behind a 'veil of ignorance' as to what our own capabilities, social position and opportunities might turn out to be. Additionally, we should imagine we do not know what gender, race or ethnicity we might have. Using such a scenario our aim is thus to formulate what conception of justice would best achieve a cooperative scheme that would offer the opportunity for an 'overlapping consensus' given potential and actual differences. As Rawls puts it: 'The parties are trying to guarantee the political and social conditions for citizens to pursue their good and to exercise the moral powers that characterize them as free and equal' (p 76).

Before describing the principles of justice Rawls believes would emerge from such a thought experiment, one key question remains to be raised: according to what principle would it be legitimate for the outcome of these deliberations to result in a *coercive* political authority? For Rawls, where 'political power [is] the power of citizens as a collective body', its exercise is

> fully proper only when it is exercised in accordance with a constitution the essentials of which all citizens as free and equal may reasonably be expected to endorse in the light of principles and ideals acceptable to their common human reason.
>
> (p 137)

This, he says, is the liberal principle of legitimacy.

Rawls argues that two principles of justice would be selected in the original position. The first principle is this: 'each person has an equal right to a fully adequate scheme of equal basic liberties which is compatible with a similar scheme of liberties for all' (Rawls 1993, p 291). These basic liberties will include freedom of thought, conscience, association, the person, and what he calls 'the rights and liberties covered by the rule of law' (ibid). While Rawls acknowledges that these basic liberties might conflict with one another, and hence one be limited for the sake of another, they have a special status which requires that they should *never* be compromised for the sake of utilitarian calculations about utility or efficiency. They must be secured *equally*, for all citizens, all the time. Using the distinction we employed earlier from Kant, Rawls argues that 'these liberties are beyond all price' and their inalienability is a core constituent of the basic structure of society (p 366).

The second principle is explained this way:

> Social and economic inequalities are to satisfy two conditions. First, they must be attached to offices and positions open to all under conditions of fair equality of opportunity; and second, they must be to the greatest benefit of the least advantaged members of society.
>
> (1993, p 291)

It may seem surprising that in putting forward a theory of justice, there appears to be a central role for justifying inequality. But with respect to the first condition of the second principle, we can see that there are undoubtedly justifiable differences of authority and responsibility attached to different jobs or official roles that we can understand as reasonable: unequal powers, for example, associated with judicial or ministerial roles, or those required for doctors or social workers to carry out their work. The key point about this condition, however, is that, as a matter of fairness, no one is excluded from the equal opportunity to attain those offices or positions. They may not in fact attain them, but so long as the opportunity is not denied them (on the basis, for example, of legalised racial- or gender-based criteria) then the process is fair. There can be inequalities, in other words, but they need not amount to injustices.

The second condition of the second principle of justice marks a decisive contrast with libertarianism. Rawls refers to it as the 'difference principle'. Unlike Nozick, Rawls acknowledges that even if we assume an original distribution of equal shares, and just procedures for transfer, the theory of justice should not stop there. The key reason for this, which we might think of by reference to the Wilt Chamberlain example, is that 'the upshot of many separate transactions will eventually undermine background justice' (1993, p 284). Therefore, we must incorporate, 'an ideal form for the basic structure in the light of which the accumulated results of ongoing social processes are to be limited and adjusted' (1993, p 281, emphasis added). This will include, for example, redistributive taxation on earnings and property holdings, and a range of other forms of state intervention. But for Rawls, because any such conditions can be clearly set out in advance and therefore be made predictable and foreseeable, they do not amount to the 'capricious interference with private transactions' (p 283) in the way Nozick described.

But again we might ask how, as a matter of justice as fairness, Rawls selects a second condition which justifies 'social and economic inequality'. The answer lies with the veil of ignorance in the original position. In imagining the society to come, we do not know if we will be rich or poor, talented or capable, or not. In these circumstances of ignorance, a rational stance would be to be reasonably risk-averse: imagine you were in the position of the worst-off in the community – what conditions would you reasonably assent to as those governing the community as a whole? In thinking this through we can deploy the 'maximin rule' that 'we are to adopt the alternatives the worst outcome of which is superior to the worst outcomes of the others' (Rawls 1971, p 133). So, if you were to be in the worst-off position would you really prefer no distribution of wealth other than that offered from the charity of the wealthy, should they choose to be charitable? Would you be content to see agglomerations of wealth occur, albeit legally, to the point where a handful of rich citizens could monopolise access to political debate or employment opportunities? Would you choose the principle that it be the amount of private property you have – or do not have – that should determine the chances of you or your family gaining access to education or health care? From considerations such as these (and many others), from behind the veil of ignorance Rawls argues that the second condition of the second principle is one that all people would reasonably endorse. In this way, therefore, the 'difference principle' will be justified and will operate in this way: 'however great inequalities are, and however willing people are to work so as to earn their greater return, existing inequalities are to be adjusted to contribute in the most effective way to the benefit of the least advantaged' (Rawls 1993, p 7).

Given the legitimacy of these principles of justice as fairness, how do they relate to each other? According to Rawls, when it comes to *ranking* the principles among themselves there is a clear priority: the first principle – of equal liberties – takes primacy and should not be traded in for other supposedly equalising benefits, including, for example, increased material equality. Liberty may be restricted but only, as we have seen, 'for the sake of liberty'. This priority of the first principle lies at the heart of Rawls's theory as one of political *liberalism*. Subsequently, the first condition of the second principle – fair equality of opportunities – must also be satisfied first *before* any redistributive mechanisms can be invoked. That is, a fair society must guarantee equality of opportunity and should not gainsay this for the purposes of addressing other types of inequality. Any programme of wealth redistribution can, in other words, only be instituted to the extent that it is still consistent with the principles of equal liberties and opportunities. If it is not, it should be rejected.

Rawls's theory is therefore one that attempts to promote both liberty *and* equality. A liberal society would enact the principles of justice in establishing the basic structure of society, and it would identify and uphold those 'social values – liberty and opportunity, income and wealth, and the social bases of self-respect', that for Rawls constitute the 'social primary goods': the necessary social conditions required by individuals to pursue their own lives and goals (1993, p 307). Rejecting the versions of utilitarianism and libertarianism considered in the previous section, Rawls therefore defends a version of political liberalism that sees coercive state power as legitimate in upholding liberty, but also and only where it addresses equality in the form of justice as fairness.

Socialism

One of the most influential political theories from the nineteenth century onwards is socialism. From its inception and development in various versions, socialism was initially rooted less in abstract theorising than in observing the effects of exploitation, inequality and injustice experienced by so many people in a capitalist society. Responding to this experience, socialist thinkers and activists sought to understand and challenge the problematic features of the order which engendered such suffering, and they endeavoured to replace it with institutions that would no longer tolerate exploitation and injustice. The collective action that socialism pursued produced successes with respect, for example, to workers' rights, access to health care based on need, equality of educational opportunities and the like, reforms which were often historically opposed by liberals as well as conservatives.

We noted in earlier sections how the doctrine of the rule of law and the liberties it can secure are nonetheless compatible with great social inequalities and injustices. This observation may be recast as a problem of formal justice versus substantive (or material) injustice. Formal justice – the requirement of equal treatment before the law based on the principle that like cases be treated alike, and different cases differently – can, and often does, co-exist with widespread material injustice. Such injustice is also compatible with extensive liberties, at least where liberties are defined in a 'liberal' way such as in Rawls's first principle. Moreover, in upholding formal justice, law not only allows material injustice to continue; it *legitimates* this continuance by reference to the claims of formal justice. This is part of law's ideological function and was taken up in more detail in ch 5, Part I. But law also plays a more direct *coercive* function in maintaining material injustice. We do not need to draw on socialist writings for this, but find it already clear in the writing of Adam Smith, a founding thinker of modern capitalism. He observed that:

> When . . . some have great wealth and others nothing, it is necessary that the arm of authority should be continually stretched forth, and permanent laws or regulations made which may [secure] the property of the rich from the inroads of the poor, who would otherwise continually make incroachments upon it . . . Laws and government may be considered in this and indeed in every case as a combination of the rich to oppress the poor, and preserve to themselves the inequality of the goods which would otherwise soon be destroyed by the attacks of the poor, who if not hindered by the government would soon reduce the others to an equality with themselves by open violence.
>
> (Smith 1978/1762, p 208)

That the poor need to be 'hindered by the government' from achieving equality acknowledges the direct relation between law, governmental coercion and material inequality. But socialists responded to this by seeking to address not only governmental power, but rather, and primarily, the material conditions and relations that produce wealth and inequality. And it is here that socialists differed most markedly from the liberal approach to justice. Liberals have traditionally been concerned with securing and maintaining liberties against the powers of government to intrude on people's lives. They are usually more concerned, that is, with political power and the dangers associated with the abuse of that power: hence the importance to them of political constitutionalism. They have traditionally been less concerned with other forms of power, and in particular economic power, arguing that freedom from government interference also requires leaving to the market or private realm economic activity. Socialists, by contrast, put the economy at the heart of their analyses of power and hence of any response to the inequalities in society.

Cohen thus sums up three essential elements of socialism as follows:

> instead of the class exploitation of capitalism, economic equality; instead of the illusory democracy of class-based bourgeois politics, a real and complete democracy; instead of the alienation from one another of economic agents driven by greed and fear, an economy characterized by willing mutual service.
>
> (Cohen 1995, p 253)

Let us take each of these aspects – equality, democracy and community – in turn and compare them with the other models of justice we have considered.

Socialism has been criticised, along the lines of Nozick's argument, for taking away private property and individual freedom in the name of the community. The socialist response is two-fold: first, that under capitalism property and labour is *already* taken away from those who produce value. As Marx and Engels put it: 'Does wage-labour create any property for the labourer? Not a bit of it. It creates capital' (Marx and Engels 1977, p 232). Capitalism does *not* in fact protect what people labour to create; it protects the right of capitalists to make profit from the value of *other people*'s work. Second, to prioritise the rights and liberties of the individual to private property is to misunderstand the nature of production in society and indeed the nature of society itself. Socialists point out that the production of value through labour is *not* an individualistic process; it is an inescapably *social* one. To valorise individual rights, property and commodities as if they existed independently of social activity is to put, so to speak, the cart before the horse. To protect such rights is to protect something that has been created by social cooperation but which has been artificially separated off from it. Capital, said Marx, 'is not a thing, but a social relation between persons which is mediated through things' (Marx, p 932). The aim of the socialist then is not to get rid of property as such. It is to return to the collective what is properly theirs through co-operative activity. It is to get rid of a form of property – private property under capitalist conditions – that in fact *deprives* the vast majority of people of that which they create. Hence it does not reduce individual liberty either but enhances it, granting people free access to the common wealth that would otherwise be fenced off from them.

Contrary to the liberal understanding then, under capitalism legally protected rights promote inequality and unfreedom. Moreover, the 'free market', far from being 'free', in fact requires constant government *intervention*. We can understand this in two senses. First, besides keeping the poor in line, as Smith noted, it also requires constant administrative supervision to maintain its supposed 'freedoms'. One need only think of the massive institutional effort required to maintain a 'free market' in the European Union to see the extent of intervention required. The bureaucracies, laws and policies, and enforcement mechanisms required to guarantee economic freedoms suggest that in practice the 'nightwatchman' state is likely to be nothing more than a fantasy. But it also requires intervention in a second sense. Historically, capitalism is subject to periodic but regular crises. When this happens, when the market 'collapses' as it did in the financial crisis that began in 2008, for example, the 'free market' requires an astonishingly high level of public intervention in the form of money in order to revitalise the possibility of making profit. In the recent crisis this required a massive redistribution of wealth: not from rich to needy, but from the vast majority of the people to the institutions necessary to sustain capitalist wealth. Intervention was required then to secure profit while those least responsible for the crisis had to pay: with their homes, pensions, jobs or public services. From a socialist perspective there can be few clearer examples of the way in which capitalism requires intervention in order to maintain relations of inequality.

At another level this may be understood as a problem of inequality of participation, and this takes us to the second aspect: democracy. In the political realm we expect political power to be legitimate only when those who are affected by it have an equal say in electing those who will exercise it. In a democracy we expect, in other words, to be both the subject and the author of political authority. As Rawls described it (above), political power is

> fully proper only when it is exercised in accordance with a constitution the essentials of which all citizens as free and equal may reasonably be expected to endorse in the light of principles and ideals acceptable to their common human reason.

And yet such a liberal principle of legitimacy in government does not apply in the economic realm. Here again, socialists diverge clearly from liberals. To address all the forms of power that sustain injustice in capitalist society requires attention not just to political power. It requires facing up to the way in which economic power works and responding to it. Hence, just as liberals (and others) sought to make political power accountable through democratic means, it seeks to remedy economic power by making it democratically accountable.

This leads us to think about how socialism seeks to rectify the problems it describes. Now socialist thought comes in many different forms, but we might usefully distinguish here between *affirmative* and *transformative* redistributive remedies to socio-economic injustices. Affirmative remedies are 'aimed at correcting inequitable outcomes of social arrangements without disturbing the underlying framework that generates them' (Fraser 1995, p 82). These may include certain aspects promoted by Rawls's difference principle, but will usually go further than this due to a clearer understanding of the social nature of the production of value. Hence they may be less concerned with the primacy of liberty and more concerned with securing equality across a full range of social needs and so aim to ameliorate the worst excesses of a market society by ring-fencing the fulfilment of certain needs from the predations of private wealth and the profit motive. But in essence affirmative approaches deal with *effects* of the problem, rather than striking at the causes.

Transformative redistributive remedies by contrast strike directly at the *causes* of socio-economic injustice. They aim to restructure socio-economic arrangements in a more fundamental way. They commonly include a combination of the following policies:

> universalist social-welfare programmes, steeply progressive taxation, macro-economic policies aimed at creating full employment, a large non-market public sector, significant public and/or collective ownership, and democratic decision-making about basic socioeconomic priorities.
>
> (Fraser, p 85)

These latter two policies in particular correspond directly to the need to make economic relations and practices democratically accountable. But more than this, transformative remedies demand that attention be paid to other structural causes of injustice that do not so readily appear, if indeed they appear at all, in the individualism of the liberal approach to justice. We highlight two here that are of key importance for the transformation of society: *gender* and *race*.

The centrality of these two factors to socio-economic injustice lies in the fact that each of them is a 'basic structuring principle of the political economy'. First, with respect to gender, Fraser notes how 'it structures the fundamental division between *paid* "productive" labour and *unpaid* "reproductive" or domestic labour, assigning women primary responsibility for the latter' (Fraser, p 78, emphasis added). Hence the 'naturalisation' of domestic labour as a lesser form of labour both justifies it being unpaid while simultaneously providing a 'free' (and exploitative) basis for the practices of paid labour. On the other hand, within paid labour, gender structures the division 'between higher-paid, male dominated, manufacturing and professional occupations and lower-paid, female dominated "pink-collar" and domestic service occupations' (ibid). It also structures discrimination within paid employment with respect to pay and conditions. Because these gendered injustices tend to continue even where legislation has been enacted to prohibit direct and indirect discrimination, it suggests that such affirmative remedies have clear limits in terms of their inability to abolish the gendered division of labour between unpaid and paid labour and within paid labour itself.

Second, race plays a structuring role in capitalist societies. The roots of this ongoing problem lie in the history of colonialism and slavery, racial segregation and discrimination. It is important to note in this regard that these practices, abhorrent as they are to many liberals, were not independent from the rise of political liberalism in the powerful Western nations, nor were they 'lawless' but commonly proceeded under the auspices of the law. As Mike Davis has written of the policies of British imperialism in the context of famines in nineteenth-century India and elsewhere: 'Millions died not outside the "modern world system", but in the very process of being forcibly incorporated into its economic and political structures. They died in the golden age of Liberal Capitalism' (Davis 2001, p 9). This historical trajectory plays a significant role in the persistence of racialised socio-economic injustices. Thus there continue to be extensive racialised divisions and hierarchies within paid employment, and race also has an influential role with respect to access to, or exclusion from, official labour markets themselves. Hence, as well as class-based divisions there continue to be '"race-specific" modes of exploitation, marginalization, and deprivation' (Fraser, p 80). Once again the effectiveness of ameliorative remedial programmes may be questioned where racialised injustices continue to pervade even the best-intentioned affirmative policies and laws. A transformative socialist response therefore requires, says Fraser, 'abolishing the racial division of labour' (ibid).

With respect to the structural causes of injustice there is one further level that socialists necessarily engage with, and it is one that has differentiated their approach from most mainstream theories of justice for some time. If the injustices of capitalism are to be overcome, then any remedies must track the nature of how these injustices are produced. Where capitalism is, and has been for some time, a mode of exploitation that spreads across the globe, then it would be wrong and artificial to stop the analysis of justice and remedial action at the territorial borders of any one state. Under conditions of globalisation, 'People in relatively affluent countries act within a transnational system of interdependence and dense economic interaction, which has systemic consequences for the relative privilege and disadvantage that people experience in different parts of the world or within particular locales' (Young 2004, p 372). This transnational system includes forms of power – transnational corporations, trading organisations and treaties, and so on – all of which are not readily captured in a liberal model of individual entitlement or fairness. But more importantly these constellations of wealth and power, and the interdependencies of the global economy that constitute contemporary economic practices, mean that questions of justice and remedial transformation can no longer plausibly be addressed solely at the level of any one individual state's policies and their political processes. In fact, to act as if they could is to perpetuate a further, if often less visible, injustice, one that Fraser identifies as misframing. As she puts it: 'By partitioning political space along territorial lines, [the state-territorial principle] insulates extra- and non-territorial powers from the reach of justice. In a globalising world, it is less likely to serve as a remedy for misframing than as a means of inflicting or perpetrating it' (Fraser 2005, p 81). This larger frame has therefore to be accessed in a way that addresses and overcomes the nature of practices of global injustice today. In terms of remedies the socialist arguments for economic democracy within a framework and tradition of internationalism may be offered as a resource for transformative remedial action. ('Conservative' and liberal 'progressive' debates on global justice are further explored in chapter 2.)

We come to our third and final aspect, community. As we noted at the start of this section, the essence of the socialist position lies in observing the fundamentally destructive nature of subjecting human lives to the principle of profit that drives capitalism. To deploy Kant's distinction, human relations, we might say, can be valued according to either a price or a dignity. For socialists a community that adequately respects human dignity cannot be built on the foundations of price. People cannot live free and equal lives when the basis of their social lives are grounded in the 'fear and greed', the inequality and unfreedom, that capitalism compels. Even something like Rawls's difference principle comes, so to speak, too late: it accepts capitalism and inequality and then asks how it might be ameliorated. For socialists, however, just as there is no common good – no 'good community' to speak of – between master and slave, or lord and peasant, neither can there be a proper community of dignity among equals built on capitalist social relations. As Alasdair MacIntyre noted, in such conditions 'It becomes impossible for workers to understand their work as a contribution to the common good of a society which at the economic level no longer has a common good, because of the different and conflicting interests of different classes' (MacIntyre 2006, pp 147–148). Moreover, given the underlying exploitative relationship – the *conditio sine qua non* of capitalism – even increased material prosperity is 'irrelevant as a rebuttal' (ibid, p 149). In fact, says MacIntyre, the incentives capitalism requires and deploys (in particular *pleonexia*, the vice of seeking more and more), corrupt the materially *wealthy* as much as anyone. For socialism, therefore, there is an elementary contradiction in seeking to build equality on inequality, or expecting that from relations of exploitation a community of genuine human solidarity could be realised. As one early, pre-capitalist, account famously put it: it is easier for a camel to go through the eye of a needle than for a rich man to enter the kingdom of heaven (Matthew 19: 24).

Reading

Nozick (1974) and Rawls (1971) and (1993) are the first place to start with their ideas. They have both spawned a huge amount of commentary. Two of the best collections are, respectively, Paul (1982) and Daniels (1975). Wolff (1991) also provides an extensive engagement with Nozick, as does Cohen (1995). Cohen (2000) is a lively engagement with Rawls's theory of justice from a socialist perspective, while the title of Cohen (2009) raises the question the book answers.

Fine (1984) offers a critical analysis of the rule of law from a Marxist perspective, and Sypnowich (1990) provides a treatment of socialist law. You should also consult the relevant topics of this book for an analysis of Marx's work.

Bibliography

Cohen, GA, 1995, *Self-ownership, Freedom, and Equality*, Cambridge: Cambridge University Press.

Cohen, GA, 2000, *If You're an Egalitarian How Come You're So Rich?*, Cambridge, MA: Harvard University Press.

Cohen, GA, 2009, *Why Not Socialism?*, Princeton: Princeton University Press.

Daniels, N (ed), 1975, *Reading Rawls*, New York: Basic Books.

Davis, M, 2001, *Late Victorian Holocausts*, London: Verso.

Fine, B, 1984, *Democracy and the Rule of Law: Liberal Ideals and Marxist Critiques*, London: Pluto.

Fraser, N, 1995, 'From Redistribution to Recognition? Dilemmas of Justice in a "Post-Socialist" Age', *New Left Review* 68.

Fraser, N, 2005, 'Reframing Justice in a Globalizing World', *New Left Review* 69.

Kant, I, 1993/1785, *Groundwork for the Metaphysics of Morals*, trans by JW Ellington, 3rd edn, Indiana: Hackett.

MacCormick, N, 1982, *Legal Right and Social Democracy*, Oxford: Oxford University Press.

MacIntyre, A, 2006, 'Three Perspectives on Marxism: 1953, 1968, 1995', in A MacIntyre (ed), *Ethics and Politics: Selected Essays*, vol. 2, Cambridge: Cambridge University Press.

Marx, K, 1976, *Capital*, vol. 1, Harmondsworth: Penguin.

Marx, K and Engels, F, 1977, 'The Communist Manifesto', in D McLellan (ed), *Karl Marx: Selected Writings*, Oxford: Oxford University Press.

Nozick, R, 1974, *Anarchy, State and Utopia*, Oxford: Blackwell.

Paul, J, 1982, *Reading Nozick*, Oxford: Blackwell.

Rawls, J, 1971, *A Theory of Justice*, Oxford: Oxford University Press (revised ed 1999).

Rawls, J, 1993, *Political Liberalism*, New York: Columbia University Press.

Smith, A, 1978, *Lectures on Jurisprudence*, Oxford: Clarendon.

Sypnowich, C, 1990, *The Concept of Socialist Law*, Oxford: Clarendon.

Waldron, J, 2005, 'Torture and Positive Law: Jurisprudence for the White House', 105 *Columbia Law Review* 1681–1750.

Wolff, J, 1991, *Robert Nozick: Property, Justice and the Minimal State*, Cambridge: Polity.

Young, IM, 2004, 'Responsibility and Global Labor Justice', 12(4) *Journal of Political Philosophy* 365–388.

Chapter 2

Global justice

The central issue and some terminology

This section discusses the question of global justice. In a nutshell, the question asks whether obligations of justice apply to the global level in the same way that they apply to the state level. The stakes raised by this question are extremely high: a *conservative* answer suggests that there exist no obligations towards those who are not fellow-nationals to redistribute resources from the rich to the poor. On this view, the standards of justice are not relevant for appraising imbalances in the allocation of resources between people living in different countries. At the opposite end lies the progressive view, which submits that obligations of justice pertain across boundaries, provided people living in different countries have reached a high density of mutual interdependence. To illustrate the contrast between the two views you may think of the conservative answer as suggesting that I am in the justice relation with the person who irons my shirts in Glasgow, but not with the Brazilian who grows the coffee I drink; in contrast, the progressive view suggests that there is no difference *justice-wise* between the two cases.

A good point to start is with some terminology: justice is the standard against which we evaluate allocations of resources among people, where resources can be understood as comprising any goods which are needed in order to realise a good life (Dworkin 1981). On this understanding any allocation of resources between two or more people can be just or unjust. Understood as the standard for evaluating such allocations, justice involves two dimensions: first, an account of the conditions for an allocation to count as just. This aspect concerns the *content of justice*; second, an account of which allocations are subject to the standard of justice (i.e., are subject to the evaluation just/unjust); this aspect concerns the *scope of justice*.

Content and scope of justice

When it comes to the contemporary debate on global justice, there is relative agreement on the *content of justice*. Most would agree that the standard of justice is some variant of *fairness*. The understanding of justice in terms of the requirements of fairness was prominently developed by John Rawls in his seminal work *A Theory of Justice* from 1971. For our purposes, two aspects are key to Rawls's project: first, the method he proposes for arriving at principles of justice; second, the content of those principles.

With respect to the method, Rawls, as we have noted in the previous chapter 1, demonstrated that, under conditions of fairness, persons are likely to arrive at the same set of principles of justice for the regulation of their common life within a society. These conditions of fairness take the form of a complex conceptual device (the *original position* in Rawls's parlance) that aims to filter out contingent features of persons and their situations, which are likely to bias their judgment when choosing the principles (e.g., race, sex, social position) (Rawls 1971, ch 3, §§ 20–30). When it comes to the content of the principles of justice, Rawls argued that fairness requires that any inequality in the distribution of resources be justified specifically to those who end up being worse off. This justification, again as we have seen earlier, comes in the form of the celebrated second principle of justice, which comprises two sub-principles: first, the *difference principle* or the requirement that inequalities must turn to the benefit of the least advantaged; and, second, the principle of *fair equality of opportunity*:

> Social and economic inequalities are to be arranged so that they are both: (a) to the greatest benefit of the least advantaged, . . . and (b) attached to offices and positions open to all under conditions of fair equality of opportunity.
>
> (Rawls 1971, § 46)

However, Rawls imposed a crucial limitation on the scope of his account. From the outset he declared that principles of justice apply only to the major institutions of a *domestic* society, or its basic structure:

> [The subject of justice] is the basic structure of society, or more exactly, the way in which the major social institutions distribute fundamental rights and duties and determine the division of advantages from social cooperation.
>
> (Rawls 1971, §2)

Consequently, the most controversial question of global justice has become the one about its *scope*. In this respect people disagree fiercely over the boundaries of justice as fairness: should it remain a standard for allocations only at the domestic level of the state, in line with Rawls's explicit commitment? Or should it be understood, consistently with the spirit of Rawls's account, as a standard of appraisal that ranges over the current allocation of resources among people who live in different countries and regions of the world? A recent example will help dramatise what is at stake in the disagreement: in September 2017, hurricane Irma hit the Caribbean with great force, leaving major destruction in its wake. The US allocated (some limited) resources to Puerto Rico which counts as part of US territory, but none at all to the inhabitants of Saint Martin, a small neighbouring island that belongs in part to France and in part to the Netherlands, despite both territories having suffered heavy losses by the hurricane. Did the US have an obligation to allocate resources fairly between the two territories? Leaving aside other details which might complicate the picture, we can distinguish between two responses: the *conservative* response says that the US was obligated to respect fairness only in the case of Puerto Rico, because of a special relationship its inhabitants bear to those living in the US mainland. On the other hand, the *progressive* view on the issue would argue that the

allocation of resources by the US was unjust and that there was another possible allocation which would have been fairer.

Let us turn to the justifications for each of these views.

The conservative view

Both the conservative and the progressive views, given their agreement on fairness as the
standard for justice, take John Rawls's *Theory of Justice* as their starting point. However, each
places the emphasis on different aspects of his theory, in a manner that generates oppos-
ing results.

The conservative view argues with Rawls that obligations from fairness apply to the
basic structure of a society, or else 'the way in which the major social institutions dis-
tribute fundamental rights and duties and determine the division of advantages from
social cooperation' (Rawls 1971, §2). Leaving out a lot of detail, what many have interpreted Rawls as saying is that justice has a claim over our lives only for those allocations
that are the result of an institutional structure which has been set up to allocate resources.
In other words, the *scope of justice* requires the existence of a structure with a particular
form. On this interpretation, the *scope* of justice is restricted by a *site* that takes a unique
form, i.e., that of the basic structure. The conservative view adduces further evidence to
support its claims by referring to Rawls's late writings on international relations where
he explicitly states that obligations of justice do not extend beyond the state, citing as
the main reason the absence of anything resembling the basic structure at the global level
(Rawls 1999).

In recent years this view has been augmented through an additional and, as it were,
more substantive justification. The basic structure of social institutions is taken to be
proof of a special relation among those whose lives are regulated by its institutions. This
special relation arises when people are *associated* in the form of a *political community*, by
setting up the type of institutions which Rawls associates with the basic structure. The
main point in this move is to show that political association generates a type of personal
interaction between those involved in it, which is salient for justice. Crucially, what
draws justice as fairness into this picture is that political associative relations are mediated by rules that can be coercively enforced, together with the fact that their enforcement is claimed 'in the name' of the rules' subjects. When this happens, then those 'in
whose name' coercion is claimed have a demand of justification (Nagel 2005). This is
precisely the moment when standards of justice as fairness are triggered: they become
the standards of appraisal for the allocation of resources to the members of the association, which the coercive structure undertakes 'in their name'.

On this *refined conservative view*, what makes the basic structure the exclusive site of
justice is not the fact that it takes a particular form, but that the form that it takes places
all those living under it in a *dense associative relation* which requires that the allocation of
goods among them be distributed in a fair way. In contrast, other interpersonal relations,
which enable different possible allocations of resources, are not subject to the demands
of justice as fairness, because they fail to do so coercively and 'in the name of' their
members. Take for instance relations between family members or friends, but also – and
here is the rub – relations between people inhabiting different states, or engaging at
arm's length in trade or other economic transactions across states. In none of those cases

is the allocation that amounts from the interaction relevant, because it fails the test of a political association.

So, to return to our initial example of hurricane Irma, on the conservative view the US did not have any obligation to allocate fairly resources to those living in Saint Martin. Perhaps there were involved some other duties to assist them, but none of these would have the stringency of justice. Examples abound: on the conservative view, whereas I owe duties of justice to the immigrant who irons my shirts locally, I do not owe them to her compatriots who make my shirts back in their country. Another example: governments which negotiate international trade agreements or labour standards are not required to treat each other's citizens fairly. All they are doing is engaging in bargaining with a view to maximizing their own benefit.

The progressive view

The objection to the conservative picture is powerful and has recently found new passionate voices (Abizadeh 2007; Julius 2006). We turn now to discuss it as the *progressive* view of justice.

The key premise that is the starting point of the progressive view submits that the problem of allocation persists despite the existence of a basic structure of allocation. The intuition is simple: to the extent to which there remain other possible allocations of resources, aside of the one performed by the basic structure, the question about the *scope* of justice is left open. For, recall, that any allocation of good things between two or more people is subject to the evaluation of justice (i.e., can be deemed just or unjust). But if that is true, any purported restriction of the *scope* of justice should tell us exactly why some allocations enjoy a privileged status over all other possible ones.

Presumably the conservative view, in its refined variant, would want to revert to the idea of the political association in order to restrict the scope of justice only to allocations that arise from the particular form of personal interaction, which takes place within the coercive scheme of the basic structure 'in the name of' those who live under it. Confronted with this claim, the progressive view turns to show that associative personal interaction does not merit a special role when compared to other instances of personal interaction that amount to alternative allocations of resources. To do so, it looks deeper into the structure of all personal interaction and aims to explain its significance for the *scope* of justice. The argument becomes more complex at this instance, but no less worth visiting for that reason.

It would seem that the key disagreement between the conservative and the progressive view and, to that extent, the key determinant of the *scope* of justice is the idea that personal interaction cannot give rise to duties of justice, unless it is performed 'in the name' of those who are involved in it. Thus 'in the name of' becomes the trigger for justice. But why exactly? The simple answer is that only when some act claims to be 'in the name of someone', then that someone has a 'standing' to ask for justification of the action: e.g., if you step in front of me, so that I have to change course in order to avoid running into you, then I have a standing to ask for a reason why you are blocking my path. Not any reason you quote will be a good justification. Relatedly, for it to be a good justification, the reason you will quote must be a reason not only for you, but also for me (e.g., that you were trying to guard me against falling into a pit). Crucially, it must be a reason for me independently of the fact of what you did (i.e., stepping in front of me), because if it were only that, then my action of avoiding you would merely be a *reaction* to your act and your unilateral reasons for having acted as you did (Julius 2006, p 188).

The upshot of the argument is that in personal interactions the reasons that make for a good justification cannot be 'unilateral' but need to be 'shared' by everyone who is involved in the interaction. Such 'shared' reasons prominently include reasons from *justice as fairness* for the justification of any allocation of resources which amounts from the relevant interaction. But if this holds true, then it follows that the *scope* of justice extends well beyond the *site* of the basic structure to comprise a wide variety of personal interactions which generate allocations of goods.

Thus, the progressive view has shown both that the claim to justification attaches to all personal interaction and that a wide range of personal interactions allocates resources to their participants. It follows that any practice of personal interaction that has allocative results is sufficiently *dense* to be subject to standards of justice (Julius 2006, p 187). To deny this conclusion the conservative view must adduce some evidence beyond repeating its claim that only allocations within the political association demand justification.

The way forward

In an age of intense global interaction it is more urgent than ever before to identify and address problems of justice. The argument that justice is restricted to only one form of personal interaction, i.e., state-based political association, comes under severe pressure when it is demonstrated that a wide range of personal interactions allocate resources to their participants and in so doing become sufficiently *dense* to be subjected to standards of justice. Of course the controversy over the scope of justice will not subside soon. Understandably so, for the political (and financial) stakes that are involved are enormous: just think of the resources that need to be transferred in order to address global poverty. But also those more limited cases, such as our example of hurricane Irma: here too, the resistance to accept responsibility for those living beyond one's community will remain strong, not least because of the considerable material sacrifice it implies.

For all these psychological barriers, however, there seems little point left in re-debating the scope of the requirements of justice. Instead, the agenda of the theory of global justice should focus on more productive challenges, such as identifying the distributive implications of transnational practices and other networks of global interaction whose impact often eludes us (global trade and markets, transnational labour, immigration, environmental policies and so on); further, debunking the idea that we are still operating in disconnected networks and show that, even if the globe has not yet 'closed' under a complete network of, salient to justice, interactions, it already fails to 'fall apart into mutually disconnected sub-networks' (Julius 2006, p 189).

On this view, failing to believe that justice applies to a wide variety of personal interaction beyond the established borders of states is not just a cognitive failure. It is a practical failure that inflicts pain, suffering and humiliation on fellow human beings in a manner that makes us responsible. It suggests therefore, that as a matter of justice, we must do better.

Reading

The starting point for any debate on global justice is Rawls's *A Theory of Justice* (Rawls 1971). While *A Theory* serves as the basis for either of the conservative and progressive accounts of global justice, Rawls himself put forward in his mature work *Law of Peoples* (Rawls 1999) a view of international law and governance that restricts the application of justice to the domestic level.

Amongst more recent defenders of the conservative view most prominent are Blake (2002), Miller (1998) and Nagel (2005); the foremost recent defenders of the progressive view are Beitz (1999), Cohen and Shabel (2006), Julius (2006), Pogge (1989) and Sangiovanni (2007).

A good compass to the debates on justice (more generally) and global justice are offered by Kymlicka (2001), Blake and Taylor (2015) and Brock (2009).

Flikschuh (2017) offers a sustained critique of the limitations of global justice theorising in terms of its tendency to apply domestic political experiences to the global context and, instead, proposes a reorientation of global reasoning in terms of context-sensitivity to local reasons of action.

Bibliography

Abizadeh, A, 2007, 'Cooperation, Pervasive Impact, and Coercion: On the Scope (Not Site) of Distributive Justice', 35 *Philosophy & Public Affairs* 318–358.

Beitz, CR, 1999, *Political Theory and International Relations*, 2nd edn, Princeton, NJ: Princeton University Press.

Blake, M, 2002, 'Distributive Justice, State Coercion, and Autonomy', 30 *Philosophy & Public Affairs* 257–296.

Blake, M and Taylor, SP, 2015, 'International Distributive Justice', in EN Zalta (ed), *The Stanford Encyclopedia of Philosophy*, Spring 2015 edn, https://plato.stanford.edu/archives/spr2015/entries/international-justice/

Brock, G, 2009, *Global Justice: A Cosmopolitan Account*, Oxford: Oxford University Press.

Cohen, J and Shabel, C, 2006, 'Extra Rempublicam Nulla Justitia?', 34 *Philosophy & Public Affairs* 147–175.

Dworkin, R, 1981, 'What Is Equality? Part 1: Equality of Resources', 10 *Philosophy and Public Affairs* 185–246.

Flikschuh, K, 2017, *What Is Orientation in Global Thinking? A Kantian Inquiry*, Cambridge: Cambridge University Press.

Julius, AJ, 2006, 'Nagel's Atlas', 34 *Philosophy & Public Affairs* 176–192.

Kymlicka, W, 2001, *Contemporary Political Philosophy*, Oxford, Oxford University Press (second edition).

Miller, D, 1998, 'The Limits of Cosmopolitan Justice', in DR Mapel and T Nardin (eds), *International Society*, Princeton, NJ: Princeton University Press.

Nagel, T, 2005, 'The Problem of Global Justice', 33 *Philosophy & Public Affairs* 113–147.

Pogge, TW, 1989, *Realizing Rawls*, Ithaca, NY: Cornell University Press.

Rawls, J, 1971, *A Theory of Justice*, Oxford: Oxford University Press (revised ed 1999).

Rawls, J, 1999, *The Law of Peoples*, Cambridge MA, Harvard University Press.

Sangiovanni, A, 2007, 'Global Justice, Reciprocity, and the State', 35 *Philosophy & Public Affairs* 3–39.

Chapter 3

Transitional jurisprudence and historic injustices

In this section we consider some of the jurisprudential implications of how countries have faced up to histories of extensive suffering, discrimination, human rights violations and other large-scale injustices. In the first part we identify a number of such problems in the context of political transitions, typically from authoritarian to democratic forms of government. In the second, we consider the issue of how democratic societies address a past, and an ongoing legacy, of colonialism by looking at a case study: Australia.

The rule of law in political transitions

Dilemmas of the rule of law

In recent decades a theme has come to prominence in legal studies concerning the role of law and legal institutions in political transitions. Under the title of 'transitional jurisprudence', scholars have paid close attention to the various ways in which law has been involved in facilitating countries – from as far apart as Central and South America to Africa – in moving from non-democratic forms of political organisation to democratic ones. With the fall of the Berlin Wall and the so-called 'velvet revolutions' of the early 1990s, Europe also saw a burgeoning of jurisprudential reflection on problems of 'how to deal with the past'. What made these recent transitions so interesting – and so important – was due, in part, to the kind of problems thrown up for new governments who wanted to instil a faith in the belief that they would uphold the rule of law. Yet these governments were simultaneously faced with many competing demands to hold to account those who had perpetrated 'historic injustices' under the previous regime. As many people saw it, this produced a kind of rule of law dilemma: on the one hand, as we have already seen, the rule of law means (among other things) securing legal certainty by upholding legal expectations as they have been set out, in advance, by legislatures, courts and constitutions. On the other hand, many of the despotic policies of the previous regimes had been carried out by governments acting under the guise of the laws they had established. Now if the ideal of the rule of law as the upholding of legal expectations was to be respected and aspired to by the new regime, this would mean recognising the laws and legal expectations established by the previous regime, no matter how much suffering they might have caused. For example, in the well-known cases of the East German border guards, soldiers who had shot at escapees were to be prosecuted under the reunified German legal process for the shootings, which were deemed to be criminal offences; yet, the soldiers argued, these actions had been carried out under legally sanctioned orders at the time of their actions and for which they had been rewarded under the East German regime. Would it be legal or fair to find them guilty of criminal acts? Was this not a breach by the new democratic regime of the rule of law (and basic human rights) principle that no one should be punished for an act that was not a crime at the time of its commission? This, in a nutshell, was the dilemma: how to respond to prior injustices of a regime that claimed to be legal at the time. And it presented itself not only in criminal law, but in public and private law too (for example, as claims to restitution in property law). Moreover, bringing in another dimension to this, if reconciliation is important as an ideal for the emerging nation, what are the best approaches to justice and the rule of law in that regard and, significantly, might legal adjudication in these matters not in fact undermine the promise of and conditions for reconciliation, for example, between victims and former oppressors or between victims and current beneficiaries? At the very least we can note that how issues of reconciliation are presented will impact on jurisprudential questions in ways that are not experienced in non-transitional situations.

In this section we will explore in a little more detail some of the jurisprudential issues arising out of such 'transitional' problems. But it should be noted at the outset that although they have become, and remain, highly relevant to contemporary societies throughout the world, these problems are not entirely new. People have always had to deal with the issues of despotic governments and the consequences of their injustices, with problems of coming to terms with the aftermath of wars, civil conflicts and liberation from colonial rule (whether in America in the 1770s, Africa in the second half of the twentieth century, or post–Second World War Europe), and writers and political and legal actors have always had to engage with these problems. The social contract tradition, for example, most vivid in the work of such key thinkers of the modern era as Hobbes, Locke, Kant and Rousseau, was itself centrally concerned with how to establish legitimate government in a transition from what they described (in their different ways) as the state of nature. In that sense, problems of transitional justice are not new. Arguably what is new, though, is the legal and international backdrop against which recent transitions have taken place. In a context where the rule of law, democracy and human rights are deemed to establish fundamental values that place limits on the actions of governments, and where – potentially in tension with this – an increasingly powerful and legally established global capitalist economy attempts to set the terms of national and international relations and commerce, the nature of political transitions is itself, we might say, in transition. The point has been reached, it could be argued, where it is law and legal norms in a global setting, rather than simply local politics or violence, which sets the terms of engagement for societies going through radical social and political upheaval. Where this is so, special attention needs to be paid to how the involvement of law and legal mechanisms operate either to limit or create possibilities for genuine social transformation.

In order to make some headway in this broad area of enquiry, we will identify a few key thematic issues in the area of transitional jurisprudence. Mainly, we are concerned here with highlighting the kinds of jurisprudential problems raised, rather than trying to address them in detail.

Difficulties in establishing accountability and responsibility

Where a country has experienced despotic government and injustice resulting in widespread harms, and that regime has now been replaced by a democratic one, one of the key questions faced is how to establish accountability for the harms suffered; that is, who, or which institutions, are to be held to give an account for causing the harms? Establishing accountability in this sense is the first step towards assessing the nature and extent of responsibility for the harms. While at first glance this might appear reasonably straightforward, in countries where this question is asked, a number of problems – some common, others unique to a particular place and time – make it less easy than it may at first seem. When atrocities have occurred on a massive scale, for example, in the commission of genocide or crimes against humanity, establishing accountability and responsibility requires analysing the complex causes, which together facilitated the commission of the harms, and for which conventional criminal law categories may not be adequate. Hannah Arendt, in her famous study of the 'banality of evil', quoted the judgment of the Israeli court in the trial of Adolf Eichmann for his role in the perpetration of the Holocaust:

> in such an enormous and complicated crime as the one we are now considering, wherein many people participated, on various levels and in various modes of activity – the planners, the organizers, and those executing the deeds, according to their various ranks – there is not much point in using the ordinary concepts of counselling and soliciting to commit a crime. For these crimes were committed en masse, not only in regard to the number of victims, but also in regard to the numbers who perpetrated the crime, and the extent to which any one of the many criminals was close to or remote from the actual killer of the victim means nothing, as far as the measure of his responsibility is concerned.
>
> (Arendt 1963, pp 246–247)

It is the extent of the harms, the difficulty of establishing exactly who is to be called to account, and which social institutions (for example, the military or government or the court system) might do this that make establishing responsibility for them commonly such a daunting task. Despite this, however, there is the desire to see that some kind of justice is done and that impunity – that is, blanket immunity from being held responsible – does not prevail.

Forms of justice

But what kind of justice? Here we encounter different possibilities. One is a form of *retributive justice*, which holds that those who committed or ordered the crimes ought to suffer proportionate punishment for the harm they have caused, that is, they ought to be held criminally liable – assuming they are found guilty by a duly constituted court – and punished accordingly. This was the model adopted post–Second World War in the

Nuremberg trials. Again, however, prosecutors and courts face an invidious task. They must establish in the first case the relevant jurisdiction over the offences and the accused, and they must establish that the alleged offences exist as crimes. (In the case of Nuremberg, one of the key crimes to be established was 'crimes against humanity'.) Otherwise, there may be a tendency, rightly or wrongly, to see the prosecutions as merely victors' justice, amounting to the imposition of retroactive laws on the defeated and overlooking offences committed by the victorious side. Moreover, given the further problems of identification and capture of offenders, the potentially vast number of the accused, and the difficulties surrounding evidence adequate to the high standard of the criminal trial, the very real possibility exists that only a few people will be brought to justice. Thus in some contexts there may be a sense that some people are being treated as scapegoats, and that a few convictions will work to expiate the crimes or complicity of many others who remain free, while in other contexts it may be perceived that the 'foot soldiers' rather than the senior political agents behind the policies of the regime are singled out unfairly for prosecution. In many such situations, then, courts have to engage with the identification of actual perpetrators under conditions in which the 'normal' operation of criminal law seems to be unsettled, since it is often the case that in such scenarios 'the degree of responsibility increases as we draw further away from the man who uses the fatal instrument with his own hands' (Arendt 1963, p 247).

This problem of unequal or uneven treatment is another element of the rule of law dilemma – whether and whom to prosecute and for what – and it plays out particularly in the context of criminal law. If the new regime wants to establish its credentials as a rule of law State, then it must be seen to be objective, procedurally proper and not politically biased in its stance towards the prosecution of crime. But in transitional settings, which are often still highly unsettled, it is almost impossible to establish the conventional distance between politics and the criminal law. Would the establishment of the International Criminal Court (ICC) help in dealing with these questions? This is debatable. Even with the establishment of this Court, these doubts and difficulties do not disappear. Moreover, not all states have accepted its jurisdiction – perhaps most problematically the United States of America – and even those that have may well argue that prosecutions are liable to be politically skewed.

These are perhaps some of the reasons why alternative means of holding to account have arisen in the context of recent political transitions. Under the broad banner of *restorative justice*, there has been an acknowledgement of the limits – though not the complete redundancy – of criminal law as a means of dealing with past injustices, and so attempts have been made to provide a different sense of doing justice to past injustices. Restorative justice is centrally concerned with restoring dignity to victims of injustice and is also based on a concern that the community itself is in some need of restoration. One of the ways in which this has been promoted is through the use of different forms of tribunal which break the link between a finding of responsibility and punishment. Here, it is argued, it is necessary still to hold to account and find responsible those who committed atrocities, but due to a sensitivity to the conditions of the transition it is deemed desirable, for the sake of social reconciliation, to establish the truth and give the victims and community a role in ways that criminal trials would not be able to achieve, and to understand the consequences of findings of responsibility in a way that goes beyond punishment and promotes social healing.

Perhaps the most prominent contemporary example of this is the Truth and Reconciliation Commission (TRC), established in South Africa in 1995 after the end of apartheid. The TRC was given the task of finding out the nature and causes of the offences committed under the apartheid regime, and one of its most important mechanisms for doing so was to provide amnesties for those who came forward and gave full disclosure of offences committed that were associated with the conflict between the apartheid government and anti-apartheid resistance. Thus, in order to establish the truth about past injustices, and so to begin to promote the possibility of reconciliation in a deeply divided society, it was seen as necessary to sever the link between a finding of responsibility and punishment.

This was controversial, and a number of victims of apartheid policies objected that it failed to take seriously the gravity of the offences, and denied them the right to have justice – of the criminal or tortious variety – established by a court. If wrongs had been committed, they argued, then justice and the law demanded that they be prosecuted. The TRC responded, and the South African Constitutional Court upheld, that unlike blanket amnesties that give no form of accountability for past offences, amnesty of this conditional form was not a denial of justice, but rather provided for an alternative form of justice. This was legitimated by the TRC performing the difficult balancing act between victims' grievances and the need to determine the truth of the past in order to begin to overcome its divisions. This type of conditional amnesty – amnesty on condition of truth-telling – was seen as instrumental to the goal of seeking a shared and peaceable future. Of course, there is a paradox to amnesties in this form: from the same root as 'amnesia' they are about forgetting at least the legal consequences of past acts; but in order to forget, one must first know what to forget, that is, it is necessary to establish the truth about the past. In this tension lies what has been called the 'risk of reconciliation': exposure of too much truth about the past may undermine the restorative process, yet a complete covering over of the past fails to take seriously the injustices of the past and risks ongoing social disharmony and trauma for that reason.

Both these forms of justice in transitional scenarios have, however, been criticised from a third perspective. Where there is a focus on criminal law sanctions, or on amnesties and reconciliation processes, it has been argued that there tends to be inadequate attention paid to a third form of justice, namely *distributive justice*. Distributive justice is concerned with the distribution of goods, opportunities and liabilities in society. After the fall of the old regime, one of the important sets of decisions to be taken is the extent to which the new democratic regime will upset the distribution of such goods and opportunities as were established prior to the transition. For example, questions will be raised about whether to maintain the existing regime of property rights or relations, and the extent to which the effects of systemic discrimination against racial or ethnic groups ought now to weigh heavily in favour of redistribution. We might compare, say, the very different approaches taken to land distribution in Zimbabwe and South Africa after white minority rule came to an end in these countries.

In these instances the new government, or, as is often the case, the courts, will face another version of the rule of law dilemma: on the one hand, to uphold legal expectations rooted in the already extant law, and on the other, to deal with the fact that these laws legitimated distributively unjust patterns which, if left in place, would merely continue the legacy of the prior regime. This problem usually reaches its height with regard to property law. Where the right to property is enshrined in the new democratic constitution, then those holding property at that time could – again according to a principle of the rule of law – reasonably expect to have their legal rights secured and their property protected. But since this fails to address the problem of material injustice on behalf of the victims of the prior regime, competing claims emerge that challenge the *status quo ante* and demand that redistribution based on redressing past injustice trump the right to property.

One of the important jurisprudential aspects of this involves consideration of what might be called a 'temporal' dimension to justice. This raises the question of whether the existence of prior injustice is relevant to doing justice now. Consider the following two arguments. One is that if there is a group in society who is at the moment disadvantaged, this means they should have a valid claim in distributive justice to address their needs now, and, that this is so, regardless of how their disadvantage has historically arisen. In that sense, doing justice to their needs is no different from any other group in a society. By way of contrast, the other argument suggests that the disadvantaged group has a *special* claim in distributive justice, based in the nature of their experience in the past, that is, that their claim should be treated differently from others, because the historical causes of current disadvantage need to be taken into account in order that a full understanding and response to contemporary injustice be made meaningful.

Think, for example, of the case of those in the United States who seek reparations for the effects of slavery. Many argue that the historical injustice that was slavery creates special obligations to descendants of that institution that ought to be taken into account in addressing their needs in the present.

Among other things, they argue that were the existence of current disadvantage not in fact to take into account the prior injustice that was slavery, then there would be a failure to fully understand and grapple with the nature of the current social and economic inequalities suffered by many descendants of slaves. Of course, we would encounter questions of identity and causation across times that are not easily addressed in legal categories. And for that reason, among others, many suggest that the disadvantages suffered by many contemporary African-Americans should be dealt with merely as a matter of contemporary distributive justice, oriented to current need, irrespective of why or how that need came about. These are urgent debates that often require difficult choices over priorities in the distribution of resources and goods.

Hence the rule of law dilemmas in political and social transitions show up across a range of areas of legal practice, such as criminal, property and human rights law. But they also encounter more fundamental questions, in two senses: first, that these areas of law themselves may conflict as to their demands and benefits and that negotiating such conflicts may overload the legal categories themselves with political or moral pressures, which, in turn, may undermine the claim to any impartial or objective rule of law; second, as such, the value of the rule of law itself may well turn out to be only one factor among many competing social forces and so not only will the benefits of the rule of law itself be unable to negotiate the making of compromises, but that it too may need to be compromised in order to ensure a relatively stable transition.

These deeper problems are ones that are commonly taken to have been settled in stable societies. But it is one of the benefits of thinking about the rule of law in transitional periods that they expose to the light what exactly these 'settled' assumptions are. And this should constantly remind us that, despite them having receded into the background, they never entirely disappear, and this is particularly so in circumstances where past injustices may rear their head again for consideration, or where contemporary conditions may be deemed to be entering a period of insecurity or instability.

Addressing colonialism: judging in an unjust society

Systematic and profound racial discrimination may occur in societies that are committed to principles of formal equality, democracy and the rule of law. It is necessary to try to understand how the operation of basic principles of conventional legal reasoning may be complicit in this situation by operating to entrench injustices, both of the past and present. Australia provides one such contemporary example, and in this section we will look at the High Court decision in *Mabo v The State of Queensland* (No 2) (1992) (hereafter *Mabo*, paragraph references in parentheses). The *Mabo* decision is important for many reasons, including what it exposes about the assumptions on which legal reasoning rests, as well as the limits of law in addressing its colonial past, and present.

Australia was colonised by the British in 1788. Sovereignty over the territory was claimed under the doctrine of *terra nullius*. According to this doctrine, which means literally 'no-one's land', land that was uninhabited could be acquired for the colonial power – in this instance, technically the British Crown – upon being 'settled'. Of course, the Australian continent was not uninhabited; European 'settlers' encountered the presence of an extensive Aboriginal population and, often, their resistance to invasion. In such instances, however, an 'enlarged' doctrine of *terra nullius* could still be applied by the colonising power, if the following assumption was made: that 'the indigenous inhabitants were not organized in a society that was united permanently for political action' (33). In essence, this involved an assessment by the imperial power, as the Privy Council put it in *In re Southern Rhodesia* in 1919 (quoted in *Mabo*, 38) that, 'Some tribes are so low on the scale of social organization that their usages and conceptions of rights and duties are not to be reconciled with the institutions or the legal ideas of civilized society. Such a gulf cannot be bridged.' In other words, the inhabitants of *terra nullius* and their form of society were seen, from an openly racist understanding, as inferior: as Brennan CJ put it: 'The indigenous people of a settled colony were thus taken to be without laws, without a sovereign and primitive in their social organization' (36).

In *Mabo*, the High Court of Australia was asked to adjudicate a claim on behalf of the Meriam people living on the Murray Islands in the Torres Strait that they had native title to their land, which survived the acquisition of sovereignty by the British Crown. This claim involved the Australian High Court re-evaluating the nature and consequences of this original racist assumption on which Australia was founded, and which had, for over 200 years, denied in law the existence of any such title. As Brennan CJ wrote:

> According to the cases, the common law itself took from indigenous inhabitants any right to occupy their traditional land, exposed them to deprivation of the religious, cultural and economic sustenance which the land provides, vested the land effectively in the control of the Imperial authorities without any right to compensation and made the indigenous inhabitants intruders in their own homes and mendicants for a place to live.

(28)

However, continued Brennan CJ: 'Judged by any civilized standard, such a law is unjust and its claim to be part of the common law to be applied in contemporary Australia must be questioned' (28). Thus, there was

> a choice of legal principle to be made in the present case. This Court can either apply the existing authorities and proceed to inquire whether the Meriam people are higher 'in the scale of social organization' than the Australian Aborigines whose claims were 'utterly disregarded' by the existing authorities or the Court can over-rule the existing authorities, discarding the distinction between inhabited colonies that were terra nullius and those which were not.
>
> (39)

According to Brennan CJ, overruling the precedent cases was necessary since otherwise their authority

> would destroy the equality of all Australian citizens before the law. The common law of this country would perpetuate injustice if it were to continue to embrace the enlarged notion of terra nullius and to persist in characterizing the indigenous inhabitants of the Australian colonies as people too low in the scale of social organ-ization to be acknowledged as possessing rights and interests in land.
>
> (63)

On the one hand, therefore, Brennan CJ acknowledged that, 'Their [Aboriginal] dispos-session underwrote the development of the [Australian] nation' (82). On the other, however, he observed that 'the peace and order of Australian society is built on the legal system' (29) and that the court was

> not free to adopt rules that accord with contemporary notions of justice and human rights if their adoption would fracture the skeleton of principle which gives the body of our law its shape and internal consistency.
>
> (28–29)

In other words, the clash of principles to be adjudicated involved confronting the foun-dational act that dispossessed Aboriginals of their lands, while simultaneously under-standing that that act was the very condition of the ongoing existence of the Australian nation. How then could the racist founding of Australia be dealt with in accordance with contemporary principles of justice and equality when that founding was itself the one which gave the Australian State – and hence the law and the High Court – its authority?

The court's solution to this problem involved making a key distinction between the acquisition of sovereignty and the consequences of that acquisition. The former, it said, is not subject to review by the court; that is, the sovereignty established by the initial act of colonisation is not justiciable in the Australian courts – it is that very sovereignty that gives the court its jurisdiction to hear this case. Were the matter to be justiciable – and the answer given that the act of sovereignty was invalid – then the court would under-mine its own authority to make precisely such a decision.

However, it was open to the court to review the consequences of the acquisition of sovereignty. And here was where their interpretative leeway entered. The court decided that although sovereignty had been acquired under the doctrine of terra nullius, this did not mean the Crown also acquired 'full beneficial ownership' (that is, a complete property right) to the whole territory. Rather, using a doctrine going back to feudal times, it had only a 'radical' (or ultimate or final) title, according to which it was entitled to grant full property rights under it, even though it did not itself own the land. 'What the Crown acquired was a radical title to land and a sovereign political power over land, the sum of which is not tantamount to absolute ownership of land' (55). Radical title therefore meant the Crown had sovereign jurisdiction to create property rights, but where no grant of ownership rights had been made to another party, then since the Crown did not own the land it was possible for native title to it to continue to exist 'as a burden' on the radical title. It was in this space, so to speak, between radical title and full beneficial ownership that the possibility for a native title claim could exist that survived the British acquisition of sovereignty.

In this way, where native title had not been extinguished by Crown grants of land, it was open for Aboriginal communities to show that their continued association with the land, from the time of colonisation, qualified them as entitled to native title rights on that land, despite the acquisition of sovereignty by the Crown. For the first time then – and overruling precedents to bring Australian law in line with principles of non-discrimination – the common law was able to redress the racist implications of the doctrine of terra nullius and recognise native title to land.

We might consider two very different types of interpretation of this ruling. The first is congratulatory, and celebrates the much-vaunted virtues of the flexibility of common law styles of reasoning. According to one commentator, the decision reflects the virtues – the 'genius' and 'spirit' – of the common law, in its ability to uphold basic standards of human rights and to respond in a pragmatic way to 'social, economic and political considerations' (Bartlett 1993, p 181). It also shows something more fundamental, namely how the law can embody – or fail to embody – fundamental human values. On this view, what the Mabo decision offered, for the first time in Australia, was the recognition of a full humanity that had hitherto been denied indigenous people by the law and that had in turn played a role in legitimating a broader social and political racism. Moreover, it was only once this full humanity was properly recognised that the further questions of policies directed towards alleviating the suffering that Aboriginals continued to experience could be addressed. Drawing attention to this distinction, Raimond Gaita wrote:

> Fairness is at issue only when the full human status of those who are protesting their unfair treatment is not disputed . . . The justice done by Mabo is deeper than anything that can be captured by concepts of equity as they apply to people's access to goods. It brought indigenous Australians into the constituency within which they could intelligibly press claims about unfair treatment.
>
> (Gaita 1999, pp 81–82)

But there is a contrary view. Kerruish and Purdy (1998) make three important observations. First they note that common law reasoning involves the application of general principles, chief among which in the Mabo decision were equality and formal justice (treating like cases alike). But legal equality, they argue, is intimately connected to the concept of the 'legal person'. It is this idea of modern Western law that provides a key legitimating role insofar as it operates according to the idea of treating persons as 'free and equal subjects of the law's address'. According to Kerruish and Purdy, this freedom has two aspects:

> First they are free (in the sense of stripped) of all their actual characteristics (from names to locations within basic social relations). Second they are supposed to have the capacity for choice or free will. Equality at law inheres in this dual freedom; that is, all those who come before the law are equally stripped of their actual character-istics and equally presumed to be responsible for their own actions.
>
> (Kerruish and Purdy 1998, p 150)

There are two criticisms we might draw from this. First, treating people as equal before the law — referring them to or measuring them by the same standard — is in fact to treat them differently by ignoring characteristics about their identity or the context (in this instance violent colonisation) that might be relevant under some other descriptive or normative standards. Moreover, this operation of formal legal reasoning does not in fact attribute no identity to the legal person; rather it imposes its version as an identity, in fact as the only available identity, against which there is no appeal or recourse. As Abo-riginal lawyer Irene Watson noted, the *Mabo* decision 'failed to recognise difference in [the] construction of native title so as to make it fit within a western property paradigm' (Watson 2002, p 257). And this point informs the second criticism: that the idea that those who come before the law are responsible for their own actions is not in fact self-determined, but rather is prescribed and defined by law itself. But to the extent that this misdescribes the historical reality, it does so in a way that nonetheless provides legitimacy for overlooking this fact.

Second, as we have just seen, the sovereignty established by the initial act of col-onisation was not justiciable in the Australian courts, because it is that sovereignty that gives the court its very jurisdiction to hear this case. Such apparently watertight logic marks the limitations of the court's power. But the effect of this is, however, that by refusing to engage with the acquisition of sovereignty, the original act of disposses-sion and its legitimacy (based as it was in racist doctrines) remains intact as the found-ing act. This continuity — that Aboriginal dispossession 'underwrote the development of the nation' — is now legally set in stone, but is legitimated in the present by the claim that the common law is acting in a non-discriminatory manner. Thus *Mabo* in fact whitewashes responsibility for the damage caused by the invasion of Australia since, again in Watson's terms, 'doctrines of state supremacy conjure a magic, which absolves centuries of unlawfulness and violence against indigenous peoples' (ibid, p 265).

Finally, the common law condition for recognition of native title requiring an ability to demonstrate continuous association with the land since the initial colonisa-tion involved serious drawbacks. Many Aboriginals, because of government policies, had been removed from their traditional lands either to other places or to the cities and towns, which meant that not only would connection with the land be in most cases impossible to show (because of these very colonial practices, but also because, even in those few cases where connection might be shown, the standards of proof required by the common law rely heavily on documentary evidence, which they know to be unavailable because Aboriginal culture was an oral one), but that this very fact of dispossession is now legitimated by the common law's decision in the case. These dispossessed indigenous people are now treated by the law equally as Australian citizens, their dispossession failing to register in law. As Kerruish and Purdy conclude, therefore,

> the Australian common law has now managed to strip those Aboriginal people whose connection with the land has been broken of the identity at law of native inhabitants of Australia. It is *a further act of colonisation* that compounds dispossession by non-recognition of Aboriginal identity.
>
> (1998, p 162, emphasis added; see also Watson (2015)).

From these observations, we witness the power of common law reasoning in legitimating – on the very grounds of equality, freedom and formal justice – ongoing dispossession and discrimination. This is the power of legal reasoning in a colonial context, even where democratic and non-discriminatory principles are espoused. In other words, while the damage and inequalities that exist in Australia for Aboriginal people are ongoing, the integrity of the common law remains intact.

Thus we might finally reflect on both the power and the limits of modern legal thought, by asking whether and to what extent principles of modern law and legal reasoning (of the type we saw in earlier sections) are able to redress the effects of colonial and deeply discriminatory practices, when these very principles have been and continue to be themselves complicit in the legitimation of these discriminatory practices.

Reading

1

For a good analysis of several of the main themes, see Teitel (2000) and Teitel (1997), and more generally Stan and Nedelsky (2013). For more extensive empirical analyses, see Kritz (1995) and McAdams (1997). For a series of analyses from a feminist perspective, see Fineman and Zinsstag (2013) and Bell and O'Rourke (2007).

Dyzenhaus's review article of several books on this topic gives a good introduction to the literature in this area and some of the central issues it raises: see Dyzenhaus (2003). For his work on the Legal Hearings in the South African TRC, see Dyzenhaus (1998). For a comparative study of truth commissions, see Hayner (2011), and for post-conflict issues generally, Grenfell (2013).

For a legal philosophical development of these themes, see the essays in Christodoulidis and Veitch (2001), especially – on South Africa – chapters by Dyzenhaus and du Bois. On the TRC hearings in relation to other famous SA legal proceedings, see Cole (2009) and especially Wilson (2001). The South African Constitutional Court's validation of the amnesty process in the context of the truth and reconciliation process can be found in *AZAPO v The President of the RSA* (1996) judgment by Mahomed DP. See also *South African TRC Report* (1998), especially volume 1, chapter 5 'Concepts and Principles'.

There is a wealth of literature on restorative justice; for an introduction, see Johnstone (2003) and Johnstone (2011); for its relation to transitions, see Clamp (2016).

On the border guards cases, see the essays by Alexy and Rivers in Dyzenhaus (1999). For the cases themselves, see *K-HW v Germany*, and for the military superiors, *Streletz, Kessler and Krenz v Germany*, both decisions of the European Court of Human Rights.

On the question of accountability for past atrocity and the 'banality of evil', see Hannah Arendt's classic account (1963). For a thoughtful essay on problems of justice and identity in periods of transition, see Ignatieff (1998), final chapter.

The *International Journal of Transitional Justice* provides a good resource for contemporary developments in the field. For the question of how to delineate that 'field', see Bell (2009). On the problems of overly 'legalising' it, see McEvoy (2007) and Sikkink (2011)

2

Brennan CJ's judgement in *Mabo v The State of Queensland (No 2)* is the best starting point for the legal and historical matters raised here. An early symposium on the *Mabo* decision can be found in Bartlett (1993) and ten years later, a critical symposium can be found in 13 *Law & Critique* (2002).

Watson's (2015) book provides analysis of 'the legality and impact of colonisation from the viewpoint of Aboriginal law, rather than from that of the dominant Western legal tradition'. Black (2011) is an important account of indigenous jurisprudence.

An extensive bibliographic resource referring to post-*Mabo* legislation, case law and commentary is Williams and McGrath (2014). The Australian Human Rights Commission produces an annual *Social Justice and Native Title Report*.

For questions about 'judging in an unjust society' with special reference to Ronald Dworkin's theory of legal reasoning and applied to the context of South Africa, see the special issue of *Acta Juridica* (2004) devoted to that theme. See also Mureinik (1988) for a critique of Dworkin. Also in the context of South Africa, see Dyzenhaus (1991) and Abel (2010). For an interesting discussion of the role of the judiciary in Nigeria, see Yusuf (2010), as well as the essays collected in Christodoulidis and Veitch (2001) and Kritz (1997).

Bibliography

Abel, R, 2010, 'Law Under Stress: The Struggle Against Apartheid in South Africa, 1980–94 and the Defense of Legality in the United States After 9/11', 26 *South African Journal on Human Rights* 217.

Alexy, R, 1999, 'In Defence of Radbruch's Formula', in D Dyzenhaus (ed), *Recrafting the Rule of Law*, Oxford: Hart.

Arendt, H, 1963, *Eichmann in Jerusalem: A Report on the Banality of Evil*, Harmondsworth: Penguin.

Bartlett, R, 1993, 'Mabo: Another Triumph for the Common Law', 15(2) *Sydney Law Review* 178–186.

Bell, C, 2009, 'Transitional Justice, Interdisciplinarity and the State of the "Field" or "Non-field"', 3(1) *International Journal of Transitional Justice* 5–27.

Bell, C, and O'Rourke, C, 2007, 'Does Feminism Need a Theory of Transitional Justice? An Introductory Essay', 1(1) *The International Journal of Transitional Justice* 23–44.

Black, C, 2011, *The Land is the Source of the Law: A Dialogic Account of Indigenous Jurisprudence*, Abingdon: Routledge.

Christodoulidis, E and Veitch, S (eds), 2001, *Lethe's Law: Justice, Law, and Ethics in Reconciliation*, Oxford: Hart.

Clamp, K (ed), 2016, *Restorative Justice in Transitional Settings*, Abingdon: Routledge.

Cole, C, 2009, *Performing South Africa's Truth Commission; Stages of Transition*, Bloomington: Indiana University Press.

Dworkin, R, 2004, 'Keynote Address', 2004 (1) *Acta Juridica* 1–17.

Dyzenhaus, D, 1991, *Hard Cases in Wicked Legal Systems: South African Law in the Perspective of Legal Philosophy*, Oxford: Clarendon.

Dyzenhaus, D, 1998, *Judging the Judges, Judging Ourselves*, Oxford: Hart.

Dyzenhaus, D (ed), 1999, *Recrafting the Rule of Law*, Oxford: Hart.

Dyzenhaus, D, 2003, 'Review Essay: Transitional Justice', 1(1) *International Journal of Constitutional Law* 163–175.

Fineman, M and Zinsstag, E (eds), 2013, *Feminist Perspectives on Transitional Justice: From International and Criminal to Alternative Forms of Justice*, Cambridge: Intersentia.

Gaita, R, 1999, *A Common Humanity*, Melbourne: Text Publishing.

Grenfell, L, 2013, *Promoting the Rule of Law in Post-Conflict States*, Cambridge: Cambridge University Press.

Hayner, P, 2011, *Unspeakable Truths: Facing the Challenge of Truth Commissions*, 2nd edn, London: Routledge.

Ignatieff, M, 1998, 'The Nightmare From Which We Are Trying to Awake', in M Ignatieff (ed), *The Warrior's Honor*, London: Chatto & Windus.

Johnstone, G, 2003, *A Restorative Justice Reader: Texts, Sources and Context*, Cullompton: Willan.

Johnstone, G, 2011, *Restorative Justice*, 2nd edn, Abingdon: Routledge.

Kerruish, V and Purdy, J, 1998, 'He "Look" Honest, Big White Thief', 4(1) *Law Text Culture* 146–171.

Kritz, N, 1995, *Transitional Justice: How Emerging Democracies Deal With Former Regimes*, 3 vols, Washington, DC: Institute of Peace Press.

Kritz, N (ed), 1997, *Transitional Justice: How Emerging Democracies Reckon With Former Regimes*, 3 vols, Washington: USIP Press.

Kymlicka, W and Bashir, B (eds), 2008, *The Politics of Reconciliation in Multicultural Societies*, Oxford: Oxford University Press.

McAdams, A (ed), 1997, *Transitional Justice and the Rule of Law in New Democracies*, Notre Dame: University of Notre Dame Press.

McEvoy, K, 2007, 'Beyond Legalism: Towards a Thicker Understanding of Transitional Justice', 34(4) *Journal of Law and Society* 411–440.

Mureinik, E, 1988, 'Dworkin and Apartheid', in H Corder (ed), *Law in Social Practice in South Africa*, Cape Town: Juta.

Rivers, J, 1999, 'The Interpretation and Invalidity of Unjust Laws', in D Dyzenhaus (ed), *Recrafting the Rule of Law*, Oxford: Hart.

Sikkink, K, 2011, *The Justice Cascade: How Human Rights Prosecutions Are Changing World Politics (The Norton Series in World Politics)*, New York: WW Norton & Company.

South African TRC Report, 1998, 5 vols, Cape Town: Juta Press.

Stan, L and Nedelsky, N, 2013, *Encyclopaedia of Transitional Justice*, 3 vols, Cambridge: Cambridge University Press.

Teitel, R, 1997, 'Transitional Jurisprudence: The Role of Law in Political Transformation', 106 *Yale Law Journal* 2009–2080.

Teitel, R, 2000, *Transitional Justice*, New York: Oxford University Press.

Watson, I, 2002, 'Buried Alive', 13 *Law & Critique* 253–269.

Watson, I, 2015, *Aboriginal Peoples, Colonialism and International Law: Raw Law*, Abingdon: Routledge.

Williams, R and McGrath, P, 2014, *Native Title and Indigenous Cultural Heritage Management*, Canberra: AIATSIS, http://aiatsis.gov.au/

Wilson, R, 2001, *The Politics of Truth and Reconciliation in South Africa: Legitimizing the Post-Apartheid State*, Cambridge: Cambridge University Press.

Yusuf, H, 2010, *Transitional Justice, Judicial Accountability and the Rule of Law*, London: Routledge.

Cases

Azapo v President of the RSA 4 SA 671 (CC) (1996).

K-HW v Germany, Judgment of the European Court of Human Rights, 22 March 2001 (Application no. 37201/97).

Mabo v The State of Queensland (No 2) 175 CLR 1 (1992).

Re Southern Rhodesia AC (PC) 210 (1919).

Streletz, Kessler and Krenz v Germany, Judgment of the European Court of Human Rights, 22 March 2001 (Application nos. 34044/96, 35532/97 and 44801/98).

Chapter 4

Trials, facts and narratives

The legacy of fact-scepticism

We saw earlier, when discussing the American Legal Realists, that one of the main pre-occupations of those we called 'fact sceptics' was to argue that the usual critique of law concentrated on a very limited aspect of the law in action, whereas most cases were decided on their facts. Jerome Frank, for one, pointed to the likelihood that the facts as found by judge and jury did not correspond to actual facts. While a number of writers had already pointed out that 'the personal bent of the judge' affects his or her decisions, this was seen as a factor only in the selection of new rules for unprovided cases. This, for Frank, is only a small part of the story. In his own words:

> In a profound sense the unique circumstances of almost any case make it an 'unpro-vided case' where no well-established rule authoritatively compels a given result. The uniqueness of the facts and of the judge's reaction thereto is often concealed because the judge so states the facts that they appear to call for the application of a settled rule. But that concealment does not mean that the judge's personal bent has been inoperative or that his emotive experience is simple and reducible.
>
> (Frank 1970, p 162)

We saw earlier that much of Frank's scepticism revolved around what could be called the psychology of fact-finding. Witnesses' observations and memory may be extremely hazy, but they will be pressed to produce clear and confident statements in court. Pre-trial inter-views with lawyers may even amount to a form of witness coaching, in which the witness gets an idea of which version of the facts would best suit prosecution or defence stories. Then, under cross-examination, they will be subject to many techniques of discrediting. Jackson examines in some detail the two-tier processes whereby witnesses attempt to make sense of what they say and courts and jurors attempt to make sense of the witness's act of testifying (1995, pp 357–362). Processes of perception are involved in eyewitness testi-mony, memory and recall, identification evidence, confession and expert statements. In all this,

> to observe a witness testifying in Court is not merely to make sense of what is said . . . The role of the lawyers is not limited to questioning the witnesses; they also

> initiate and frame the narrative in their opening and closing statements and provide
> a running commentary of the acceptability of the performance of the witnesses.
>
> (1995, p 15)

In fact, cross-examination serves as much to obscure as to reveal the 'truth'. One of the prevailing images of our age is that of Milosevic at The Hague, aggressively examining one of the survivors of the atrocious act of ethnic cleansing at Srebrenica to the point at which the witness broke down and was unable to recall the details of his aggressors' actions. The pattern has been repeated in numerous political and other trials.

By the end of this process, which began in uncertainty in the first place, we may be many degrees from the truth. In jury trials these psychological problems are compounded by the jury's complex perception and reaction to the facts as narrated. But it is not just witnesses and juries that Frank has in mind:

> Of the many things which have been said of the mystery of the judicial process, the most salient is that decision is reached after an emotive experience in which principles and logic play only a secondary part. The function of juristic logic and the principles which it employs seems to be like that of language, to describe the event which has already transpired. These considerations must reveal to us the impotence of general principle to control decision . . . The reason why the general principle cannot control is because it cannot inform . . . It is obvious that when we have observed a recurrent phenomenon in the decisions of the courts, we may appropriately express the classification in a rule. But the rule will be only a mnemonic device, a useful but hollow diagram of what has been. It will be intelligible only if we relive the experience of the classifier.
>
> (Frank 1970, pp 159–160)

What Frank is stressing here is the subjective and active character of decision-making that only *ex post facto* is vested in terms of classification and rule following. This says a great deal about the articulation of rule and fact, though perhaps what Frank is mostly concerned with is the active character of the intervention that is the decision. And to counter such psychological instabilities of truth-finding, Frank called upon the expertise of psychology itself. Experts could be brought in to examine witnesses for the accuracy of their perceptual apparatus and their propensity to lie (with reference to reliability and credibility). Juries should be abolished altogether but, failing that, there should be training in jury duties at school, and jury experts to accompany and advise the jury in the court.

More crucially, Frank's argument is not just about psychological reactions and human fallibility. Rather, the unreliability of fact-finding is a direct result of the institutional process of fact-finding itself. For him, the very rules of proof and procedure are antithetical to truth. The whole trial process, as developed over the centuries, is less a unified, scientific and rational method of getting at the truth and far more an archaeological site where successive systems have all left their traces. Archaic legal forms jostle with slightly less archaic forms. Frank focuses primarily on the adversarial process, which he likened to a trial by combat with each side's champions trying to do down the others – a 'fight' method of proof. While this may have made sense in the past, when we believed that God was on the side of justice and truth, it is not appropriate to the age of secular rationalism. The jury is thus an archaic element whose original task was not to judge facts and individuals they had never come across before, but to deal with a fellow member of the community.

Other writers have made related points. Weber described methods of proof by combat, ordeal and oracle as formally irrational – there was no logical connection between the facts and the outcome (means – end). Substantive irrationality was found in systems of 'khadi' justice typical of traditionalism, individualised decisions pronounced with the wisdom of Solomon or the common law magistrate (see chapter 13). For Weber, such formal and substantive irrational elements still persisted particularly in the lower courts. Britain had developed what he saw as a 'two-tier' system of justice, legal and rational at the higher level where the powerful (notably capitalists) were seeking to find clear and predictable rules for commercial dealings, yet irrational and summary where the less powerful (notably workers) had their crimes assessed. Other writers have described the Roman-canon system, which replaced trial-by-combat-and-ordeal with elaborate rules of evidence (and confession as the centrepiece), maintaining a horror of circumstantial and hearsay evidence and a grading of witnesses by their status credibility. On the Continent at least, the use of torture was seen as a small price to pay for the certainty of confession: in replacing absolute divine knowledge with human sources, only the highest standards were acceptable. Modern methods of extracting confessions from suspects, and ranking the credibility of witnesses (the doctor the highest, the unchaste woman the lowest), show that the past is far from superseded. In fact the use of torture has reappeared on the agenda in the context of the West's waging the so-called 'war' on terror. The use of torture in practice (typically the West's practice of 'extraordinary rendition') and the discussion over its 'justifiability' in theory have made a spectacular, and spectacularly alarming, reappearance in the last few years.

As we have become more willing to accept inferences and indirect human knowledge, we have also increased the number of protections against error and injustice by introducing strong corroboration rules (especially in Scotland) and exclusionary rules concerning admissibility of evidence, for example of bad disposition and so on. Of course for Frank, as for Bentham in the nineteenth century, this series of reforms, undertaken in the very name of fairness and rationality, merely compounds the problem. The whole lot should be swept away in the name of modern scientific rationalism. Such protections could be abolished, he said, if the remnants of the archaic past were totally eliminated and we adopted an inquisitorial system of free proof in which the judge was an investigating magistrate and the jury was no more. Frank's inquisitorial system would include better training of legal officials, impartial government officials to dig up all the facts, specialisation of judges and State administrators to deal with the complex facts of modern society and increasing use of expert witnesses.

It may well be that today Frank's belief in the value of scientific expertise, free proof and the managerial legal official may seem naive, costly and politically worrying. But Frank's basic points have had considerable influence in disturbing the formalist presumption that 'law' divides neatly from 'facts' and that the jury can easily master them. The incorporation of facts in narratives, the possible limitations of legal procedures, the intelligibility of legal language, and the aspiration that the courtroom may function as the forum for the establishment of the truth and of genuine communicative exchange are all deeply contested issues in legal theory. It is to these issues, also at the core of legal reasoning, that we now turn.

Trials and perceptions of fact: language and narrative in the courtroom

The law of evidence provides the structure within which facts may be 'found' and established as legally relevant. There is of course much that is filtered out in the process. There are rules about the admissibility of evidence, ruling out evidence that is unreliable because, for example, it is 'hearsay', and there are rules about the criteria for the allocation of the burden of truth and the threshold – 'beyond reasonable doubt' – that establish what has to be proven as true. Judgments as to whether something counts as relevant or as to whether the case has been proven occur 'within this outline structure', as Jackson (1995, pp 390ff) characterises it, and at the point where that judgment must be made, 'common sense' is called to complement 'legal sense', judges often explicitly instructing juries to use it. At that point of confluence of the two, of 'legal' and 'common sense' construction of meaning, neat analytical distinctions become blurred in practice. Inferences and intuitive judgements come to play a crucial role in the reconstruction of the story, and they are different criteria from those stipulated in the rules of evidence that take centre stage.

In his important work in legal semiotics, Jackson (1988, 1995) surveys linguistic, semiotic and psychological accounts of sense construction in some depth. For present purposes it suffices to raise only a few of the basic arguments, in each case stressing the constructive – rather than given – elements in the perception of facts and of how that perception is translated in enunciation in the courtroom. Semiotics alerts us to the dimension of 'signification' – how meanings are constructed within contexts of interaction. Indicatively:

> Judgements as to the truth of the evidence of witnesses, made by jurors who have no direct or personal knowledge of the events, is based in part on the plausibility and coherence of the stories told by the witnesses: such plausibility is a function of the relative similarity of the rival accounts to narrative typifications of action already internalised by the jurors.
>
> (Jackson 1995, p 392)

What are these 'typifications' and in what sense do they determine perception and allow selective communicability? Let us take a step back here to look at the kind of stock narratives or stock stories, which, as ordering structures, allow us to rationalise or make sense of how things 'hang together', as it were, as meaningful wholes. In *Rethinking Criminal Law* (1978), Fletcher made use of the term 'collective images', which serve as a kind of 'paradigm': the collective image for an offence against property is the 'thief', and 'collective image' of the thief is the nocturnal burglar. These paradigmatic images collect and orient understanding and allow also a certain sharing of understandings (hence 'selective communicability' above). The crucial thing, of course, is that all collective images are temporally and culturally contingent, and, even where those contingencies are shared, often class-specific. This may explain why jurors will be more attuned to picking out certain elements of a situation before them on this basis. This may explain why certain forms of offences against property in their eyes are 'privileged' (housebreaks) and others command lesser 'fit' (forms of fraud), why jurors may be keener to see certain offences punished more than others in the sense that they feel more vulnerable to them (to breaking and entering, for example, rather than fraudulent undertakings in financial circles), or, in extreme cases – like the jury in the Rodney King trial in which a community of peers acquitted police officers for a grave assault on a black man in the aftermath of the violent riots in Los Angeles – why they are willing to leave offences unpunished. Collective images, obviously, while allowing selective understanding, carry tacit evaluations. Jackson's notion of action typifications can be understood on the same continuum: they provide the necessary and sufficient conditions for recognition of fact situations; they allow recognition of what lies within and what outside the situation; they come laden with evaluation; and they are relative to 'semiotic groups', whether these are determined along class, professional, cultural or other social lines (1995, pp 141–163, and for the discussion of examples, pp 163ff). Knowledge is not conveyed in some 'unmediated' way, but through the narration and behaviour of those who present the case in court. We add 'behaviour' here because signification and meaning are not of course limited to what is said, but to a wealth of other factors (body language, signs of sincerity, reliability, nervousness, pace, etc) to which we attach meaning. Going back to our discussion of truth-telling, these images, typifications, 'frames', 'schemas', or whatever we want to call the narrative frames that 'collect' sense-data as information for us, determine the ways in which we decide who is telling the truth, when and under what circumstances.

In their pioneering early work on narratives in the courtroom, Bennett and Feldman analyse the form of stories in terms of central (a 'setting-concern-resolution' sequence) and peripheral action. Battles in court are about who can define the central action successfully and – they claim – success in this matter depends on:

1   narrative strategies by prosecution and defence (definitional, inferential and validational; defence also uses challenge, redefinition and reconstruction as rhetorical strategies);
2   the cognitive and social functions stories play in everyday life in organising complex information and codifying normative value. Apart from being used in 'narrativising' practices, juries also have stock stories that prosecution or defence may appeal to. Stories thus mediate between law and social life.

Thus, unlike MacCormick for example, they see social bias as a potential element in constructing narrative coherence – but this is no crudely realist account of prejudice distorting law from the outside (for example, gut reactions to individuals on the basis of class, race, sex and stereotypes). Rather, bias is structured into stories in terms of 'plausible' action.

Bennett and Feldman also look at another important aspect – *narration* – the way the story is told, particularly the success of witnesses in getting 'their' story across. They draw here on the work of sociolinguistics. From Bernstein (1971), they take the distinction between elaborated codes used in (middle class) formal languages and the restricted codes of (working class) public language. Elaborated codes involve many abstract terms with defined meanings and alternative words to convey and explain; the object of discussion is clearly specified (context-independent). Elaborated codes are thus more mobile in that everything in principle can be explained and defined. They are also more inner-oriented and individualistic. Restricted codes are seen as closed, inflexible and context-bound because they have a fixed vocabulary where knowledge of meanings often depends upon being a member of a particular group (for example, slang) and hence use of this code is also status-oriented. Supposedly, the language used in court by legal professionals is an elaborated middle-class code and working-class witnesses are therefore disadvantaged ('linguistically incompetent') in the courtroom. (But is law really an elaborated code? Perhaps a better use of Bernstein would be to see law as a restricted code.) Bennett and Feldman also draw a contrast between 'narrative' and 'fragmented' testimony styles – the extent to which the witness is permitted utterances long enough to constitute an independent narrative string, as against mere responses to questions, and find psychological evidence that the first style is more persuasive and successful.

There lies implicitly, and sometimes explicitly, in these theories of the trial a more radical, philosophical, objection to correspondence theories of truth that presuppose some single truth 'out there' waiting to be discovered, perhaps distorted by story forms and linguistic incompetence. For our writers, it is a naive realism that does not recognise that facts are constructed by and within different discourses and thus do not have an independent status. If witnesses suffer cognitive dissonance between their understanding of the facts and the law's understanding, then this is a clash between legal and everyday discourses. Writers from varied perspectives (and not just relativists and postmodernists) challenge the whole notion that there is a distinction between law and fact, arguing that legal norms already determine what can count as legally relevant and indeed how that fact is defined. However, does this necessarily mean that law is a totally closed-off, sealed system? There still seems some plausibility in the idea that stories in the courtroom are mediating between legal and social discourses. Or, as Jackson argues (1988, pp 94–97), that there may be narrative structures that occur in both: he cites a judgment of Lord Denning's (Miller v Jackson) involving cricket and analyses, following Greimas, the story involved in terms of paradigms (community) and oppositions (young/old) and narrative sequence in which tradition is disrupted by newcomers. The narrative involves 'value-laden associations [which] are not legally relevant, yet they are inextricable from the narrative understanding of the situation'.

Trials, regulation and justice

Let us finally, in this section, take a step back from the level of interaction in the courtroom to the function of the trial and look at how the imperatives of State regulation have affected the character of the trial. The question that becomes central from this perspective is this: is there a growing conflict between the bureaucratic organisational form and due process? For Weber, describing late-nineteenth-century State bureaucracies, there was not a conflict but a fruitful convergence between bureaucratic structure, the spread of formal rationality and the rule of law. These provided a social and administrative guarantee of formal justice and control of the judiciary. The hierarchy of supervision and division of labour was also the most efficient way to handle cases. The uniform and regular application of rules was an effect of the institutional structure. Conversely, however, this guarantee may turn into a threat to the rule of law, for the connection between efficiency and due process is only contingent. If the situation of the administration changes – for example, through increased volume of work – then formal rationality may cease to be the most efficient form of administration. The guarantee has no inherent stability.

Many contemporary analyses of legal administration have thus focused on a general trend towards mechanical regulation and bureaucratic goal displacement. Internal administrative goals conflict with due process. The increasing volume of work and decreasing resources put the legal system under severe pressure to increase productivity or even to maintain level 'throughput' in processing cases – 'conveyor belt justice'. The response is, on the one hand, to increase the pitch of the bureaucratic logic of standardisation where due process has to be observed in the trial and pre-trial decisions and, on the other hand, to seek ways of avoiding contested trials:

1   simplification techniques: no-fault liability; reducing the need to investigate the mental element in crime; standardising sentencing tariffs;
2   diversion techniques: pre-trial and post-trial diversion; decriminalisation; plea-negotiation; substantial shifts in decision-making powers to the 'paralegal' sphere – police, procurators-fiscal, social workers involved in production of social enquiry reports.

Critics argue that legal decision-making thus becomes almost a parody of formalism since legal outcomes will be increasingly uniform and predictable, while leaving the rule of law an empty shell. Legal rationality has no simple protection against this trend since the form of law still remains the 'general application of known [administrative and legal] rules' – the form of the rule of law. Yet simplification techniques mean that crimes and delicts are increasingly put into meaningless categories; for example, the pressure to lose the concept of fault is a major shift away from traditional views of responsibility. Transfer of responsibility to paralegal spheres means decisions are increasingly being made on an extra-legal basis and hence are discretionary in the sense of not being controlled by strictly legal rules. (Their source is no longer internal to law.) Moody and Tombs argue that, in the Scottish prosecution service, this does not mean an increase in individual discretionary powers, but rather an increase in bureaucratic rigidity, control and form-filling, which they characterise as 'extra-legal formalism' and a loss of external accountability.

The second trend associated with the growth of the modern State converges with the first in involving an alleged increase in discretionary powers and a shift away from rights-based law to social management. State bureaucracies have increasingly involved themselves in substantive ethical and policy issues associated with a welfare interventionism. This often involves legal formulations that take an overtly discretionary form, thus requiring judges to bring in open-ended considerations. This expansion of judicial discretion is associated with:

1   the increasing abstractness or open-endedness of statutory provisions and standards, whereby inherently discretionary concepts such as 'the best interests of the child' replace fault-based legal actions;
2   therapeutic and hence offender-specific calculations in respect of sentencing and the consequent reliance on paralegal judgements of social workers;
3   the increase in short-term government-of-the-day policy uses of law – the use of criminal law provisions in industrial disputes, 'football hooliganism', drug abuse and so on;
4   the blurring of the boundaries between broad policy, administrative and narrowly legal aspects of legal administration, in the expansion, for example, of welfare law, or the use of equal opportunities legislation. Judges are increasingly expected to adjudicate in fields of expertise – social and economic policy – that lie outside their

competence. Increasing use is made of tribunals and regulatory agencies, such as the Equal Opportunities Commission, that rely on informal procedures. Conciliation procedures are increasingly important in family law.

Weber suggested that the features of law that dominated its liberal era – formality and neutrality – would pervade future development. Neutral rules, thought Weber, were particularly conducive to the workings of bureaucracies and they would persist and expand to new ground without challenge, due to their apparent indispensability to the logic of bureaucratic organisation. While post-liberal law has shifted significantly from legislatures to administration, its form remains what Weber predicted it would remain, formal rational. But that of course is only part of the story. Let us say that between bureaucratisation and welfarism in law there is both a tension and a convergence. Tension because bureaucratic law is rational law, its form that of general abstract rules, while welfarist regulation is substantive, particular and casuistic. Convergence because often welfarist concerns key in with bureaucratic ones, for example, the welfarist shift away from fault (as socially inappropriate) meets with the efficiency demand of bureaucracy, the speedy processing of cases thus far inhibited by the requirement to explore *mens rea*. Other tensions and compatibilities may be traced.

Let us then briefly identify some of these here. First, the 'materialisation' of law marks the tendency towards particularised legislation: the movement towards breaking up the general categories into sub-categories towards which law applies differentially. The grand category of the legal person gives way to a specification of categories, and the formal equivalence of the legal subject gives way to a proliferation of different legal statutes: consumer (consumer law), worker/trade union member, employee, welfare recipient, business franchisee. In each case the law addresses the legal subject under that more specific description and there is a move from the formal to the material. But further, natural and artificial persons grouped together under liberal law become differentiated for specific legal purposes, so that, for example, the privacy of the natural person is protected where that of company is not (access to data, freedom of information). Second, the separation of powers, that other lynchpin of liberal law, is eroded, for example, once courts are called upon to determine whether a government has acted in the public interest; equally, when the legislature delegates responsibility for fixing the terms of what appear as general directives because the executive state machinery has the resources to do the job better. Finally, formal equality is eroded by 'reverse discrimination' or 'affirmative action', that is, a reverse preference to a disadvantaged group becomes institutionalised in law in order to redress existing inequalities.

Reading

See Cotterrell (1992) for a concise account of the changing forms of regulation (pp 161–166). For an in-depth, comprehensive semiotic approach to narrative construction, see Jackson (1995), and generally for the role of narratives in trials, see Burns in Duff et al (2004). For an analysis of juries, see Redmayne and Schafer and Weigand in Duff et al (2005). On the relationship between truth, standing, participation and due process in the trial, see Duff et al (2007).

For one of the most striking examples of the use of cross-examination for political purposes, see Bilsky (2001) on the Kastner trial, and Boas (2007) and Christodoulidis (2010) on the Milosevic trial. On the political uses of the court-room, see Koskenniemi (2002) and the classic (though still untranslated into English) Vergès (1968).

Bibliography

Bennett, W and Feldman, M, 1981, *Reconstructing Reality in the Courtroom*, New Brunswick: Rutgers University Press.

Bernstein, B, 1971, *Class, Codes and Control*, London: Routledge and Kegan Paul.

Bilsky, L, 2001, 'Justice or Reconciliation? The Politicisation of the Holocaust in the Kastner Trial', in E Christodoulidis and S Veitch (eds), *Lethe's Law*, Oxford: Hart.

Boas, G, 2007, *The Miloševi'c Trial: Lessons for the Conduct of Complex International Criminal Proceedings*, Cambridge: Cambridge University Press.

Christodoulidis, E, 2010, 'Political Trials as Events', *Events: The Force of International Law* 130.

Cohen, LJ, 1977, *The Probable and the Provable*, Oxford: Clarendon.

Cotterrell, R, 1992, *Sociology of Law*, 2nd edn, London: Butterworths.

Duff, A, Farmer, L, Marshall, S and Tadros, V (eds), 2004/5, *The Trial on Trial*, vols 1 (2004) and 2 (2005), Oxford: Hart.

Duff, A, Farmer, L, Marshall, S and Tadros, V, 2007, *The Theory of the Trial*, Oxford: Hart.

Fletcher, G, 1978, *Rethinking Criminal Law*, Boston: Little, Brown & Co.

Frank, J, 1970, *Law and the Modern Mind*, Gloucester, MA: Peter Smith.

Jackson, B, 1988, *Law, Fact and Narrative Coherence*, Liverpool: DC Publications.

Jackson, B, 1995, *Making Sense in Law*, Liverpool: DC Publications.

Koskenniemi, M, 2002, 'Between Impunity and Show Trials', *Max Planck Yearbook of United Nations Law* 1–35.

Moody, S and Tombs, J, 1982, *Prosecution in the Public Interest*, Edinburgh: Scottish Academic Press.

Vergès, J, 1968, *De la Stratégie Judiciare*, Paris: Minuit.

Chapter 5

Displacing the juridical

Foucault on power and discipline

Our discussions of legal modernity up to this point have accorded a central role to the law. In analyses such as Weber's, for example, the development of modernity is linked to the law playing an ever more central role in the constitution of political power, in the regulation of economic transactions and in the government of social life. These replicate the arguments in, say, liberal political theory that emphasise the role of the law in developing human rights and democracy and protecting the autonomy of the individual. This is challenged by theoretical approaches which seek to displace the centrality of the law in the development or analysis of modernity. These approaches go beyond merely attempting to displace the centrality of State law, such as we see in Santos's discussion of globalisation and legal pluralism, to the argument that in the development of modernity law is transformed in such a way as to reduce the significance of juridical categories. It is argued that law is no longer a category through which we can understand or analyse the operation of power in modernity. We shall examine these types of claims through an examination of the work of the French philosopher and social theorist Michel Foucault (1926–1984).

Foucault famously, and controversially, contended that the period of modernity is a 'phase of juridical regression', and that a focus on the constitutions and legislation that had been passed since the eighteenth century would prevent us from understanding fundamentally important shifts in the nature of the operation of power in modernity (1979, p 144). He argues that new techniques of government that developed in the modern period were distinct from the traditional juridical forms of sovereignty. The juridical, he suggests, has been displaced as a principle of power, and modern society should be analysed in terms of the development of a 'governmentality', which constitutes both 'society' and the individual as effects of the operation of power.

Foucault's work has been important and influential, and though it rarely focuses on the law directly, it raises radical questions about the social role and function of law in modern society. In this section we will first of all examine the key terms of discipline and biopower, and their place in the complex of techniques that Foucault called 'governmentality'. We will then look at the concept of power in Foucault's work before addressing the question of how his work can contribute to our understanding of law in modern society.

Power and the law

Some of Foucault's most intriguing and important remarks on power and the law are contained in the short section entitled 'The Right of Death and the Power Over Life', which concludes volume I of *The History of Sexuality* (1979, pp 135–159). Here Foucault sets out two models of political power: the pre-modern, or classical, model of juridical power, and the modern normalising power. In the juridical model, the sovereign had the right to take the life of those who threatened the internal or external order of the State, or to demand that his subjects give up their lives in the defence of the State. This power could be characterised as a right of seizure (of things, time, bodies, even life itself): a power of life and death exercised by a sovereign over his subjects. The normalising model, by contrast, is characterised by its power over life: to administer, sustain, develop and multiply the life of the population of a particular territory. This did not necessarily exclude the right to take life, but to the extent that it remained, it was part of a complex of forces that were aimed primarily at the fostering or production of life – the administration of bodies – rather than its seizure or negation. Thus if juridical power was characterised by negativity (the prohibition), exemplified in the use of the death penalty, this new form of power was productive or positive in its effects, and subtle and diverse in the techniques and strategies that it employed. Where juridical power relied on the single intervention, these new powers were continuous and regulatory in their effect. Most important of all, he claims that these new apparatuses of power increasingly incorporated and transformed the judicial institution, leading to the decline, or regression, of the juridical.

> [The normalising power] evolved in two basic forms . . . two poles of development linked together by a whole intermediary cluster of relations. One of these poles . . . centered on the body as a machine: its disciplining, the optimization of its capabilities, the extortion of its forces, the parallel increase of its usefulness and its docility . . . [A]ll this was ensured by the procedures of power that characterised the disciplines: an anatomo-politics of the human body. The second, formed somewhat later, focused on the species body . . . [S]upervision was effected through an entire series of interventions and regulatory controls: a bio-politics of the population.
>
> (1979, p 139)

These two forms, then, are discipline and biopower. While the former operates on individuals located in institutions such as prisons, factories, schools and hospitals by surveillance and control with the constant aim of the more efficient distribution and use of power, the latter is concerned with the management of populations through the science of statistics and techniques of political economy.

Discipline

Foucault's analysis of discipline is developed in what is probably his most famous book, *Discipline and Punish*, first published in France in 1975 (Foucault 1977). Although the primary subject of the book is the birth of the prison, that is to say an analysis of the dramatic shift that took place in the early nineteenth century towards the systematic and large-scale use of incarceration as a form of punishment in its own right, Foucault's main concern is with how institutions such as the prison were based on (and in turn fostered) new techniques for the disciplining or control of the body. He is concerned here with the question of how power operates in institutions such as the prison, for he observed that the modern prison did not seek simply to segregate the prisoner from society. The prison, he argued, developed techniques that sought to operate on the mind or soul of the prisoner, placing them in a network of power relations aimed at creating a new kind of individual. It was, in short, a form of discipline. This, he argued, comprised three techniques or modalities of power: hierarchical observation, normalising judgment and the examination (1977, pp 170–194).

Hierarchical observation enabled coercion through the means of surveillance or monitoring. While observation, of course, was not new, what was distinctive about the modern period was the way that it became embedded in the architecture and design of certain institutions. Prisons were designed in such a way as to make the prisoner physically visible to other inmates or to prison officers, who were themselves being watched and supervised. At the same time, the network or hierarchy of management was an apparatus that placed individuals in a field of relations in which all were continuously supervised by their superiors and inferiors. These institutions and networks made possible the exercise of a continuous control over conduct. Normalising judgment, by contrast, refers to the breaking down of actions and behaviours into evermore distinct elements, the normal (or average) way of behaving or performing an action, the departure from which is corrected by discipline aimed at training or instilling in the individual the proper way of acting. Corresponding to the deviations from the norm, there was a new microeconomy of penality, of rewards and punishments, according to which individuals could be compared, differentiated, hierarchised, homogenised and excluded (1977, p 183). Last, Foucault suggests that these first two techniques are combined in the examination. The importance of the examination (the physical examination of the patient or prisoner, the assessment of the student and so on) lies in the fact that it constitutes the object of the examination as a field of knowledge, something that is to be known. The examination, then, made possible the gathering of a certain kind of knowledge (of individuals, of cases), that could be systematised, made more scientific, and which would in turn enable more effective future examination and control. The examination thus 'linked to a certain type of the formation of knowledge a certain form of the exercise of power' (1977, p 187). The aim of all these techniques was the production of more efficient distributions of power or mechanisms of control, but central to them was the constitution of the individual as both the object of power and the instrument of its exercise.

The importance of these 'modest' techniques goes well beyond the analysis of the prison, for Foucault argues that these represent a new political technology of the body, that is to say, a set of techniques and forces that aimed at maximising the productivity and obedience of the individual. Indeed, he took Jeremy Bentham's model of the panopticon – the prison in which the prisoners are continually visible to their jailer, and must believe themselves to be observed even when they are not – as a model for the operation of this form of power throughout the social body (1977, pp 200–209; Bentham 1995). The mechanism could be used for the surveillance of prisoners and patients, but also of workers in a factory to increase their productivity. This form of constant observation was more effective, inducing people to act as though they were always being observed, and thus to internalise the operation of discipline. It was a form of police power, systematic, far-reaching and intense that allowed the government of society as a whole without the need of recourse to repression or the outward display of force. The panopticon internalised the operation of disciplinary power, while maximising the number of people on whom it could be exercised. Most important of all, it was capable of being transferred between different contexts or institutions, making possible a generalised surveillance. It was, in this sense, 'the diagram of a mechanism of power reduced to its ideal form' (1977, p 205).

Biopower

Where discipline works on the individual, 'biopower' is aimed at the administration and production of life. This, Foucault proclaims rather grandly, was 'nothing less than the entry of life into history' (1979, p 141), by which he meant that the conditions of biological existence became the concern of politics.

Foucault remarks here that the modern period sees the development of a new kind of concern with public health. States and sovereigns had had to contend throughout history with disease and epidemics, and their damaging consequences. Famine and natural disaster had caused economic slumps. However, he noted that the eighteenth century saw the beginning of attempts to regulate or manage public health, and to adjust the life and well-being of the population to the needs of economic production. This was made possible by the development of three techniques. First, the collection of social statistics allowed the monitoring of the size and well-being of the population, the recording of birth and death rates, and the measuring of the incidence of disease. It was observed that there are regularities or patterns in these figures at the level of the population – in birth or mortality rates, or the incidence of certain illnesses – and that the social body has a life that can be studied and regulated. Second, interventions in public health could improve collective welfare or security at the level of the population. Thus, for example, improvements in drinking water and sewage disposal eradicated certain diseases; mass vaccination programmes led to dramatic improvements in health and mortality rates; the provision of public housing led to improvement of the collective health of the working classes; and the regulation of sex and the family, through programmes of contraception and sex education, could alter birth rates and infant mortality. Third, population dynamics have economic effects – the size, health, level of education and wealth of the population are all, more or less, directly linked to the economic capacity of the State. The new science of political economy arose out of the perception of these links between population, territory and wealth, and was accompanied by new forms of intervention: managing economic production through the provision of social infrastructure such as roads or housing; establishing systems of public education for an educated workforce; the provision of benefits to workers to sustain the workforce even during economic slumps and so on.

We can thus see how this biopower was central to the development of capitalism: inserting bodies into the machinery of production and adjusting the phenomena of population to economic processes. However, Foucault wants to contend that this was neither the outcome of the process of economic development nor a process that was directed by the State. It was, he argued, a new rationality of government, or governmentality, based around techniques for the management of individuals and populations, but which was not reducible to changes in the form of State institutions.

Governmentality

Governmentality, he argued, is a specific and complex form of power (institutions, procedures, analyses, tactics), which 'has as its target population, as its principal form of knowledge political economy, and as its essential technical means apparatuses of security' (2000, p 220). There were thus certain techniques of individualisation and totalisation that characterise the operation of power in modern society: the production of knowledge through statistics as a means of establishing the social as a field of intervention; the production of collective welfare, health, wealth; the production of the citizen through discipline as a certain way of relating inner being and outer behaviour; and the production of new apparatuses of security and surveillance (the prison, the hospital, the asylum, police) that created and regulated social space.

The importance of these forms of power is that they do not necessarily emanate from the State, nor are they employed exclusively in State institutions. Indeed, he is at pains to contrast governmentality with traditional juridical forms of sovereignty centred on the State. There are three important differences between the two forms of power. First, while juridical power is repressive and negative, Foucault argues that normalising power is productive. It is an action upon an action, not upon a thing, and through action it produces or constructs knowledge about its object and the processes of its application. It thus constructs society and the individual as the targets of power. Second, it is not a property, but a strategy. Power is not located at a particular point in the social body (the sovereign, the constitution), and it cannot be possessed, either in itself (as a right) or as a consequence of the ownership of something else (such as the means of production). Power is a relation and it operates through clusters of individual relations or nodal points in the social body. And third, then, its operation is always localised rather than centralised. Power is not handed down from the great institutions of State, but operates through diverse and multiple networks. Thus in his radical formulation, the State and the rights-bearing individual appear as an effect of power rather than as its source.

However, while this analysis does not take the State and State institutions as its starting point, it is also important to note that Foucault sees the State as having been 'governmentalised' in the sense that problems of sovereignty, such as the competences of the State, come to be thought of within the matrix of powers and knowledge that have been produced by governmentality (2000, p 221). In a more specific sense, governmentality goes hand in hand with the modern liberal State and capitalist economy as the means by which population and individuals are managed so that individuals can become the self-governing subjects of the liberal legal order. However, where traditional political theory has interpreted sovereignty in juridical terms – founded on a contract, and structured by rights – the analysis of governmentality argues that political and social relations cannot be reduced to the legal relation, and that we should additionally focus on the governmental practices that shape the subject as the self-governing, rational actor presumed by political theory (Dean 1999, ch 6).

A theory of legal modernity?

Let us now return to the question with which we started: to what extent can Foucault's theory contribute to our understanding of the place of law and modernity? We can now see that Foucault is making two claims about the law. First, that with the development of governmentality the law is transformed by normalising power. Second, that the basis of sovereignty, which before the modern period was constituted in juridical terms, requires to be rethought. Let us look at each of these in a little more detail.

The characteristic form of modern law, Foucault argues, is not the absolute rule or prohibition, but the norm, as 'the judicial institution is increasingly incorporated into a continuum of apparatuses (medical, administrative and so on), whose functions are for the most part regulatory' (1979, p 144). Consider, for example, the end of life. Death no longer merely marks the limit of sovereign authority, but is surrounded by detailed legislation regulating the point of legal death, how a person may die (euthanasia, medical intervention), the responsibility for the well-being of the terminally ill patient, and even the disposal of the body so as to protect public health. The norm is not an absolute rule, referable to an external source of authority, but is produced through the logics of discipline and government; a norm of behaviour is established through observation and then applied to the same objects that it seeks to govern. The norm as a standard of behaviour is thus strictly self-referential, not emanating from a sovereign power. The strengths of the norm, however, are that it is a common, even objective, standard of measurement, and that it can measure and adjust the behaviour of different individuals. Modern law thus operates as a series of continuous regulatory and corrective mechanisms, rather than on the basis of the sovereign prohibition. It is constituted with reference to the object of regulation rather than according to a set of universal principles. And the sources, objects, institutions and practices of law are necessarily plural. Law in this sense must be understood as a medium rather than a principle of power.

We can now see that claim about modernity as a phase of juridical regression is not necessarily a claim about the declining importance of law so much as a claim about the declining significance of a particular form of sovereignty. The juridical should thus be taken as a way of describing a particular historical form of monarchical sovereignty. However, this is important because this conception of sovereignty has been of importance in shaping our theoretical understanding of the concept. On this view, law is increasingly sidelined, as it is no longer the principle of power: real power is neither constituted nor defined in legal terms, but operates through non-legal strategies and mechanisms. The importance of law may be merely that of legitimising certain actions of the State; indeed, Foucault suggests at various points that formal legal liberties are founded on the corporeal disciplines, and that these were the forms that made normalising power acceptable (1977, p 222, 1979, p 144). We believe power is constituted in legal terms (rights, constitutions, etc) and so are distracted from the real operation of power in society.

The claim of juridical regression is, however, significant in two further and closely linked senses. On the one hand it is a claim about the declining capacity of the categories of the law to capture or define the nature of society (Murphy 1991). On this view law is neither a measure of rationality nor an index of social solidarity; the study of law can reveal nothing essential or fundamental about the nature of society. On the other hand it raises a question about how sovereignty is to be constituted in the absence of an external source of power such as the monarchical sovereign, for we cannot start from any assumptions about the nature or proper function of law as distinct from its actual operations. How, that is to say, can we theorise a sovereignty that is referable only to its own practices? How do we theorise law if it possesses no fundamental characteristics? And how, as a question of politics, can law limit the operation of power in the knowledge that there is no space 'outside' in which law can stand against power? These questions are not easily answered, but the importance of Foucault's theory is that he raises them in particularly acute form.

Reading

The starting point for any understanding of Foucault must be the original texts, because of his distinctive style. The most accessible are probably *Discipline and Punish* (1977) and Volume I of *The History of Sexuality* (1979). Of his shorter texts his 'Two Lectures' (in Foucault 1980) and 'The Subject and Power' (2001) are key, and important points of reference. It is also worth bearing in mind that Foucault published a number of interviews, which also provide short, accessible introductions to his work. Many of these have now been reproduced in the three-volume *Essential Works* (2000). You will also find a selection in Foucault (1980). Gordon (1987) offers a useful comparison with the work of Max Weber. There is little secondary literature directly on Foucault and law, but Ewald (1991), Murphy (1991) and Golder and Fitzpatrick (2009) are most useful. Golder has also written an important book on Foucault and rights (2015) and has edited a volume on this theme (2013). Whyte (2012) and Dean and Villadsen (2016) discuss the role of rights in the context of the exercise of State power.

On governmentality, you should begin with Foucault (2000), while Dean (1999) provides a very useful summary and discussion of the ideas and of the literature spawned by the lecture. The lecture is also published in Burchell et al (1991), together with a number of other essays discussing and applying the ideas; see also Joyce (2003).

Finally, it is worth reading some of the more recent attempts to extend and apply Foucault's thought. The themes of governmentality and police are explored in the essays in Dubber and Valverde (2006), and the legal construction of categories of gender in medicine and law in Sheldon (1997). Hardt and Negri (2000) and Agamben (1998) are influential attempts to address the questions of sovereignty and biopower in a globalised world. For further elaborations and extensions of Foucault's theory of biopolitics, see in particular Deleuze (1992) and Rose (2001); also Villadsen and Wahlberg (2015), Loader and Walker (2007, ch 4) and Neocleous (2008, chs 2 and 3).

Bibliography

Agamben, G, 1998, *Homo Sacer: Sovereign Power and Bare Life*, Stanford: Stanford University Press.

Bentham, J, 1995, *The Panopticon Writings*, ed by M Bozovic, London: Verso.

Burchell, G, Gordon, C and Miller, P (eds), 1991, *The Foucault Effect: Studies in Governmentality*, London: Harvester Wheatsheaf.

Dean, M, 1999, *Governmentality: Power and Rule in Modern Society*, London: Sage.

Dean, M and Villadsen, K, 2016, *State Phobia and Civil Society: The Political Legacy of Michel Foucault*, Stanford: Stanford University Press.

Deleuze, G, 1992, 'Postscript on the Societies of Control', 59 *October* 3–7.

Dubber, MD and Valverde, M (eds), 2006, *The New Police Power*, Stanford: Stanford University Press.

Ewald, F, 1991, 'Norms, Discipline and the Law', in R Post (ed), *Law and the Order of Culture*, Berkeley: University of California Press.

Foucault, M, 1977, *Discipline and Punish: The Birth of the Prison*, Harmondsworth: Penguin.

Foucault, M, 1979, *The History of Sexuality. Volume I: The Will to Knowledge*, Harmondsworth: Penguin.

Foucault, M, 1980, *Power/Knowledge: Selected Interviews and Other Writings 1972–77*, ed by C Gordon, Brighton: Harvester.

Foucault, M, 2000, 'Governmentality', in JD Faubion (ed), *Essential Works of Foucault 1954–1984: Volume III Power*, New York: New Press.

Foucault, M, 2001, 'The Subject and Power', in J Faubion (ed), *Power*, London: Allen Lane.

Garland, D, 1990, *Punishment and Modern Society*, Oxford: Clarendon Press, chs. 6 and 7.

Golder, B (ed), 2013, *Re-reading Foucault: On Law, Power and Rights*, New York: Routledge.

Golder, B, 2015, *Foucault and the Politics of Rights*, Stanford: Stanford University Press.

Golder, B and Fitzpatrick, P, 2009, *Foucault's Law*, London: Routledge.

Gordon, C, 1987, 'The Soul of the Citizen: Max Weber and Michel Foucault on Rationality and Government', in S Whimster and S Lash (eds), *Max Weber, Rationality and Modernity*, London: Allen & Unwin.

Hardt, M and Negri, A, 2000, *Empire*, Cambridge, MA: Harvard University Press.

Joyce, P, 2003, *The Rule of Freedom: Liberalism and the Modern City*, London: Verso, esp. chs. 1, 5 and 6.

Loader, I and Walker, N, 2007, *Civilizing Security*, Cambridge: Cambridge University Press, ch. 4.

Murphy, WT, 1991, 'The Oldest Social Science? The Epistemic Properties of the Common Law Tradition', 54 *Mod LR* 182–215.

Neocleous, M, 2008, *Critique of Security*, Edinburgh: Edinburgh University Press, chs. 2 and 3.

Rose, N, 2001, 'The Politics of Life Itself', 18 *Theory, Culture & Society* 1–30.

Sheldon, S, 1997, *Beyond Control: Medical Power, Women and Abortion Law*, London: Pluto Press.

Villadsen, K and Wahlberg, A, 2015, 'The Government of Life: Managing Populations, Health and Scarcity', 44 *Economy & Society* 1–17.

Whyte, J, 2012, 'Human Rights: Confronting Governments? Michel Foucault and the Right to Intervene', in M Stone et al (eds), *New Critical Legal Thinking: Law and the Political*, New York: Routledge.

Chapter 6

Legal pluralism

The question at the heart of legal pluralism is that of what separates law from non-law. For many students, teachers and practitioners of law, the instinctive answer to this is that law is the formal product of the State, consisting primarily of statutes made by legislatures or the decisions of courts. According to this view, special training is required to become 'learned in the law', and so be able to administer and use it. Legal pluralism contends that this view of law – sometimes referred to as 'lawyers' law' – gives us only a partial account of the nature and scope of law. Instead it is argued that there are many other non-official, often unwritten, normative orders operating in society – whether setting standards for conduct in workplaces, within clubs and associations or among neighbours – which should also be regarded as sources and forms of law.

Legal pluralism presents an alternative paradigm of law to that of legal modernity. As discussed above, the dominant legal understanding that emerged from the eighteenth century onwards saw law as one of the principal achievements of Enlightenment rationality. This view emphasised law's singularity, its universality and its effectiveness. Law was regarded as a coherent body of norms, emanating from a single source – the State; rational law was the culmination of human progress and the aspiration and mark of all 'civilised' societies; and law was one of the primary instruments of social engineering available to the State, shaping society through various inducements and sanctions. Legal pluralism challenges not only the State-centredness of legal modernity, but also its main attributes. In place of singularity and unity, legal pluralism sees multiplicity and relative disorder; in place of universality, legal pluralism sees legal modernity as but one, deeply contingent, way of imagining law, tied to a particular (European) time and place; in place of effectiveness, legal pluralism highlights the ways in which State law is often stymied by non-State law, and so fails to live up to its own standards of instrumental rationality.

Renewed interest in ideas of legal pluralism is generally attributed to anthropological research, conducted in colonial societies in the mid-twentieth century. The nature of this work – often focused on the customary habits of tribal communities – led to legal pluralism being depicted as 'exotic,' and so kept on the margins of legal study. However, in the 1970s, interest in non-State forms of law extended to the mainstream law and society movement, and more recently ideas of legal pluralism have become a central feature of debates about globalisation. While much of this scholarship was conducted over the past fifty or so years, it is important to note that exponents of legal pluralism claim that they are recovering an older tradition, which was temporarily displaced by legal modernity (cf Benton and Ross 2013). We now consider some of the key claims from each of these periods to illustrate the more specific arguments advanced by legal pluralists.

Classical and contemporary legal pluralism

The issue of the basis of legal authority in colonial societies crystallises some of the principal themes of legal pluralism. The paradigm of legal modernity played an important role in justifying European colonialism. According to the Europeans, if land was unoccupied – *terra nullius* – it was open to settlement and governed according to the law of the coloniser. But the territories that the settlers encountered were still occupied by their original inhabitants, and in many cases had been for thousands of years. This problem was overcome by contrasting the stage of development of European societies, with their formal, rational laws, with indigenous forms of social organisation that were deemed 'so low in the scale of social organisation' that they could not be 'reconciled with the institutions or legal ideas of civilized society'(see chapter 3). Without law, there could be no rights of ownership on the part of aboriginal peoples and so, as John Locke put it, there could be no injury to them by the assertion of European sovereignty.

Various legal–anthropological studies over the past century have disputed the idea that law arrived in modern-day North America, sub-Saharan Africa or Australasia with the European settlers. These studies – often referred to as 'classical legal pluralism' – emphasised two points. First, that indigenous peoples formed relatively complex societies with their own normative structures and forms of political organisation. Legal anthropologists identified many developed systems for regulating social life (Moore 1973), whether for exchanging goods, raising children, exploiting the land or settling disputes. These rules were often expressed through (to Western eyes) unfamiliar forms, such as woven belts, and operated within different cultural assumptions – private ownership of land is simply incomprehensible to many indigenous peoples (Galanter 1981). The settlers did not recognise this as law because it failed to meet their own cultural predispositions (as would be the case with Western law for the aboriginals). The second argument running through classical legal pluralism is that indigenous forms of law did not disappear in the colonial state. Indeed, the coexistence of both formal and indigenous law is said to be the more accurate account of the colonial era (Asch 1997). For example, the early settlers often entered into treaties with aboriginal groups, adopting the latter's rites of solemnification, such as exchange of wampum belts (although, when inconvenient, these treaties were dispensed with by asserting the ultimate authority of the colonial state). Moreover, colonial officials often found it more pragmatic to license the use of customary norms, which in many cases continued to be followed by the local population, to govern areas of social life such as the family (Chanock 1985). Thus legal pluralists argue that claims that official State law provides the sole criterion for legal order simply do not accord with reality. In sum, the lessons that are possibly shared by almost all classic legal pluralist authors are at least three: theorists must be aware of their ethnocentric biases; legal concepts emerge out of a historically and spatially bounded experience; there cannot be only one universal legal discourse which would capture all social realities.

The key development that marked a move from classical to 'new' or 'postcolonial' legal pluralism was the growth in empirical socio-legal studies. This research adopted a different approach to traditional legal scholarship, concerned less with doctrinal analysis – 'law in the books' – and more with how it operated in practice – 'law in action'. This led many to conclude that an exclusive focus upon State law only gave a limited picture of legal relations in developed countries. An important impetus here was research on forms of alternative dispute resolution (ADR). This demonstrated that citizens who lacked the wherewithal to have access to the formal machinery of justice often cultivated their own informal means of settling disputes (Abel 1982). The idea that informal law was not only to be found in colonial societies was taken forward by other studies, for example in the field of industrial relations. Legal pluralists here contrasted State labour law with the 'indigenous law of the workplace', such as codes of conduct, informal agreements and customary patterns of behaviour, and argued that the latter were often more important in shaping workers' day-to-day activities (Arthurs 1985b).

The advent of globalisation has further refocused attention on plural forms of legal ordering. This is unsurprising, given that the principal argument across the globalisation literature is that the nation-state should no longer be the privileged object of study. Some commentators highlight the profusion of sites of formal political authority in the global era, and suggest that citizenship is now necessarily multiple, and that we negotiate our rights and obligations within overlapping legal orders at the subnational, national and supranational levels (see ch 8, III, Part I). Others argue that the new legal forms, which have helped lubricate the operation of the global economy, can only be explained by a pluralist perspective. For example, an important feature of contemporary economic activity is global *lex mercatoria*, which includes various business practices, codes of conduct, standard form contracts and arbitration awards, all of which can be described without reference to State law. Economic globalisation may also recast what we regard as sources of law, and see multinational corporations as exercising significant normative authority, for example, in setting standards in the fields of agricultural production or medical research (Hertz 2001).

Strong and weak legal pluralism, and the position of the state

It should already be clear that legal pluralism itself takes many forms. One way in which we might characterise different approaches adopted in the various phases is the distinction between 'strong' and 'weak' legal pluralism. According to John Griffiths, 'weak' legal pluralism entails the 'formal acquiescence by the state' in accepting 'different bodies of law for different groups in the population' (1986, pp 7, 5). The archetypal, but not only, example of this is the coexistence within the colonial state of Western and indigenous legal rules, with the State's courts authorising reliance on customary law to resolve disputes before it. Griffiths argues that this situation should not count as proper legal pluralism, as it accepts the State as the ultimate sovereign authority: in our example, customary norms apply because the State legal system 'recognises' them. He contrasts this with 'strong' legal pluralism, which he defines as 'that state of affairs, for any social field, in which behaviour pursuant to more than one legal order occurs' (1986, p 2). Accordingly, State law is but one legal order, whose authorisation is unnecessary for the empirical operation of other forms of law.

A leading account of 'strong' legal pluralism is found in the work of Boaventura de Sousa Santos, in particular his complex 'structure-agency map' of modern capitalist society. Santos posits six structural places – the householdplace, the workplace, the marketplace, the communityplace, the citizenplace and the worldplace. Each generates its own distinct form of law: for example, the domestic law of the householdplace refers to the unwritten codes that govern social relations within the family, while the exchange law of the marketplace denotes the trade customs and normative standards operating among producers, merchants and consumers. For Santos, the actual legal rules that apply at any one time are not dependent on one type of law, but will necessarily be a combination of the different forms. For example, the legal regulation of the family includes a mixture of formal State law and informal domestic law.

The distinction between strong and weak legal pluralism is a controversial one, and not everyone accepts Griffiths's dismissive stance towards the latter. It highlights, though, that attitudes towards the State remain an important fault line within legal pluralist scholarship. This raises important methodological and normative issues. Regarding the former, legal pluralists have sought to provide a definition of law that captures the full range of legal phenomena. However, Brian Tamanaha (1993) claims that many of these attempts underscore the difficulty of conceiving of law without reference to the State. He argues that legal pluralists tend to posit their criteria for law by focusing on what appears essential to State law – whether the enforcement of norms or the resolution of disputes – but then subtracting the indicia of the State from this equation. For him, this shows that the State remains the starting point even for some leading pluralist accounts of law.

A related question is whether, even if legal pluralism could escape the analytical framework of State law, it is desirable that it should. This addresses the connection between description and prescription in legal pluralism. While Griffiths argues that legal pluralism is simply a fact, it is part of his mission to debunk the 'ideology' of centralising approaches that hold that law ought to be the law of the State. It would seem to follow that legal pluralists think that law ought to be regarded other than in State-centred terms, and some writers appear to valorise non-State forms of law for their own sake. Others, though, are concerned by the normative implications of this position. First, they suggest there is no special reason to believe that plural forms of law will be necessarily progressive: for example, some socio-legal scholars saw the rise of ADR as problematic as it potentially restored the advantages of the financially and socially powerful, which the formal law had sought to equalise. Moreover, to confer the term 'law', with its connotations that what is lawful is right or moral, on some aspects of social life, is to confer upon them a legitimacy that they do not deserve (for example, the often oppressive regimes generated within prisons) (Tamanaha 2000).

These are important questions, but to some extent, they are unanswerable in their own terms: how, for example, do we 'prove' what law is? Rather, they direct us to an enquiry into the usefulness of plural understandings of law, and the objectives that they serve, to which we now turn.

Empirical, conceptual and political approaches to legal pluralism

The points just discussed highlight the importance of the qualifying adjective. In traditional terms, State law is simply 'law,' while plural forms of law, such as indigenous or informal law, require qualification or demotion, so that they are customs, or habits, or social norms, but not law. There are various strategies that legal pluralists employ to cast off the burden of the qualifying adjective, and so affirm that they are indeed talking about law. We might categorise these strategies on the basis of their empirical, conceptual and political emphases (although these categories are far from watertight, and overlap in practice).

Empirical approaches to legal pluralism seek to provide a more comprehensive account of the actual norms that influence everyday life, and argue that this requires a broader research field than an exclusive focus on State law. This engages with the influential command theory of law, that is, that through people's subservience to law, the State can direct the future shape of society. Legal pluralists argue that if this is what distinguishes State law as law, then it frequently fails to live up to this ideal. Moreover, other forms of normative order often seem better to approximate the special characteristics claimed for State law. In place of the model of (State) law acting upon a passive society, legal pluralists see it as constantly interacting with other legal orders. For example, to return to the example of relations in the family, the limitations of State law in addressing problems such as domestic violence can be attributed to the fact that it does not wholly displace the (often patriarchal) norms of domestic law. The objective here is to understand better how the interaction between these different forms of law may facilitate or impede different policy objectives.

While empirical approaches may lead to a more nuanced account of State law, with more feasible expectations, it could still be objected that we lose conceptual clarity if the category of law becomes overbroad. Conceptual approaches to legal pluralism respond by arguing that the singularity associated with State-centred views provides a distorted basis for legal study, and necessarily gives way, once we accept that law reflects the society within which it is embedded. This approach is grounded in a pluralistic social theory, which views social life in terms of a disorganised struggle between different groups. Seeing law as one part of a larger web of varied and complex social relations, it is argued that legal relations must also be asymmetrical (Sampford 1991). This goes further than some empirical approaches: not only is law decoupled from the State, but also all forms of law tend towards disorder and incoherence. From this perspective, even if our focus is on State law, this has to be recast as inherently plural, with full account taken of its crosscurrents and contradictions (and so the difference between strong and weak legal pluralism may not be as pronounced as has been suggested).

One might accept that the empirical and conceptual approaches present important challenges to traditional legal thought, but still insist there is value in maintaining the distinction between law and other social norms. This brings us to the political dimension of legal pluralism, which reverses the enquiry so far conducted, and asks what purposes are served by presenting State law as the sole category for legal study. For Santos, this reflects less an analytical imperative and more the operation of a politics of definition designed to portray the State as the only form of political authority in society. He argues that the main consequence of this politics of definition is to mask other sites of social power, and their attendant forms of law, such as the market. Thus the political purpose of pluralising law is not to suggest a moral equivalence, say, between norms produced by states and multinational corporations; rather, it seeks to expand questions about the legitimate use of power across all those institutions (State and non-State) which exercise coercive power.

Future directions in legal pluralism

Ideas of legal pluralism now occupy a more prominent place in legal scholarship than has historically been the case and have recently been employed to address mainstream subjects such as constitutional law (Walker 2002; Anderson 2005), transnational law (Buchanan 2006) and legal ethnography. With this expanded interest, debates within and about legal pluralism have continued to adapt. We conclude by briefly discussing three key innovations in the literature.

The first, usually termed global legal pluralism, is an adaptation of the discourse of legal pluralism to some legal questions posed by globalisation. Working under the assumption that State law cannot capture the fragmentation of law in the global age, global legal pluralists propose an epistemology which is attentive to the proliferation of legal sources and respectful of the autonomous capacities of social groups. However, despite all the proclamations on the importance of protecting autonomous sites of 'juris-genesis', it is arguable that the main concern of global legal pluralism is how to manage (rather than enhance) the plurality of global legal fragments through either norms of interaction (typically conflict-of-laws) among legal sources (Krisch 2013, p 297) or procedural mechanisms 'that aim to manage, without eliminating, the legal pluralism we see around us' (Berman 2012, p 10). A regional variation of this approach has also been developed in European studies, where the notion of constitutional pluralism (a coupling of constitutionalism and legal pluralism beyond the State) has been one of the most successful in explaining the development of European integration and in particular the behaviour of the highest courts adjudicating on EU law. In this case, too, the element of pluralism captures only conflicts among modern State-legal institutions.

A second approach follows the 'linguistic turn' in political philosophy, and seeks to develop a form of legal pluralism that both is sensitive to the limitations of the State-centred conception and retains a distinction between law and social norms. The solution, it suggests, lies in the coupling between autonomisation of certain social systems *qua* normative systems. Gunther Teubner, one of the leading exponents of this view, argues, for example, that global commercial practices (*lex mercatoria* discussed above) should be seen as a form of law as the binary coding 'legal/illegal' is used by key actors such as international arbitrators (Teubner 1997, p 4). The same applies to many other legal fragments which have just been upgraded to the global level (Teubner 2012). While this approach may provide a relatively straightforward threshold test for the existence of law, it has been criticised on the grounds that it retains the view that certain functions are essential to law – in Teubner's terms, the controlling and co-ordinating of behaviour – which are ultimately derived from the State-based understanding (Tamanaha 2000, pp 308, 312–321); the same type of criticism has been made of the binary code legal/illegal, deemed also to be a replica of State-based legal rationality (Roberts 2005, p 20).

An approach that seeks to avoid any preconceived notion of how law should be defined comes under the rubric of critical legal pluralism (Kleinhans and Macdonald 1997). This departs from empirically based scholarship, arguing that techniques of mapping tend to see law in positivist terms as something that can be measured 'out there', apart from the human agents who created it. Critical legal pluralists reject this view of law as external knowledge, and instead highlight the role of knowledge in creating our perception of reality. This results in a different test for legal order. The focus is no longer simply on which external legal order exercises normative authority over individuals; we also have to ask within which legal order individuals regard themselves as acting. This places more emphasis on the legal subject, who is not just a passive recipient of law, but has an active role in producing and shaping legal knowledge. As we perceive ourselves to be working within different legal orders at different times, according to the various views canvassed in this section, the legal knowledge produced will be necessarily and irretrievably plural.

Reading

A helpful overview of the principal differences between legal pluralism and State-centred accounts of law is found in Arthurs (1985a, ch 1). For a discussion of the shift from 'classical' to 'new' legal pluralism, see Merry (1988, pp 872–874), and for the application of ideas of legal pluralism in the context of globalisation, see Santos (2002, pp 194–200) and Twining (2009, ch 12). For a review of the debate concerning the utility of the distinction between strong and weak legal pluralism, see Woodman (1998). Davies (2005) highlights the various empirical and conceptual strands within legal pluralist scholarship, and for an elaboration of the 'politics of definition', see Santos (2002, pp 89–91). For a discussion of critical legal pluralism and its responses to some of Tamanaha's criticisms, see Kleinhans and Macdonald (1997, pp 30–43).

On the concept of legal pluralism, see the classic statement by Griffiths (1986); also Tamanaha (2000) and Melissaris (2009). A recent edited collection (Roughan and Halpin 2017) describes the current state of the art in jurisprudential debates about legal pluralism. For an overview of the main voices in the debate on constitutional pluralism, see Avbelj and Komárek (2012); on global legal pluralism, see Berman (2012), Michaels (2009) and Walker (2014).

Bibliography

Abel, R (ed), 1982, *The Politics of Informal Justice*, vols 1 and 2, New York: Academic Press.

Anderson, GW, 2005, *Constitutional Rights After Globalization*, Oxford and Portland, OR: Hart.

Arthurs, HW, 1985a, *Without the Law*, Toronto and Buffalo: University of Toronto Press.

Arthurs, HW, 1985b, 'Understanding Labour Law: The Debate Over "Industrial Pluralism"', 38 *Current Legal Problems* 83.

Asch, M (ed), 1997, *Aboriginal and Treaty Rights in Canada: Essays on Law, Equality and Respect for Difference*, Vancouver: University of British Columbia Press.

Avbelj, M, and Komárek, J (eds), 2012, *Constitutional Pluralism in Europe and Beyond*, Oxford: Hart.

Benton, L, and Ross, R (eds), 2013, *Legal Pluralism and Empires, 1500–1900*, New York: New York University Press.

Berman, PS, 2012, *Global Legal Pluralism: A Jurisprudence of Law Beyond Borders*, Cambridge: Cambridge University Press.

Buchanan, R, 2006, 'Legitimating Global Trade Governance: Constitutional and Legal Pluralist Approaches', 57 *Northern Ireland Legal Quarterly* 1.

Chanock, M, 1985, *Law, Custom and Social Order: The Colonial Experience in Malawi and Zambia*, Cambridge: Cambridge University Press.

Davies, M, 2005, 'The Ethos of Pluralism', 27 *Sydney Law Review* 87.

Galanter, M, 1981, 'Justice in Many Rooms: Courts, Private Ordering, and Indigenous Law', 19 *Journal of Legal Pluralism and Unofficial Law* 1.

Griffiths, J, 1986, 'What Is Legal Pluralism?', 24 *Journal of Legal Pluralism* 1.

Hertz, N, 2001, *The Silent Takeover: Global Capitalism and the Death of Democracy*, London: Heinemann.

Kleinhans, M-M and Macdonald, RA, 1997, 'What Is a Critical Legal Pluralism?', 12 *Canadian Journal of Law and Society* 25.

Krisch, N, 2013, *Beyond Constitutionalism*, Oxford: Oxford University Press.

Melissaris, E, 2009, *Ubiquitous Law: Legal Theory and the Space for Legal Pluralism*, Aldershot: Ashgate.

Merry, SE, 1988, 'Legal Pluralism', 22 *Law & Society Review* 869.

Michaels, R, 2009, 'Global Legal Pluralism', 5 *Annual Review of Law and Social Science* 243.

Moore, SE, 1973, 'Law and Social Change: The Semi-Autonomous Social Field as an Appropriate Subject of Study', 7 *Law and Society Review* 719.

Roberts, S, 2005, 'After Government? On Representing Law Without the State', 68 *Modern Law Review* 1.

Roughan, N and Halpin, A, 2017, *In Pursuit of Pluralist Jurisprudence*, Cambridge: Cambridge University Press.

Sampford, C, 1991, *The Disorder of Law*, Oxford: Blackwell.

Santos, B, 2002, *Toward a New Legal Common Sense*, 2nd edn, London: Butterworth.

Tamanaha, BZ, 1993, 'The Folly of the "Social Scientific" Concept of Legal Pluralism', 20 *Journal of Law and Society* 192.

Tamanaha, BZ, 2000, 'A Non-Essentialist Version of Legal Pluralism', 27 *Journal of Law and Society* 296.

Teubner, G (ed), 1997, *Global Law Without a State*, Gateshead: Athenaeum Press.

Teubner, G, 2012, *Constitutional Fragments*, Oxford: Oxford University Press.

Twining, W, 2009, *General Jurisprudence: Understanding Law From a Global Perspective*, Cambridge: Cambridge University Press.

Walker, N, 2002, 'The Idea of Constitutional Pluralism', 65 *Modern Law Review* 317.

Walker, N, 2014, *Intimations of Global Law*, Cambridge: Cambridge University Press.

Woodman, GR, 1998, 'Ideological Combat and Social Observation', 42 *Journal of Legal Pluralism* 21.

Chapter 7

Legal institutionalism

In the history of legal thought, legal institutionalism is a twentieth-century creation born in reaction to two dominant streams of scholarship, legal positivism and natural law. The social and intellectual context that gave birth to legal institutionalism explains many of the concerns at the forefront of legal institutionalists' work. On one hand, the crisis of the liberal State under the pressure of demands for inclusion put forward by the masses (Romano 1910) and the tragedy of World War I provided a context where a formalist understanding of the law would come across as untenable. On the other hand, the rise and consolidation of sociology as an academic discipline pushed legal theorists to focus their attention on the link between societal formation and the legal order. Coupled to the rise of sociology was the creation of a new field, 'social law', which found in legal institutionalism an obvious theoretical ally. In particular, theorists that would later be associated with legal institutionalism began to conceive the relation between society and law as an *internal* one, overcoming the comprehensive liberal conception of a legal world made up of State and individuals. In other words, the legal order began to be conceived as part of society's formation. Gunther Teubner has captured this peculiar trait of legal institutionalism in the following terms: 'Institutionalist theories and, in particular, the new discipline of sociology then came up with a more complex self-description of society' (Teubner 2012, p 21). While opening up legal analysis to a multiplicity of social spheres, legal institutionalists maintained that they were pursuing legal ('juristic' is their preferred term) knowledge as a 'complex self-description of society', meaning that the formation and development of society was not detachable from the juridical dimension. Nonetheless, in adopting this approach, they did not recognise any specific role to morality in determining the validity and content of the law.

In light of these brief remarks, it should not come as a surprise that the paradigmatic texts of legal institutionalism have been produced in France, Italy and Germany (although one might make a case for a parallel development in the US during the New Deal), where legal positivism had become hegemonic within legal circles. One may find antecedents of the institutionalist approach in the work of Montesquieu and, later, Emile Durkheim, but the founding authors of legal institutionalism are without doubt Maurice Hauriou and Santi Romano. The former, a student of Leon Duguit (the founding father of social law in France), taught and published important treatises in public and administrative law (e.g., Hauriou 1916), and only in the last part of his career formalised his key idea of institution.

According to Hauriou, neither the social contract nor the rule of law can be thought of as the real basis of the legal order; only the notion of the institution can provide this basis (Hauriou 1918, p 813). Institutions can be of two types: 'person-institutions' and 'thing-institutions'. The former represent the most basic element of the legal order and it is the type that really interests Hauriou. The definition of institution contains three constitutive elements:

> An institution is an idea of a work or enterprise that is realized and endures juridically in a social context; for the realization of this idea, an organized power equips it with organs; on the other hand, among the members of the social group interested in the realization of the idea, manifestations of communion occur and are directed by the organs of the power and regulated by procedures.
>
> (Hauriou 1970, p 99)

In short, one can detect three defining tenets of an institution: (1) its existence is directed by and towards a driving or ordering idea (*idée directrice*); (2) there is an organisation which endows the institution with proper power and organs for realising the idea; and (3) there are forms of solidarity which hold the institution together. It should be made clear that the ordering idea does not play the role of a teleological function or of a fundamental objective of a social group. All three elements are essential, but the distinctive one (the one that gives to the institution its own specific identity) is the 'driving' or 'ordering idea'. This might be generated by certain fundamental aims, but in time it allows a transformation of what is at the beginning only a psychological intention into social reality. The temporal extension of the driving idea is key for making the idea autonomous and independent of the connected fundamental political objectives. At the same time, in order to become autonomous, the driving idea needs to gather enough and constant consensus from the members of the institution. By consensus here Hauriou is not invoking a collective will; instead

> it is individuals who are moved by their contact with a common idea and who, by a phenomenon of interpsychology, become aware of their common emotion. The centre of this movement is the idea that is refracted into similar concepts in thousands of minds and that stirs these minds into action.
>
> (ibid, 107)

Taken together, the three elements make up the constituent process of formation of the institution itself. Indeed, the process can be divided into three phases. First, the introjection of the driving idea; second, the incorporation of the idea into an organised power; and, finally, the moment of specification, in which 'the group members are absorbed in the idea of the work, the organs are absorbed in a power of realization, the manifestation of communion are psychical manifestations' (ibid, 101).

In a classic institutionalist gesture, Hauriou draws a distinction between institution and positive law: 'institutions make juridical rules; juridical rules do not make institutions' (ibid, 93). Institutions are therefore 'jurisgenerative' whereas legal rules 'only stand for ideas of limitation instead of incarnating ideas of enterprise and of creation' (ibid). Such a distinction suggests an affinity between Hauriou's theory and legal pluralism (see chapter 6). Hauriou, however, makes clear that the State represents the most accomplished form of institution (it is the 'institution of institutions') and, accordingly, implies that the most developed institutions are those that resemble the State and its internal organisation.

Romano's masterpiece *The Legal Order*, originally published in 1917–1918, contained a fully fledged theory of law as institution. Unlike Hauriou's work, Romano's book was not conceived as a substantial defence of the State (although the State was recognised as an 'institution of institutions'). Against normativism, Romano argued that the original and foundational concept of each and every legal order is the institution. Hence, the legal order can never be reduced to an aggregation of norms, not even to a system of norms. For Romano, the idea of a system remains too abstract, and makes legal positivism's understanding of the law as a system of norms (see in particular Kelsen's Pure Theory of Law, ch 11, Part II) inaccurate. Rather, the legal order is a *concrete* unity, which is held together by an effective social organisation defined by Romano as 'institution'. The notion of institution is neither a requirement of reason nor an abstract principle: it is an integral part of social reality. Interestingly, the relevant concept of organisation does not entail a relationship of superiority and corresponding subordination. Not every organisation qualifies as an institution. For Romano, to qualify as an institution, four distinctive aspects need to be met: (1) the entity has to possess an objective and concrete existence, which, even when immaterial, must be visible; (2) the entity must be a manifestation of the social nature of human beings; (3) it must be individuated, that is, it must have a recognisable distinct existence (this, of course, does not mean that it cannot be related to other institutions, as complex institutions are); and (4) the institution should be a firm and permanent unity (Romano 2017, p 19). In this scheme, norms are necessary but not sufficient features of the institution. They are determined by but not determinant of the institution. This means that

> the law cannot just be the norm established by the social organization . . . if it is true that the legal character of the latter is conferred by the social power that issues it, or at least sanctions it, it follows that this character must be already present in the institution, which could not assign such a legal character to the norm if it did not have it itself.
>
> (Romano 2017, p 25)

In fact, Romano is convinced that an institution can have all its norms changed and still remain identical to itself. Not even legal relationships (what were, at that point, known as *jural* relationships) can define an institution. Romano thus does not conceive of the law in the terms of imperativism; an imperativist conception of the law considers the latter as a command issued usually by a sovereign or one of its delegates, backed by the threat of sanction or coercion. Romano does not accept this conception of the law because it underestimates the creative and constitutive aspects of legal orders. If the legal order were made only of norms backed by sanctions, its connection with society would be lost, and law would be conceived, in the end, as external to social relations, and as a coercive imposition upon society. Instead it is its capacity to generate social power that defines the institution. Hence, while norms remain part of institutions, it is the attribution and distribution of roles and functions that are the institution's distinctive factors. This is because institutions contain ordering properties as intrinsic to the organised form: to put it in simple terms, an organised entity is logically endowed with internal ordering properties, otherwise it would not be capable of assuming the form of an organisation. And without taking up that form, it could not generate social power. For this reason, the legal order always presents itself as a construction internal to society: *ubi ius ibi societas* (where there is law there is society) and *ubi societas ibi ius* (where there is society there is law).

The above discussion brings us to the question of the monopoly of legal force and the role of the State in his theory. Romano does not discard the State as an accomplished institution, though he is certainly more ambiguous about it when compared to Hauriou. He openly criticises Hauriou for having

> limited the concept of institution to only one type of social organization, which would reach a given degree of development and perfection . . . Hauriou was moved by the intent to shape his institutions in the image of the state, or better, of the modern state, while one should have rather outlined a very general figure, whose contingent traits can vary.
>
> (ibid, 33)

But although his institutionalism contains the seeds of a legal pluralist approach in the suggestion that there are as many legal orders as there are institutions, he underplayed this aspect. In the end, if somewhat contradictorily, he draws a distinction between superior and hierarchically inferior institutions, which is parallel to the distinction between autonomous and derivative legal orders (cf Loughlin 2017, ch 7). States and churches represent, for Romano, more complex and accomplished institutions.

Hauriou and Romano produced their most important works in the first three decades of the twentieth century. In the following two decades, their reflections proved inspirational to a cohort of scholars dealing in particular with issues of constitutional and administrative law. The ordering properties of institutions were later taken up as a key premise by Carl Schmitt, who after having read Hauriou and Romano appeared to convert to an institutionalist conception of law (Schmitt 2004a/1934). During the 1920s, Schmitt became the most important advocate of *decisionism*, an approach to law famously epitomised by the idea that sovereign is he who decides on the state of exception (Schmitt 2005/1934). Famously, Schmitt remarked that 'the exception is more interesting than the rule. The rule proves nothing, the exception proves everything. It confirms not only the rule but also its existence, which derives only from the exception' (ibid, 15). Such an approach provided a theory of law grounded on sovereignty as political decision and expanded this into a fully fledged conception of the constitution. In *Constitutional Theory* (2008/1928), Schmitt drew a distinction between the constitution and constitutional law: the former he deemed to be the fundamental decision on the political unity of a constitutional regime, while the latter constituted a mere collection of constitutional norms. In this sense, for Schmitt, a decision preceded the formation of the legal order as a whole, an 'exceptionalism' that created order *ex nihilo* (from nothing) and from the *outside* (in other words, a political decision that was outside the legal order that it generated). However, Schmitt soon understood that political unity could not be bootstrapped to a single decision out of nothing and, under the influence of Hauriou and Romano, started to shift the emphasis of his argument by highlighting the critical role of unity and order. He explained that all legal theories contain necessarily three fundamental elements: norms, decisions and institutions. But what makes distinctive a legal theory is the priority given to one of these three elements. In the preface to the second edition of *Political Theology*, Schmitt wrote: 'I now distinguish not two but three types of legal thinking; in addition to the normativist and the decisionist types there is the institutional one . . . which unfolds in institutions and organizations that transcend the personal sphere' (Schmitt 2005/1934, p 2). The perspective of the institution defines what Schmitt calls 'concrete order': a series of institutional practices that positive law incorporates and qualifies as legal. Schmitt had come to see that the State could be stabilised only if social normativity, which in his account is prone to generate a plurality of institutions, could be kept under control (meaning: constrained) by politics and law. What is necessary, according to Schmitt, is a law which is both selective and exclusionary in protecting key institutions of society from internal and external threats. The process unfolds by selecting the standard instantiations of an institution and by excluding those that are not compatible. Legal norms ought to try to determine and stabilise what in a given context is deemed to be a normal case (Croce and Salvatore 2013, p 39). Of course, unlike Romano, Schmitt still conceives of law as an imperative, that is, in the most part as a command backed by sanction or coercion. Later, Schmitt would expand his interest in legal institutionalism and concrete order thinking by using the idea of *nomos* as a specific conception of the legal order tied to space (Schmitt 2006/1950) and three movements of appropriation, distribution and production. This late work will confirm the importance of the role of institutions for his reflection on the concrete order (Loughlin 2017, ch 5).

The last institutionalist writer that we will visit is Italian constitutional lawyer Costantino Mortati, who adopted legal institutionalism in order to expose the limits of formalism in describing constitutional orders and to develop a politically realist conception instead. Mortati recognised his debt to Hauriou and Romano, but still deemed their theories to fall prey to a rigid dualism between fact and norm. For Mortati, Hauriou still separated into two different spheres the driving idea and the social organisation behind it, as if they belonged to two different levels. Romano, on the other hand, underestimated the normative elements intrinsic to the process of social organisation: functions and roles still retain important normative aspects, which were unjustly underplayed by Romano. Mortati concedes that each institution is animated by a driving idea/telos, but this

> cannot perform its function . . . if it [does] not have the character of uniformity and constancy, that is, if it is not a norm; this norm would be without doubt different from those disciplining directly behaviours, but still similar in its function.
>
> (Mortati 1998), p 46)

In other words, Mortati believed that legal orders necessitate unity and the latter can be realised only if there are (ultimate) foundational norms. These norms should not be conceived as deontological constraints, but as norms with a teleological core. Mortati makes an Aristotelian point here: the existence of legal orders is driven by a final cause that it is the function of the basic norm to give expression to.

Norms and institutions can be distinguished for analytical purposes but they are always mutually implicated. The point of convergence which makes possible to conceive both of them as co-implicated is what Mortati considers as a synonym of constituent power: the idea of *normative fact*. This is a fact which contains in itself a norm (in the form of a rule or a principle) and the conditions of its persistence in the future. Normative facts are not abstract entities, but concretely organised (i.e., ordered) entities with juridical features. Mortati, like the other legal institutionalists, emphasised the internal relation between societal formation and the legal order. The latter is therefore conceived as something that can be cognised in terms of juristic knowledge from its inception. And in this way, the methodological strict distinction between facts and norms collapses. However, this means that for proper legal knowledge, it is necessary to go beyond the level of formal norms, as the latter won't tell much about the basic framework of social relations.

In light of these remarks, it is understandable why Mortati needed to introduce the notion of the '*material constitution*' as the concrete legal order which would breathe life into the formal legal order. This notion allowed Mortati to shed light on the defining traits of a constitutional order beyond the formal constitution; studying the material constitution would force the lawyer to address also the basic structure of society. Unlike Hauriou and Romano, Mortati did not concede much to the spontaneous 'jurisgenetic' properties of social relations. Only an active political intervention, already juridical in essence, can actually bring about a properly organised social order. Mortati postulates that the political unity of an order can be achieved only with the positing of fundamental political objectives and the emergence of a social group or collective subject as the 'bearer' of the material constitution, that is, the social force behind the realisation of those objectives. Political parties, at least in the first phase of his thought (see, later, Mortati 1998) would play the role of the bearers of the material constitution, as they would function as critical agents in processes of differentiation within society among those who rule and those who are ruled (Mortati 1998, pp 60–62).

While Schmitt and Mortati adopted some of the fundamental intuitions of Hauriou and Romano, they differ on two essential aspects: first, they maintain an imperativistic conception of positive law which was functional to a more politically inclined approach to the concept of law. Only a strict selectivity of concrete (i.e., tied to the social context) institutions or a hegemonic political group can create and maintain the legal order. Second, as a consequence, they did not concede much to what we might call the 'autopoietic' properties of social systems (see section below), failing to recognise the emergence of a more spontaneous order of social law.

In the second half of the twentieth century, legal institutionalism either morphed into different disciplines (legal anthropology, the cultural study of law, etc) or, as an autonomous theory of law, steadily declined in influence and importance (La Torre 1993). It was only with the publication of Neil MacCormick and Ota Weinberger's *An Institutional Theory of Law* (1986) that the idea of law as an institution was revived. It should be noted that MacCormick and Weinberger's project was more concerned with an updating of legal positivism than a revival of the old version of institutionalism. MacCormick and Weinberger shared with Hauriou and Romano the idea that there exists a legal reality which is distinct from brute reality. They also adopted the notion of normative facts, but three crucial differences set the 'new institutionalism' apart from the old one. For the 'new' institutionalists, first, the main unit of analysis of the link between society and law is not the institution, but social facts; second, these social facts do not pay attention to or afford any specific significance to the lived experience of institutions and their concrete orders; third, the main legal form studied by Mac-Cormick and Weinberger are rules, and not roles or functions. In particular, resorting to an idea originally introduced by John Searle (1995), they are interested in exploring the constitutive, regulative and terminative function of rules vis-à-vis legal institutions. The complete absence of any engagement with authors such as Hauriou and Romano in the last restatement of the theory by MacCormick (2007) confirms that this revival of legal institutionalism does not share much with the work of its founding fathers.

Reading

The foundational texts of legal institutionalism are now available in English: a key text published by Hauriou in 1925 is contained in an edited collection of French institutionalism (Hauriou 1970), and another, originally published in two parts between 1917 and 1918, has been recently translated (Romano 2017). Schmitt's key institutionalist texts are from the 1930s, but they are now all available in English: see Schmitt (2004a, 2004b, 2005) (in particular, the preface to the second edition). See also his classic *Nomos of the Earth* (2006). Mortati published an essential work on the function of governing (Mortati 2000) which contains early traces of his ideas, but these are mostly spelled out in Mortati (1998) and Mortati (2008).

Amongst the older sources, a good introduction to legal institutionalism is provided by Ivor Jennings (1933). For an introduction and an analysis of Hauriou's legal theory in English, see Gray (2010); in French, see Millard (1995) and Blanquer and Millet (2015). As for Romano's legal institutionalism, a solid analysis in English is available in Stone (1966, ch 11) and Fontanelli (2011); see also the foreword by Martin Loughlin and the afterword by Mariano Croce to Romano (2017). The secondary literature in English on Schmitt has grown rapidly in recent years: see, among many titles, Bendersky (1983), MacCormick (1997), Dyzenhaus (1998), Croce and Salvatore (2013) and Schupmann (2017). On the legal thought of Mortati not much is available in English, but for a very good edited collection in Italian, see Catelani (2001).

For an in-depth confrontation between old and new institutionalism (with a clear preference for the latter), see La Torre (1993, 2010). An assessment of the legacy of new institutionalism is offered in Del Mar and Bankowski (2009). Two recent proposals formalised as partly inspired by old legal institutionalism are Lindahl (2013) and Loughlin (2017). An analysis of the links between legal institutionalism and legal pluralism is put forward in Croce (2012). On the potential application of old legal institutionalism for a philosophical reflection on Europe and the EU, see Esposito (2018).

Bibliography

Bendersky, JW, 1983, *Carl Schmitt: Theorist for the Reich*, Princeton: Princeton University Press.

Blanquer, M, 2015, *L'invention de l'État: Léon Duguit, Maurice Hauriou et la naissance du droit public moderne*, Paris: Odile Jacob.

Catelani, A (ed), 2001, *La costituzione materiale: Percorsi culturali e attualità di un'idea*, Milano: Giuffré.

Croce, M, 2012, *The Self-Sufficiency of Law*, Dordrecht: Springer.

Croce, M and Salvatore, A, 2013, *The Legal Theory of Carl Schmitt*, London: Routledge.

Del Mar, M and Bankowski, Z, 2009, *Law as Institutional Normative Order*, Farnham: Ashgate.

Dyzenhaus, D (ed), 1998, *Law as Politics: Carl Schmitt's Critique of Liberalism*, Durham, NC: Duke University Press.

Esposito, R, 2018, *A Philosophy for Europe: From the Outside*, London: Polity.

Fontanelli, F, 2011, 'Santi Romano and *L'ordinamento Giuridico*', 2 *Transnational Legal Theory* 67–117.

Gray, CB, 2010, *The Methodology of Maurice Hauriou*, Amsterdam: Rodopi.

Hauriou, M, 1916, *Principes de droit public*, Paris: Sirey.

Hauriou, M, 1918, 'An Interpretation of the Principles of Public Law', 31 *Harvard Law Review* 813–821.

Hauriou, M, 1970, 'The Theory of the Institution and the Foundation: A Study in Social Vitalism', in A Broderick (ed), *The French Institutionalists*, Cambridge: Cambridge University Press, 93–124 (original ed 1925).

Jennings, I, 1933, 'The Institutional Theory', in I Jennings (ed), *Modern Theories of Law*, London: Oxford University Press, 68–85.

La Torre, M, 1993, 'Institutionalism Old and New', 6 *Ratio Juris* 193.

La Torre, M, 2010, *Law as Institutions*, Dordrecht: Springer.

Lindahl, H, 2013, *Fault Lines of Globalisation*, Oxford: Oxford University Press.

Loughlin, M, 2017, *Political Jurisprudence*, Oxford: Oxford University Press.

MacCormick, JP, 1997, *Carl Schmitt's Critique of Liberalism: Against Politics as Technology*, Cambridge: Cambridge University Press.

MacCormick, N, 2007, *Institutions of Law*, Oxford: Oxford University Press.

Millard, E, 1995, 'Hauriou et la théorie de l'institution', 30 *Droit et société* 381–412.

Mortati, C, 1998, *La costituzione in senso materiale*, Milano: Giuffré (original ed 1940).

Mortati, C, 2000, *L'ordinamento del governo nel nuovo diritto pubblico italiano*, Milano: Giuffré (original ed 1931).

Mortati, C, 2008, 'Costituzione', in Mortati, C (ed), *Una e indivisibile*, Milano: Giuffré (original ed 1962).

Romano, S, 1910, 'Lo Stato moderno e la sua crisi', *Rivista di diritto Pubblico* 3.

Romano, S, 2017, *The Legal Order*, London: Routledge (original ed 1918).

Schmitt, C, 2004a, *On the Three Types of Juristic Thought*, Westport: Praeger (original ed 1934).

Schmitt, C, 2004b, *Legality and Legitimacy*, Durham, NC: Duke University Press (original ed 1932).

Schmitt, C, 2005, *Political Theology*, Chicago: University of Chicago Press (original ed 1934).

Schmitt, C, 2006, *The Nomos of the Earth*, New York: Telos Press (original ed 1950).

Schmitt, C, 2008, *Constitutional Theory*, Durham, NC: Duke University Press (original ed 1928).

Schupmann, B, 2017, *Carl Schmitt's State and Constitutional Theory*, Oxford: Oxford University Press.

Searle, J, 1995, *The Construction of Social Reality*, London: Alle.

Stone, J, 1966, *Social Dimensions of Law and Justice*, London: Stevens.

Teubner, G, 2012, *Constitutional Fragments*, Oxford: Oxford University Press.

Weinberger, O and MacCormick, N, 1986, *An Institutional Theory of Law: New Approaches to Legal Positivism*, Dordrecht: Kluwer.

Chapter 8

Law and deconstruction

Deconstruction is a mode of philosophical thinking, literary criticism and socio-political critique associated with the work of the French philosopher Jacques Derrida. The *Cardozo Law Review* published a long essay by Derrida in 1990 under the title 'Force of Law: The "Mystical Foundation of Authority"' (Derrida 1990). Derrida's work had enjoyed the attention of legal scholars long before 'Force of Law' appeared, but the publication of this essay marked the beginning of a period of legal theoretical scholarship during which the work of Derrida received widespread attention among legal theorists, especially in English-speaking countries. This legal theoretical engagement with Derrida's work ranged from strong enthusiasm and endorsement, on the one hand, to serious scepticism, on the other. However one might feel about the reception of deconstruction in legal theory today, a contemporary textbook on jurisprudence can hardly claim to be a comprehensive engagement with the prominent trends in this field of scholarship without paying due attention to the implications of deconstruction or Derridean thinking for legal theory.

Thirteen years after the publication of Derrida's essay in the *Cardozo Law Review*, the Italian philosopher Giorgio Agamben published a little book of which the English translation appeared two years later under the title *State of Exception*. In this book he commented on the continuing failure of legal theorists to arrive at some cogent interpretation of the title of Derrida's essay 'Force of Law: "The Mystical Foundation of Authority"' (Agamben 2005, p 37). Agamben then proceeded to articulate his own understanding of the title of Derrida's essay in which he linked it to states of exception in which the *force of law* is suspended for the sake of maintaining or sustaining the law. Agamben's interpretation of Derrida's essay is forceful and convincing in many respects. Constraints of space preclude an engagement with this interpretation in what follows. Suffice it to observe in this regard Agamben's crucial insight that Derrida's essay and deconstruction in general is concerned with *a state of exception in which the law is observed but not applied* (Agamben 2005, pp 35–40). Why this state of exception concerns 'the foundation of authority' and why these foundations can be described as *mystical* are questions that Agamben nevertheless addresses only indirectly or implicitly. The engagement with Derrida's essay 'Force of Law' and with his work in general that follows here endeavours to address these questions expressly and directly so as to explain and scrutinise the possible significance of Derridean thinking for legal theory. Derrida's invocation of the mystical foundation of authority in the essay is taken from an observation of Pascal regarding the 'the mystical foundation of law' to which the law cannot be traced without annihilating it (Derrida 1990, pp 938–939). It is this annihilating source or foundation of law that legal theory must come to understand should it wish to respond to Agamben's challenge.

A meaningful engagement with Derrida's work requires considerable background knowledge. It is impossible to come to grips with Derrida's thinking without some understanding of the way core thoughts of those such as Martin Heidegger, Edmund Husserl, Ferdinand de Saussure, Sigmund Freud, Karl Marx, Friedrich Nietzsche and Emmanuel Levinas impacted on his work. The short engagement with Derrida's thinking that follows here cannot pay attention to all these influences, but some of them will become evident in the course of the discussion. It is instructive, however, to highlight the influence of Heidegger's work on Derrida (arguably by far the strongest of the influences mentioned here). Derrida would take over from Heidegger a critique of Western philosophical thinking as a thinking that invariably and predominantly gives priority to the stable presence of the *existence* (*Being*) of all things (*beings*) at the expense of a regard for the way *existence* concerns the primordial and temporal *emergence* of things from 'origins' or an 'origin' that cannot be described in terms of presence or present existence. *Being*, for Heidegger, 'is', then, the non-present (which is not the same as absent) origin of all things (beings) that eventually become present.

The philosophical disregard for the temporal emergence of all things, argued Heidegger, is the defining characteristic of the long tradition of Western philosophical thinking that, according to him, started with Plato and Aristotle and continued right up to and into Nietzsche's identification of the *will to power* as the source of all things. This whole history of philosophy, he maintained, pivoted on the disregard for the way things are never simply *infinitely present* but the outcome of a *finite event of disclosure*. Heidegger accordingly referred to this long tradition of Western thinking as the history of the *metaphysics of presence*, and he presented his own philosophical endeavour as a *destruction* of this metaphysics of infinite presence for the sake of recovering the regard for temporal and finite emergence or disclosure of things that, according to him, was still evidently prevalent among the pre-Socratic Greek philosophers. These essential themes in Heidegger's work emerged from a vast oeuvre to which more specific references are not necessary for present purposes. (For more specific bibliographical references to these thoughts and a more comprehensive engagement with Heidegger's work from a legal theoretical perspective, see Ben-Dor 2007 and Van der Walt 2011.)

Heidegger's selection of the word *destruction* for purposes of recovering the sense for the way things are not simply present and do not simply exist but come to presence and emerge into existence played a crucial role in Derrida's characterisation of his own thinking as *deconstruction*. For Derrida too, *deconstruction* concerned the recovery of the regard for the way things come to presence and are not simply present. It is not only crucial for philosophers and theorists who wish to engage more fully with Derrida's thought to understand this aspect of his thinking incisively. It is also crucial for legal theorists who may only want to engage with Derrida's thoughts about law or the implication of his thinking for law. This is so because the concern with the finite and temporal emergence, as opposed to the stable and infinite presence of existence, goes to the heart of Derrida's thoughts on justice and the law, as will soon become clear.

The emergence of existence, for Derrida, concerns a *textual event*. According to him, dominant texts structure the prevailing forms of consciousness and understanding of an era. Fundamental texts (for instance, religious and philosophical works or political documents like constitutions, international treaties, human rights declarations, classic literary works, etc) constrain the variety of present possibilities of human existence and hold them in place. They maintain *the presence* in which any given era of human existence unfolds and proceeds; hence his provocative assertion that 'there is nothing outside the text' that met with much opprobrium among literal-minded philosophers who did not share Derrida's affinity for probing rhetorical phrases that often capture penetrating thoughts more economically and effectively than laborious prose. What Derrida meant by this assertion 'there is nothing outside the text' concerned an insight that would, in the wake of the work of especially Ludwig Wittgenstein, become common currency in contemporary theories of language. In contrast to earlier analytical theories of language, which pivoted on the idea that accurate language mirrors and reflects in the human mind a world that is already in place outside the mind, post-Wittgensteinian theories of language, as especially articulated in the work of Donald Davidson, turn on the insight that language does not reflect or refer to a world that exists independently outside language and outside the human mind. Language *constructs* the world in which human beings live. Already in an early work that is still closely associated with the picture, correspondence or reflection theory of language elaborated above, Wittgenstein observed that 'the limits of my language mean the limits of my world' (Wittgenstein 1922, 5.6). There may well be things or obstructions 'out there' against which humans bump into mutely, uncomprehendingly and often disastrously (violation of human dignity and environmental pollution were surely 'around' for some time before definitive language introduced it into our normative and physical worlds), but these 'things' or 'obstructions' do not become part of the human world until such time as they become integrated into a coherent and comprehensible human environment. And the work of integrating coherent and comprehensible human environments is done by language. Pre-Wittgensteinian legal philosophical sentiments may still want to object that this work of integration is done by human individuals *with the help* of language. In doing so they would be clinging to the idea of language as a mere tool with which the human being's subjective experience of objective reality can be ordered and integrated so as to render it coherent and integrated. They would be suggesting that both the subjective and the objective pillars of the subject–object reality come first and that language comes second. Their suggestion would be that human beings (subjects) first live in the world (objective environment) and then resort to language to make better sense of themselves and their environments. With this suggestion, however, they would be ignoring something that takes place 'right under their noses', so to speak, namely, the way they rely on already available and constraining language to describe the very notion of subjectivity, objectivity and the whole array of linguistic tools with which the former can 'reflect the latter accurately' or 'through which everything can be integrated into a comprehensive and comprehensible whole'. Heidegger had already observed that the human being does not speak. Language speaks; humans only answer to the speaking of language. Humans are not capable of a single or first thought without language making that thought possible in the first place. And one might add: humans are not humans before the articulation of the first thought that language makes possible for them.

One cannot understand Derrida's thought and more specifically his assertion that 'there is nothing outside the text' without due consideration of these developments in twentieth-century philosophy of language and the way this philosophy of language came to understand the human world as constructed by language. Derrida's concern with deconstruction must be grasped as a concern with the de-construction of the world or worlds constructed by language. Deconstruction is the textual event under the sway of which new worlds, new possibilities of observation and new modes of assertion become possible. Deconstruction, broadly definable as the picking at the seams of dominant texts that hold existing worlds in place, seeks to solicit the textual event through which new worlds may emerge. It is a picking at the textual seams that sustains present realities in the hope that they may unravel, come apart and begin to release new ways and new forms of understanding. A regard for this fundamental point also allows one to grasp a remarkable twist that Derrida's thought would bring about in the development of contemporary theories of language outlined above. Having realised that all words and all linguistic signs are arbitrary denotations that bear no unique, necessary or non-conventional relations to the things they denote, mainstream analytical philosophers of language started to emphasise the stabilising linguistic practices (conventional rules of grammar, exigencies of contextual coherence, etc) that secure linguistic meaning despite the arbitrariness of linguistic signs. Derrida, quite to the contrary, focused microscopically on the dynamics of language for purposes of discovering and emphasising the destabilising potential of this dynamics. What was his motive for doing so?

The answer to this question lies in the concern with the emergence or disclosure of existence that Derrida took from Heidegger. To get to the point quickly, let us repeat two sentences on which we have already relied above: the emergence of existence, for Derrida, concerns a textual event. According to him, dominant texts structure the prevailing forms of consciousness and understanding of an era of history. The concern with the emergence or disclosure of existence can evidently not be or not only be a concern with the stabilising dynamics of the texts that construct prevailing modes of consciousness in any given era or epoch; it is also and predominantly a concern with the ways in which dominant texts of an era or epoch become unstable. Deconstruction is a concern with the way dominant texts of an era become unstable and, thus, susceptible to the inauguration of unprecedented modes of consciousness and understanding. And this points to the second twist that Derrida's thought would bring about in contemporary philosophy of language. Derrida may have underlined and emphasised along with and not against his major contemporaries that the world is constructed through language and that 'there is nothing outside the text' constructed by the dominant language or languages of a particular era of history, but the fact that he was concerned with the deconstruction of the text constructed by dominant languages points to an acute concern with the outside of that text, the nothing outside that text. In other words, deconstruction is acutely concerned with that which is not constructed by the text, that which is excluded from the text.

One might say deconstruction suffered from semantic claustrophobia. It experienced the worlds of readily available linguistic meaning as suffocating. It gasped for a breath of fresh 'meaning' that is not yet contaminated, or not yet fully contaminated, with the stale air of recirculated linguistic meaning. Provided one does not read into it a suggestion that Derrida returned to a reference theory of language that scrutinised the conditions for accurate referential relations between language in the world, one can risk the following suggestion: in a very surprising and different way (different from referential theories of language), Derrida was much more of a 'realist', much more concerned with some independent 'reality' that exceeds the worlds of linguistic construction, than were most of his contemporaries. Strictly speaking, this 'reality' cannot be named at all. It can hardly be alluded to. This is so because all naming and all allusion take place within language, within the constraints that existing languages impose on knowledge and understanding. The 'reality' at issue here cannot be named from within language and can only be alluded to indirectly from within language, because it concerns the very emergence of language that precedes whatever naming or allusion may take place from within established language and established linguistic practices.

Derrida knew the bounds of the metaphysics of presence, the bounds of languages that define things, give meaning to things and render them present as some or other established form of existence, human or animal, animal or vegetative, organic or inorganic, spiritual or material, and so on, that cannot be crossed or transgressed. He was well aware that these are the bounds of the typical binary oppositional ways in which humans constructively understand their worlds. He knew that there is no escape from these bounds. There is nothing beyond the metaphysics of presence. Language allows for no escape and no transgression. He would emphasise this repeatedly throughout his career. And yet, his whole philosophical endeavour obsessively and relentlessly scrutinised possibilities of alluding, at least indirectly or obliquely, to the emergence of language to which no direct allusion is possible. For this purpose his writings experimented, over a period of four decades (starting in the 1960s and ending with his death in 2004), with a number of key concepts such as différance, trace, supplement, event, coming (the irreducibly coming or arriving nature of things), spectre, hospitality and justice. Let us very briefly look at the first three of these concepts. We return to the last four later.

Derrida's insight into the arbitrariness of linguistic signs was not instilled by Wittgenstein or post-Wittgensteinian philosophy of language, as might well have been the case. It derived from his engagement with the work of structural linguists, especially that of Ferdinand de Saussure. And it is in response to especially De Saussure's work that Derrida would develop the concepts of différance and trace. De Saussure had already articulated the insight into the lack of any necessary relation between the signifier and the signified, that is, between the linguistic sign and the object or product of its signification. The signified, De Saussure argued, was a product of differential relations between signifiers. It was the outcome of how linguistic signs related to one another. It was not an outcome of any referential relation to any specific signifier. Meaning, argued De Saussure, is the outcome of interaction between signifiers; it was an outcome of interplay between acts of signification. It is against the background of this insight that Derrida would argue that language turns on the dynamics of différance. The word différance was a neologism (like the word deconstruction, it no longer is one) with which Derrida denoted the double dynamic of differentiation and postponement, that is, of differing and deferring. This dynamic suggested that meaning never enjoys any anchorage in some or other positive and present signifier. The meaning of any present signifier is always the product of its difference from other signifiers (a is a because it is not b and c, etc; cat is cat because it is not dog or fish or monkey, etc). As a result of this incircumventible differentiation from other signifiers, the meaning of any one signifier is always deferred or postponed. The meaning of any one signifier only comes to the fore once other signifiers have also been in play. And considering this basic dynamics of interminable differentiation and deferring, argued Derrida, positive meaning is never positively present at any given point in time. Meaning is nothing but the interlacing of *traces*.

The remarkable reversal at stake here must be noted. The *trace* is not the lingering remainder of any nodal point or chunk of fully present meaning that happened to have disappeared just recently, as the common understanding of the word 'trace' would suggest. Quite to the contrary, any nodal point of present meaning is nothing but the effect of an interlacing of traces that never were anything but traces. The same dynamic is evident in the phenomenon of the *supplement* and *supplementation*. Close analysis of the practice of constructing texts into main parts and supplements led Derrida to a similar insight into the reversed dynamics between main and supplementary parts of texts. To the extent that they are acts of significant or pertinent *supplementation*, supplements *alter* and *re-organise* main bodies of texts. If they do not do this, they serve no real purpose and may just as well be omitted from the text. This again leads to the remarkable insight that textual meaning is the product and result of supplementation. It does not precede the supplement. The supplement becomes the origin which, in turn, has its origin elsewhere. (For Derrida's elaboration of these themes, see especially Derrida 1982, 1973, 1978.)

Meaning thus never has any solid purchase in any present reality. It is the product of spectral events of differing, deferring, tracing and supplementation. The concern with *spectres* and *ghosts* and *haunting* would come to mark a later phase of Derrida's thinking and most expressly so in his engagement with Marx (Derrida 1994). He suggested in this regard that philosophy should replace *ontology*, the study of existence, with *hauntology*, the study of ghostly haunts. But his acute regard for the way fully fleshed 'present' realities derive from a spectral play of ghostly realities that defy the categories of both presence and absence is already abundantly evident in his early engagement with structural linguistics and the notions of différance, trace and supplementation that he developed in these earlier works. The brief engagement with these key concepts in Derrida's early works should nevertheless make clear that the haunting 'reality' with which deconstruction might be said to be concerned does not entail something or some thing beyond language. It simply concerns the spectral event or events and the primordial or early structuration that sustain language. The deconstructive analysis of this primordial structuration – Derrida also called it *arche-writing* – is the closest that language can move to its ineffable outside, the closest that it can come to saying something about its outer limits without falling into utter incomprehension.

Wittgenstein famously observed that language must remain silent with regard to that which it cannot articulate (Wittgenstein 1922, p 7). Considered from this Wittgensteinian position, the outer boundaries or outsides of language fall within this ineffability because language would have to reach beyond itself to articulate the film or membrane of its outer limits. And the moment it would do so, it would no longer be able to articulate anything. Unlike Wittgenstein, or perhaps only in a different way, Derrida nevertheless pressed on with a relentless endeavour to say something about the limits of language, to say the unsayable. As will become clearer in the next paragraph, the linguistic engagement with the unsayable is not as such a Derridean invention. It has been the mark of mystic contemplation and poetry that is as old as language itself, and Wittgenstein, too, was not impervious to this mystic concern with origins that cannot be articulated (Wittgenstein 1922, 6:552: 'There are things indeed that cannot be put into words. They make themselves manifest. They are what is mystical'). And as we shall see in the next paragraph, the mystic concern with ineffable origins can plausibly be said not to be the exclusive inclination of unique individuals. It is plausible to say that language itself posits, alongside the register of clarity and clear communication the register of an irrepressible curiosity regarding the mists and mysteries from which its clarity emerges.

These reflections on language and the deconstructive concerned with the boundaries of language provide a telling clue to what Derrida may have wanted to express with the title of the essay 'Force of Law: The "Mystical Foundation of Authority"'. We shall presently turn to this essay, but one more observation is important before we do so. Careful readers of everything said above might still want to raise the objection that *someone* is experimenting here; *someone* is picking at the seams of texts; *someone* is intervening to solicit the textual event; *someone* is doing deconstruction and using language or experimenting with language to do so. The old subject–object constellation of the metaphysics of presence, in terms of which language is nothing but the tool of a pre-existing subject, is still conspicuously present in all of this. Derrida's reply to this objection would be ambivalent. He would concede that this is correct to the extent that the language of the metaphysics of presence indeed holds us captive and constrains us to repetitions of its essential linguistic schemas. The philosophy of deconstruction, to make its point, also has to resort to language that is largely conventional and common. We have already mentioned this. There is indeed no transgression possible, not even for deconstruction and deconstructionists. But the language that holds us captive in this way remarkably also allows for, grants, and even solicits, the experimentation and exploration that resist this captivity. Deconstruction is not some extra-textual philosopher's brainchild. It is not just a smart idea or thought that one of the ingenious thinkers of our time plucked from his undoubtedly highly productive and creative mind. Derrida knew that deconstruction is the product of a language or languages that has and have been around long before him. His entire oeuvre consisted of painstakingly following and tracing leads already followed by other thinkers before him. He knew that his own creativity was a textually *provoked* creativity, a creativity *solicited* by the creative possibilities that the language of his predecessors (especially, as mentioned above, Heidegger, Husserl, De Saussure, Freud, Nietzsche, Marx and Levinas) offers. Deconstruction is an event of language, an event in which language gives itself, as it has done for ages, to the possibility of an impossible resistance to its own constraints. That this resistance of language to itself is as old as language itself is attested by ancient instances of mystic poetry, philosophy and theology that sought to explode or transgress language for the sake of a direct, or at least more direct, experience of existence. It has always been evident whenever significant poetry resisted conventional ways of saying in order to say what has hitherto remained unsaid. Heidegger found a telling instance of this mystic resistance to language in Parmenides's poetic probing of a thinking that would be close enough to existence to become *boundless* and to warrant the assertion of the *oneness of thinking and existence*, the oneness of *thought* and *Being* (Heidegger 1982). He also found this resistance to be evident in the work of several poets, especially in the poetry of Friedrich Hölderlin (Heidegger 1971). Derrida found and explored this resistance in the writings of the medieval mystic theologian/poet Angelus Silesius (Derrida 1995) and in the poetry of Paul Celan (Derrida 1986b), among many others.

The mystic and poetic resistance of language to itself has indeed all along been a regular feature of language, a regular feature of significantly innovating philosophy, theology and poetry. Might this mystic and poetic resistance of language to itself also be evident in, or pertinent for, legal theory and thinking about law? This is the question that Derrida's essay 'Force of Law: The "Mystical Foundation of Authority"' added to the concerns of contemporary legal theory. The lively response and wide acclaim that this essay found in contemporary legal theoretical scholarship would suggest that this is a worthy legal theoretical and jurisprudential concern. Is this so, or has a considerable contingent of contemporary lawyers and legal theorists just succumbed to the allure of something that is completely foreign to law and should have remained foreign to legal theory? Might one not argue that the concerns of legal theory are circumscribed by the clear language of law? Should legal theory therefore not confine its concerns to the register of clear communication and, at that, to a very clearly defined sub-category of this communication that complies with the even higher levels of linguistic clarity exacted by the demands of law and the ideal of the rule of law? Has the legal theoretical reflection upon the social and political origins of law in the course of the twentieth century (legal realism, sociological theories of law, critical legal studies, etc) not already bitten off more than it can chew by venturing much too far beyond the proper province of jurisprudence? Has it not already moved much too far beyond clear primary rules of legal obligation backed up by clearly defined secondary rules of legal recognition, application and change (Hart)? Has this introduction of political and sociological impurities not polluted the concern with pure law enough; has it not already introduced enough troubled water into the transparency of pure law, the transparency of legal norms that are clearly validated by higher norms and ultimately by a clearly defined foundational norm that insulates the law from all extra-legal impurities (Kelsen)? And if this circumscription of the domain of jurisprudence is perhaps too narrow, should one not then let the matter rest with the respectable and relatively transparent integration of some fundamental moral considerations into law and legal theory (Dworkin)?

The concern with a well-circumscribed domain of jurisprudence or legal theory that is reflected in these questions must surely turn into dismay when the question of deconstruction's relevance for legal theory comes to the fore, for deconstruction is not just concerned with the political, sociological and moral origins of law. As if these origins are not already worrying enough, deconstruction is concerned with the origins of these origins; the origins of the social, the political and the moral; the origins of social, political and moral languages. It is concerned with origins of origins, moreover, that can never be pinned down anywhere but are ever again displaced, suspended, deferred or supplemented by other originating moments; origins that are mere traces of traces that are lost in the mists of linguistic differentiation. No rule of recognition stands a chance here. No foundational norm and no moral principle can hope to arrest the abyssal chaos of the primordial event of language.

Had it not been for Agamben's challenge, one might not have needed to elaborate the matter to this extent. The mystic curiosity of deconstruction is mentioned right up there in the title of the essay that catapulted deconstruction into the concerns of twentieth-century legal theory – the mystical foundation of authority. Derrida was upfront and considerate enough to state the concern of the essay straight away. Anyone for whom the foundation of legal authority begins and ends with a rule of recognition, foundational norm, fundamental moral principle or considerations of social legitimacy and so on could have turned away immediately. But the essay 'Force of Law' made its mark on legal theory and continues to do so. Why is this?

The essay is in the first place an engagement with Walter Benjamin's (1978) essay 'The Critique of Violence'. We cannot do justice here to the richness of either Benjamin's text or Derrida's engagement with it. Suffice it to highlight some of the key themes of Derrida's essay. The first theme concerns Benjamin's analysis of the law in terms of a recurring cycle of two forms of authority and violence (the German word *Gewalt* which Benjamin employs denotes not only authority, but also violence), law-*founding* authority and law-*preserving* authority. This analysis is in itself already interesting to Derrida because of the way it reflects the split origins of law. It reflects the fact that the authority or violence required to found the law (for instance during a popular revolution) is never enough. The resulting order of law or rule of law does not terminate the authoritarian and violent origins of law so as eventually or subsequently to inaugurate what might be called non-violent and non-authoritarian governance or non-violent authority. The rule of law repeats the authoritarian violence of its origins incessantly in the form of law-conserving violence (Derrida 1990, especially pp 948ff). Derrida also discerned and highlighted the split and repetitive origins of law in the relation between the initial drafting and ratification of the American Constitution. The initial draft was unlawful for it was not yet mandated by law and only became law as a result of ratification. But the ratification necessarily remains haunted by a lack of law, for the unlawful cannot be ratified without contaminating the lawful with the unlawful (Derrida 1986a). What, after all, ratifies or legitimises the act of ratification? The ultimate foundations of law and legal authority can evidently never be pinpointed with reference to a single and clearly definable origin that is in itself sufficiently authoritative. The foundation of authority is mystical because it is never fully present. As is the case with the materialisation of linguistic meaning that we described above with reference to Derrida's early works, authority always emerges from split origins, repetitions, traces and supplementations. It emerges from the mists and mysteries of multiple moments of lawmaking of which no single moment is authoritative. Authority is therefore also always significantly extra-legal or non-legal. Regular legal authority itself thus always involves, in significant respects, a state of exception.

The second theme in Benjamin's essay that interests Derrida is Benjamin's invocation of a third kind of violence that breaks completely with law-founding and law-conserving violence. Benjamin calls this third kind of violence *divine violence* to contrast it with law-founding and law-conserving violence, both of which Benjamin subsumes under the category of *mythical violence*. *Divine violence* differs from *mythical violence* because it has no relation to law. It neither founds, nor conserves, law. Benjamin identifies the possibility of such divine violence in the revolutionary practice of the *general strike*. Derrida's interest in Benjamin's analysis should be evident when one keeps in mind deconstruction's concern with the outer limits of language or the *outside of the text* that we outlined above. Benjamin's notion of *divine violence* evidently seeks to articulate a source of authority or violence that transcends the law and the language of law. Benjamin's concern with *divine violence* is a concern with absolute transgression and the absolute outside of law; something one might want to call *divine justice*. Derrida's regard for the impossibility of complete transgression and the impossibility of transcending the limits of language, irrespective whether this language is legal, political, moral, revolutionary, theological or poetic, nevertheless renders him highly critical of Benjamin's idea of *divine violence*. The last part of the essay turns, in fact, into a sharp critique of Benjamin. One might comment in this regard that Derrida had a mystical curiosity regarding the ineffable foundations from which things emerge, but he had little tolerance for any mysticism that would hold these foundations accessible.

This brings us to the third theme of the essay: *law is not justice, justice is impossible*. The insight that legal authority is interminably caught up in cycles of law-founding and law-conserving authority/violence precludes the law from any claim to justice. The law cannot be just. Not only is the law not just, justice is impossible. The insight that language and legal language preclude direct access to divine authority and divine justice demands the recognition that justice between humans is impossible. No legal rule and no application of a legal rule can be just because all law is always caught up in some form of authoritarian violence or violent authority and no revolutionary destruction of law can save or deliver us from law and the violent authority embodied in it. We can at best, claims Derrida, have an *oblique* or *indirect* experience with justice (Derrida 1990, p 935). How might one have this indirect experience with justice? One might have an experience with justice through the deconstructive regard for the differential relation and tension between an incircumventible need for law and legal rules, on the one hand, and the impossibility of justice, on the other. Derrida articulates this differential tension further under the second aporia of justice elaborated in the essay: *justice would demand that one simultaneously follow and not follow a rule* (cf Derrida 1990, p 961). At issue here are two contradictory demands of justice that render the present materialisation or embodiment of justice impossible. A complete disregard for rules cannot be just. The just decision must follow the applicable rule. But the mere application of rules, however equitable, can also not do justice. It will presently become clear that these two irreconcilable demands of justice may well relate directly to two irreconcilable conceptions of justice in the history of Western or European legal thought.

How might this deconstructive articulation of the relation between justice and law be contextualised in the history of legal theoretical conceptions of the relation between law and justice? One must answer this question by considering the broader context of the late phase of Derrida's work to which the essay 'Force of Law' belongs. At issue here is the phase of Derrida's thinking in which the Levinasian concern with *hospitality* played a key role. According to Levinas and Derrida (leaving aside the differences between them for now), *hospitality* concerns the selfless submission to the demands of others upon us. It concerns, further, the absolute gift that expects or demands nothing in return. It concerns the selfless giving of that which one does not have to give. It concerns a completely asymmetrical relation in which the self gives itself to the demands of the other (Derrida 2000). This giving and this hospitality, just like justice, are impossible. There is no pure gift and no pure hospitality. Earthly relations, however generous or giving they may claim or aspire to be, always take place with the expectation of a return, an expectation of symmetry. There are key passages in the essay 'Force of Law' that clearly evince a direct connection or association of the impossibility of justice at stake in the essay, and the impossibility of the gift and of hospitality at stake in Derrida's engagement with Levinas in this phase of his thinking (Derrida 1990, pp 959, 965). Doing justice to others would require nothing less than absolutely selfless hospitality and giving. As we saw above, Derrida invoked 'nothing outside the text' to denote, obliquely, the limits of all language. This early concern with the limits of language takes an ethical turn in the works that would relate to his engagement with Levinas. The language that remains language in the wake of its poetic or mystic encounters with its own limits, the language that survives that encounter without giving way to incomprehensible delirium (Derrida often observed that deconstruction is an exploration of madness), is the precursor of the mad ethics of giving articulated in his later work. The ethics of giving articulated in this work evinces a deep fascination with the possibility of an insane disregard for mundane concerns of economic survival (Derrida 1990, p 965).

Evident in this ethics and in the deconstructive understanding of justice which Derrida articulates in 'Force of Law' is a clear departure from the Aristotelian understanding of justice in terms of just proportions that give to everyone that which is due to them (Aristotle 1981). This understanding of justice found its way into Roman law in the form of Ulpian's definition of justice as *jus suum cuique tribuere* – 'justice is to give to everyone his own' (*The Digest of Justinian* 1.1.10) – and can be argued to have remained, ever since, one of the pillars of Western legal thinking. The gigantic weight of the legal tradition that is challenged by the concept of asymmetrical justice articulated in 'Force of Law' should be clear. But 'Force of Law' is not the first articulation of this challenge. The Aristotelian concept of justice in terms of just reciprocities gave way for many centuries to the Christian ethics of asymmetrical giving and forgiving, the ethics of forgiving seventy times seven and of turning the other cheek. It was introduced to Western moral thinking by the works of St Augustine in the fourth to fifth century AD and it displaced the Aristotelian tradition of justice right up to the eleventh century. Aristotelianism experienced a revival in the twelfth century, and from the twelfth to the fourteenth centuries these two pillars of Western legal thinking, Greek/Roman and Christian, competed fiercely with one another for the soul of Western or European morality and law. From the thirteenth to fourteenth centuries St Francis of Assisi and his followers articulated a remarkable example of the moral mysticism of selfless giving that haunts the Derridean concern with justice in 'Force of Law'. It gave rise to the famous poverty debate between the Dominican and Franciscan orders of the Catholic Church. Hotly contested was the question whether Jesus and his disciples owned property, whether they owned the clothes they wore and the food they ate, or just used and consumed these necessities without any claims to property. Like Benjamin, the Franciscans were aspiring to a life beyond property, beyond law (Villey 2003, pp 212–268).

Derrida's concern with the ethics and justice of selfless giving does not derive from this Christian background. He took it over from Levinas who, in turn, articulated it with reference to Jewish conceptions of ethics and justice. We cannot go into the difference between the Jewish and the Christian traditions here. Suffice it to say that both these traditions, together with the secular articulations they would find in the tradition of Marxism, embody a counterpoint to the Aristotelian (and Kantian) understandings of justice which today, perhaps in a fundamentally distorted way (one can presently basically forget about the ethics of selfless giving as modern legal systems can hardly claim in good faith to afford to each what is due to them), still inform dominant modes of legal thinking. One might say that these contrapuntal tensions in Western legal thinking evince the way legal language, like all language, incessantly resists itself and explores its own boundaries. Fundamental conceptions of law emerge from these and many other tensions. Only an anachronistic and recalcitrant metaphysics of law would endow them with stable and infinite presence.

Aspirations and claims to justice always emerge from the tensions of restless legal languages that explore and resist their own boundaries. The concern and experience with justice always *comes* from renewed instantiations of these tensions, explorations and resistances. Considered from this background, justice can never exist as a positive presence. It *comes*. It is *always to come* (Derrida 1990, p 969).

The contribution of deconstruction to legal theory is bound to remain controversial. But it is fair at least to credit Derrida with some of the most probing analyses of the precarious spectral dynamics and non-presence of law and legal language in recent philosophy and legal theory. The fact that a highly non-jurisprudential theoretical project such as deconstruction – something so far beyond the domain of rules of recognition, foundational norms, basic principles of morality, social and political legitimacy, and so on – has come to make such a forceful impression on legal theorists may well itself be explained in Derridean terms. Jurisprudence too is an unstable and restless discipline that continues to resist and explore its own outer limits and the outsides of its foundational texts. It is important to stress again in this regard the deconstructive regard for the fact that deconstruction is not something that some individuals or some legal theorists have done or are doing to law and legal theory. Deconstruction is what happens. It happens in law and legal theory because of the law's irreducible susceptibility to deconstruction. There is little point in dismissing these restless boundary explorations of jurisprudence as irrelevant or inappropriate as far as the 'proper domain of jurisprudence' is concerned, for there is little point in dismissing or being judgmental about that which happens, has happened and is likely to happen again. It is much more prudent and therefore also much more *jurisprudent* to endeavour to understand what really happens in law and legal theory. And it is for this reason that Derrida might be said to have made a huge contribution to *jurisprudence*, not only *notwithstanding* but perhaps also *because* of the obvious distances between his philosophical concerns and the more regular concerns of legal theory. If it is an aspiration of jurisprudence or legal theory to understand its own concerns more comprehensively, let alone fully, it cannot shy away from also exploring the outer limits of its fundamental textual organisations and constructions. And this may well require the traversal of considerable distances.

Reading

Students who wish to do more reading on deconstruction can consider the following books and articles:

Drucilla Cornell et al (eds), *Deconstruction and the Possibility of Justice* (1992) (Derrida's essay 'Force of Law' discussed above is also republished in the volume along with many other essays by other legal theorists who engage with Derrida's work).

Jonathan Culler, *On Deconstruction* (1985).

Christopher Norris, *The Deconstructive Turn* (2010).

Christopher Norris, *Deconstruction, Theory and Practice* (1982).

Christopher Norris, 'Law, Deconstruction and the Resistance to Theory', 1988 *Journal of Law and Society* 166–187.

Neil MacCormick, 'Reconstruction after Deconstruction. A Reply to CLS', 1990 (10) *Oxford Journal of Legal Studies* 539–558 (more broadly a response to the Critical Legal Studies movement than specifically a response to Derridean deconstruction).

Bibliography

Agamben, G, 2005, *State of Exception*, Chicago and London: University of Chicago Press.

Aristotle, 1981, *Nicomachean Ethics*, Harmondsworth: Penguin Books.

Ben-Dor, O, 2007, *Thinking About Law – In Silence With Heidegger*, Oxford and Portland: Hart Publishing.

Benjamin, W, 1978, 'Critique of Violence', in W Benjamin, *Reflections*, ed. P Demetz, New York: Schocken Books.

Cornell, D et al (eds), 1992, *Deconstruction and the Possibility of Justice*, New York: Routledge.

Culler, J, 1985, *On Deconstruction*, New York: Cornell University Press.

Derrida, J, 1973, *Speech and Phenomena*, Evanston: Northwestern University Press.

Derrida, J, 1978, *Writing and Difference*, Chicago: University of Chicago Press.

Derrida, J, 1982, *Margins of Philosophy*, Chicago: University of Chicago Press.

Derrida, J, 1986a, 'Declarations of Independence', *New Political Science* 7–15.

Derrida, J, 1986b, *Schibboleth*, Paris: Galilée.

Derrida, J, 1990, 'Force of Law: The "Mystical Foundation of Authority"', 11 *Cardozo Law Review* 919–1726.

Derrida, J, 1994, *Specters of Marx*, New York and London: Routledge.

Derrida, J, 1995, *On the Name*, Stanford: Stanford University Press.

Derrida, J, 2000, *Of Hospitality*, Stanford: Stanford University Press.

Heidegger, M, 1971, *Erläuterungen zu Hölderlins Dichtung*, Frankfurt am Main: Vittorio Klostermann.

Heidegger, M, 1982, *Parmenides*, Frankfurt am Main: Vittorio Klostermann.

MacCormick, N, 1990, 'Reconstruction After Deconstruction. A Reply to CLS', 10 *Oxford Journal of Legal Studies* 539–558.

Norris, C, 1982, *Deconstruction, Theory and Practice*, London and New York: Methuen.

Norris, C, 1988, 'Law Deconstruction and the Resistance to Theory', 15(2) *Journal of Law and Society* 166–187.

Norris, C, 2010, *The Deconstructive Turn*, London: Taylor & Francis.

Van der Walt, J, 2011, 'The Murmur of Being and the Chatter of Law', 20(3) *Social & Legal Studies* 389–400.

Villey, M, 2003, *La formation de la pensée moderne*, Paris: Quadrige/PUF.

Wittgenstein, L, 1922, *Tractatus Logico-Philosophicus*, London: Kegan Paul.

Chapter 9

Juridification

The meaning and scope of juridification

A development that has preoccupied many recent theorists of legal modernity has been the growth in the scale and scope of legal regulation in the modern State, a phenomenon that can be described as the *juridification of social relations*. This, indeed, has become a central theme in contemporary political debates over the role of the State, with (broadly speaking) politicians of the right decrying the over-regulation of the economy and society and arguing for a reduction in the amount of legal regulation, and politicians of the left defending the necessity of such regulation as a means of remedying social inequalities produced by the operation of the market. This is a debate that has taken on added significance in the context of globalisation. On the one hand, the emergence of supranational bodies such as the European Union (EU), which seek to regulate the conditions of labour and production at a supra-State level, has led to political clashes over questions of national sovereignty and the 'democratic deficit' in European institutions. On the other, the globalisation of the economy has greatly facilitated the capacity of economic players, such as multi-national corporations, to evade or shape particular regulatory regimes, leading to concerns about the impact of certain practices on the environment and on the health and working conditions of workers in particular industries. It is not our intention to take sides in this particular debate, though it is important to understand the way that these debates are connected to jurisprudential themes. Our purpose is rather to open a different perspective on these debates by situating them in the context of our understanding of legal modernity.

The central issues here are, first, how to explain the growth of legal regulation, and second, what this can tell us about the place of law in the modern State. Underlying these issues, there is the broader question – a theme that runs through the whole of this part of the book – that of whether the development can be understood and explained within the paradigm of modernity, or whether we need to develop new theoretical resources in order to understand these processes. Before we go on, however, we must set out a basic description of the phenomenon of juridification.

We can imagine juridification as having both horizontal and vertical dimensions. Horizontally, we can observe that in modern society law increasingly spreads its regulatory reach across an increasingly diverse range of social activities – a feature that corresponds to Weber's observations about the instrumentalisation of modern law. It has spread, for example, into areas that were formerly considered private and beyond the proper reach of the law, such as aspects of domestic and family relations; it has spread into the area of what were once considered as matters purely of nature, such as the environment, genetics and life and death (as one English Court of Appeal judge put it, 'Deciding disputed matters of life and death is surely and pre-eminently a matter for a court of law to judge') (Re A [2000]);and it has spread increasingly – though incompletely and unevenly – into the political realm. This has led public law theorist Martin Loughlin to comment that one of the most important features of this, our 'age of rights', is that the 'politicization of law' goes hand in hand with the 'legalization of politics' (2000, ch 13). In each realm legal norms gain prominence as a means of organising factual and normative aspects of social relations, which were previously under- or unregulated by law. The vast increase in legislation in recent years (at subnational, national and supranational levels, for example), as well as more popular perceptions of ours being an increasingly litigious society, are both symptomatic of this trend.

In tandem with this, the vertical aspect concerns the ways in which legal norms not only tighten their hold on already or newly regulated areas through increased legislation or judicial activity, but do so by way of increasingly detailed normative standards. That is, rather than legal standards being general principles of reasonably broad coverage, there is an observable tendency for these standards to become more detailed in their specification of the factual circumstances that are being legally regulated. Again, this is observable across a broad range of areas of legal practice, such as administrative, corporate and criminal law: the United Kingdom, for example, has seen the creation of more than 3,000 new criminal offences in the last fifteen years – offences that tend to be concerned with detailing more and more precisely the operative facts, rather than in responding to whole swathes of new forms of criminality.

Habermas on juridification

Juridification in the words of Jürgen Habermas, one of the leading analysts of this phenomenon:

> refers quite generally to the tendency toward an increase in formal (or positive, written) law that can be observed in modern society. We can distinguish here between the expansion of law, that is the legal regulation of new, hitherto informally regulated social matters, from the increasing density of law, that is the specialized breakdown of global statements of the legally relevant facts into more detailed statements.
>
> (1987, p 357)

Habermas argues that the process of juridification can generally be understood as part of a series of processes by which the modern State and economy developed as distinctive bodies or systems that operate subject to their own distinctive rationalities. While the spheres of politics and the economy are increasingly subject to the instrumental demands to reproduce systems of power and money, the rest of society – which he designates by the term the lifeworld – operates according to a non-instrumental, communicative rationality. Juridification, then, is a process by which system and lifeworld, and the relationships between them, are legally structured and regulated. This process facilitates the growth of the capitalist economy but also, and crucially, establishes and guarantees political and social liberty as the State seeks to legitimise its actions through the concession of political rights and freedoms.

He designates four distinctive epochs or thrusts of juridification. These begin in the seventeenth century with the emergence of the bourgeois State and the capitalist market economy. Here law is primarily concerned with regulating relations between individual commodity or property owners, and the authorisation of a 'sovereign state power with a monopoly on coercive force as the sole source of legal authority' (1987, p 358). That is to say that the legal order formally guarantees both the capacity of private individuals to own and alienate commodities in the market, through the laws of contract and property, and the political liberty and security of the individual, to the extent that it does not conflict with the security of the State. What is crucial here is the drawing of the distinction between public (the State) and civil society or the private, which is left unregulated. The succeeding epochs see the expansion of the scope of civil society vis-à-vis the State, as the lifeworld makes demands on the State for greater political freedoms, but these come at the cost of the increasing legal regulation (juridification) of social relations.

The second and third epochs, then, are the development of the constitutional State and the democratic constitutional State. In both these stages 'the idea of freedom already incipient in the concept of law as developed in the natural law tradition was given constitutional force' (1987, pp 360–361). In general terms, State power was first constitutionalised, giving citizens rights against the State (for example, not to be detained or punished except by due process of law), then democratised, as citizens were given rights to political participation (with, for example, the extension of suffrage and the freedom to organise political associations and parties). Political power is thus made subject to law and then, with the juridification of the legitimation process, its legitimacy is anchored in the democratic process.

While the first three stages mirror Weber's account of the achievements of legal modernity, as in Weber's account we see a more complex and ambivalent picture emerging in the fourth epoch. Here Habermas suggests that while the welfare state continues the line of freedom-guaranteeing juridification of the earlier epochs by 'the institutionalizing in legal form of a social power relation anchored in class structure' (1987, p 361), it does so in ways that, in fact, restrict freedom. Where the capitalist economy, supported by the laws of contract and property, had permitted the unlimited pursuit of self-interest and tolerated the resultant inequality and social deprivation, the welfare state sought to regulate the economy and intervene in the social sphere (or lifeworld) to mitigate the worst effects of the capitalist system. Classic examples of the juridification of economic relations would be measures to improve working conditions, the right to unionise and collective bargaining, and so on – all of which seek to protect or enhance the freedom of labour. Other social welfare measures can be described as the 'juridification of life-risks', including measures such as State provision of pensions and benefits, socialised health care, public education and so on – measures which seek to secure individuals against economic risks and to improve equality of opportunity. While these measures aim to guarantee freedom, Habermas contends that bureaucratic interventions in the lifeworld may also limit freedom by creating new forms of dependency. This occurs because bureaucracies must, of necessity, intervene in ways that require individuals to conform to general legal conditions in return for monetary compensation. This abstracts individuals from their life-situations, obscures the more general social conditions that might have given rise to particular problems, and damages pre-existing networks of social support or communication. Juridical intervention demands a restructuring – or 'colonisation' – of the lifeworlds of those entitled to social security. As he puts it generally:

> The negative effects of this wave of juridification do not appear as side effects; they result from the very form of juridification itself. It is now the very means of guaranteeing freedom that endangers the freedom of the beneficiaries.
>
> (1987, p 362)

He thus concludes by pointing to the dilemmatic structure of this type of juridification:

> [W]hile the welfare-state guarantees are intended to serve the goal of social integration, they nevertheless promote the disintegration of life-relations when these are separated, through legalized social intervention, from the consensual mechanisms that coordinate action and are transferred over to media such as power and money.
>
> (1987, p 364)

Juridification and the 'regulatory trilemma'

Where Habermas sees the problem of juridification in the dilemma of under- or over-regulation, Gunther Teubner's analysis of juridification suggests that it should rather be understood in terms of a 'trilemma'.

Teubner begins by asking why it is that many regulatory initiatives, such as attempts to limit polluting emissions, fail. He suggests that among the many reasons why such a measure might fail – expensive and inaccurate means to detect marginal violations, corruption, excessive budgetary costs on industry due to enforced slowdowns, and so on – is a response that we might even deem expected. Industry's typical response will be to deal with the penalties of breaching the law as an added cost. And, more often than not, such costs enter the balance sheets and are returned to consumers in terms of higher prices for the products without any effect on environmental damage. Or, to take another perhaps more complex problem, a government committed to fair housing policies may introduce measures to prevent landlords from raising rents. As a direct economic result of such a policy, capital is redirected away from the housing industry towards more lucrative ventures. As a result, tenants find themselves in a housing market where the rents may be affordable, but there is very little supply of rented accommodation.

Note that in these scenarios we have crossings of boundaries between the political, legal and economic systems. A political demand (for cleaner environment, for cheaper housing) is translated into a legal measure, operating a distinction between what is legal and illegal (penalties, fair rents), which is then retranslated by the economy into a language of prices and costs. Teubner identifies the problem of regulatory failure as the mistranslations that have occurred from each system using a different register to translate the 'stimulus' they receive: in the political system in which the demand is generated it is about the use of power; the legal system 'picks up' that demand as one that has to do with acting legally or illegally; the economic system picks it up in terms of what makes good economic sense. In this process the systems (political, legal, economic) do not operate causally on each other, but through what Teubner, following Niklas Luhmann, calls 'structural coupling'. It is a moment of reciprocal interference that sends each of the 'interacting' systems in the direction that the limited range of its own possible responses pre-ordains. Regulatory failures are a direct result of this inevitable mismanagement, inevitable because of the change of register that any 'structural coupling' between systems involves.

Teubner thus invites us to think about 'juridification' in the context of the increased instrumentalisation of law in the regulatory State. This use of law stumbles, he argues, on a 'regulatory trilemma', which confronts it with three possibilities – all three detrimental: 'either [to be] irrelevant, or produce disintegrating effects on the social area of life or else disintegrating effects on regulatory law itself' (1987, p 21). What do these three options mean? The first – indifference – denotes an absence of impact: the law has failed to make its demands felt at all and has had no regulatory effect. In the second case, regulation has a disintegrating effect on the field it attempts to regulate: under the bombardment of regulation the field loses its distinctive character, and becomes in a sense 'colonised' by the legal medium. Examples of this kind of failure abound: think of the family and the way the legalisation of reciprocity within it in terms of rights and duties erodes what we value most about it; or systems of childcare, where bureaucratic–legal criteria come to colonise and substitute for what are hugely nuanced and difficult judgements over what is in the best interests of the child in any concrete case. In the final horn of the trilemma it is law itself, the regulatory mechanism, that in a sense becomes 'colonised' by its object. If the law, in order to avoid riding roughshod through the societal field it is called to regulate, attempts instead to introduce too much complexity in order to respond more sensitively to its object, it runs the risk of undermining itself as a system. That is because the law draws its identity from introducing general standards and subsuming individual cases under them. If it is responding on an ad hoc, case-by-case basis, readjusting itself as it goes, then it no longer provides that certainty and stability of expectations that it must produce and guarantee, leading to the disintegration of what was distinctive about law.

In locating the problem in the specific context of regulatory law, Teubner (unlike Habermas) invites us to understand juridification as a pathology associated with this type of law. Juridification becomes an umbrella term to cover questions of the function, legitimacy, structure and success of this 'managerial' type of law. Teubner pursues the explanation as a question of 'structural coupling' between the political system, where regulatory strategies are hammered out, the legal system, which is the former's means of implementing that policy, and the social field to be regulated, each with its own autonomous logic that defies direct manipulation. Problems of juridification then appear as failures to respect the boundaries and logics of the systems involved. It is all too easy to overstep boundaries on all sides in this delicate process; the result of such overstepping is experienced as juridification.

From within this theoretical framework, only two options remain open in respect of our ability to act through law to fashion our own future. The first is a conservative, laissez-faire option, espoused by Hayek and renewed by Luhmann, which calls us to respect differentiation and the autonomy and integrity of different systems. A functionally differentiated society is one that has no 'centre' remaining from which social demands can be articulated and directed to other systems. If we do not, however, want to give up on the possibilities of intervention, Teubner's social democratic alternative attempts to base such possibilities in the concept of 'reflexive' law – a procedural alternative to substantive intervention. This circumvents the regulatory trilemma by avoiding direct intervention and instead seeking to guarantee the conditions for autonomy and self-reproduction in the system under regulation.

Juridification as depoliticisation

These two approaches to juridification identify it as a crisis of the legal system, a problem that emerges with the growth of regulatory law in the welfare state. The instrumentalisation of law damages social relations (Habermas) or undermines the function of the legal system (Teubner); the response to this must be to limit the function of law by respecting the autonomy of the legal system. An alternative approach, however, sees juridification as a political problem – that is to say a problem that arises as a result of the legal system appropriating, or juridifying, conflicts that should more properly be dealt with politically. On this view, political disputes or problems are distorted by being made to fit legal categories; legal reasoning (which is oriented towards fitting particular cases within pre-existing general rules) excludes the possibility of a consensual or future-oriented resolution. This view does not start from an assumption of the autonomy of the legal system, but sees law as a tool (or strategy) that might be used by the State for the control or management of social relations. The crisis, then, is not one of law, but one that legal regulation brings about in the social field to be regulated (Santos 2002, pp 55–61).

Perhaps the most revealing historical examples of this kind of expropriation are in the area of labour law and industrial relations. It is in fact in this context that the term itself originates, in the polemical writings of early labour lawyers in Germany for whom 'juridification' was explicitly a moment of depoliticisation of industrial conflict, which could only properly be conceived and played out in political, class-conflictual terms. To use legal categories instead of political ones in the workplace not only alienates workers from a conflict that is vital to their sense of identity and their plight, but also hands it over to legal experts and disempowers them further.

The idea that juridification involves 'depoliticisation' is not of course confined to the sphere of industrial relations and labour law. It is in fact possible to establish that the increasing density of law can be witnessed in the regulatory modes employed generally by governments, national and supranational. These modes may themselves be more or less public, may themselves exist in regulatory competition, and overall will tend to an increasing specialisation of knowledge and norms in comparison with traditional legal principles. Of greatest importance here is the observation that while a range of legal mechanisms is used to discipline actors and practices, there is no necessary correspondence – in ideal or practice – to furthering goals of political freedom, in particular since the trajectory of freedom-enhancing measures in the pursuit of social or public goods is no longer paramount. Instead, the density of regulation, and the importance of private law mechanisms in this juridical matrix, is geared largely or almost exclusively to economic or efficiency ends.

What are we to take from all this? One response is to see these developments as symptomatic of a general decline in politics, what Isaiah Berlin (1969) saw as the demise of genuine political disagreement and its replacement with debate over means only. Evidence of this is normally of the kind that draws attention to voter apathy, the decline of differences between political parties, and the almost total demise of genuinely influential public political deliberation. However, what is significant is the way that the adherence to particular regulatory regimes or frameworks is used to 'depoliticise' certain issues. So, for example, the augmented and privileged role of private law as an institutional mechanism in public and economic life (in private finance initiatives (PFIs) or the contracting out of government services) acts to signal a decline in political participation in favour of corporate influence and demands.

These changes are not only taking place at a national level, but are replicated at the transnational and global level. The 'constitution of global capital', as Stephen Gill calls it, is made up of institutional mechanisms that discipline markets and states, forcing states, for example, to restructure market and regulatory institutions internally in return for loans or investment. This is done, says Gill, to accord with the 'Three Cs': confidence of investors, consistency of policies and credibility of governments (2000). In this sense, national, but also EU, institutions and policies have to adapt to transnational networks and deregulated markets, such as agreements on competition in services and intellectual property in formerly locally protected markets. Significantly, these forces are locked in through more or less formal legal agreements and conventions, and are implemented by a range of legal institutions – EU, WTO, IMF, central banks – operating at different levels of locality. For these reasons it is appropriate to talk about a 'constitution' of global capitalism.

It is arguable, however, that rather than representing a depoliticisation, these trends could also, or perhaps better, be understood as an immense repoliticisation in favour of a certain style of politics. This politics is geared to the naturalisation of unequal distribution of resources and opportunities, to its enforcement through disciplinary mechanisms (including law and the sanctity of contracts and private governance regimes) and in which democratic participation, where it exists at all, tends to be merely formal. Pierre Bourdieu talked insightfully of this 'new' politicisation as

> a conservative revolution ... a strange revolution that restores the past but presents itself as progressive, transforming regression itself into a form of progress. It does this so well that those who oppose it are made to appear regressive themselves.
>
> (Bourdieu and Grass 2002, p 65)

A fifth epoch?

The analysis so far has analysed juridification from the perspective of regulatory law in the welfare state, but it could be contended that recent developments, such as those referred to in the last section, require us to develop a new theoretical framework for the analysis of juridification. Should we, in other words, be asking whether we have entered a fifth epoch?

The starting point for this would be the observation that the welfare state is variously seen in many westernised countries as being in decline, under pressure, or, more actively, being dismantled. The post-war ideals and institutions that saw its establishment and development, and around which there existed a broad political consensus, have decayed to a point where the very existence of the welfare state might be in doubt. Such developments, it is important to note, do not signify the triumph of the free market over the State. Rather the State has realigned itself in relation to capital (and in particular corporate capital) in such a way as to demonstrate that the State and the market are not in competition. We can thus identify an increased 'marketisation' of social life in areas formerly considered public. This takes many forms, but is most commonly carried through by the privatisation of the delivery of public goods and services (and in some cases the privatisation of these as public goods themselves). The UK in particular has successfully pioneered and exported models of 'private finance initiative' (rechristened 'public private partnerships (PPP)' by New Labour) where companies pursue profit through the provision of public services, such as schools and hospitals, both in terms of investment capital and ongoing management and delivery. The processes of individual-isation and monetarisation established in the fourth epoch continue, but no longer simply in the guise of public welfare entitlements, but rather as part of a complex web of private or 'public–private' economic relations.

Central to this process is the re-embedding of private law mechanisms – contract and property law in particular – within formerly public, State-owned areas. These carry with them techniques (such as commercial confidentiality clauses, etc) that exclude more conventional public supervision. In addition, these mechanisms themselves are structured within competition law frameworks, which draw on supranational legal sources, and which at the academic level have seen demands for the convergence of private law at a conceptual level: the development of European private law codes, har-monisation of trade and contract laws, UNIDROIT, and so on. Together, these signal a decentralisation of power in contrast to the welfare state model, but also a reconfigura-tion of power at the supranational level. As MacNeil has put it:

> These 'private' institutions [such as corporations] are delocalized, being almost totally mobile. Many dwarf half the 'sovereign' countries of the world. By their power over money, information and communication they can and do manipulate and control even the largest of 'sovereigns'.
>
> (MacNeil 2000, p 431)

One could say more about these processes, but together they might suggest that a new epoch of juridification is upon us. If we map these changes onto Habermas's definitions we may note the following. First, there can be little doubt about the increased volume of formal law within particular states and in the EU more generally. This might best be seen as part of a longer trajectory, that in itself does not amount to a new epoch. How-ever, when we consider that aspect, which identifies the expansion of law, we find that regulatory activity has in fact expanded into new areas. To take only one, emblematic, example: the regulation of biomedical sciences and, in particular, those relating to genetics – human, animal and plant – exemplifies a rethinking of the very means and modes of the reproduction of basic social and material life.

Crucially, however, regulation in this and other areas is driven by private enterprise and the desire for commodification, and only secondarily as a public welfare concern. It is for this reason that we can speculate whether the fourth epoch of juridification iden-tified by Habermas is giving way to a fifth.

Reading

For a general account of the epochs of juridification and the problems encountered by law in the fourth epoch, see Habermas (1987, pp 357–373). Teubner (1987) presents a challenge to this interpretation of the problems of juridification. There is some useful background discussion in Cotterrell (1992, pp 65–70 and ch 9), and the debate between Rottleuthner (1989) and Smith (1991) and the response in Teubner (1992) provide further illustration of the issues here.

For historical accounts linking juridification to the development of the welfare state, see Kamenka and Tay (1975) and Unger (1976, pp 58–66, 192–223), and for a critical dismissal of the whole debate, see Santos (2002, pp 55–61).

The question of whether we have entered a fifth epoch of juridification is addressed in Veitch (2012).

Bibliography

Berlin, I, 1969, 'Political Ideas in the Twentieth Century', in I Berlin (ed), *Four Essays on Liberty*, Oxford: Oxford University Press.

Bourdieu, P and Grass, G, 2002, 'The "Progressive" Restoration: A Franco-German Dialogue', March/April *New Left Review* 62–77.

Cotterrell, R, 1992, *The Sociology of Law: An Introduction*, 2nd edn, London: Butterworths.

Gill, S, 2000, 'The Constitution of Global Capitalism', www.theglobalsite.ac.uk/press/010gill.pdf.

Habermas, J, 1987, *The Theory of Communicative Action. Volume 2: Lifeworld and System*, Cambridge: Polity.

Kamenka, E and Tay, AE, 1975, 'Beyond Bourgeois Individualism: The Contemporary Crisis in Law and Legal Ideology', in E Kamenka and RS Neale (eds), *Feudalism, Capitalism and Beyond*, London: Edward Arnold, 127–144.

Loughlin, M, 2000, *Sword and Scales*, Oxford: Hart.

MacNeil, I, 2000, 'Contracting Worlds and Essential Contract Theory', *Social & Legal Studies* 431–438.

Rottleuthner, H, 1989, 'The Limits of the Law: The Myth of a Regulatory Crisis', 17 *International Journal of the Sociology of Law* 273–285.

Santos, B de Sousa, 2002, *Toward a New Legal Common Sense*, 2nd edn, London: Butterworths.

Smith, SC, 1991, 'Beyond "Mega-Theory" and "Multiple Sociology": A Reply to Rottleuthner', 19 *International Journal of the Sociology of Law* 321–340.

Teubner, G, 1987, 'Juridification: Concepts, Aspects, Limits, Solutions', in G Teubner (ed), *Juridification of Social Spheres*, Berlin: de Gruyter.

Teubner, G, 1992, 'Regulatory Law: Chronicle of a Death Foretold', 1 *Social & Legal Studies* 451–475.

Unger, RM, 1976, *Law in Modern Society*, New York: The Free Press.

Veitch, S, 2012, 'Juridification, Integration and Depoliticisation', in D Augenstein (ed), *Integration Through Law*, Aldershot: Ashgate.

Case

Re A [2000] 4 All ER 961.

Chapter 10

Autopoietic law

The concept of autopoiesis

The term 'autopoiesis' was borrowed by German social theorist Niklas Luhmann from biology and introduced to help understand social (rather than biological) systems. The concept, which was coined by biologists Maturana and Varela, in order to describe the self-reproduction of organic life – the production of living cells from living cells – was transported by Luhmann to the study of society, significantly not as a metaphor. Luhmann insists that social systems are autopoietic in as real a sense as living systems are: they too produce their own elements from their own elements, the difference being that their elements are not cells but communications.

The distinction of system and environment (common to, and constitutive of, living and social systems) is fundamental to this approach to society. The system identifies itself in an environment and maintains itself in constant relationship to that environment. The system organises its own processes and reproduces its own elements (hence autopoiesis: self-production), and its environment is that against which it defines itself and in constant 'coupling' with which it reproduces itself. This maintaining itself alongside an environment is a key to understanding one of the most important insights systems theory has to offer, over the idea of closure (from the environment), openness (to it) and the relationship between closure and openness in the operations of a system. This dialectic of closure and openness is crucial across the typology of systems Luhmann distinguishes: living systems, psychic systems and social systems. The autopoiesis of living systems has to do with the self-reproduction of life, of psychic systems with that of consciousness, and of social systems with that of communication. We will limit ourselves to the discussion of the latter only, and out of the range of social systems primarily with the social system of law.

The theory of autopoietic social systems is admittedly difficult and pitched at a challengingly abstract level; it demands 'high entry costs' as Luhmann himself put it once, and we cannot hope but simply to introduce some of its main tenets here. And yet the theory, despite its complexity, has generated an extraordinary level of interest, in particular in Continental Europe, and a considerable amount of controversy, not least in Anglo-American legal theory. We will try and say something here both about what makes it so useful to the study of law as well as to what makes it controversial. To do so we will need initially to set up an inventory of key notions: the key analytical distinction between operations and observations, and that between communication and action, the notions of complexity and contingency, and of coding and programming. After that we will look at what systems theory takes to be the function of law, and then explore more concretely 'how the law thinks', to use Gunther Teubner's famous formulation (Teubner 1989).

An inventory of concepts

Operations and observations, communication and action

Autopoiesis means self-reproduction and is consequently defined at the level of *operations*: operations whereby elements reproduce elements of the system. It is because the system exists as the linking up of operations that Luhmann sees as the most important question relating to the concept of society: 'which is the operation that produces the system of society and, we must add, produces it from its products, that is, reproduces it?' He says:

> My proposal is that we make the concept of communication the basis and thereby switch sociological theory from the concept of action to the concept of system. This enables us to present the social system as an operatively closed system consisting only of its own operations, reproduced by communications from communications.
>
> (Luhmann 1992, p 71)

Thus Luhmann identifies communication as the operation that reproduces the social system and designates society, the most comprehensive social system of all, as *the totality of communications*. By positing communication as the element, Luhmann proposes something much more precise than the social category 'relations' and side-steps the problems associated with employing individuals, conflict/co-operation and most significantly action, as the basic units or categories of sociological inquiry.

The shift of sociological inquiry *from action to communication* is treated by Luhmann himself as a 'conceptual revolution'. Society is for Luhmann the totality of communications, not of individuals or groups, nor of their relations, nor of their actions. Unlike Habermas for whom communication is a way of acting, Luhmann conceives of acting as a way of communicating. This reversal brings far richer possibilities into sociological inquiry, he argues, and circumvents some fundamental problems of action theory. Importantly it circumvents the problem that action is not necessarily social, which has made it necessary for sociologists (e.g., Weber) to impose criteria upon actions as to what counts as their *social* meaning. Secondly because it addresses the problem of treating in the framework of action the active decision to *abstain from action*; maintaining one's silence in the courtroom, to use an important example, can be fruitfully thematised in the context of communication rather than action. Finally it redresses the problem that the focus on action screens off an essential social aspect of action, that is the *impact of the action*, that is something – what else? – *outside* the action (someone is talked *to*) but not outside the communication that always involves communicators (in the plural). These are not mere problems that are avoided in the shift from action to communication, but are in fact *brought back into sociology as questions that enrich sociological inquiry*.

Because the communication is always unfinished, it is in anticipation of a response. The system exists not as an aggregate of communicative acts, but as a linkage of new communicative acts to those past. Between the two there is a sense in which meaning is pending, because without memory or anticipation there can be no meaning. It is through this 'capacity for linkage' (Anschlussfähigkeit) that the system exists and its autopoiesis consists of this generation of new elements from existing ones.

To summarise: the operations of the social system are communications. A social system is autopoietic in that it produces and reproduces its own elements, new communications from a network of existing communications. The system does not exist as the aggregate of its elements but as their succession: it exists as dynamic, in the continuing linkage of new communications to ones already communicated. Systemic meaning is thus based on the instability of elements, their connectability, the opportunities they raise, the potentiality that is actualised in linkage.

Observation is defined by Luhmann as the unity of an operation that makes a distinction in order to indicate one or the other side of this distinction. A system's operation is tied to a system's observation. Operations are communications about system and environment, internal and external reference, therefore observation. Observation, on the other hand, equips communication with a reference in terms of which it can continue, link up, and thus allows the system to effect its operations, produce new elements from existing ones and continue its autopoiesis. The system 'observes' (the law 'thinks') with the help of distinctions, and we will return to this below.

Complexity and contingency

The world is infinitely complex, it admits of a variety of ways it can be talked about, it possesses many aspects and possibilities of its description. New perspectives displace older ones, the false necessities of 'natural' descriptions are shaken as they do; every such new description reminds us of the world's complexity but also increases that complexity by adding to the possibilities of describing it. So every time that a new system draws a boundary and establishes a specific difference of system and environment it of course adds to the overall complexity but also, importantly, reduces it to that specific difference of system and environment. This reduction of complexity is a reduction of the possible states and events to ones that can be envisaged by the system as determined through its specific means of making selections and establishing relevance. Not every societal communication, not every state of affairs that can be talked about, may become the subject of each system's communication. More importantly competing categorisations, interpretations of events will not all find expression in the system's terms; each system will restrict the modes in which the world can be talked about by perceiving it in a categorically pre-formed way. That is how the reduction of complexity occurs and is managed by each system. Much of what happens in its environment the system remains indifferent to. Some of it it picks up as relevant to what it is 'attuned' to. The system creates 'order from noise' by drawing selectively on the surplus of possibilities – the domain of high complexity – potentially available in the environment. 'Noise' is what is not yet reduced. In the process of this selective depiction the system constructs the external world that it could not conceive in its complexity. A system knows by simplifying, and then by choosing among, manipulating and combining these self-produced simplifications that stand in for that which is too complex for the system to conceive. Systems are agents of reduction only in terms of which the unbearable complexity of the world becomes meaningful. This reduction, as Gianfranco Poggi puts it well, allows the system 'a simple hold upon possibly highly complex stretches of reality' (Poggi 1979, p x). As complexity in the environment increases, the system adapts its own capacities for resonance by building up its own complexity; but it will never match that of its environment (or it would merge with it).

To summarise: meaning is always system-specific according to Luhmann. It depends on a reduction of complexity, a reduction in the scope of possibilities of all that may be communicated. A system comes about as a specific, reductive, selective way of observing a complex world, with a surplus of possibilities, is established. When a system observes its environment, it observes it through a form of selection that has to do with the distinction that guides it. Put another way, the world is a horizon; it is not yet meaningful except as a background against which certain possibilities are actualised. This is what Luhmann is saying too, except in the more precise terms of infinite complexity (horizon, the World) and reduced complexity (the system). Systems are thus islands of reduced complexity in a world of infinite complexity. Significantly, complexity is not eliminated in the process but reduced. It needs to be preserved, like the horizon, not only to furnish further selections but more importantly to make present ones meaningful. The dimension of time is also of the essence here: every actualisation as selection transforms the system and forms the basis for future selections. It is the specific form of selectivity-in-progress that constitutes the identity of the system.

The coding of social systems

Systems observe by introducing a guiding difference and by making the world relevant to this guiding difference. The guiding difference organises, permeates and 'over-determines' the network of differences, the set of further distinctions and demarcations that meaning requires. Semantic codes specify the differences which form the basis for something to be received as information. The world is, in the case of each system, submitted to the difference that, for that system, makes a difference. A pattern of difference lies at the basis of the system's observation of the environment. The idea of the 'code' of the system is pivotal to this.

At the very root of the matter, then, the possibility of cognition for the system, springs from difference-controlled observation. According to Luhmann, 'the formulation of the concept of difference makes it possible for events to appear as information and to leave traces behind within the system'. In view of this, the interesting question is: 'with the aid of what distinctions can a [social] system observe internal and external objects?' (Luhmann 1985, p 393).

Binary codes are simply a difference between a yes and a no, the difference between a positive and a negative value. The value and counter-value of the code, unlike 'thick' values, have formal equivalence for the system: designating something as legal or true is not a more likely or favoured choice for the legal and scientific system respectively, than deeming it illegal or false. The power of the code lies in the notion that the very constitution of the identity of a system involves the play between positive value and negative value: the designation of every position is always identified in relation to (in the mirror of) its counter-position. 'Communication x is legal, y is true', claim the lawyer and the scientist. How could things be different? They could be different in being illegal or false. The identity of x as legal involves situating it in the difference between legal/illegal. Only by reflecting it in the mirror of its negation does the identity of x as legal come about.

This is how the identity of the system comes about: identity as tautology (legal is what is legal) is replaced by identity as difference (the law is the difference between legal and illegal). It may be true that this 'identity as difference' means very little before it can be shown how through the latter the system can relate to the world. But it is crucial to note that in whatever context the legal/illegal dichotomy may be used in communication, it will underpin, cause, raise and furnish the identity of any information. This is what the theory's critics do not see when they criticise the theory's exaggerated reliance on the code.

The point is that the code gives a communication in law its very identity as legal, allowing in the first place any further state of information about concepts, conditions, incentives, strategies, etc, to appear, and all this in an immediate way. However legal information is to be processed, and the variety here is immense, it first comes about as such through coding. Experience, action, facts are grasped through difference, by virtue of their being submitted to the guiding distinction; information is possible only in this situating, this channelling into a pattern of difference. It is in the situating of a stimulus (noise) in the pattern of 'this rather than that' that codes can be understood as duplication rules. They duplicate the reality they observe. Reality acquires a dimension other than that of being normal. When exposed to the code difference, say the legal code, the 'facticity' of the world becomes information. Actions become legal or illegal, events become legally relevant. How they are allocated to either value is itself not a matter for coding. What duplication means is that the very identity of x as legal involves its negation, that is its reflection in the counter-value (x is not not-legal). A statement about x can be made meaningfully, the system activates a perspective by duplicating reality and making 'x is legal' meaningful because it could be the case that 'x is not legal'. It is this duplication that determines in what sense things could be different. Reflecting in the counter-value enables observation, by setting an assertion against the background of another possibility (this rather than that). Pure fact now acquires the possibility to register, to be observed.

At the same time the duplication through the negative value opens up a contingency space: x could be legal or illegal. The negative value allows us to see how things could be different. In view of this everything is neither necessary nor impossible, therefore contingent. This is a contingency that is bound by the bivalency of the code; it is, in other words, a 'first-order contingency'. There are other levels too at which we encounter contingency and we must be careful to keep these distinct.

We will look at an example of how this works in the final section below.

Society, sub-systems and the law

Society, as we said earlier, is the sum total of communications. In Luhmann's words, 'society is the closed system of connectable communications'. But a paradoxical situation arises. Whatever unity the formula 'all communication' makes apparent is in fact dispersed; for within society's ambit there develop a multitude of sub-systems, each developing a selective and exclusive mapping of the world. Where society cannot communicate with its environment, since it already consists of all that is communicable, between sub-systems there does develop a communication of sorts. Each system of the 'social' type is a sub-system of society and each makes sense of the world in different, mutually overlapping, mutually undercutting ways. Sub-systems are not strung together in any pattern of co-ordination. Society's sub-systems are not patterned in a whole/part schema, but instead each system repeats a system/environment distinction within society, distinguishing itself from society through that distinction. For Luhmann, 'the unity of the world is not the unity of an assemblage . . ., but rather the unavoidable, indestructible possibility of moving from one thing to another – not an aggregation, but rather a correlation of meaningful experience and action' (Luhmann 1975, p 411). Every formation of a sub-system is nothing less than a new exposition of the unity of the whole social system from its perspective. And yet, every formation of a sub-system breaks that unity of the whole system into a specific difference of system and environment.

How does this differentiating out of a sub-system occur? As far as functional sub-systems are concerned, these are differentiated-out of society on the basis of performing a unique function in society. Luhmann writes:

> I propose to characterize modern society as a functionally differentiated social system. The evolution of this highly improbable social order required replacing stratification with functional differentiation as the main principle of forming subsystems within the overall system of society. In stratified societies the human individual was placed in only one subsystem. . . . This is no longer possible in a society differentiated with respect to functions such as politics, economy, intimate relations, religion, sciences and education. Nobody can live in only one of these systems.
>
> (Luhmann 1986b, p 318)

Functionally differentiated systems are not 'manned' or 'lived in'. They consist of sets of differentiated and specialised resources and activities each articulating with others and each contributing through its own operation to the functioning of the whole. Each develops its own partial rationality, options and demands, goals and means. Partial rationalities do not combine in a comprehensive social rationality as such, however, and in one sense at least, the sum of the parts is more than the whole. No system is of primary importance to the functioning of the whole, none provides a 'summit' (as was the case in stratified societies) or a 'centre' for society. Finally, according to the principle of functional differentiation each sub-system performs a function that is unique: were that exclusivity to be compromised the principle of differentiation itself would give way. Sub-systems do not simply perceive the world in different and competing ways but also perceive their differences in different ways. As Teubner (1993, ch 7) describes it, society is a *unitas multiplex*: a society that is at once unity (all communication as distinct from life and consciousness) and multiplicity. And at the same time, in the current evolutionary phase of functional differentiation, it is also a 'heterarchy'; the multiplicity of descriptions of society cannot be co-ordinated hierarchically. This is how Luhmann summarises this:

> Each system is universally competent and at the same time a system within the world, able to distinguish and observe and control itself. It is a self-referential

system and thereby a totalizing system. It cannot avoid operating within a world of its own. Societies [social systems] constitute worlds. Observing themselves, that is communicating about themselves, societies cannot avoid using distinctions which differentiate the observing system from something else. Their communication observes itself within its world and describes the limitation of its own competence. Communication never becomes self-transcending. It can never operate outside its own boundaries. The boundaries themselves, however, are components of the system and cannot be taken as given by a pre-constituted world.

(Luhmann 1986c, pp 178–179)

How does 'the law think'?

Let us now try and apply all that we have seen so far to the legal system, to understand in what sense it might constitute a 'reduction achievement', what constitutes its specific operations, what furnishes its observations, and how to understand its function. It is in this sense, in particular, that we might begin to untangle, then answer, Teubner's challenge:

What is the precise meaning of the somewhat ambiguous statement that law constitutes an autonomous reality? Similarly, what is meant by saying that the individual is a mere construct of society and law? And, above all, how does the law 'think'?

(Teubner 1989, p 730)

Like every other social system, the legal system's operations are communications. They are communications that are 'coded', that is aligned to the code of the legal system legal/illegal. Any communication that concerns the allocation of one of those values qualifies as legal, whether it be someone asserting their right ('I have a right to speak'), assuming a duty ('I will deliver the merchandise tomorrow') or interpreting a legal provision ('surely the law cannot be interpreted to authorise the killing of innocent civilians'). Of course certain communications will be pivotal and others less so. Decisions of courts, officials and parliaments, interpretations of the law offered by courts or legal academics, promises, offers and verbal transactions, and so on, fall into the first category; lay communication invoking the law, falls into the latter. But all communication thematised along the legal/illegal coding is 'part' of the legal system, the world of legal communication.

In what sense does this system, thus broadly understood, constitute a *reduction achievement* and what accounts for its *'closure'* as a system?

If the world, as we discussed earlier, admits of a variety of ways it can be talked about, every system restricts on its own terms the ambit of what is meaningful by filtering communication through system-relevance established by the code. Competing categorisations and interpretations of events will not all find expression in the system's terms; out of the infinite possibilities of describing a person's action, for example, the legal system addresses what is relevant to deeming it legal or illegal. Only on that basis can a person's will further be thematised as intention or motive on the basis that it is conducive to a legal characterisation of his/her action. The economic system may recast that expression of the will as economic-rational preference, the political system will assess it in terms of support or disaffection to Government or Opposition, and so on.

Each system will restrict the modes in which the world can be talked about by perceiving it in a categorically pre-formed way. Further distinctions (programming) build on the code: intended/not-intended, fault/strict liability, incitement/free expression, occupational/political demand, speech/action. All the distinctions on the one hand draw on the system's reduction of the world to a single difference (legal/illegal), while at the same time building up the system's internal complexity, that allows it to 'see' more things, and cope more adequately with external reality.

In this sense the code enables the system to 'construct' its environment, to set itself in context; it enables it to observe environmental stimuli on the basis of the distinction and deal with them by each time indicating one side of the binary schema. The structural technique that makes this possible is a 'difference technique'.

The system introduces its own distinction and on that basis grasps states and events as information. The 'difference technique' is the device that the system employs to decipher complexity by enacting a system-specific reduction which results in a system-centric representation of reality. It is thus that the distinction 'establishes a universe, sets up systemic boundaries, structures a discourse'. Together coding and programming provide the cluster of differences through which the world is localised within the system. Primacy of course lies with the code that underlies the identity of the system and ultimately generates information; it does not determine, however, 'which pieces of information are called for and which selection they trigger'. Programming provides criteria for fixing the conditions for the suitability of selections. In science, for example, the requirement of suitability belongs to theory and method, on the basis of which the truth or falsity of scientific statements can be assessed. Structures themselves can be changed at the level of programming, as is ultimately the case with a paradigm shift in science, without the system thereby losing its identity, which depends on the coding. To move this to law: norms (programmes) provide the correctness of the allocation of legality and illegality (code), method (programme again) here consisting of rules of interpretation of norms; structural variations, in law, occur when norms are varied through new legislation or new constitutional interpretations.

To recapitulate: the identity of the system comes about at the level of the code. The system's identity as tautology (legal is what is legal) is replaced here by identity as difference (the law is the difference between legal and illegal). But the symmetry has to be broken because it is otherwise unproductive for the system. On the basis of programming (the deployment of other schemes of differences aligned to coding) the system is allowed to steer its operations by allocating events to either side of the contrast-schema. Together coding and programming allow the system to see the world in a certain way (it can be legal or illegal), and to operationalise its mode of seeing. We do not need any more background information in order to make sense of those cryptic and controversial descriptions of systems as 'closed and open at the same time'; of the legal system, for example, as 'cognitively open because normatively closed'. It is the difference of coding and programming that makes possible the combination of closure and openness in the same system. These are flip-sides of the same coin, internally linked, mutually supportive, reciprocally enabling: it is the very structural constraints that enable the system to relate to the environment. The system's capacity for reaction to the environment, 'resonance', which is steered through programming, rests on the closed polarity of the code. The possibility that the environment registers at all is due to the code, and in that sense closure is a precondition for cognitive openness.

The function of law, for Luhmann, is the very rule-of-law-like imperative to provide for the 'stabilisation' of normative expectations. Let us explain this. Contexts can be fixed at a number of levels. Simple interactions between, say, friends, lovers or colleagues develop as contexts that allow reciprocal perspective-taking and thus expectations to articulate. Interactions in wider settings also develop elementary contexts that allow meaningful interchange. But the greatest constancy of the context of reciprocity is achieved at the level of functional systems like science, the economy, and of course law. Law has a special, enhanced role here. Law secures this constancy by narrowing the *expectability* of expectations, by abstracting from various 'irrelevant' contingencies of the pragmatic situation, by providing norms that involve sanctions should the other not conform, but, most importantly for present purposes, by abstracting from the concrete parties involved and the reciprocal perspective-taking that in turn would involve knowledge of the other party and the contingencies that entails. It renders this context independent of the indeterminacy that comes from concrete interactions: it allows people to encounter each other as role-players, here, as legal actors.

Motive, identity, implied reciprocities that stem from role are always-already aligned to systems. For Luhmann role-indeterminacy as context-indeterminacy becomes settled by the system but only for the system. Legal expectations allow uncertainty in specific, controlled ways and immunise the system towards other uncertainties it cannot control. The legal system reduces the complexity of possible contingencies: it allows for some, and reproduces itself by responding to them. By the same token it immunises itself against others, that are precluded because expectations are not attuned to them. A system modulates its reaction to its environment by changing expectations and controlling this change at the level of expectations of expectations.

The legal system's *openness* to the world consists, therefore, in its reading disappointment or fulfilment of the expectations it itself projects. Of course the system is neither static nor insensitive to change; to remain responsive to a changing world the system must also vary the expectations it projects. New legal possibilities need to be projected to respond to new situations. New expectations test new patterns of conflict around new issues, and their fulfilment or disappointment is fed back into the law as valid new premises for future decisions. The legal system thus varies its structures, reconstructs and alters them, and in the process 'learns' and evolves. It does this by providing legal answers to the conflictual expectations that face it requiring litigation. Conflict is necessary for law because it provides input into the reproductive process without which the system of law would stagnate. But in dealing with conflict, law only achieves a new return to order. It pushes back the threat of disorganisation by conceiving and resettling disturbed practice on the basis of uncontroverted practice. Law conceives of conflicts as disturbances that must be overcome. The conflictual pattern is transitory; a destabilisation that allows legal evolution through successive steps of return to order. The uncertainty of expectations that face law in a situation of social conflict is fruitful ground for internal innovation and simultaneously for the regeneration of legal order. The system overcomes the turbulence that it sees conflict as presenting it with, by resettling disturbed practice and sanctioning the resettlement with permanence for the time being. For the legal system the conflictual pattern is a pathology in the healing of which law evolves.

Note that the only way in which a claim for change may register is if it manages to surprise projections of expectations. Following the principle that we can only see what we know how to look for, perception must be based upon an already existing preconception of what is to be seen or understood. For a challenge to register, that is, the system's memory has to be tapped. The degree to which the system is open to learning is, of course as always, an internal matter. In Luhmann's terms this would be expressed in the following way: the system itself controls the balance of redundancy and variety. It is a distinction that bears on the system's readiness to vary its structures in the face of an evolving environment. Variety is about increasing responsiveness, redundancy about suppressing it.

It is *because* the system needs to react to, and keep up with, a changing environment that 'variety' comes into play. Significantly the practice of distinguishing and overruling 'occasionally invents new [grounds] to achieve a position where the system can, on the basis of a little new information, fairly quickly work out what state it is in and what state it is moving towards' (Luhmann 2004, p 291). The reason why it requires 'a special effort' to shake the redundancy of the system and stretch its imagination is because the system tends to 'reduce its own surprise to a tolerable amount and allow information only as differences added in small numbers to the stream of reassurances' (Luhmann 1993, p 291). In an extract that could easily have been written by critical legal scholars had it not preceded them by a decade, Luhmann says:

> Suitable information . . . must be specially produced, brought to light by uncovering some latent aspect of existing order, or retrieved from the existing decision-making process by incongruent questions.
>
> (Luhmann 1990, pp 33–34)

'How the law thinks', then, has to do with the opportunities and limitations that pertain to what is specifically institutional about it: the imposition and entrenchment of certain reductions in the possibilities of describing and talking about the world. Law as such an institution gives us a language to conceive of identity, interdependence, conflict, benefit and harm, concepts of risk and time, what is owned and what is due. These are precisely the kinds of reductions in the possibilities of communicating about the world that give rights their specific legal nature as an institutional achievement. The selection of what is legally relevant occurs over and against the background of other possibilities that remain legally underdetermined. The system actualises something over and against other possibilities – that is the crux of institutionalisation, of the drawing of the legal system's boundary.

How the legal system controls that boundary, to what extent it stands to 'learn' from the changing environment or to remain indifferent to it by reproducing the same set of expectations and immunising itself from 'noise' from it, is a matter for the law and the law alone. There is, as has often been discussed, something profoundly self-referential about this, tautological even: 'the law is what the law is' or, put differently, 'the law is what it says it is'. This is positivism radicalised. But Luhmann insists that we should not shy away from the self-reference that one encounters at the foundation of things but instead focus on the way it is 'breached', unfolded and made productive. And Teubner will add this:

> The theory of autopoiesis deals with these paradoxes of self-reference in a different way: Do not avoid paradoxes, but make productive use of them! If social discourses are autopoietic systems, that is, systems that recursively produce their own

elements from the network of their elements, then they are founded on that very self-referentiality. As autopoietic systems, discourses cannot but find justification in their own circularity and cannot but produce regularities that regulate themselves and that govern the transformation of their own regularities. The paradox of self-reference then, is not a flaw in our intellectual reconstruction of discourse that we have to avoid at all costs, but is its very reality that we cannot avoid at all.

(Teubner 1989, p 736)

Reading

Luhmann's *opus magnum*, where he introduces the term 'autopoiesis', is his *Social Systems* of 1984, which appeared in English in 1993. His major work on the legal system, *Das Recht der Gesellschaft*, was translated into English (*Law as a Social System*) in 2006. For a concise account of how coding works and how it links to programming, see Luhmann (1986a).

The application of systems theory in law is connected primarily with the work of Gunther Teubner. See in particular (1989) and (1993) and in connection to theories of global law and constitutionalism (2012).

Among the growing secondary literature on systems theory in English, see Nobles and Schiff (2002, 2006) and King and Thornhill (2006), who provide a very good introduction to Luhmann's theory of law and politics. For an early, highly creative, introduction to autopoiesis, see Smith (1991), and on the concept of 'redundancy' in legal reasoning, Smith (1995). For an application of systems theory to the relation between law and politics, see Christodoulidis (1998). See also the monograph on Luhmann's legal theory by Andreas Philippopoulos-Mihalopoulos (2009).

Bibliography

Christodoulidis, E, 1998, *Law and Reflexive Politics*, Dordrecht: Kluwer.

King, M and Thornhill, C, 2006, *Niklas Luhmann's Theory of Politics and Law*, Basingstoke: Palgrave Macmillan.

Luhmann, N, 1975, *The Differentiation of Society*, New York: Columbia University Press.

Luhmann, N, 1985, 'Some Problems With Reflexive Law', in G Teubner and A Febbrajo (eds), *State, Law, Economy as Autopoietic Systems*, Milano: Giuffré.

Luhmann, N, 1986a, *Ecological Communication*, trans by J Bednarz, Cambridge: Polity.

Luhmann, N, 1986b, 'The Individuality of the Individual: Historical Meaning and Contemporary Problems', in T Heller et al (eds), *Reconstructing Individualism*, Stanford: Stanford University Press.

Luhmann, N, 1986c, 'The Autopoiesis of Social Systems', in F Geyer and J van der Zouwen (eds), *Sociocybernetic Paradoxes; Observation, Control and Evolution of Self-Steering Systems*, Beverly Hills: Sage.

Luhmann, N, 1990, *Essays on Self-Reference*, New York: Columbia University Press.

Luhmann, N, 1992, 'The Concept of Society', 31 *Thesis Eleven* 67.

Luhmann, N, 1995a, *Social Systems*, Stanford: Stanford University Press.

Luhmann, N, 1995b, 'Legal Argumentation: An Analysis of Its Form', 58 *Modern Law Review* 285.

Luhmann, N, 2006, *Law as a Social System*, Oxford: Oxford University Press.

Nobles, R and Schiff, D, 2002, *The Autonomy of Law: An Introduction to Legal Autopoiesis*, Oxford: Oxford University Press.

Nobles, R and Schiff, D, 2006, *A Sociology of Jurisprudence*, London: Bloomsbury Publishing.

Philippopoulos-Mihalopoulos, A, 2009, *Niklas Luhmann: Law, Justice, Society*, London: Routledge.

Poggi, G, 1979, 'Introduction', in N Luhmann (ed), *Trust and Power*, Chichester: Wiley.

Smith, SC, 1991, 'Beyond "Mega-Theory" and "Multiple Sociology": A Reply to Rottleutner', 19 *International Journal of the Sociology of Law* 321.

Smith, SC, 1995, 'The Redundancy of Reasoning', in Z Bankowski, I White and U Hahn (eds), *Informatics and the Foundations of Legal Reasoning*, Dordrecht: Kluwer.

Teubner, G, 1989, 'How the Law Thinks: Toward a Constructivist Epistemology of Law', 23(5) *Law & Society Review* 727–758.

Teubner, G, 1993, *Law as an Autopoietic System*, Oxford: Blackwell.

Teubner, G, 2012, *Constitutional Fragments: Societal Constitutionalism and Globalization*, Oxford: Oxford University Press.

Index

Note: Page numbers in italic indicate a tutorial on the corresponding page.

accountability in political transitions 253

acts, subjective and objective meaning of 141

adjudication, rules of 138

administration *see* bureaucracy

Agamben, G. 299–300

Alexy, R. 152–153

American legal realism 173–181; critique 182–184; fact-scepticism 178–179; faith in science 179–181; 'Path of the Law' 174–176, 179; prophecy/prediction 175; rule-scepticism 176–177

analogy: argument by 187–188; hospitality and justice 308–309

Anti-terrorist Act 2001 163–164

Arendt, H. 253–254

Aristotle 154

Arthurs, H. W. 284

Austin, J. 49–50, 133, 137

Australian Aborigines (*Mabo* case) 257–261

Authority: mystical foundations of 299–300, 305–307; political 73–75, 77, 92, 100–102; and violence 307–308

autopoiesis 321–331; coding of social and legal systems 324–325, 327–328; concept of 321–322; how does the 'law think' 327–331; related concepts 322–324; society and sub-systems 325–327

Bartlett, R. 259

basic goods 154–155

Benjamin, W. 307

Bennet, W. and Feldman, M. 269–270

Bennion, F. 166

Bentham, J. 49–50, 167, 230, 276

Berman, H. 166

Bernstein, B. 269–270

Bingham, Lord 164

biopower 275, 277–278

Bourdieu, P. 31, 318

Brennan, Chief Justice 257–258

Browne-Wilkinson, Lord 158–159

bureaucracy 96; and justice, conflict between 270–272; and political authority 73–74, 81

capitalism: critique of 238–242 (function of law 66–67; legal ideology 67–70); historic development 35–39; and welfare state 93–99; *see also* globalisation

change, rules of 138

citizen-government reciprocity 147–148, 206

citizenship 283

civil rights 197

class conflict 63–70, 83, 92; *see also* capitalism, critique of

classification, relevancy and interpretation 184–185, 201–203

coding of social and legal systems 324–325, 327–328

Cohen, L. J. 234, 238

coherence – and legal reasoning 187, 189, 191

Collins, H. 68, 197

colonialism 251, 257; Australian Aborigines (*Mabo* case) 257–261; legal pluralism 283–284

commodification 40, 42–43, 66–67

common good(s) 30–32, 153–155
communication: codes 324–325, 327–328;
    operations, observations and action
    322–323
community: and capitalism 154–155,
    242; and society (Gemeinschaft and
    Gesellschaft) 84–86, 94, 97
complexity and contingency 323–324, 329
consistency and legal reasoning 187, 191
constitutionalism: beyond the state
    105–107; paradox of 50
constitutional legitimacy 50
constitutional state, elements of 50–53
contract law 95, 195–197; historical
    perspective 38, 84–85, 86–87, 94–95
courts 149; fact-scepticism 178–179;
    language and narrative of 268–270
critical legal pluralism 288
critical legal studies (CLS) 193–198

Davis, M. 241
deconstruction 299–310
deduction: and legal formalism 170–172
democracy 99, 148, 239
depoliticisation, juridification as 317–318
derogation of rights 164
Derrida, J. 299–310
dignity 148–149, 151–152, 232, 242
discipline see under power
discretionary powers 96–97, 271
distributive justice 255–256
Durkheim, E. 83–88
Dworkin, R. 188–192, 219, 220

economy: and advent of modernity 35–44;
    and rational legal system 79–81; see also
    capitalism; globalisation
emancipation and regulation 12–13
emancipatory concept of law 12,
    107–110
emergency powers see state of emergency
'entitlement' theory of justice 233–234
equality/ fairness issues 237–241;
    discrimination and legal reasoning
    219; gender 201–203, 240–241; and
    liberty 234–237; racial 241, 257–261;
    and social conflict 92; and welfare

state 97–98; see also capitalism, critique
    of; feminist critique of legal reasoning
European Union (EU) 101–102, 104, 140,
    239, 312
Ewing, K. 80–81
'extended formalism' 184–188, 189

facts and rules in legal reasoning 165–166
fact-scepticism 178–179; legacy of 265–267
fairness see equality/fairness issues
feminist critique of legal reasoning
    198–205; challenges 198–199; form
    199–201; relevancy, interpretation and
    classification 201–203
Finley, L. 201
Finnis, J. 147–148, 153–159
Fletcher, G. 268
'focal meaning' of law 156
formalism see legal formalism
Foucault, M. 274–280
Frank, J. 173, 178, 265–267
Fraser, N. 201, 240–242
Fuller, L. 112, 145–148, 148–149, 206, 208

Gaita, R. 259
Gemeinschaft and Gesellschaft 84–86, 94, 97
gender inequality 201–203, 240–241; see
    also feminist critique of legal reasoning
'general public norms' 149
Gill, S. 106, 318
Gilligan, C. 200
Glasman, M. 98
globalisation: and constitutionalism 105–
    107; and emancipatory concept of law
    12, 107–110; and injustice 241; and
    juridification 121, 312–320; and legal
    pluralism 284–285; and reconfigured
    state 101–102; sovereignty after
    103–105; and welfare state 97–99
global justice 244–248; central issue and
    terminology 244; conservative view
    246–247; content and scope 244–246;
    progressive view 247–248; 'way
    forward' 248
governmentality 278
government-citizen reciprocity 147–148,
    206

Grass, G. 318
Griffiths, J. 284–285

Habermas, J. 98, 313–319, 322
'hard' cases 188–190, 215
Hart, H. L. A. 137–141, 147, 149–150, 182–184, 206, 208, 214, 220
Hauriou, M. 290–296
Hayek, F. A. 173, 316
Hegel, F. W. G. 48
Heidegger, M. 300–302, 305
Hobbes, T. 19–23, 25, 27, 48, 83, 113–114
Holmes, O. W. 174–176, 179
hospitality and justice analogy 308–309
human rights see rights
Human Rights Act 1998 164
Hume, D. 135, 212–214, 229

ideology, legal 67–70
industrial revolution 13, 35–36, 39, 42
inequality see equality/ fairness issues
injustice and invalidity of law 151–153
inner morality of law 145–148
institutionalism, legal 290–296
instrumental and justice reasons for rule of law 144–145
integrity of law 190–192

Jackson, B. 265, 26–70
judicial discretion, expansion of 96, 271
Julius, A. J. 247, 248
juridical regression 274–275, 279
juridification 312–319, 121; as depoliticisation 317–318; epochs 314; and globalisation 312, 318; horizontal and vertical 312–313; and 'regulatory trilemma' 315–317
jurisdiction, state and legal system 17–18
justice: and bureaucracy, conflict between 270–272; deconstructionist perspective 308–309; distributive 230, 236–237, 240; fairness and liberty 234–237; global 244–248 (central issue and terminology 244; conservative view 246–247; content and scope 244–246; progressive view

247–248; 'way forward' 248); and instrumental reasons for rule of law 144–145; retributive 37, 230, 253; socialist perspective 237–242; types 229–230 (in political transitions 251, 253–257); utilitarianism vs. libertarianism 230–234

Kant, I. 11, 232, 242
Kelsen, H. 140–143, 151, 155, 156, 168–169, 208

Lacey, N. 202
Language: deconstructionist perspective 301–310; elaborate and restricted codes 269; and narrative of courtroom 268–270; 'open texture' of legal language 182–184
law and morality, the differentiation 133–136
legal formalism 167–173; critiques 173–176, 200; and deduction 170–171; definition 167; 'extended' 184, 189; promise of 167–168; see also American legal realism; pure theory of law
legal ideology 67–70
legality: characteristics of 145–146; and validity of law 133–136
legal norms 140–143
legal pluralism 282–283; classic and contemporary 283–284; concept of 282–283; empirical, conceptual and political approaches 286–287; future directions 287–288; strong and weak: position of state 284–285
legal positivism 133–135, 137, 140; critiques 151–153
legal profession 77, 78, 80
legal rationality 71, 74, 77; forms 74–77; and modernity 77–79
legal realism see American legal realism
legal reasoning 161–203, 211–222; colonial context 257–261; relevancy, interpretation and classification 184–185, 201–203; see also feminist critique; moral reasoning

legitimacy: modern natural law 93
legitimation, concept of 85–86
Levinas, E. 308–309
lex mercatoria 17, 101, 284
libertarianism, utilitarianism vs. 230–234
liberty 234–237
Llewellyn, K. 173–174
Locke, J. 24–28, 32–34, 56, 113–117
Loughlin, M. 21, 23, 27, 45, 103–105,
  113, 123, 293–294, 313
Luhmann, N. 72, 316, 321–327, 329–330

MacCormick, N. 103, 139, 140, 142,
  144, 150, 170–172, 184–188, 201,
  211–217, 295
MacIntyre, A. 242
MacKinnon, C. 200, 203
MacNeil, I. 319
market system 39–44; institutional
  dimension 37–39
Marx, K. 26, 37–39, 42–44, 63–70, 79,
  83, 118, 193, 238–239; and Engels, F.
  67, 238
materialisation of law 91–92, 97, 272
Meiksins Wood, E. 38, 43
Mill, J. S. 230
modernity/legal modernity 118–120;
  advent of 11–58; globalisation and
  emancipatory concept of law 12,
  107–110; and legal rationality 71, 74–77;
  materialisation 91–92, 97, 272; power
  as medium of 279–280; and social
  solidarity 83–87; 'unthinking' modern
  law 107–109; see also capitalism;
  juridification; power; welfare state
morality and law, the differentiation of
  133–136
morality of law, inner 145–148
moral reasoning 153–159
Mortati, C. 294–295
mystical foundations of authority 299–300,
  305–307

Nagel, T. 246
narrative of courtroom 268–270
natural law 153–154; formal and
  substantive legitimacy 93; and legal

positivism 155; question of content
  151–159; question of form 144–151
natural rights 25–26, 28, 57, 154
new constitutionalism 106–107
Nozick, R. 26, 233–234

'open texture' of legal language 182–184

Pashukanis, E. 66–67
'Path of the Law' 174–176, 179
Poggi, G. 324
Polanyi, K. 40, 43, 83
political and legal power 47, 74
political authority 73–75, 77, 92,
  100–102
political transitions 251–257;
  accountability and responsibility issues
  253; dilemmas 251–253; forms of
  justice 253–257
politics: and law, relationship between
  45–59; of legal pluralism 286–287
positivism see legal positivism
'positivity of law' 150
post-sovereignty 103–104
Pound, R. 173–174
Power: biopower 275, 277–278; and
  discipline 275–277 (techniques
  276–278); and exploitation
  (see capitalism); governmentality 278;
  juridical regression 274–275, 279;
  political and legal 47, 74; theory of
  legal modernity 279–280
prediction/prophecy principle 175
prisons 275–276
privatisation 319
progress, the idea of 12–13;
  emancipation and regulation 12–13
property: historical perspective 24–28,
  31, 33, 37–38, 43, 66–67, 69, 87,
  239; rights 37, 87, 95, 115–116, 117,
  209, 210, 259
psychology of fact-finding 178, 265
'publicness' of law 150
public-private relationship 105, 180,
  202, 319
pure theory of law 140–143, 169; and
  self-containment notion 168–169

racial inequality 241, 257–261
Radbruch, G. 151–154, 206
rationality *see* legal rationality
Rawls, J. 234–237, 239–240, 244–246
realism *see* American legal realism
reciprocity between government and
    citizens 147–148, 206
recognition, rule of 138–141, 208
regulation and emancipation 12–13
'regulatory trilemma' of juridification
    315–317
relevancy, interpretation and classification
    184–185, 201–203
responsibility in political transitions 254
restorative justice 254–255
retributive justice 37, 253
'right answer' 190–192
Rights: derogation in state of emergency
    164; Human Rights Act 1998 164;
    legalisation and politicisation 313;
    Marxist perspective 69–70; origins of
    24–28; positive and negative 56–58;
    as restraints 56–58; utilitarianism vs.
    libertarianism 230–234
Roman law 17, 78–79, 167, 309
Romano, S. 290, 292–296
Rousseau, J. J. 28–33, 47–48, 114–115,
    117; commons 29, 30, 32–33, 114
rule of law 54–56, 91–109, 206;
    formalism 172–173; and inner
    morality of law 145–148; justice and
    instrumental reasons for 144–145;
    validity 148–151
rules: and facts in legal reasoning
    165–166; and 'open texture' of legal
    language 182–184; primary and
    secondary 137–138
rule-scepticism 176–177

Sale of Goods Act 1979 172
Santos, B. de Sousa 12, 18, 22, 107–110,
    285–286
Sassen, S. 104–105
Saussure, F. de 300, 303, 305
Schmitt, C. 45, 293–295
Science: American legal realism 179–181;
    and modernity 13–14, 35–36

self-containment notion 168–169
separation of powers 45, 50, 51–54, 55,
    144, 165, 177; erosion of 97
simplification and diversion techniques
    271–272
Singer, J. 180
Smith, A. 1, 38, 39–40, 64, 238–239
'social contract' 17–34
'social contract law' 94–95
socialism 237–242
social rights 94
social solidarity 83–87
social systems and sub-systems 324–327
society and community (*Gesellschaft* and
    Gemeinschaft) 84–86, 94, 97
sociology 71–73, 83, 173, 290, 322
sources of law 101, 165
sovereignty 47–51; attribution of
    49–50; and the exception 293; after
    globalisation 103–105; and identity
    of 'the people' 49; modernity and
    juridical regression 274–275, 279;
    post-sovereignty 103–104; *see also*
    colonialism
specialisation of knowledge and the
    individual 13–15
state: constitutional, elements of 45–47;
    constitutionalism beyond 105–107;
    position in legal pluralism 284–285
    ('Westphalian state' 17–18)
state of emergency 164; derogation
    of rights 164; sovereignty and the
    exception 293
Steyn, Lord 221
supra-national constitutionalism
    105–107
supra-national law: EU 103–106, 140;
    and international law 47, 65, 101–102,
    104, 254
surveillance 276, 277, 278
'systematicity' of law 150–151

Tamanaha, B. 285, 287
'temporal' dimension to justice 256–257
territorial validity of law 46–47, 73
terrorism and derogation of rights
    163–164

Teubner, G. 287, 290, 315–317, 322, 326–327, 330–331
Thompson, E. 37, 41
Thompson, J. 68
Tönnies, F. 84, 86
Torture 16, 57, 209–210, 230–231, 267
trials *see* courts
Truth and Reconciliation Commission (TRC), South Africa 255

Unger, R. 167–168, 195–198, 207, 219
'unthinking' modern law 107–109
utilitarianism *vs.* libertarianism 230–234

validity of law 148–151; injustice and invalidity 151–153; legal positivist perspective 137–143; territorial 46–47, 73
Violence, authority and 307–308

Waldron, J. 148–152, 206, 229, 231
Walker, N. 103–106, 287
Ward, Lord Justice. 188
Weber, M. 40–41, 43, 71–82, 83, 85, 91–93, 118, 120, 134, 168, 267, 272, 314
welfare state 93–96; bureaucracy, justice and instrumentalism 96; and capitalism 94, 312–320; discretionary powers 96–97; erosion of separation of powers 97; and globalisation 98; and juridification 318; particularised legislation 97
Westphalia, Peace/Treaty of 18
'Westphalia as marker of transition' 17–18
witness testimony 265, 270
Wittgenstein, L. 182, 301, 303–304

Yntema, H. 180
Young, I. M. 241